'HONEST ENOUGH TO BE BOLD':
THE LIFE AND TIMES OF SIR JAMES PLINY WHITNEY

On a promise of 'Clean, Uncorrupt, and Incorruptible Government,' James Pliny Whitney became premier of Ontario in 1905. His victory marked the end of an era of Liberal rule that had lasted for over three decades, and introduced to the province a new, 'progressive' brand of conservatism.

As this lively biography demonstrates, Whitney was a gruff and forceful leader. He had a keen understanding of the social and technological forces that were changing Ontario so dramatically in the early twentieth century; he also understood, better than the Liberals, the political implications of those forces. The policies of his government extended to hydroelectric power, bilingual schools, northern development, automobile regulation, temperance (he dealt with the advocates of prohibition 'through gritted teeth'), imperial unity, housing, workmen's compensation, and the suffrage movement. (In a lapse from progressiveness, he argued that women should not be exposed to 'the unlovely influence of party politics.') He had a lasting influence on higher education in the province through the establishment of a Board of Governors for the University of Toronto, then unmistakably the provincial university of Ontario, and the provision of tenure for its full professors.

Whitney liked to describe himself as 'bold enough to be honest... honest enough to be bold.' Humphries concludes that as premier from 1905 to 1914 Whitney lived up to his self-description. The boldness of his legislative programs recognized the evolution of a new industrial society and paved the way for government to intervene in economic and social affairs. The success of his progressive conservatism laid the foundations for decades of Tory success in Ontario.

CHARLES W. HUMPHRIES is Professor of History at the University of British Columbia.

James Pliny Whitney (Ontario Hydro Archives)

CHARLES W. HUMPHRIES

'Honest Enough to Be Bold': The Life and Times of Sir James Pliny Whitney

Published by University of Toronto Press
Toronto Buffalo London
for The Ontario Historical Studies Series

ISBN 978-0-8020-3420-5 (cloth)
ISBN 978-1-4875-9188-5 (paper)

Canadian Cataloguing in Publication Data

Humphries, Charles W. (Charles Walter), 1932–
  'Honest enough to be bold': the life and times of Sir James Pliny Whitney

  (Ontario historical studies series, ISSN 0380-9188)
  Bibliography: p.
  Includes index.
  ISBN 978-0-8020-3420-5 (bound) ISBN 978-1-4875-9188-5 (pbk.)

  1. Whitney, James Pliny, Sir, 1843–1914.
  2. Prime ministers – Ontario – Biography.
  3. Ontario – Politics and government – 1905–1919.*
  4. Ontario – Politics and government – 1867–1905.*
  I. Title. II. Series.

FC3073.I.W53H8 1985   971.3'03'0924   C85-098038-0   FI058.W53H8 1985

This book has been published with funds provided by the Government of Ontario through the Ministry of Citizenship and Culture.

Cover photo: James Pliny Whitney (Ontario Archives s 305)

IN MEMORY OF DOREEN

Contents

The Ontario Historical Studies Series

For many years the principal theme in English-Canadian historical writing has been the emergence and the consolidation of the Canadian nation. This theme has been developed in uneasy awareness of the persistence and importance of regional interests and identities, but because of the central role of Ontario in the growth of Canada, Ontario has not been seen as a region. Almost unconsciously, historians have equated the history of the province with that of the nation and have depicted the interests of other regions as obstacles to the unity and welfare of Canada.

The creation of the province of Ontario in 1867 was the visible embodiment of a formidable reality, the existence at the core of the new nation of a powerful if disjointed society whose traditions and characteristics differed in many respects from those of the other British North American colonies. The intervening century has not witnessed the assimilation of Ontario to the other regions in Canada; on the contrary it has become a more clearly articulated entity. Within the formal geographical and institutional framework defined so assiduously by Ontario's political leaders, an increasingly intricate web of economic and social interests has been woven and shaped by the dynamic interplay between Toronto and its hinterland. The character of this regional community has been formed in the tension between a rapid adaptation to the processes of modernization and industrialization in modern Western society and a reluctance to modify or discard traditional attitudes and values. Not surprisingly, the Ontario outlook is a compound of aggressiveness, conservatism, and the conviction that its values should be the model for the rest of Canada.

From the outset the objective of the Board of Trustees of the Series has been to describe and analyse the historical development of Ontario as a distinct region within Canada. The series as planned will include some thirty volumes covering many aspects of the life and work of the province from its original establishment in 1791 as Upper Canada to our own time. Among these will be biographies of several premiers, numerous works on the growth of the provincial economy, educational institutions, minority groups, and the arts, and a synthesis of the history of Ontario, based upon the contributions of the biographies and thematic studies.

In planning this project, the Editors and the Board have endeavoured to maintain a reasonable balance between different kinds and areas of historical research, and to appoint authors ready to ask new questions about the past and to answer them in accordance with the canons of contemporary scholarship. Nine biographical studies have been included, if only because through biography the past comes alive most readily for the general reader as well as the historian. The historian must be sensitive to today's concerns and standards as he engages in the imaginative recreation of the interplay between human beings and circumstances in time. He should seek to be the mediator between the dead and the living, but in the end the humanity and the artistry of his account will determine the extent of its usefulness.

The biography of Sir James Pliny Whitney is the ninth volume in the Series to be published. It depicts the life and times of the first Conservative premier of Ontario, whose electoral victory in 1905 brought to an end the long reign of the provincial Liberals. Whitney took many bold initiatives which challenged many of the powerful forces in his society and which had an enduring impact on the economic, social, and political development of the province. We hope that this study will illuminate the character and the accomplishments of James Whitney and thereby deepen our understanding of twentieth-century Ontario.

The Editors and the Board of Trustees are grateful to Charles Humphries for undertaking this task.

Goldwin French
Peter Oliver
Jeanne Beck
Maurice Careless, Chairman of the Board of Trustees

Toronto
28 October 1984

Preface

This work is a political biography without adulteration through any attempt at psycho-biography: the personal papers of J.P. Whitney, mercifully, contain nothing on his rearing or his reactions to it. Thus my attempt in this volume has been to see the problems of his time through his eyes and, in consequence, interpret his answers. I do not claim to be endowed with any extraordinary powers in this regard, but should note – as have other biographers – that I probably now know more about my subject than he could himself have recalled at any given moment in his life. I would have been happier had I been able to explore his relationships with his family at any length, but material in this area is abysmally tiny: there is not, to my knowledge, a solitary letter extant between Whitney and his wife, Alice, or his three children. One can presume, rather tritely, that these people stood by him; but one cannot say much more with any sureness. The writer, however, cannot moan too much, because the Whitney papers are, for most years, full to overflowing on matters of politics and policy. This, in turn, simply reinforces what was said above: this end product is very much a political biography.

This book has been a long time – too long, my friends would wearily amend – in gestation, and for that I owe apologies to a host of persons who cannot be enumerated. I can offer thanks, however, to a range of people for their contributions to this work. Maurice Careless supervised the thesis from which this book sprang and his cheerful guidance and support over the years are gratefully acknowledged. The state of twentieth-century Ontario history was small indeed when I first began to plough this field, and it is only fitting to salute those who have since rolled back its boundaries and, in so doing, have assisted the author: H.V. Nelles, Michael Piva, Margaret Prang, and Peter Oliver. I would be remiss if I did not note the work, on my behalf, of Bill Magney, who, in particular, focused my attention and research on the Ontario Railway and Municipal Board.

To the editors of the Ontario Historical Studies Series, Goldwin French, Peter Oliver, and Jeanne Beck, I owe a large vote of thanks, because they possessed the patience of Job and the compassion of angels when I was laid low by a host of personal woes. At the same time, they quietly and firmly insisted that the work be finished. Behind them stands the Ontario Historical Studies Series' Board, to whom they had to explain my tardiness and who, in light of those explanations, went several extra miles, which included freeing me from teaching for six months while I concentrated on Whitney.

Then, there are those generous people of the public archives of Canada and Ontario who fetched files and dispensed advice over too many summers. And there are the stalwarts who never lost confidence in the author when he, at times, misplaced his: Carl Berger, Keith Ralston, Syd Wise, Norb MacDonald, and, especially, Mary Vickers picked me up, dusted me off, and, sometimes, dressed me down. I hope they still think I deserved their support.

My children – Mary, Andrew, and David – grew up with the book and I trust that none is really any worse for the experience. Lastly, it must be observed that much thanks is owing – but cannot be said – to the person to whom this book is dedicated. She bore with J.P.W. and the author through the bad times and the good times.

CWH
25 January 1985

Cornwall legal lights. Back row, left to right: Henry Sandfield Macdonald, John Greenfield Macdonald, John Bergin, J.P. Whitney. Front row, left to right: Dr Derby Bergin, John Ban Maclennan

Adam Beck, cabinet minister and horseman (Ontario Archives s 4481)

Whitney (hand to mouth) at the opening of the Toronto General Hospital
(Ontario Archives s 794)

Robert Allan Pyne, Whitney's minister of education (Ontario Archives s 493)

James Joseph Foy, Whitney's Roman Catholic right-hand man and his attorney-general (Ontario Archives s 737)

Samuel Nelson Monteith, Whitney's first minister of agriculture, 1905–8 (Ontario Archives s 2598)

William John Hanna, Whitney's provincial secretary (Ontario Archives s 2600)

Whitney on the campaign trail (Metropolitan Toronto Library Board)

Whitney on the platform (Metropolitan Toronto Library Board)

Whitney checking his public appearance (Metropolitan Toronto Library Board)

E.C. (Ned) Whitney, the premier's millionaire brother (Public Archives Canada C 21862)

Whitney engaging in informal banter with US Vice-President Fairbanks at the Quebec tercentenary, 1908 (Public Archives Canada PA 24751)

Plotting the 1911 federal election campaign in Ontario. Left to right: Robert Borden, Edmund Bristol, Frank Cochrane, Joseph Octave Reaume, and J.P. Whitney (Public Archives Canada C 17945)

Whitney receives the gift of a car from fellow Tory legislators, 1913 (City of Toronto Archives, James Collection 1036)

Chancellor W.R. Meredith and President Robert Falconer of the University of Toronto
(City of Toronto Archives, James Collection 1383)

Robert A. Pyne, Whitney's minister of education, at his office desk in the west wing of Ryerson Hall, 1910 (City of Toronto Archives, James Collection 8208)

MADE TO ORDER   Old Man Ontario: 'Well, there may be an alteration or two necessary, but it's a big improvement on some of the "hand-me-downs" I be'n gettin' across the street lately.' (Toronto *World*, 16 March 1906; Public Archives Canada NL 13775)

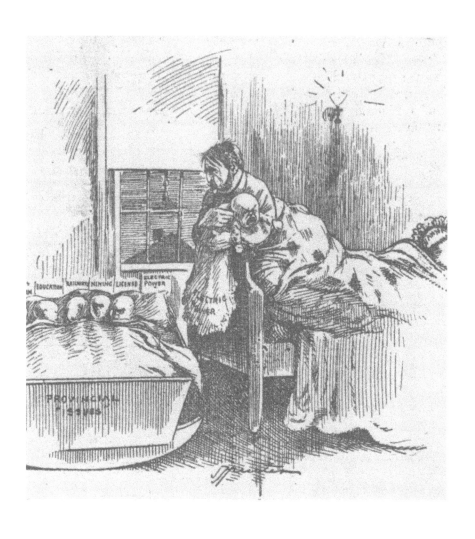

A LARGE FAMILY   Mr Whitney: 'I'll be glad when the holidays come and I can get away from 'em for a while.' (Toronto *World*, 1 May 1906; Public Archives Canada NL 13774)

'HONEST ENOUGH TO BE BOLD':
THE LIFE AND TIMES OF SIR JAMES PLINY WHITNEY

1

'I Come from Liberal (Baldwin) Stock':[1] 1843–1890

Tuesday, 31 January 1888, had been a fine winter's day for the provincial by-election in Dundas County, Ontario: crisp air, clear skies, bright sunshine. Zealous Liberal and Conservative partisans had busied themselves on behalf of their respective candidates. The evening before, a Tory supporter had been spirited westward out of the county to Prescott and lodged in the Revere Hotel. The night clerk, Conservative to the marrow, tipped the plot to party friends, and they shipped the victim back to Iroquois on the next Grand Trunk train – in time for him to cast his ballot. Then, turning on the abductor, they whisked him across the ice of the St Lawrence to Ogdensburg, New York. An inquiring telegram located him and he, too, was returned to vote. Such activity was one ingredient in the mix that was late-nineteenth-century Ontario politics.[2]

Once the polls had closed, crowds began to gather in the streets of Morrisburg and, ten miles upriver, Iroquois, to await the posting of results. Not only did the residents of the two riverside villages turn out but, because interest ran high and sleighing was excellent, people arrived from the surrounding farms and cross-roads. Any sound Tory in the crowds was not misled into despair by the early returns which gave an initial lead to Dr T.F. Chamberlain, the Liberal candidate, because he knew full well that Morrisburg, Iroquois, and Williamsburg Town-ships would go against the Conservative, James Pliny Whitney. The latter's hope for victory rested on the proven Tory strength in the townships of Matilda, Mountain, and Winchester.

By eight in the evening, the main street of Morrisburg was jammed with people and the Tory cheers grew louder as those distant Conservative polls produced the anticipated support for Whitney, while Liberal strength in Morrisburg and Iroquois sagged ever so slightly. Suddenly, the counting was over and Whitney was the member-elect for Dundas – by the slim margin of twenty-five votes. Jubilant Conservatives grabbed the winner and, hoisting him onto their shoulders, carried him 'amidst deafening cheers and the tooting of horns' to the Morrisburg music hall where the new member and other Tories delivered impromptu 'spirited addresses.' Then, 'at the close of the proceedings Mr. Whitney was escorted to his residence by a body guard of about 100 enthusiastic supporters.' James P. Whitney was on the road to the provincial legislature in Toronto; but, now in his forty-sixth year, he had already travelled some considerable distance toward that particular goal.[3]

I

Richard Whitney, James's American-born father, had migrated into Dundas County, Upper Canada, from St Lawrence County, New York, sometime after the War of 1812. In 1828, at the age of twenty-two, the young blacksmith had married a local girl, Maria Doran, and settled in Williamsburg Township. Three years later their only child, a girl, was born, but mother and infant lived just three months after the birth, dying within days of each other. The young widower was obliged to remarry in 1834, taking as his second bride Clarissa Jane Fairman of Chateauguay, New York. Over the next twenty years this union produced ten boys, three of whom died in infancy. The fifth of these offspring was James Pliny, born on 2 October 1842, less than a mile west of the site of the Crysler's Farm battlefield. Eleven weeks later, the boy was baptized into the Church of England with Mary and John Pliny Crysler acting as sponsors. Thus a prominent local lumberman-merchant and future Conservative legislator gave the baby both his blessing and his middle name.[4]

When young Whitney was five years old, his father changed location and, in part, occupation, moving across the Dundas-Stormont county line into the south-west corner of Osnabruck Township, where he devoted more time to farming and spent fewer hours as a blacksmith. Richard Whitney worked a portion of his waterfront lot of two hundred acres and produced a comfortable living for himself and his growing family from his efforts at mixed farming. Although he secured a steady income over the years, a number of his neighbours owned farms of comparable size that were valued higher than his. In light of this and of the advantages he was able to provide for his sons, he must have continued to earn some money as a smith. In this setting young James grew to adolescence. There were, of course, the customary farm chores that had to be performed and the daily trek to school that had to be made; but there were also the more exciting trips to the riverside village of Aultsville where James would stand on the wharf, waving frantically at the mate of the freshly docked steamer, the *Jenny Lind*.[5]

There were sufficient family funds to send the boy to the Cornwall Grammar School for the completion of his formal education. While he was there, a particular episode provided some evidence of Whitney's capacities as a leader and organizer. In December of 1860, a student of the grammar school charged in the columns of the Cornwall *Freeholder* that the school's headmaster, H.W. Davies, had referred to the common school in town as the 'ragged school.' Other students reacted in defence of Davies and a committee was struck to draft a reply to the unfair charge. The burden of its composition fell on *ad hoc* secretary Whitney; but the editor of the *Freeholder* denied the students the right of rebuttal. Consequently, James and his followers descended on the rival Cornwall *Economist* and persuaded its editor to print their reply. In that letter, the young secretary ably defended the headmaster, carefully uncovered the source of the inaccurate account, questioned the honesty of the complainant, and practically demolished his story.[6]

Earlier in that same year Whitney had been one of those who had signed an agreement to organize a volunteer militia infantry company at Cornwall. Membership in that body over the next few years gave shape and firmness to some of his beliefs and prejudices. When the American Civil War erupted, Whitney performed a tour of duty at the time of the *Trent* affair and was surely caught up in the emotions spawned by those events in December 1861. When this particular crisis had passed, Whitney continued as a member of the militia, attending the frequent drills that were called throughout the years of that most bitter American conflict.[7] It was, however, the threats and activities of the Fenian brotherhood that provided Whitney with his longest active period of militia duty. On 6 March 1866 – the day after the Canadian government called out ten thousand volunteers – the twenty-three-year-old militiaman went on active service in the Cornwall Volunteer Battalion as a private at the pay rate of twenty-five cents per day. Evidently displaying some talents – and honesty – Whitney was promoted to the rank of pay sergeant in mid-March, and his daily allowance rose by fifteen cents. Because Cornwall was judged to be an 'advanced frontier' post, Whitney was not discharged at the end of March when Canadian numbers on duty along the border were cut; rather, he remained on guard until the conclusion of the first Fenian scare on 23 July 1866.[8]

Militia activity in the Cornwall area intensified during the month of June when the Fenians undertook an assault on Canada West in the Niagara region. Canadian military men, convinced that the Niagara attack was but 'a prelude to cover more formidable attacks along the line of the St. Lawrence,' judged the Cornwall situation to be 'exceedingly serious,' because 'possession of the canals' was the chief goal of the Fenian leadership. Consequently, 'a patrol was established for ten miles up and down the river [from Cornwall] by the local companies, and navigation on the river and through the canal was stopped.' But the enemy never came.[9]

Undoubtedly these were exciting times for the young pay sergeant, who probably tramped his share of that twenty-mile patrol almost eagerly searching for signs of Fenians. There was more to it than that, however, for these stirring events surely assisted the development of two strong convictions in the young man: a firm belief in the value of the imperial tie and an intense wariness of things American. After all, in the brief space of five years – when the teenage boy was becoming a young adult – there had been a series of military threats directed at Canada West from south of the border because of a combination of imperial policies and American attitudes. Given such circumstances, plus his membership in the militia, there was little room for shades of grey in Whitney's maturing mind: Britain was the benevolent parent and the United States the hostile continental partner.

It would have been difficult for a youth, raised in the Loyalist upper St Lawrence valley, to have been immune to such ideas, which were born of the American Revolution and nurtured by both the War of 1812 and the aftermath of the Rebellion of 1837. Whitney, however, was not of Loyalist stock. And, although he was exposed to these Upper Canadian views along the riverside, it probably took his personal experiences during the American Civil War and the Fenian fulminations to root them firmly in his mind. It is interesting to note that in later descriptions of him, for which he must have provided some information, stress was laid on his militia activities and on his descent from a seventeenth-century Herefordshire Englishman, Henry Whitney, who migrated to the Thirteen Colonies long before the American Revolution. No mention was made in these sketches of his father's much later river crossing, and there was but a solitary reference to the fact that his grandfather had been a captain under George Washington. In later life Whitney never seemed anxious to acknowledge his American heritage or to admit that he was the son of a 'new Canadian.'[10]

II

While militia activities absorbed some of his time and attention in the early years of the 1860s, Whitney also completed his education at the Cornwall Grammar School and cast about for a promising occupation. He was now a young man who still resisted the style of the day by remaining clean-shaven. His unadorned and handsome face displayed penetrating eyes, high cheek-bones, a fine but strong nose, tightly pursed lips, and a firm jaw; there was little trace of weakness in his facial characteristics. His somewhat unkempt hair was generally covered by a cap, set at a jaunty angle. Standing five foot nine, he had a well-proportioned, moderate frame made strong through those days of labour on the farm and in the blacksmith's shop. With shoulders back, he stood erect and walked with a firm step at a brisk pace. Thus equipped with a pleasant appearance and substantial formal education, he chose law as his vocation and entered the offices of two prominent Cornwall lawyers, John Sandfield Macdonald and John Ban Maclennan. His entry into this firm was undoubtedly facilitated by the contacts that he had made through his attendance at the Cornwall Grammar School and his membership in the militia. He was certainly acquainted with Sandfield Macdonald before he entered his offices.

For much of the time that Whitney was with this firm, Sandfield Macdonald had much larger concerns before him than the operation of his law office; nevertheless, he found time – probably after the events of March 1864 had thrust him out of the

Canadian premiership and onto the political sidelines – to tutor Whitney in politics in addition to law. It is difficult to say just how great Macdonald's influence was upon Whitney; no known correspondence between the two exists. But the younger man was always insistent upon the point that the older political maverick did much to influence and modify his political thinking. Later, much later, Whitney was to write that he was 'one of the few men now living, who understood something of ... MacDonald's [sic] mental methods.' He judged Macdonald lacking in the power and inclination 'to conciliate men' and therefore not a completely successful politician. But, Whitney insisted, he found himself 'acting occasionally' in a manner which he learned from Macdonald; and he regarded himself as Sandfield's 'immediate successor.' At another time, in discussing Macdonald, Whitney observed that his 'political views and ideas' were 'largely founded upon' Sandfield's. The younger politician viewed the older as a 'Baldwin Liberal' who, after Baldwin's retirement, had moved 'slowly but surely' away from the Reform party and into the Liberal-Conservative camp of John A. Macdonald. And Whitney saw himself as a political descendant of that transition.[11]

While insisting upon the Liberal strain in his political composition, he would acknowledge that he was, in terms of party, strictly a Tory, and then he would add that this did '*not* mean Toronto Tory necessarily.' This deliberate qualification was designed to suggest that he was not an ultra-Conservative, that he was not a captive of the Toronto 'machine' and that he was not tainted by the strong anti-Catholicism of some Toronto Tories. Whitney had no particular fear of association with Roman Catholics. After all, his political education came in part from a Roman Catholic, although Sandfield Macdonald was a rather unorthodox one. Among his Cornwall cronies were Catholics of both Scottish and Irish descent, such as Sandfield's sons, Henry Sandfield and John Greenfield, and John and Dr Derby Bergin. At the outset of his political career, some might have suggested that Whitney could live with individual Catholics, not the entire faith, but his mind was generally open on the subject of Roman Catholicism and the basis of a more understanding attitude was present. He possessed and developed a flexibility on the subject which could easily distress rigidly Protestant Tories.[12]

Cornwall life, however, was not straight politics and law. Alcohol provided a most congenial mixer; and the members of the Macdonald and Maclennan law office were well known for their drinking parties. Whitney was certainly a participant in such affairs and, because of them, he early acquired a reputation as a heavy drinker. Whether or not he deserved this judgment is debatable; in part, the community may have rendered a verdict of guilty by association. Nevertheless, in his early days he seldom turned down the offer of a drink.

This habit – some local residents would have insisted upon the word 'problem' – may have been responsible for Whitney's 'lost years.' Some time in the late 1860s, he gave up the study of law and disappeared from sight, surfacing occasionally in Aultsville, his father's place of residence, then vanishing once more. Regardless of his whereabouts, he did continue to take an active interest in politics and, on one occasion, served as an intermediary for a Conservative candidate who hoped to gain the vote of Whitney's Liberal father. He was at least in his thirtieth year when he resumed his legal studies in Cornwall, but something was now apparent: whatever difficulty had driven him from town was now resolved. James Whitney had found himself and he returned to Cornwall with a purpose and determination that were missing before. The end product of his experience had been personal growth.[13]

This time he finished his labours and was called to the bar at Osgoode Hall in the Easter term of 1876. He decided to strike out on his own in the practice of law and, in May, opened his own office in Morrisburg where his parents were then living. The population of the village numbered about sixteen hundred but, located at the foot of the Rivière du Plat canal and on the main line of the Grand Trunk railway, its citizens had high hopes for Morrisburg's population growth and economic development, hopes that could be found in dozens of small Ontario communities in the same period. Consequently, a feature of the village's life was its constant boasting, which cited its excellent water power, local exports, and commercial and manufacturing potential. But, despite such boosting, the town actually survived as a service centre for the surrounding farms and from them obtained one of its chief exports, butter, which was often destined for the manufacturing cities of England. Despite the declarations of prosperity, there was another side to life in Morrisburg which revealed 'several families' on 'the verge of starvation' because of unemployment.[14]

When Whitney arrived in the spring of 1876, the village contained four churches to serve the needs of the Anglicans, Lutherans, Methodists, and Roman Catholics; the Presbyterians, fewer in numbers, made do with a rented hall. In spite of such manifestations of religiosity, the adult males of the village had decided, three months prior to the new lawyer's arrival, to live with the reality of their needs, and had voted out the Dunkin Act, returning the village to the category of a wet municipality. That development had, in turn, spawned a reaction: a team of temperance workers descended on the town and, after a week's labour, signed hundreds to a pledge of total abstinence, thus focusing local attention on one of the outstanding questions in politics and religion for Ontarians over the next half century. Such was Morrisburg when Whitney opened his office in Barry's block and readied himself for legal business.[15]

Work was not long in forthcoming and Whitney soon established himself as a tough, able lawyer. In the course of one civil suit, late in 1876, he so shattered the defendant that the judge felt obliged 'to stop Mr. Whitney's crushing and merciless cross examination of the witness,' and to find for the plaintiff. 'The admirable management of this case by Mr. Whitney, and his instant seizure upon the [flaw in the] witnesses' story ... scattered the defence to the winds, and evoked highly favorable comments from the spectators.' One did not need many such cases or nods of approval from the press in order to commence the building of a successful law practice in a village. Subsequently, additional printed words of praise marked Whitney's advance in his profession.[16]

There was another matter on Whitney's mind at that time, in addition to the development of his legal business. During his Cornwall period, the student lawyer had met and fallen in love with Alice Park, some three years his junior. Her parents, William (a watchmaker and sometime life insurance agent) and Margaret, had scarcely been overjoyed when the romance had first blossomed: they were well acquainted with the stories of the drinking bouts staged by some of Cornwall's legal lights. Alice was not to be denied, however, and, applying pressure on Whitney, had considerably slowed his alcoholic intake. Further, James was making progress in his field and this must have impressed her parents because, when Whitney travelled down from Morrisburg to Cornwall to marry Alice on 30 April 1877, the wedding was held in her parents' home with her sisters as attendants.[17]

III

In addition to his profession and his marriage, another factor gave shape to Whitney's early months in Morrisburg, and that was politics. Already a convinced Conservative, he plunged into labour on behalf of the party in Dundas County and was soon rewarded by being elected secretary of the county's Liberal-Conservative association, a post which made him, in effect, the local organizer for the party in federal and provincial elections. When John A. Macdonald began his comeback along the picnic trail in 1877, it was Whitney who wrote and urged him to place Dundas on his itinerary for eastern Ontario. The federal chieftain did so and addressed the county's Tories at Winchester Springs late in September.[18]

Through such work Whitney came to understand his county thoroughly. He knew that his village, Morrisburg, was hopelessly Grit, that Iroquois was no better, and that Williamsburg Township always managed to show a majority for Reform. But the three remaining townships of the constituency – Matilda, Mountain, and Winchester – were on the Liberal-Conservative side by a substantial margin; and these townships generally provided the narrow margin for Tory victories in the riding. This was an era when any shrewd poll-watcher could furnish almost exact voting results before the ballots were counted; not because of any corrupt practice – although that was always a possibility – but because party allegiances were generally very firm, particularly in eastern Ontario. Dundas County, then, was a Liberal-Conservative riding; barely so, but Liberal-Conservative nevertheless.[19]

This was the political setting in which Whitney worked and spoke for his party; in which he met people, making political and personal friends of some and bitter enemies of others; and in which he became acquainted with Andrew Broder, butter shipper and Orangeman from West Winchester, who had first been elected to the Ontario legislature as a Conservative in 1875. Broder and Whitney became fast lifelong friends, doing battle together for almost forty years. The pair complemented each other: Broder was gregarious and hearty, if not physical, in his greetings; Whitney was more aloof, the organizer and analyser, whose bluntness was not always appreciated. At one meeting, when Broder scrambled down from their carriage to shake hands, engage in political banter, and greet all by their first names, Whitney sat in the vehicle. Broder urged him to join the group; the lawyer gruffly declined, commenting that any attempted imitation of Broder's techniques would only give him the appearance of a 'damn fool.' There was about Whitney a cold edge of detachment which could only be thawed by the warmth of good friends or the hot anger he directed at an enemy. Generally, however, the wall of reserve kept him very much a private person. So he remained 'J.P.' or 'James' or 'Whitney' to even his closest associates; no one ventured to call him 'Jim,' let alone 'Jimmy.' He was, in fact, an autocrat by temperament and a democrat by conviction.[20]

The political enemies which Whitney faced in Dundas County were not all of a Liberal stripe; some he encountered within the ranks of his own party. This problem developed in 1878, when the local executive split over the method of selecting a standard-bearer for the federal general election, and was likely intensified by the knowledge that the nominee would probably capture the constituency for the Tories. The Whitney group triumphed in this petty brawl – and their man did become MP – but wounds were opened which plagued the county organization for the next four years. The division probably accounted for Broder's reduced majority when he successfully retained his provincial seat in the election of 1879, when Whitney campaigned diligently on behalf of his party ally.[21]

Whitney thus cut his political teeth on battling Grits and in-fighting with Tories. His activities as secretary and county organizer did create some Conservative opponents, but they also provided him with a following in party ranks; consequently, when Liberal premier Oliver Mowat called a provincial election for February 1883, the forty-year-old lawyer saw his name go forward at the Dundas Conservative nominating convention. But Broder and three others were also nominated, and Whitney, after accepting the salute, declined the honour out of respect for his friend. He laboured on Broder's behalf in the ensuing campaign, however, and the produce merchant was returned to the Ontario legislature for the third time. Elsewhere in the province the Conservatives did not fare as well and Mowat's government received the endorsement of the electorate for a third time.[22]

In addition to warring with Grits – and some Tories – Whitney had to find time to earn a living as a lawyer in order to support himself and a growing family. Much of his business came from estate work and real estate transactions, but he was also involved in larger cases which provided him with a wider reputation and legal contacts outside the county. One such was the dispute which arose out of a drainage scheme for Dundas County, an issue made more complex by clashing personalities and by the fact that a portion of the county drains towards the St Lawrence while the remainder drains toward the Ottawa. In 1884, those in favour of pressing ahead with the project found themselves confronted by legal barriers raised by their opponents. Whitney was retained as counsel by those favouring action, but the legal fight soon escalated and Samuel Blake, Edward's brother, was called upon to head the fight for the proponents of the scheme, who were ultimately successful. The whole affair brought Whitney into contact with a leading Liberal legal light and, of course, he also encountered the chief lawyer for the other side, D'Alton McCarthy, the rising Conservative star. None of this was harmful to Whitney's legal career.[23]

Not quite content with all this activity, Whitney successfully sought the post of high school trustee in the 1880s, and he took sufficient interest in sports to become president of the Morrisburg lacrosse club. Nor did he break his long association with the militia, advancing to the rank of major in the Dundas reserve during this period. All the while he remained an active layman in the Church of England.[24]

Politics, however, remained very much a prime concern and when, in the late fall of 1886, Mowat called another provincial election and Broder decided against running, Whitney was prepared to come out of the shadows of the backroom and seek the Conservative nomination for Dundas. At the Winchester Springs nominating convention, Whitney's was but one of five names put forward. When his turn came to speak, he wasted little time and simply promised, if chosen as candidate, 'to give a good account of himself.' Voting on the five nominees followed, but it was a mere formality because Whitney secured an overall majority on the first ballot.[25] The Morrisburg lawyer became the Conservative candidate for Dundas because he had served the party and the local association for over nine years and, in that time, had established a wide range of political contacts throughout the county; those acquaintances now paid dividends. Beyond that he had a deserved reputation as a forceful and forthright speaker. Last, but not least, Whitney wanted the nomination this time: he was not averse to seeking a stepping-stone to power or to placing himself in open competition with his peers.

The Dundas candidate entered the provincial election campaign under the leadership of William Ralph Meredith, the party's Ontario chieftain. The latter, a London lawyer, had come to his position in 1879 and had led the party unsuccessfully against Mowat in the elections of that year and 1883. As it turned out, Meredith's chances of victory were not better in 1886. Dundas County, however, did provide a bright spot in the midst of dreary Conservative prospects. After all, it had returned Andrew Broder in two previous provincial contests, and a man thoroughly familiar with the constituency was the candidate on this occasion. Robert Birmingham, the party's Ontario organizer – a man who generally gave more of his time to federal matters – encouraged Whitney: 'With zealous work and good organization your riding will be safe for W.R. Meredith and good government.' The Conservative nominee probably felt reasonably confident of success; but this did not prevent him from visiting every nook and cranny of the riding and generally speaking twice a day over the next three weeks.[26]

The Ontario election campaign of 1886 was not a particularly attractive one. Although the Conservatives put forward a platform containing both criticisms of the Liberal administration and positive proposals for the future, much speech-making revolved around that most divisive subject, Roman Catholicism. The Toronto *Mail* led the way, charging that a concordat existed between Archbishop John Joseph Lynch of Toronto and Premier Oliver Mowat, which meant that Liberals were subservient to Roman Catholics particularly in educational matters and held office by virtue of their support. Many Conservatives followed the harsh lead of the *Mail*, out of either conviction or desperation; but others, with an eye to federal politics, were alarmed by the Toronto paper's language. John A. Macdonald, in receipt of a host of dire predictions about the fate of the federal Tories in Ontario unless the *Mail* was silenced, was finally obliged to repudiate the paper and its opinions.[27]

Meredith, caught up in this furore, tried to play it to his advantage without alienating Catholic Tories. He hinted that somehow Roman Catholics were receiving advantageous treatment, but noted that the separate school system was guaranteed by the constitution. His posture, however, was too awkward for wide public acceptance and for his own peace of mind. He tried to talk of other things – retrenchment in government spending, conservation of the forests, enforcement of local prohibition, a truly secret ballot, and manhood suffrage – but he could not be heard over the religious cry which he could not control. His critics were able to label him as strongly anti-Catholic.[28]

In Dundas County, Whitney faced his Grit opponent, Dr T.F. Chamberlain. Standing squarely behind his leader, the Morrisburg lawyer took up the religious issue and argued, as did many other Conservatives, that it was not his party that had raised the question but, rather, the Liberals by way of their actions. He insisted that favouritism to Roman Catholicism had produced religious inequality in Ontario and that all he was demanding was a correction of this imbalance. At the same time, Whitney contended that he bore no ill will towards Roman Catholics as such; rather his hostility was directed at the Mowat government which had caused all the trouble. Whitney was confident there was logic in his argument: he was not being anti-Catholic, simply anti-Mowat. Such reasoning was not always accept-able to Catholics, however, because they could not see the fine line that was drawn. Whitney knew, of course, that Orangeman Andy Broder had preceded him in provincial politics and had survived; one could assume then that Whitney's position would not be fatal to his cause.

The Tory candidate did give time and attention to other matters. He insisted that the Grits were opponents of the British tie, favouring an end to the Empire and its institutions. He argued that the Liberals were stripping the people of their liberties through a string of gerrymanders, the failure to extend the franchise, and the lack of a real secret ballot. He assailed the government for its extravagance, and contended that parents were victims of a school-book ring that, because of a publication monopoly and the absence of a tendering system, overcharged for texts used by their children. And he frequently concluded his speeches by insisting that the Liberal-Conservative party was the party of progress; the inheritor of the best from the old Reform and Tory groups.[29]

Despite his vigorous campaigning, Whitney did not win. When the ballots were counted on the evening of 28 December, the Tory candidate had lost by the narrow margin of twenty-five votes. In light of Broder's earlier successes, it seems unlikely that the provincial religious issue was much of a factor in Whitney's defeat. What did haunt the Morrisburg lawyer was the intra-party strife in the constituency of the preceding years. One of his Tory opponents was quick to suggest that Whitney was not 'a popular candidate,' and that he had secured the Conservative nomination in a closed convention. There were even dark hints that the Morrisburg lawyer did not have 'clean hands,' but there was no substance to such a charge; rather, this accusation simply indicates that the continuing division within Dundas Tory ranks had not served the purpose of their nominee. The suggestion, however, that Whitney lacked popularity was not without merit. The outgoing dentist who opposed him – and who had held a wide range of public posts – probably was better known than Whitney, who could not boast a comparable public service record. As well, when viewing the Conservative candidate against the warm personality of Chamberlain, no one would have seen the former as gregarious. Whitney thus became just one more Tory loser as Mowat swept to victory for the fourth time.[30]

IV

Defeat was not that bitter a pill for Whitney. He could return to the status of full-time lawyer and seek to recoup losses in business and money which the campaign had undoubtedly caused. In any event, two fresh developments meant that he was not long removed from the political arena. A federal election was called for early in 1887, and the Dundas Conservative association managed to stage one more internal battle before deciding to nominate the sitting member, a decision which Whitney supported. Then the Tory constituency secretary laboured diligently to secure the election of his candidate in the ensuing campaign.[31]

A second political matter also seized Whitney's attention: there appeared to be sufficient evidence to warrant protesting Chamberlain's election on the grounds of corruption and bribery. In due course the information was assembled and the protest entered. Then Whitney's cause survived another hurdle: the 'saw-off,' an arrangement whereby Conservatives would drop proceedings in one riding in return for a similar Liberal favour in another. Such action was sometimes dictated by a shortage of funds, because protests always involved legal fees, and sometimes by the inadequacy of the case. But Whitney's protest proceeded, delayed only by the slow movement of the law.[32]

The trial of the election petition requesting the unseating of Chamberlain opened in the Morrisburg music hall in mid-December 1887, with Whitney represented by the redoubtable D'Alton McCarthy. The latter's intention was to demonstrate that the Liberals had exercised undue influence on some voters, had purchased the votes of a few, and had treated others to liquor during the 1886 election. Before the first day's examination of witnesses was concluded, McCarthy was well on his way to firmly supporting these charges. His cause was aided by the confession of a supposed Tory that he had left a prayer meeting to accept a five-dollar bribe to vote for Chamberlain; that done, he had returned to his prayers.

When the second day of the hearing began, Chamberlain's counsel admitted that there was sufficient evidence to warrant upsetting the election result and declaring the Dundas seat vacant. The judges concurred, thereby paving the way for a by-election. The Conservatives were quick to point out that the Liberal concession was probably made to avoid the presentation of further evidence. Had that occurred, they argued, they could have proven that Chamberlain was an agent in this corruption, and thus ineligible to contest the riding in another election. As it was, Chamberlain was unseated, but because guilt had been laid at other feet he could run in the by-election. The Conservatives could afford a smile: the riding had been opened; the counter-petition against Whitney was dropped; and the seven guilty Liberal zealots were each either fined two hundred dollars and costs or faced with the prospect of six months in jail – for their excesses in campaigning.[33]

Before the Mowat administration had chosen 31 January 1888 as the Dundas by-election date, the eager Tories held their nominating convention and once more selected Whitney as their standard-bearer. The forty-five-year-old lawyer again trekked the campaign trail. January was devoted to canvassing the county, first in the north concessions and then south along the river. Unemcumbered by a provincial campaign and its religious disputes, the Conservative candidate was able to wage his own particular battle, centring it largely on one point: the court-established corruption of the Grits. He argued that Dundas residents had been 'robbed' of the 'right to be represented by the man' of their choice, and asked for their support in order to 'teach' the Grits that 'the liberties of the people of Dundas' were 'not to be trifled with.' There was a call to put purity ahead of party in support of the Tory nominee. This honesty versus corruption issue, highlighted in this campaign and accompanied by a plea for bipartisan support, became a theme which Whitney played in subsequent elections and over which he achieved such mastery that he was ultimately able to orchestrate the collapse of a Liberal administration around it.[34]

This emerging picture of Whitney's essential honesty – initially self-sketched and then filled in by others – was drawn in sharp colours thanks to his forceful, blunt, and aloof manner. He had the look – and, for that matter, the sound – of incorruptibility. The accuracy of this portrait can be debated, but without much profit. The point is that it was increasingly accepted in Dundas and, once accepted there, it was soon accepted in a larger scene. Whitney was gathering the reputation of a politician who would not stoop to conquer.[35] Exuding righteousness, Whitney constantly retold the tale of Grit corruption to his Dundas listeners who, by their reaction, gave him increasing confidence that this time victory would be his. And it was. The path to the Ontario legislature had been cleared. On a February day in 1888, the Morrisburg Tory emerged from a train in Toronto, ready to start his new work.[36]

Friends of the new arrival in the provincial capital would, of course, have described him as a honest man, and warned that no one should dare to challenge him on that point. They might have complained that he could be withdrawn and noted that he could be pained by over-congeniality. He could be stubborn, possibly to the point where this trait might prove a weakness. He had a good mind and had shown a talent for political organization. He seemed to possess the ingredients of a tough politician. And, above all, he was a Liberal-Conservative, descended, he would have undoubtedly hastened to add, from Reform political stock.

v

Whitney took a room at the Walker House, that hotel at York and Front streets which was the favourite temporary home for members of the legislative assembly. On the afternoon of Friday, 10 February, he made his way east on Front Street to the red brick parliament buildings, built in the 1830s but still serving the provincial legislators. Externally, the structures were not impressive: 'too modern to pass muster as old ruins,' and looking 'not unlike a factory of some kind.' And, inside, they had 'a faded shabby-genteel, boarding-house appearance.' But the newest member was quite content to be there.[37]

Supported by two fellow Liberal-Conservatives, Whitney was admitted within the bar of the assembly and introduced to the speaker; that done, he took his seat. He then could survey the occupants of the house. Sitting across the aisle was Oliver Mowat, premier of the province since 1872, looking relaxed and comfortable as he leaned back in his seat with just the trace of an indulgent smile about his lips; on a table beside his desk sat 'his invariable attendant': 'a small grip sack ... full to the brim with papers.' The 'next most comfortable looking member of the government' was Arthur Sturgis Hardy, provincial secretary for the past eleven years and member of the assembly since 1873. Hardy, a lawyer by profession like the premier, was the most powerful speaker in the cabinet; powerful not only in the force of his argument but in its delivery, a characteristic which had earned him the title of 'little Thunder.' Then there was George W. Ross, the minister of education from Middlesex West, who could usually 'be found in his seat, wearing a hard felt hat tipped well over his nose, and nervously pulling at his whiskers.'[38]

On Whitney's side of the legislature the most impressive figure was the leader of

1879 Election Results			
Popular vote			Seats
Liberal	119,124	(48.06%)	57
Conservative	118,536	(47.83%)	29
Other	10,196	(4.11%)	2 (Ind. Cons.)
Total	247,856	(100.00%)	88
1883 Election Results			
Liberal	126,633	(48.73%)	50
Conservative	121,085	(46.60%)	35
Other	12,125	(4.67%)	3 (2 Ind. Libs and 1 Ind.)
Total	259,843	(100.00%)	88
1886 Election Results			
Liberal	153,290	(48.42%)	57
Conservative	148,969	(47.05%)	32
Other	14,355	(4.53%)	1 (Ind.)
Total	316,614	(100.00%)	90

the opposition, William Ralph Meredith, the member from London. An exceptionally able lawyer, almost fifty-eight years of age, Meredith had sat in the house since 1872 and had served as leader of the Ontario Liberal-Conservative party since 1879. Whitney came to be a fast personal and political friend of this man and developed a deep admiration for him, his policies, and his principles. In fact, Meredith became the dominant influence in the development of James Whitney as a politician.

After failing in three successive provincial elections to topple the Grits from power, the Tory chief seemed almost doomed to be the perpetual leader of the opposition. He simply could not match the Liberals' strength, which rested on their talented leader, the sagacious use of patronage, cautious legislation, tight political organization, loyal followers in south-western Ontario, and a perceptive awareness of the Ontario character. For his part, Meredith, a man not always admired by his supporters, led a party weakened by shortcomings in men, money, and organization, handicapped by Tory dominance nationally, sapped by religious controversy, and frustrated by continual failure. This being the state of Ontario politics, prospects for the freshman member from Dundas seemed limited indeed.

Whitney's maiden speech was made in the course of the debate on the resolutions before the assembly on proposed amendments to the British North America Act; these had come out of the interprovincial conference held at Quebec City in the previous autumn. Acknowledging that a new member should not be rash in entering the discussion of matters before the legislature, he argued that he had to 'protest against concurrence by the House in the findings of the Provincial

Premiers assembled in secret conclave at Quebec.' Whitney then moved on to defend vigorously the federal power of disallowance, the exclusive federal right of making senatorial appointments, the federal government's right to determine its own franchise, and the existing dominion-provincial financial relations. In passing, he also supported the protective tariff and condemned reciprocity. He condemned Mowat's failure to request representation at the gathering for Ontario's opposition party; but he then went on to demonstrate why the premier had not done so when he stated that Tories would not be party to tinkering with the constitution, preferring 'the establishment' 'of permanent institutions.' The newest Conservative legislator had just revealed once more a congenital weakness in his provincial party: it had to stand with the federal Tories on this subject and thus could not gather support with the cry of provincial rights, thus creating the impression of being controlled by Ottawa.[39]

Discussion on the need for revision of the constitution was a rather heady introduction to the matters that came before the Ontario legislature. Generally, the topics were on a smaller scale and it was these which largely occupied the attention of the Tory back-bencher. Like his leader, Whitney welcomed the decision by Mowat to extend the provincial franchise to provide manhood suffrage, a proposition for which Meredith had long fought. The Morrisburg member also busied himself with opposition to amendments to the Municipal Act which would prevent municipalities from granting bonuses in efforts to attract manufacturing industries. It was finally decided to delay implementation of these clauses for six months and this provided municipalities, concerned about sluggish growth, some time in which 'to induce some large manufacturing establishment to locate in their midst.' Whitney, in fighting such changes, undoubtedly shared a Dundas County view that, unless some industries were secured, the 'outlook' was 'gloomy enough.' The Conservative legislator, seeking support for the retention of bonuses, tried to stir the reeves of Morrisburg and Iroquois to send petitions denouncing the amendments which he thought were 'tyrannical' and 'an extreme exercise or application of the doctrine of protection.' In this matter he was very much the constituency man, playing to the concerns of a region beset by assorted economic difficulties, not the least of which was growth.[40]

As might have been expected, Whitney took time during his first session to denounce corrupt election practices. His own experience, of course, provided him with the chart for such a course. He troubled the government with questions about the number of convictions under the Controverted Elections Act and suggested 'that it was practically without effect.' 'There surely should be some punishment for these offences,' he continued, 'and he thought it would be agreed that the punishment should be in the nature of a deterrent, or one calculated to bring about a prevention of the practice.'[41]

Whitney's success in regaining Dundas County meant that he was given the task of assisting in the organization of the eastern corner of the province. Such labour was made essential by the advent of manhood suffrage: it was necessary to ensure that the name of every male – or, at least, of every Conservative male – who was twenty-one, British by birth or naturalization, and a nine-month resident of Ontario appeared on the voters' lists. These lists were produced by Grit and Tory assessors and since each tended to be forgetful of known opponents' names, constant vigilance was required. Whitney, in agreeing to supervise these matters in Stormont and Glengarry and to report on conditions to Meredith, protested that his own riding would keep him busy enough. George F. Marter, a fellow Conservative legislator, urged him to get on with the job and argued the party could 'carry the province' if it had 'good Candidates, Lists in good shape and ... the Protestant horse.' Then, remembering that Roman Catholics constituted half of Glengarry's population and a third of Stormont's, Marter lamely added that 'this would be a difficult programme' in these two ridings but that it would take in 'the majority of cases.'[42]

The Dundas member grudgingly began the chore, corresponding with neighbouring Tories and receiving mixed political reports. Some were positive in reply, noting that a particular assessor was a 'Friend' whose only flaw was a desire for exactness which meant Grit names made the lists. Others detailed stories of Tory inertia and lack of local organization, factors that were bound to aid the Liberals. A Glengarry resident, mindful of the events of the previous provincial campaign and aware of the Catholic composition of his constituency, advocated that the party run an independent Conservative candidate in his riding and thus perhaps slide over religious difficulties. Aside from Dundas, the Conservatives were clearly not in good shape in the eastern end of the province. Whitney obviously had a major task before him if he was to win people, particularly Catholics, to his party.[43]

Even in Dundas, the local party rift continued, with fresh trouble erupting when each faction sought a railway charter. Whitney supported the cause of the projected Ottawa, Morrisburg, and New York railway and appealed to John A. Macdonald for a favourable decision. Here was one more scheme to lift up the region's economy, and the provincial member noted the strong local feeling on the subject. He also warned of serious trouble at the next federal election if positive action were not forthcoming. In the end, Macdonald smiled on the project because, in part, the 'MPP for Dundas' was 'a good friend.' Whitney, however successful, was still left with his Conservative enemies in the home constituency. It was true that their numbers were dwindling, but it remained a situation that required careful observation.[44]

VI

Such a close watch on Dundas affairs was pertinent because Whitney would have to face the electorate once more in a general election in 1890. And that election, when called, was dominated by cries of race and religion. Pressed by the creation of the Equal Rights Association in 1889, Meredith edged perilously close to a 'no-popery' position when he vigorously denounced Grit catering to the Catholics, as if they held the balance of power between the two parties. He did not pledge himself to the abolition of separate schools, but he stood next to that position when he asked for the use of the ballot in separate school trustee elections and when he came down hard against the use of French, except where absolutely necessary, in the schools of Ontario. He said he simply wanted – and here he deliberately chose his words – equal rights for all, with favouritism to none. Meredith's stance had been shaped by personal conviction, irritation with Grit policies, and of course, a desire for power.[45]

Although there was praise for the Tory leader's decision to break 'away from the traditions of Ottawa conservatism,' he was damned by Conservative Roman Catholics and candidates who faced large numbers of that faith in their constituencies. Tory Catholics drifted in the direction of the Liberal party or else simply chose to sit out this election contest. Orangemen, of course, were delighted and declared that the party was bound to 'make great gains' because, finally, the heather was on fire. The danger here was that anyone could get burned in the blaze, which was fanned by a rousing exchange of open letters between Meredith and Archbishop James Vincent Cleary of Kingston. Bigotry on both sides produced a most unattractive election campaign.[46]

Whitney came to the battle without having made a major speech on either separate schools or the use of the French language; but he left no room for doubt about his position at his nomination meeting. After being selected without opposition by the Dundas Conservatives, he unhesitatingly 'adopted the platform of Mr. Meredith as laid down on the lines of his London Speech.' If, by chance, this statement did not clarify his position, his election letter certainly did when it called for an imprecise limit to church control over separate schools and announced that Ontario was 'an English province ... in every respect.' Whitney called for every man to battle the provincial government which was 'under the influence of ... the tremendous power of the Roman Catholic Hierarchy.' A staunch supporter of Meredith, the Morrisburg man completely accepted his leader's platform. In Whitney's eyes these ugly issues had been raised by the Liberals, through their deliberate pandering to Roman Catholics and through their prejudicial favours to the separate school system. As a result, he could ask: 'And what other consequences could be expected than the state of affairs we have now?'[47]

The questions of religion and race did not adversely affect Whitney, who encountered no serious trouble in defeating the Liberal candidate, Morrisburg *Herald* editor George P. Graham, by more than one hundred and fifty votes. Despite the increase in his majority over the by-election result, the Tory winner still failed to capture the Grit strongholds of Morrisburg, Iroquois and Williamsburg township.[48]

Elsewhere in the province the Conservatives were not so fortunate, and barely improved upon their seat strength at the dissolution of the legislature. Even more indicative of trouble was the fact that the Tories' share of the total vote had

1890 Election Results			
Popular vote			Seats
Liberal	165,470	(50.65%)	56
Conservative	146,631	(44.89%)	34
Equal Rights	9,817	(3.00%)[49]	1
Other	4,758	(1.46%)	0
Total	326,676	(100.00%)	91

declined, and, even allowing for the future return to the fold of those who had voted for straight Equal Rights candidates, the gap between the triumphant Liberals and the beaten Conservatives in terms of share of the total vote was growing. 'The result,' wrote Meredith, 'generally is not satisfactory but did not surprise me though some of the gains & losses did so. We had tremendous odds to fight against and our Presbyterian friends seemed to have preferred their party to their principles.' Undoubtedly Meredith's campaign had given offence to a goodly number of Conservative Catholics, and they had opted to vote Liberal or remain at home; but other observers, seeking to explain the outcome, put their fingers on the old Tory weaknesses of inadequate local and provincial organization, anemic federal support, and poor-quality candidates. Whitney's success under these circumstances could only serve to elevate his status in the party's legislative ranks, which still remained 'a Spartan band.'[50]

2

Dismounting from 'the Protestant Horse': 1890–1898

I

Following the election of 1890, Whitney rose steadily in Ontario Conservative ranks. His own abilities played a part in this development, but so did the departure of some able Tories from the political scene and the absence of considerable talent on the opposition benches. Despite this advancement, Whitney had some temporary reservations about remaining active in politics. After the campaign, he initially declared his eagerness for the next legislative session; by late 1891, however, he was casting about for something else – possibly a patronage appointment – but was unsuccessful in his quest. In mid-1892, he contemplated 'quitting public life.' Meredith advised against it, observing that 'it would be a mistake for one like you who enjoys it and has such good prospects ... in his party to withdraw.' Whitney accepted his leader's advice, shook off his gloomy mood about his political future, and settled into active work on behalf of his party both in and out of the legislature.[1]

He soon demonstrated growth in the job by taking up larger issues and serving as his party's critic on education, justice, and, of course, electoral corruption. As an ex-school trustee, a practising lawyer, and a victim of electoral corruption, he chose fields of interest that were not particularly surprising. On the other hand, he offered little on subjects where his background and training left him without strong or informed opinions; thus he said almost nothing on prohibition and contributed rarely to debates on economic affairs.

In speaking on education, he argued that the government should increase the grants to and thus the efficiency of Ontario's public and high schools, particularly those in rural areas; but he found that enough was being done to aid the university level. He even attempted to have the number of lecture days extended at the University of Toronto, until George Ross read him a short lecture on the wear and tear of the university year on faculty and students. Anxious to see a maximum effort put forward to the benefit of the public school system, Whitney sharply questioned the cost and usefulness of the Ontario Agricultural College at Guelph. Whatever good might come from that institution, he remarked, 'was sprinkled so thinly over the country as to be scarcely perceptible to the naked eye. Some scheme should be devised by the minister of agriculture whereby information upon agricultural subjects could be imparted to the people at various points throughout the province.' Being Tory schools critic, he also kept a sharp eye open for purely political appointments in the educational field and watched for the 'political wirepuller' who was 'not properly qualified for the position.' Whitney's primary concern was to secure adequate educational opportunities and facilities for the lower grades of the system. He was not opposed to higher education, but he did want it placed second in any order of priorities. Given his own background and that of most of his constituents, Whitney's position on educational matters was scarcely surprising.[2]

Turning to the field of judicial administration, he suggested that there was a need for the decentralization of the courts so that the cost and inconvenience to the little man could be reduced. With some eastern Ontario hostility, he noted that the 'atmosphere of Toronto seemed to choke off' any implementation of his proposal. But he reserved his strongest words for the questionable abilities of rural magistrates whom he judged to be 'unfit for their positions' which they secured as political rewards. 'Nine out of ten of them' were simply 'unmitigated' nuisances in their communities.[3]

As he had done in sessions prior to the election of 1890, Whitney attempted to have the penalties for election bribery stiffened. He wanted imprisonment a definite consequence of conviction, not just an alternative to be employed when the fine could not be paid. The latter arrangement 'simply put a premium upon corruption' and sent only the poor man to jail. Whitney failed to secure his goal but, as before, he forced a division on the issue and thus created the impression that the government favoured corruption, despite Mowat's protests that the Morrisburg lawyer's proposals 'would be injurious rather than beneficial.' And at least one Liberal was sufficiently troubled by the issue to vote with Whitney and the Tories. A year later, in 1892, the rising Conservative attempted to have the two-year imprisonment penalty for impersonation restored to the election laws; again, he failed but forced a division on the question. His doggedness in this matter inevitably drew increasing public attention and cast him in a very favourable light. Further, his stance was inadvertently providing him with a growing reputation for incorruptibility; not that a public position and a personal attribute should necessarily be equated, but in this instance they were, and that development certainly aided Whitney's political career.[4]

When the legislature was not sitting, Whitney attended to other political chores. He established himself as a capable speaker and was soon taking up invitations to address by-election audiences in constituencies far distant from his own. He pitched into party work in the federal election of 1891, and assisted the Dundas member of Parliament, H.H. Ross, in sorting out local patronage. When John A. Macdonald died, Whitney expressed the hope – as did others – that in the ensuing cabinet reorganization a place would be found for Meredith, thus strengthening Ontario's representation; but this was not to be. And, beyond all this, there was a law practice to maintain because it remained the base of Whitney's financial security.[5]

II

In the early 1890s, while Whitney busied himself with the dual chore of earning a growing reputation as a politician and a satisfactory income as a lawyer, the nation in general – and more especially Ontario – entered a crisis of confidence, particularly in the matter of political leadership. There developed a deep-rooted conviction that Canada had failed to achieve its destiny, although visions of that destiny were as varied as the shades of an Ontarian autumn. On every hand, so it seemed, there was evidence of failure and trouble. The federal government, after the death of Macdonald, was irresolute in the face of the Manitoba school question and beset by a growing list of scandals. French- and English-speaking Canadians were divided in the wake of the hanging of Louis Riel and the quarrels over the Jesuit Estates Act. Disillusioned farmers, notably in Ontario and Manitoba, became increasingly sour over the consequences they saw flowing from a protective tariff. Toronto workers challenged the supposed unity of Canadian society with an angry march on city hall under the black flag of anarchy – an event witnessed by Whitney and hundreds of others. Impoverished urban families, headed by an unemployed breadwinner, huddled through harsh, bleak winters on the handouts of unorganized social welfare. The Working Women's Protective Association of Toronto supported the efforts of female glove factory workers to maintain – not increase – their incomes, and was destroyed for its pains. A growing body of temperance workers viewing alcohol as the cause, not the symptom, of social ills, flayed away at the demon rum with increasing vigour. The Salvation Army, looking to earlier evangelicals and the military for inspiration, invaded the quiet comfort of residential areas in half a hundred Ontario towns with drum and voice early – too early – on Sunday mornings. And militant Protestants and rigid Catholics converged once more for a running donnybrook in Ontario.

The solutions offered to end the unease were as numerous as the signs of it; some had rhyme, some had reason, some had neither. Prohibition, salvation, abolition of separate schools, strong trade unionism, assimilation of Franco-Ontarians, and free trade were all advanced as the means of getting the country – and the province – back on the tracks. There were also calls for fresh political leadership and new parties to lead the way out of the slough of social decay. 'The spirit of independence in political matters is steadily growing,' wrote one Ontario editorialist in 1893, hoping to shape public opinion through this judgment; he then proceeded to point to one factor back of such a mood: both national party leaders, Thompson and Laurier, were Roman Catholics. Having begun the cry for independent politics with an assault on the religion of the two chieftains, he broadened his attack to argue that partyism negated the free thought that was so necessary to 'light up the national questions of Canada, and usher in an era of statesmanship.' While this argument was rooted in anti-Catholicism, it nevertheless contained the concept of independent politics, and in the early 1890s the idea had sufficient appeal to result in the creation of two new provincial political parties. These parties were to rearrange the allegiances of many Ontarians and make for the greatest fluidity in provincial politics since the days of Sandfield Macdonald.[6]

The Patrons of Industry, a farmers' movement, arrived in Ontario from the United States in 1889 and early indicated that it might take political action in order to secure redress for the grievances of the province's agriculturalists. This organization, severing its American connection in 1891, proceeded to denounce the protectionist aspects of Macdonald's national policy, deplore the worrisome signs of rural depopulation, search for the road to rural economic recovery, and condemn the impurities so obvious in the political system. The Patrons publicized these views through the pages of the *Canada Farmers' Sun* to a growing body of converts to Patronism. Encouraged by the latter development, they decided to plunge into Ontario politics, despite the obvious fact that many of their complaints could only be dealt with at the federal level.[7]

The Protestant Protective Association had different and deeper sources. It took some inspiration from a similar body in the United States, but it also had roots of a distinctively Canadian character: the Equal Rights Association, the Manitoba school question, the Ontario separate school debate, the labours of the Orange Order, the vexing fact of Roman Catholic leadership in federal politics, and long-standing Ontario Protestant prejudice. The PPA announced its determination to protect the nation and 'its free institutions against the secret, intolerant, and aggressive efforts that are being persistently put forth by the Roman Catholic Church to control the Government of the Dominion of Canada, and its provinces ...' This militant body also sounded a nativist note in the economic hard times of the day when it urged changes in immigration laws which would prevent the entry of 'cheap pauper and criminal labor' which supplanted 'free and educated Canadian citizens in every line of industry.'[8]

In December of 1893, these two new groups made their presence felt on the Ontario political scene in the results of two by-election contests. The Patrons of Industry representative, Daniel McNaughton, captured Bruce North, defeating Liberal and Conservative candidates in the process. He swept all but one rural township and left his two opponents to divide triumphs in five towns and villages of the constituency. McNaughton had been 'Secretary for the Local Reform Association when he accepted the Patron nomination.' At the same time, the voters of Lambton East returned a member of the PPA, Peter McCallum. In this instance, the Conservatives offered no opposition and the victor faced only a Liberal opponent. This result cheered many who wanted a vigorous anti-Catholic party in the province, particularly if it could be led by D'Alton McCarthy.[9]

Whitney did not remain unaffected by these changing political circumstances. Even before the by-elections of 1893, he had managed to incur the wrath of the *Canada Farmers' Sun* thanks to his early and strong opposition to the Patrons of Industry. Whitney's course in this matter had been dictated by a strong suspicion, made firmer by the report of a fellow Tory legislator, that the Patrons were little more than Grits in disguise, possessed of pro-American and anti-British feelings. Then, too, the Morrisburg lawyer was acutely aware of the growth of Patronism in his own political bailiwick; he must have found the Patron pledge of solidarity behind only their candidates particularly vexing when repeated by the Dundas County president of this farmer's party. Thus, late in the fall of 1893, after the Patrons had selected a former Conservative to do battle with him in the next election, Whitney moved into action. Speaking in the northern end of his riding, he saluted the concept of an organization designed to assist the farmers *within* the existing political structures of the province but, warming to his topic, he condemned as 'a most monstrous proposition' the attempt 'to bind the Patrons to support every candidate nominated by the society.' In Whitney's eyes there was simply no place for the conversion of a potentially useful farmers' organization into a political party, a move which might well destroy the two-party system of which he was such a firm exponent. Further, he thought he smelled about the movement an odour which was both dictatorial and annexationist. Whitney, of course, could also see a danger to himself in all of this: the selection of a Patron candidate for Dundas, supported by fervent converts to Patronism, could well place his own seat in jeopardy.[10]

Whitney's position on the other rising political force of the day, the PPA, is far less clear. It is a fact, however, that on one occasion in 1893 he moved to block Protestant extremism in Dundas when he saw danger in it for the federal Conservative party. It was feared that, at the annual county meeting of Orangemen, 'a couple of Grit members' would seek passage of a resolution condemning the Roman Catholic prime minister and two of his Orange cabinet colleagues, M. Bowell and N.C. Wallace, for their conduct in the Manitoba school question. Concerned about the consequences of such action, Whitney suggested that Andy Broder attend the meeting in order to 'prevent any rash action.' Clearly Whitney did not want to see any breach in the two-party system and was struggling – in vain as it turned out – to avoid the splintering off of unhappy farmers and Protestants.[11]

These Ontario political developments, coming as they did immediately prior to the provincial session and anticipated election of 1894, could not but colour the language of debate in the assembly and on the platform. Early in the session, James

Conmee, the Liberal Roman Catholic member for Algoma West, introduced a bill which would provide for the use of the ballot at separate school elections, if desired by the ratepayers. The move was designed, in part, to take the sting out of Conservative and PPA criticism on this point. The measure briefly threatened to split the Grit legislative ranks, but party loyalty proved stronger than religious affiliation and the bill became law. The Conservatives, arguing that the legislation was insufficiently strong, offered an unsuccessful amendment which would have made use of the ballot compulsory, not optional.[12]

Debate on this and other matters in the session of 1894 set the stage for the election campaign which followed. Meredith, in setting out his platform in May, charged the government with the reckless selling of timber limits and, as was expected in light of remarks during the preceding session, came down on the side of biennial legislative sessions and the abolition of Government House; the latter proposition was designed to woo economy-minded farmers of Patron persuasion. On the ticklish subject of prohibition, he said that any government he formed would bow to the will of the majority; but he failed to indicate how that will was to be measured. Following Whitney's lead, he favoured the use of an absolutely secret ballot. Then, he turned to those most tender problems that were related to separate schools and declared for a compulsory secret ballot for the election of trustees, the use of authorized texts, and the adequate inspection of these institutions. At the same time the Conservative leader, as he had done before, insisted that there was nothing in his programme to warrant the charge of intolerance or bigotry. He would not ask for the abolition of separate schools because, regrettable as their creation might be, they were guaranteed by the constitution.[13]

Meredith's position on separate school matters quickly drew Archbishop Cleary of Kingston into the fray, and he did nothing for the tone of the debate by provocatively suggesting that the Tory leader was a pseudo-Conservative and 'a hungry adventurer.' That was enough to ensure that this provincial campaign – like the two preceding – would be one in which the religious cry drowned out all else. 'The Separate school question was thenceforth discussed on all the public platforms, but with more particular vigour in Toronto.' On one occasion, when Samuel Blake – a critic of the Tory position – attempted to address a stormy Massey Hall meeting, police were called upon to eject hecklers before he could be heard.[14]

Thus the religious question shaped the Ontario campaign of 1894, and the presence of Patron and PPA candidates further distorted the battle and its results. Not one of the parties ran candidates in every one of the ninety-three constituencies. Local riding associations undoubtedly worked out deals to prevent split votes and triangular contests. Such arrangements depended very much on the views of the people on the ground and did not reflect directions from the leadership of the parties. For example, the Tories in the Lambton ridings decided not to run candidates against the PPA nominees, on the clear understanding that the PPA organization would support the Conservatives in the next federal election. In the constituency of Cardwell, the Tories endorsed the candidate of the PPA – who then ran as a Conservative; this manoeuvre meant that they were forced to drop their sitting member. Such local intrigues meant that provincial politics almost defied analysis and produced wildly inaccurate predictions from foolhardy forecasters.[15]

In Dundas County, the Liberals wrestled with the question of contesting the riding, given the Patron presence. Would it be wiser to name a candidate in hopes of a Patron-created split in the Tory vote, or avoid the election in the expectation that Grits, and disgruntled Conservatives, would throw their ballots to the farmer candidate? In the end they chose the latter course and left the field to Whitney and the Patron nominee. Consequently, Whitney's energies continued to be devoted to assaults on the Patrons: he denied the need for such a group, arguing that 'the agriculturalists were and always had been receiving the best of attention at the hands of the Government.' This unexpected defence of Mowat clearly indicated that the election of 1894 made for some strange bedfellows, even in Dundas County.[16]

1894 Election Results			
Popular vote			Seats[17]
Liberal	159,354	(42.46%)	47
Conservative	118,127	(31.47%)	27
Patron	67,570	(18.01%)	17
PPA	18,038	(4.81%)	2
Other	12,187	(3.25%)	1 (Independent)
Total	375,276	(100.00%)	94

Out of this confusion of parties came the election results indicated above. Any possibility of a minority government, however, evaporated when the Liberals were successful in by-elections held before the legislative session of 1895 began. Whitney, neither blessing nor blessed by the PPA, fought out his battle with his Patron opponent on Meredith's platform and was victorious. A glance at the results must have left him with mixed feelings: he had captured Morrisburg and Iroquois for the first time, but had slipped a notch in the rural sections of his riding.

III

The Ontario Conservatives, led by Meredith, had now lost to Mowat in five successive elections; future prospects were as dim as ever because the party still lacked men, money, and organization and, in recent years, had thoroughly antagonized many Roman Catholic voters. Thus it was not surprising that, when Prime Minister Thompson offered Meredith the chief justiceship of the Court of

Common Pleas, the battered leader readily accepted the place. In one move, the Catholic Thompson had honoured Meredith's service and abilities, reassured some suspicious and militant Protestants, and removed a liability to the federal party in Ontario. The manoeuvre, of course, stripped the provincial party of its head, but in that development there was opportunity for Whitney who, in six brief years, had established himself as a diligent worker, a competent critic, and a loyal lieutenant.[18]

On 23 October 1894, twenty-three of the Conservatives who had been elected to the legislature gathered in the *Empire*'s offices to select a new leader and, also, to make a run at straightening out organizational matters. Despite considerable speculation about a possible successor to Meredith, including mention of D'Alton McCarthy, only four legislative members were seriously considered: Oliver A. Howland, just elected for Toronto South; Dr George S. Ryerson, sitting for Toronto East for but two years; George F. Marter, an eight-year veteran from Toronto North; and Whitney, described as an 'able legislator' and vigorous debater. The last was also the only potential leader not from a Toronto seat.[19]

Among these men, Whitney had a slight edge over Marter and considerable margin over the other two. Meredith thought it likely that the Morrisburg lawyer would be offered the leadership and urged him not to decline, even if the thought of the work involved was overwhelming. Whitney, for his part, was sufficiently interested to start an exchange of correspondence with the retired leader on the responsibilities and possible tactics of the future leader. Meredith suggested that it would be wise for the new leader to avoid any action that might drive off the Patrons, because the 'mission' of the opposition was to destroy the Mowat government and its 'vicious' patronage system. He also advised Whitney to 'strenuously' oppose any move by the party to adopt two particular PPA planks, 'the abolition of separate schools and the blacklisting of Roman Catholics.' And he informed the Dundas member that the leadership would devour time but not money, and suggested that the 'old heads' of the party should get together before any convention in order to avoid 'a mistake in selection.' Clearly, Meredith wanted Whitney to take up the leadership.[20]

If, in his quiet moves towards the party's headship, Whitney had the discreet blessings of the former chief, he did not have those of the *Canada Farmers' Sun*. Recalling his attack on the Patrons of a year before, the newspaper made it clear that Patrons preferred – or should prefer – 'Marter or Howland rather than Whitney as leader of one of the parties.' To make matters more difficult for Whitney, the *Sun* hinted that Marter might become premier, a possibility only if the Patrons lined up with the Conservatives. So, there it was: choose Marter, and Mowat might just be tipped out of office; select Whitney, and the Liberals would have a fresh lease on life. This was the background for the meeting at the *Empire*.[21]

Just what occurred at that meeting is not altogether clear because the newspaper accounts of it vary. The *Empire* ran a story the following day which stated that

Howland, Ryerson, Marter, and Whitney were all nominated and that all allowed their names to stand. These nominees then retired and an informal discussion among the remaining legislators ensued. 'At the close of the discussion [they] took a ballot in the absence of the gentlemen whose names were proposed, resulting in the selection of Mr. Marter, which choice was afterward made unanimous amidst enthusiasm.'[22]

The *Mail* published an account somewhat at odds with the *Empire*'s report. Whitney, it recorded, would not 'accept the position on any account,' although assured 'of an almost unanimous vote.' During a recess, talks were held, and 'shortly after the meeting resumed Mr. G.F. Marter was selected leader unanimously.' There is sufficient detail in the *Mail* story to give it an air of credibility and, consequently, a problem arises. Was Whitney defeated by Marter on a ballot, or did he indicate that he would refuse the leadership? Two days later the *Empire* qualified its account by stating that 'there was nothing like a contest, but simply a consultation and consideration of what, under all the circumstances, was best to be done.' This modified story suggests that debate and discussion occurred, but not an open contest. Whitney, then, apparently did not make a strong play for the leadership, either under pressure or out of conviction. Why did he pursue this course after seriously contemplating the leadership in his exchange with Meredith?[23]

If Whitney had the party's interests at heart – and he was not the type of man to place himself ahead of the party – then he would acknowledge that he was a liability in dealing with the Patrons. As matters stood at that time – although they were to be altered before the 1895 session began – the selection of a speaker from amongst the Liberals would place the government in a minority of one against a combined opposition, if the Conservatives retained Meredith's vacant London seat. Thus, if there ever was a time for Conservative-Patron co-operation, it was then. Not a solitary Patron could be offended and Whitney was offensive to most; so the Morrisburg lawyer stood aside in favour of a man of whom the Patron newspaper had spoken kindly. Whitney's course may well have also been dictated by fears of loss of business, money, and time if he took the leadership. Finally, it has to be conceded that the post was not an attractive one at that point. Whitney did not become leader of the party in the fall of 1894; but – and this was to prove important – should Marter resign, there was little real question about who would succeed. Intentionally or otherwise, Whitney had clearly established the line of succession, if he chose to follow it.

On the day following the selection of Marter, the Conservative MPPS convened once more and this time they discussed matters that related to organization and questions of policy. When these topics were exhausted, Marter suggested the creation of an executive committee 'to consult with the chief on such matters as he may deem of sufficient import to necessitate such consultation.' In addition to Whitney, there were seven other members on this committee, including the three remaining Toronto MPPs and the one from York West. Even allowing for the uneven quality of the other Tory members of the legislature, the committee could not be described as representative, and it had the look of Toronto domination. Whitney was 'strongly opposed to the creation of an Executive Committee,' and 'also objected to being appointed a member of the Committee,' although he did not press his objection 'for obvious reasons.'[24]

Whitney left no record to explain his opposition, but he may well have been alarmed at the Toronto bias of the group. Further, he may have reasoned that this reorganization tended to place party policy-making in the hands of a select few and to ignore the caucus. He probably agreed to serve realizing that a refusal could be interpreted as either division in the ranks or a fit of personal peevishness. In any event, Whitney had found himself at odds with Marter on the latter's first day of leadership, a development quite unlike his experience with Meredith.

This modest split between the two men was widened into a visible breach by events surrounding the London by-election called to fill Meredith's former seat. Both Marter and Whitney spoke in the brief mid-November campaign, but it was Marter who rocked the party when he came down for prohibition and the abolition of separate schools. The Conservatives had suddenly, and without warning, veered onto a new course. Three days later, on 17 November, Whitney – furious with his leader but committed to speak – arrived in London. As the keynote speaker at the final Conservative rally of the campaign, Whitney had the opportunity to comment or elaborate on the Marter policy innovations; but, in a wide-ranging speech that ran from high praise for Meredith to humorous jibes at Liberal practices, there was not a word on separate schools or prohibition. In silently repudiating his leader's position, Whitney recognized the futility and divisiveness of the proposed separate school policy and made clear his lack of sympathy for the prohibition cause.[25]

Three days after Whitney's speech, the Liberals won the constituency by eight hundred votes. Staggered by the size of the defeat, the *Empire* was quick to blame 'Roman Catholic and liquor votes,' particularly the latter. Embittered by the crushing blow, the Conservative candidate lashed out at Grit 'bribery and personation' and Conservative 'treachery.' On the last point he argued that he had been deserted by the London MP, Sir John Carling, on the issue of separate schools in an attempt 'to destroy the party in Provincial matters with the intention of regaining influence for Dominion purposes.' It is likely that many federal Conservatives were distinctly displeased with Marter's new policies and thus would avoid any connection with the by-election campaign, the results of which also assured Mowat of a majority government.

Marter, left to absorb the lessons of his first campaign as leader, did just that and, consequently, moved to make amends at a Toronto Conservative meeting on 5 December. In remarks which just 'came out,' Marter disavowed the policies enunciated in London. In effect, he admitted that separate schools had a legal status which could not be overcome and then went on to concede Roman Catholics a definite say in matters of teacher certification, textbook selection and school inspection. Calling for an end to 'agitation for agitation's sake,' and fifteen years of fighting, Marter proffered the olive branch to Catholics. 'What was to be gained by keeping up the old warfare,' he asked Whitney, 'we have been defeated three times on that platform[;] I always said we just went far enough to drive away every Catholic and not far enough to get any Protestant reformers.' Marter qualified his remarkable shift by stating that he was speaking for himself, but, as party leader, he was scarcely in a position to do only that on this contentious topic. He was, in fact, laying to rest a bogey which had haunted the provincial Conservative party through a succession of campaigns. There would be protests to this course of action but, nevertheless, the deed was largely done. Marter then finished his performance by hauling the party off the prohibitionist track, observing that such a route had failed to draw temperance Grits to the Tory side. He would retain his private prohibitionist sentiments, but the party was in no way tied to them. A supposedly routine Conservative gathering had turned into a landmark in the history of party policy.[26]

The *Empire*, only too conscious of the federal political scene, quickly applauded Marter's course: 'The business of the Conservative party in the Legislature is to reform the administration of the province in toto, to give us economical government, and stop crude legislation. To go on advocating one or two questions which the electors declare they do not want and will not have would be to abdicate the functions of a political party and cripple its general usefulness.' Whitney, however, was in no mood to echo praise for his leader. He argued that 'Mr Marter's London speech was in direct opposition to the instructions of the Caucus & put the party in a false position before the people. His subsequent speech in Toronto made the matter a great deal worse.' Whitney allowed Marter's claim of misquotation in his Toronto speech but noted that his leader had not publicly corrected any errors and, consequently, the question was 'settled ... in the public mind.' The Morrisburg lawyer was thus unwilling to participate in a Kingston by-election campaign because he would be compelled to repudiate Marter's erratic course at any political meeting.[27]

Whitney's obvious irritation stemmed largely from Marter's shifts on the separate school question. Whitney would have objected to the suggestion of abolition simply because neither he nor Meredith had ever advocated that policy: respect for the constitution and fear of political consequences had steered them away from that route. Whitney apparently found fault with Marter's subsequent position because it was a dramatic and embarrassing change of stance, a betrayal of Meredith's stand, a possible source of party disunity, and an end to some useful criticisms of separate schools. In all likelihood, Whitney thought there was still merit in pressing the government on issues such as a compulsory secret ballot for separate school board elections, the use of authorized texts in separate schools, and the certification of separate school teachers in the same manner as public school ones. What Whitney apparently could not see, for the moment, was that the party might well profit from Marter's moves; the Morrisburg man was more concerned with past positions than with future prospects. Ill will, largely generated by Whitney, now existed between party leader and first lieutenant.

IV

Once the by-elections of late 1894 and early 1895 had assured the Mowat administration of an absolute majority in the legislature, the Liberals called the assembly into session, sure in the knowledge that they could not be beaten by any Conservative-Patron alliance. But such opposition unity failed to develop, even when the Conservatives put forward a motion based on a Patron plank: the payment of county officials by salary rather than fee. Mowat argued that a fee commission, appointed almost a year before, was considering this very matter but had not yet reported; thus there was no need for legislative action until the commission delivered its verdict. The Patrons, inexperienced and weakly led by Joseph Haycock, accepted Mowat's explanation and voted against the Conservative amendment. Although the Patrons were to support Marter's men on later issues, this vote was critical in the Conservative argument that Patrons were nothing but Liberals in fraternal disguise who had coldly deceived Tory farmers in order to weaken the party in the election. This point, made repeatedly over the next four years, certainly hastened the decline of the Patrons and a return to the two-party system. And such a line of argument was continued despite the fact that the Conservatives and almost all the Patrons voted together for the abolition of Government House and for the implementation of the tendering system in securing supplies. On these particular votes a few Patrons went with the Liberals and, thus, before the session was four weeks old, the new party was showing clear signs of internal division. To compound their difficulties, the Patrons lost their first post-election contest when the riding of Haldimand went to the Liberals in March of 1895. The protest party had been quickly dragged into a struggle for survival.[28]

Whenever the opportunity arose, Whitney was quick to torment and confuse the Patrons about their abandonment of principle, scornfully referring to them as 'irresponsible chatterers.' Despite his party's earlier concern about wooing the Patrons, Whitney showed no inclination to be conciliatory; after all, these people had cost him a chance at the party leadership and he seemed determined to make them pay. But Patron-baiting was not Whitney's sole concern in the session. He was up to speak on virtually every question: schools, law reform, agriculture, and the student strike at the University of Toronto. In fact, he was having more to say than the leader of the party, who only managed to keep his end up in the public accounts committee. Near the close of the session Marter fell ill with peritonitis, and Whitney had the prime position on the opposition benches to himself. He had become leader in fact, if not in title, of the Conservative party.[29]

Although Whitney spoke clearly on some educational matters – he charged the government with mishandling university affairs and urged it to pay more attention to elementary schools – he said nothing about separate schools, not a word. The absence of acrimonious debate over these schools helped produce a short, quiet legislative session, although other factors also promoted sessional brevity. No one seemed to have the strength to continue the brawling of the 1894 election campaign. Aside from an attempt to legislate greater control over the medical profession, the Patrons contributed little while occupying a sixth of the legislature's seats. Last, but not least, Meredith was gone and Marter simply could not fill his shoes. The former's departure had removed a fine legal mind from the assembly, but had also diminished the fiercely partisan quality of debate. Meredith was missed and hot issues were missing.

Whitney, however, remained hot on the subject of Marter. The precise cause of his continuing vexation is not clear. If Whitney committed any thoughts on the matter to paper, they have never come to light; only a couple of letters from old friends suggest that tension between leader and follower persisted. Shortly after the 1895 session, Meredith cautioned his ex-lieutenant not 'to take the course you suggested with regard to Marter.' The former party chief argued that by not acting in a certain way – what way is not spelled out – Whitney would avoid a responsibility, presumably for Marter's words. Meredith urged Whitney to 'delay action until the eve of next session' when, if the situation remained unaltered, his old supporter might have to take action of a 'drastic character.' This advice fails to indicate just what action Whitney was proposing, but additional counsel provided by Andrew Broder at the outset of the 1896 legislative session shows that Whitney was 'not in accord' with Marter on 'some questions.' It would appear, then, that Whitney was still upset by Marter's policy pronouncements, and particularly his dumping of the separate school question. This interpretation is open to some criticism; it seems odd that Meredith would argue against a repudiation of Marter's new separate school position. On the other hand, although Whitney had followed Meredith's criticisms and policies in the matter of separate schools, he had had remarkably little to say on the subject in the legislature. Perhaps Whitney wanted to be free to criticize the operation – not the existence – of separate schools, and thought that Marter's pronouncements prevented him from adopting such an approach. In any case, he remained distinctly hostile to his new leader.[30]

The Dundas County politician was not the only restless person in the party; there were other Conservative members of the legislature who were similarly affected. Once the 1896 session had begun, there were rumours that Whitney was going to replace the present leader. Oddly enough, the initial party caucus was held after the session commenced and it was anticipated that this meeting would produce the fireworks that would end with Marter's abdication. Whitney was evidently embarrassed by such rumours because, although he wanted to be free to criticize Marter at this caucus, he was not anxious to be cast in the role of *coup* mastermind. Andy Broder advised him to 'take little or no part' in the caucus, fearing that active opposition by Whitney to Marter would be construed as a drive for the leadership. In this way, those unwilling to depose Marter would be left 'to carry him.' And should the party drop its chieftain and offer the leadership to Whitney, Broder wanted him to ponder policies for a few days and then demand that the party follow them, if he was to lead. In this way, wrote Broder, Whitney and the party would be rid 'of all the announcements of policy made by Mr. Marter without any authority,' but which 'to some extent' were still sticking to the Conservatives. The message was clear: force the party to come to terms with Whitney, not the reverse. Whitney would then be in a position to put matters in 'better shape' and advance proposals which might hurt Marter but which would benefit the Dundas lawyer and the party.[31]

Adding confusion to this sharp dispute between Whitney and Marter is the fact that the potentially stormy caucus meeting passed without an audible rumble. Whitney attended the gathering and, apparently, nothing happened. The question of Marter's leadership 'never came before the caucus, and the leader was received with every mark of confidence and approval.' 'It was a most harmonious meeting all through.' Whitney had held his fire either for his own reasons or at the behest of someone like Meredith. The decision was a wise one because the last thing a party scarcely blessed with success needed was a nasty public brawl.[32]

The provincial Conservatives, however, were not yet clear of divisive forces: of all the issues that came before them in the 1896 session, none was more difficult than the Manitoba school question. That problem which had proven, and was to prove, so disruptive to the federal party similarly threatened the provincial group, especially following the action of Thomas Crawford, the Toronto West member who had signed the PPA obligation in the 1894 campaign. From the outset of the session, despite strong pressure from some fellow Conservatives, Crawford was determined to introduce a resolution on the subject of the proposed federal remedial legislation. Finally, on 4 March, he gained the floor and moved his resolution which, in effect, made a case for provincial rights in the matter of education and asked the Ontario legislature to look upon the remedial legislation 'unfavourably.' Then, in defending his position, Crawford declared that he did not wish to make the subject a party one but, rather, wanted the legislature to voice the wishes of Ontarians and strengthen the hand of Manitoba. Although he voiced his concern for 'the stability of Confederation,' and his desire not to 'offend anyone's religious feelings,' the Toronto cattle-dealer had clearly put the cat amongst the pigeons.[33]

Mowat rose on the government side and noted, as had Crawford, that the Judicial Committee of the Privy Council had found for Manitoba in its action of abolishing the dual school system of that province. But, he added, the Judicial Committee had also 'decided that the Act interfered with certain rights and privileges of the Roman Catholic minority of Manitoba.' He suggested that Catholic grievances should be removed by action of the Manitoba legislature.

After deploring any 'hasty action' which might menace confederation, Mowat moved a lengthy amendment, the gist of which was that 'the proposal of remedial legislation by the Dominion should not be entertained until after the request of the Manitoba legislature for thorough investigation on the part of the Dominion of all the facts is acted upon, and all reasonable and proper efforts for conciliation have been made and have failed.' Mowat was running close to the Laurier line in Ottawa. The Conservative member for Toronto South, Oliver Howland – another signatory to the PPA obligation – followed with a motion urging that each member of Parliament be permitted to decide the merits of remedial legislation according to his individual judgment and conscience, and that the subject not be treated as a party measure.[34]

Two Conservative back-benchers had thus jumped in to head the debate on the Manitoba school question. It remained to be seen what the leadership, and the rest of the party, would do in the face of the Crawford resolution and the Mowat amendment. It was Whitney who rose to provide the response. He did not propose, he said, to debate the merits of a federal bill that was beyond Ontario's jurisdiction. Arguing that others were actuated by 'narrow, partisan motives,' Whitney loftily took the high ground of principle with his amendment to the effect that 'any expression of opinion by this House relating to the legislation ... known as the Remedial bill, would be an unwise and unwarranted intrusion upon the proper domain of the Parliament of Canada, and that this House consequently refuses to express or commit itself to any opinion bearing upon or having reference to the said bill.' A Liberal member twitted Whitney about inconsistency and suggested that his 'amendment ... did not coincide with expressions of the party upon Separate schools in the past.' Whitney replied with silence, but Marter rose to endorse his stand enthusiastically. In fact, the Dundas member's public position was identical to the private one taken by George Ross, just ten days before the legislature was confronted with the problem. 'Mr. Crawford,' he wrote, '... has given notice of a motion in our House against coercion [of Manitoba]. We have not yet decided how to meet it. At present I favor a resolution to the effect that as the question is not within our jurisdiction, we should express no opinion upon it.'[35]

In view of the admitted indecision of the Liberal cabinet and the personal opinion of Ross, it seems likely that a conference between Laurier and Mowat was an important factor in shaping the policy of the provincial Liberals. For his part, Whitney was open to the charge of trying to aid the federal Conservatives at the expense of the provincial party. At the same time, his stand was considerably more correct than that of Crawford, Mowat, or Howland; and, if he was opposed to Marter's stance on separate schools, he gave no clue to that fact in his conduct in this matter. On the division which followed, Whitney carried thirteen Conservatives with him, plus the solitary Independent. Six Conservatives and all Liberals and Patrons present voted against his amendment. But, then, three-quarters of the Patrons in the assembly (though not their leader) voted with all the Conservatives against the Mowat amendment. Whitney had led the members of his party over an awkward hurdle. Not all of them had made it; yet, as it turned out, this only forced them to run harder to catch up with the Morrisburg lawyer, or drop out. He had publicly put space between himself and the separate school questions, whether of Ontarian or Manitoban origin. He had room in which to breathe and manoeuvre, and for some of that space he had to thank Marter, like it or not.[36]

At the end of the session, every Conservative member attended a most important caucus on 2 April. At that meeting Marter tendered his resignation as party leader. There was some protest, but Marter was adamant. Whitney was nominated to replace him; no one else was named and the leadership of the party was Whitney's by acclamation. It was as simple as that: no fuss, no debate, no division. The party handed the formal lead to the man who had been informally leading it.

The whole business was transacted with such speed that, initially, little was said or done about the change in Toronto. But things were different in a delighted Morrisburg. A large, non-partisan reception was tendered Whitney by his constituents on 7 April. A band was imported from Waddington, New York, and led the way to the local music hall, serving up a 'lively air' when Whitney entered the auditorium to the sound of loud, long, and lusty cheering. He took advantage of the occasion to deliver a speech on the necessity of having political parties – preferably only two of them – and the duties of those parties and their leaders. The party system had created 'the great benefits' enjoyed 'under the British system of responsible government.' Because the British had 'perfected the party system,' they were 'the freest people on the face of the earth.' Such talk on a celebratory occasion was fine, but it remained to be seen what Whitney could do in the world of real politics with a party sapped of strength through want of men, money, organization, and cohesion. Leadership of the Ontario Conservatives was not a particularly attractive position.[37]

v

After he had assumed the provincial leadership, the first call upon Whitney's services came from the federal Conservative party. Without reservation, he threw himself into the 1896 election campaign, battling in the cause of remedial legislation, and thus ignoring the warning of a friendly constituent that it was 'time to call a halt' to attempts to restore Manitoba's separate schools. During May, Whitney toured the province, speaking in places as widely separated as Carleton Place and Galt, Perth and Dunnville, and pausing in Toronto to discuss organizational matters with central Ontario Tories and to take a day at the races. His speeches were never long and always essentially the same, except for some local reference: the 'national honour' was at stake; constitutional rights were threatened; and the desirability of separate schools was not the question at issue. Regardless of that last point, he was arguing for the restoration of Manitoba's separate schools and was thus moving himself and his party another step away from militant anti-Catholicism.[38]

In addition to working for the federal party throughout the province, Whitney busied himself with electioneering on behalf of Andrew Broder, who had decided to return to the political wars in Dundas County. Whitney's labours were probably critical in Broder's ultimate success because the Conservative candidate secured only a plurality of sixty-two votes over his Liberal opponent, in a contest complicated by the candidacy of a Patron of Industry. The losing Liberal thought that 'Broder got most of the floating vote. The canal works here hurt me very much also as most of the men went for the Government Candidate.'[39]

During these weeks of activity, circumstances changed not only for the provincial and federal Conservatives but also for the Liberals. Oliver Mowat, although approaching his seventy-sixth birthday, was enticed into the field of federal politics. He campaigned for Laurier in Ontario and joined his new cabinet as minister of justice in July of 1896. This train of events surprised some observers who had expected that George Ross would return to the larger field, but not Mowat. Laurier, however, wanted the premier in order to bolster his new-found strength in Ontario and to assure Ontarians that a Quebec Roman Catholic had cabinet room for a Protestant who strongly favoured the British connection. Arthur S. Hardy, the powerful Brantford orator who had been Mowat's provincial secretary, became premier and attorney-general. Hardy's health was not the best and he had some reservations about accepting the position but, in the end, he took it. 'I concluded,' he wrote to J.S. Willison, 'not to let it pass by. There were other good men who could have taken the place, and it would not have gone begging; but you know how very difficult it is in this wicked world to let high honors pass by.' Many Liberals knew that they had sustained a 'heavy loss' in Mowat's removal to Ottawa – and so did the Conservatives. 'Our prospects,' noted a Toronto Tory MPP, 'are brighter than they have been for a long time.'[40]

If the election of 1896 brought triumph to the federal Liberals, it also brought troubles to the provincial party, troubles other than those implicit in the departure of its shrewd leader. For nearly two decades it had not mattered – in terms of party politics – if the governments at Ottawa and Toronto failed to pull together. If one seemed badly out of step, the other could simply blame it on a balkiness produced by mean adherence to partisan lines. Now the story was to be different: each Liberal government would find it advantageous to assist the other and to avoid divisions and difficulties. George Ross, alert to the new situation, saw a liability in the ranks of the Ontario members of Parliament which could do damage to the provincial party. 'I would like also,' he told Laurier, 'if some way could be found to conciliate the Roman Catholics of Ontario. Unfortunately for us, there is no representative Catholic in the Province who can be set up as a [federal] leader, and notwithstanding their confidence in Sir Oliver ... the want of such a person is somewhat embarrassing.' What was needed was an Ontario Catholic of stature in the cabinet; but Laurier, on looking over the material, might well have concluded that it was impossible to make a silk purse out of a sow's ear. Ross, aware of this, still thought there could be trouble on the point.[41]

Laurier, for his part, ventured into the affairs of the provincial Liberals and so increased the stresses created by having the same party in power in Ottawa and Toronto. Laurier's intrusion into provincial politics came with the death in August of William D. Balfour, just elevated to the post of provincial secretary from that of speaker when Hardy shuffled the old Mowat cabinet. The federal leader, seeing two provincial positions open – the speaker's chair and a cabinet portfolio – pressed Hardy with the suggestion that Francis E.A. Evanturel, a French-Canadian and provincial member for Prescott since 1886, should be given something. 'From the point of view of Dominion politics,' emphasized Laurier, 'such a step, under existing circumstances, would be of very great service to the party. It would be an offset to the School question in showing the liberality of our Ontario friends to their French brothers.' Hardy initially dismissed this argument for Evanturel by pleading that the cabinet shuffle had created 'a good deal of friction and disappointment,' and he wanted no more trouble. But Laurier would not be put off, and so Hardy pointed out that he was being called upon to satisfy the demands of James R. Stratton, publisher of the *Peterborough Examiner* and, like Evanturel, a member since 1886. Hardy feared a Conservative-Patron effort at putting Stratton in the speaker's chair, a manoeuvre without hope of success but with every prospect of embarrassing the government. The provincial premier did concede that yielding to Laurier would solidly secure 'the seven or eight constituencies in which there is a large French vote in this Province.' Laurier, however, had little patience with Hardy and his woes; he had his own problems and he wanted a firm commitment. 'A tremendous effort is going to be made to detach the French from us,' he reminded Hardy. 'The School question is to be worked up to that end, and ... it is a very ticklish one at this moment. The selection of Evanturel would in all probability, secure the French vote absolutely.' And, as for Stratton, he 'should understand that all considerations of party interest are overwhelming against him.'

In delivering himself of this strong and entirely federal lecture, Laurier spoke to the provincial premier in a manner that had little precedent. Perhaps it was a mark of Laurier's strength and Hardy's weakness, but it did not bode well for harmony between the two branches of the Liberal party in Ontario. Nor did the federal leader let the matter rest: he pursued the cause of Evanturel with John S. Willison, editor of the *Globe*. Finally, in the last week of the year, victory went to Laurier when Hardy persuaded Stratton to abandon his campaign and announce that he favoured Evanturel. Confined to bed with an attack of the grippe, Hardy had cleared the way for the nomination of Evanturel as speaker when the 1897 session began. But he surely must have recognized the disadvantages inherent in the Liberals' holding power at two levels of government.[42]

VI

Despite the fact that there might be some benefits for the Conservative leader in such Liberal tensions, Whitney would undoubtedly have welcomed the problems that power brought. The new chieftain had little time for such day-dreaming, however, as the chores of his position greedily ate into his days and nights. He had to concern himself with preparation for, and participation in, the session of 1897, his first as leader of the opposition. In it, he took on the major speaking chores, lashing the government for its policies on education (but not separate schools), natural resources, and agriculture, and charging it with gross patronage and electoral corruption, all themes he had pursued on earlier occasions. Once set in his new position, he seemed to grow in the job: his speeches were better, more slashing and confidently delivered. Meredith saluted his efforts and Speaker Evanturel echoed the praise. But reservations persisted in the minds of some Tories, particularly Toronto ones: when Whitney had been selected, John Ross Robertson of the *Telegram* had been prompted to remark that a stone thrown through the window of any country barrister would have hit the head of a better man than the Morrisburg lawyer. The newspaperman had company in that view.[43]

Despite the fewness of Conservative legislators and the multitude of problems he now faced, Whitney thought he was making inroads against the Liberals' position. 'We have hammered away as well as we could,' he wrote to W.H. Montague, 'and circumstances have aided us materially. I think Mr Hardy is worried by the responsibilities of his position.' 'It is apparent to the most casual observer that Mowat is not here,' he confided to Charles Tupper, the federal Conservative leader. Although the hard work of the session put him 'quite under the weather,' he was cheered by encouraging reports that came in from various sections of the province. He judged that the sessional labours of the Conservatives had 'attracted public attention to a marked degree.' Matters seemed to be proceeding favourably.[44]

A positive session, however, did not begin to make an election triumph, and Whitney discovered he had to devote considerable time to the business of party organization. Despite his advancing years and a clear fondness for residence in England, Tupper also had turned to this work, demonstrating a lively concern for the proper reorganization of the party on a national basis. Early in October of 1896, Whitney had been in Ottawa hard on the heels of members of Parliament who had attended Tupper's initial conference on organization, and apparently arranged with him for a provincial Conservative gathering in Toronto for later in the month. At that time Whitney met his caucus in the Queen's Hotel and discussed 'schemes for turning the Hardy-Ross Government out of power at the next elections.' Next day Tupper addressed a larger group of Ontario Conservatives on federal organization.[45]

The fact that Whitney's meeting was held before, and not with, Tupper's reflected his firm belief in the need for cooperation and consultation with federal Conservatives but avoided the public impression of Ottawa domination. He made his position on this point perfectly clear on a number of occasions. In discussing a projected Tory gathering in the nation's capital, he insisted that the meeting be addressed by himself '& one or two of our [provincial] Members' whom he would name. 'I will not consent,' he decreed, 'to have any of the late Ministers connected with the meeting in any way.' He was not going to allow his Liberal opponents to charge that the provincial Conservatives were 'merely an offshoot from Sir Charles Tupper and the other Members of the late Government.' The meeting had to be 'of a strictly Provincial character.' And when an attempt was made to tie Whitney to federal politicians and then to lecture him on the dangers of such an alliance, he vigorously asserted that he was not the mere servant of 'Tupper and Co.'[46]

Thus, while the provincial Liberal party found itself being enmeshed in a tighter relationship with the Ottawa party because of the responsibilities of office, Whitney used the freedom of opposition to avoid suggestions that his Conservatives were federally dominated. As time passed, he had less to worry about on this score, because the Liberals increasingly became the ones against whom the charge could be levelled with some effect. Party lines could be shaped into either a harness of cooperation or a rope of strangulation; Whitney wanted no part of the latter.

In addition to checking the charge of being a federal puppet, Whitney moved to strengthen himself and his following. He had to attempt to make himself and his views known and, he hoped, acceptable – particularly in that Grit stronghold of western Ontario. Further, he had to pull together the party organization, search for men of higher calibre as possible candidates, win back some of those alienated Roman Catholic Conservatives, and cut Liberal and Patron strength. In the course of 1897, he accepted all these challenges.

In late June and early July, he ventured into the central and western parts of southern Ontario: London, Chatham, Hamilton, and Guelph were a few of the places on his political itinerary. His speeches usually contained local opening references and then pursued a common course: an assault on the faults of the Hardy government and promotion of Conservative policies. In thoroughly canvassing this Liberal region, Whitney did avoid some Grit strongholds, notably Hardy's home town of Brantford; he was not at all anxious to supply the Liberal leader with a reason for a major speech in his own backyard while their tilting was still in a preliminary stage. After some hesitation, however, he did attend a Roman Catholic parish picnic at Arthur, despite the fact that no 'prominent Grit' would be present to provide the excuse, in Protestant eyes, for Whitney's appearance. It was a novel but necessary step for a provincial Conservative leader.[47]

Having expended time and energy in the party's interest, Whitney paused in Morrisburg for much of August before commencing the wearing round again with a return to western Ontario. By mid-September he was in northern Ontario, visiting the Algoma constituencies; and from then until the chill of late fall made outside meetings impossible, he toured the southern section of the province. Exhausted, a weary Whitney finally stopped in his home town in November to catch his breath. He had given the province, particularly those sections that were less than politically friendly, an opportunity to see, hear, and assess the new Conservative leader.

The revitalization of the party in certain sections of the province could not rest solely on visits by the new chieftain. Whitney had made a serious effort at infusing the party with fresh life, at least at the constituency level; but, at the provincial level, his efforts were hampered by a lack of money. Conservatives, who were willing to support the federal party financially, were loath to give funds to the losing provincial cause. Consequently, as Whitney knew only too well, there was 'very little of the former [party] machinery' left. In the autumn of 1896, there had been a fresh attempt at rebuilding this machinery, and district chairmen had been appointed throughout the province; but, almost a year later, Robert Birmingham, the secretary-treasurer of the Liberal-Conservative Union of Ontario, remained the only paid party worker. Much organizational work thus fell onto the shoulders of Whitney and Birmingham. Taking up this additional chore, the party leader penned appeals to local Conservatives, urging them to update the voters' lists and maintain the vitality of their riding associations. He tried to avoid the impression of dictating to local groups by permitting them to set their own dates for nominating conventions, and by refusing to attend meetings where the candidate was to be selected from among a field of contenders. He chose the latter course because he did not wish to become an inadvertent party to some internal dispute. Nevertheless, he did urge certain men to seek nomination in critical constituencies because he thought that they could carry the ridings concerned.[48]

Money problems continued to bedevil the provincial party and, on one occasion, led to a moment of ill feeling between Birmingham and Whitney when the latter refused to order the payment of some bills charged to the secretary-treasurer. The Tory leader insisted that money raised for purposes of campaign literature could not be redirected to pay the secretary-treasurer's expenses, and he argued that the payment of Birmingham's accounts would have to be ordered by the executive committee of the Union. Such financial strains did little for party unity.[49]

In his concern to rebuild the bases of the Conservative party in Ontario, Whitney devoted particular attention to the Patrons of Industry and the Roman Catholics. By 1897, even the Patrons' most ardent supporters were conceding that the movement was a spent force: Goldwin Smith noted that it was 'the general opinion that the Patrons Organization will not last beyond the next Provincial Election.' A Dufferin county Tory gleefully reported on the Patrons' condition in his bailiwick: in 1894, he noted, 'there were thirty four hundred Patrons and a lodge room on every four corners' and now there were 'only four or five sickly little lodges in the

County and they are just dying out.' Hazy provincial objectives, improved economic conditions, and internal disunity were pushing the Patrons into rapid decline.[50]

Some Conservatives continued to view the Patrons as a Liberal invention designed to divide the Conservative vote: 'a grit will join anything to lead Conservatives into a hole but when election time comes they all vote *Grit* and our ranks are divided and we lose.' Although suspicions about an organized Liberal plot were groundless, there were clearly close relations between some individual Patrons and Liberals. George Ross could thus write to Laurier about a patronage position for a 'Patron friend ... who served us faithfully in the by-elections.' For his part, Whitney did not relent in his pursuit of this third party in order to establish its true colours – whitewashed Liberal. 'You might take the Journals [of the Legislature] of 1895, 1896 & 1897,' he wrote to his secretary, 'search every division that was taken, copy the motion or question in each case and give the Patron Votes on it shewing how each one voted.' 'The object,' he explained, 'is to have a handy record of each Vote given by each Patron during the 3 Sessions.' Of the sixteen Patrons who still sat in the legislature, the Tory leader excluded but one from the list: James Tucker of Wellington West, who regularly supported the Conservatives. The remainder were fair game in Whitney's determination to expose them as supporters of the government and, thus, deceivers of the public.[51]

In his cautious steps towards the Roman Catholics of Ontario, the Morrisburg lawyer knew only too well he was facing a people made hostile by earlier provincial election campaigns, while at his back stood Conservatives upset by his moderate stand on the Manitoba schools question and his stark silence on Ontario's separate schools. His tentative moves soon made his goal obvious to John Willison, who informed Laurier that the province's Conservatives were on a new tack. Further, he noted that Catholics might be soured on the Hardy government for reasons over which it had little control: Laurier's settlement of the Manitoba schools question and his distribution of patronage. 'I am told,' the *Globe* editor informed the prime minister, that 'Mr. Whitney ... is determined not to ride the Protestant horse in the next election. He will probably go as far as he can in bidding for the Catholic vote.' But, he added on a more optimistic note, if 'Mr. Hardy can hold the new [Protestant Conservative] element which has joined the Liberal party over the school issue, he will probably get through safely.'[52]

The fear that some Ontario Catholic support was drifting away from the Liberal party led the provincial leaders to attempt to stem the flow by the judicious application of federal patronage and quiet suggestions that the Conservatives were still anti-Catholic. 'His Excellency, the Apostolic Delegate, was the guest of the Ontario Government yesterday,' George Ross reported to Laurier,

... His Grace, the Archbishop of Kingston, as well as Archbishop Walsh were with us and appeared to be exceedingly sympathetic and friendly. ... Our treatment of the Roman Catholics in Ontario has impressed him very favorably and he distinctly intimated that the re-opening of the [Manitoba] School Question at Ottawa might possibly endanger the Separate Schools of the Province of Ontario. I felt it my duty to say to him that a revival of the Separate School agitation at the next General Election in this Province, or even later, might mean the repeal of all the amendments made to the Separate Schools Act since confederation, as it was only by the most herculean efforts on our part at the last two General Elections that we were able to hold our ground. I am placing in his hands all the literature available on the [separate school] question, including some speeches delivered by Mr. Meredith during the last and previous campaigns and the answer of Sir Oliver Mowat and myself to the charges made against us that we favored unduly the extension of Separate Schools.

By pointedly recalling the contentious issue of the 1890 and 1894 election campaigns for the benefit of the church hierarchy, the Liberals gave notice that they did not propose to stand idly by while Whitney laboured to build the provincial Conservatives' Catholic support. And, at the same time, they tried to assist Laurier by broadly hinting at the injudiciousness of any clerical effort to reopen the Manitoba schools question. Wisely, if nervously, the Liberals were attempting to cover front, rear, and flank.[53]

Despite these efforts, the Liberals continued to sense a developing unease among their Catholic supporters. 'I find,' Hardy informed Laurier, 'that most of the unrest which appears in certain localities, – notably in Toronto, Ottawa and Kingston, – ... is in part influenced by the question of appointments.' Such a perception meant that the provincial Grits now pressed Laurier on the question of jobs for Catholics, as he had pressed them in the Evanturel case. Such demands made it clear that the mere presence of an aging Mowat in Ottawa was not enough to maintain complete harmony in Ontario Liberal ranks. What Laurier needed was a vigorous Ontario representative in the front ranks, one who could command respect from Catholics and Protestants and maintain the Liberal hold on the province, while skilfully doling out coveted positions to both religious groups. For the moment, however, Laurier had no one in sight who could adequately fill that description; there were few men that could.[54]

While the Liberals bemoaned their developing difficulties, Whitney watched the turn of events with a good deal of relish. Heightening that sensation were encouraging reports on the renewal of ties between his party and the Roman Catholics of Ontario. A Franco-Ontarian, reporting on a Tory meeting in Essex North, made the cheering observation 'that the Roman Catholic & old PPA members have amalgamated & have decided to work shoulder to shoulder and redeem our good old county from grit rule & put a man such as you are at the head of our provincial legislature.' Of course, he went on, the last goal could only be achieved if 'the religious cry' was left aside. There were other signs that Conservative Catholics were prepared to return to the fold, but Whitney checked the urge to make an open move in their direction because he did not want to precipitate either Liberal counter-manoeuvres or Protestant Conservative complaints. Convinced, by midsummer of 1897, that numerous Catholics were coming, or returning, to his party 'practically spontaneously,' the Tory leader decided that his 'best policy for the present, as far as these people are concerned would be *silence.*' Privately, however, he did recommend courses of action designed to further and consolidate the Catholic shift: a suddenly friendly priest was to be given absolutely no cause for annoyance by anyone. Quiet fence-mending, obviously so rewarding, was the order of the day.[55]

In addition to the complaints, waverings, and defections of Catholics, other woes arrived to trouble the Liberals. Occasionally their newspaper, the *Globe*, seemed to favour Whitney. J.M. Gibson, the commissioner of crown lands, bitterly complained to Willison that the paper's descriptions of the Tory chief's provincial tour were 'decidedly complimentary,' that they exaggerated the size of his crowds, and that they always gave the impression he had received 'a very hearty reception.' Another time, Hardy exploded over an editorial: 'For God's sake,' he roared at Willison, 'don't press your suggestion of this morning that we should abandon all timber dues. ... We would have the whole fraternity of lumbermen in full cry at our heels, and Whitney would probably jump at the suggestion ... which we could under no circumstances adopt. The whole country would rise in arms against us, except the lumberman.'[56]

Observant Conservatives judged the Liberals to be stumbling into tactical errors that would have been avoided in the days of Mowat. A.H.U. Colquhoun questioned the perceptiveness of the provincial premier when Laurier came to Toronto for a rally. 'Hardy,' he told Whitney, 'unwisely I thought, instead of partaking of the glory that was going sat in evening dress in a side box of Massey Hall, doing the grand with 5000 of the *hoi polloi* looking at him. Old Mowat would have waddled on with Laurier & shared the applause. There was absolutely *nothing* in the demonstration for the local Grits.' And then there was the long-standing and treacherous question of temperance legislation, invariably a source of trouble for the party in power. Encapsulating the problem, Gibson described the government as caught 'between two fires – the temperance party on the one side and the liquor party on the other.' 'It has been pretty hot for us,' he told Laurier, 'and we have been obliged to make such important concessions to the advanced wing (which seems to embody nearly the whole of the Methodist denomination) that we have incurred the dissatisfaction of the liquor trade to a rather serious extent.'[57]

On balance, then, Whitney had enjoyed good fortune in his first full year as leader of the Conservative party. In touring the province he had been well received and, just as important, had made himself known to many. Working on the problems of organization and recruitment of sound candidates, he had slowly moved towards partial solutions. And he had generally avoided attempts to link him with the federal Conservative party. The Liberals, on the other hand, had discovered that they were being lumped with Laurier and that there were hidden penalties in such a situation. Dissatisfied with Laurier's answers to the Manitoba school question and the problem of patronage distribution, Ontario Roman Catholics were looking seriously at the provincial Conservatives for the first time in years, and Whitney did nothing to discourage the flirtation. He had also found time to hammer at the crumbling organization of the Patrons of Industry. And the Liberals, obviously missing Mowat's fine hand, had managed to wander onto troublesome grounds without any assistance from the Tory leader. In all, it had been a good year.

There was one significant dark spot, however, and that was money or, rather, the lack of it. By May of 1897, Whitney was in serious financial difficulties because of the size of his personal expenditure since assuming the leadership. 'I am bound to say,' he ruefully informed Broder, 'that, when I was chosen Leader over a year ago I did not realize the consequences to me, otherwise I could not honorably have accepted the position. However, to make a long story short, I am practically at the end of my resources.' It had apparently been suggested at that organizational meeting in Ottawa in the fall of 1896 'that the sum of $2000.00 or thereabouts, should be raised and given' to Whitney to reimburse him 'for the loss of business, unusual expenditure &c for one year.' This money had never found its way into Whitney's hands, however, not because some Conservatives failed to support him but because their donations got 'mixed up' with the campaign literature fund, which had a two-thousand-dollar objective. By the time he wrote Broder, the Conservative leader was convinced that, unless this money was produced, it would be 'absolutely impossible' for him to take on the speaking engagements arranged for the summer of 1897. 'The anxiety and uncertainty,' he wrote, 'is such a strain upon me that I am afraid I will not be able to make the effort expected of me and that the meetings will be a disappointment.' Embarrassed and worried by his situation, he complained: 'It is a humiliating position in which I find myself, *but there I am.*'[58]

This development prompted the initiation of a fund-raising drive for Whitney's benefit. He estimated that '$2000.00 would suffice to cover the time [from the summer of 1897] till the Elections' of 1898 were over, and he was convinced that, without such an amount, he could not continue as party chief. But he did not want his followers in the legislature to be troubled about his plight, and regretted that at least one of them had been made privy to it. He was flustered by the discovery that his financial difficulties had been made known beyond the '5 or 6 men' who were to handle the matter quietly. Witnessing the decline in his Morrisburg law practice and his personal resources, Whitney had occasion to regret his decision to assume the Conservative leadership and was sometimes deeply disturbed by his shaky financial position. And, in the final analysis, he had only himself to blame: his own ambition, desire to serve, and need for power had egged him on. Consequently, when some foolhardy soul dared to suggest that he was not doing all that he might as leader, that intrepid counsellor was treated to a vitriolic display of temper. So, despite the bright prospects politically, there were times of frustration, anger, despair, and, possibly, self-pity.[59]

Such times had to be short, however, because Whitney had barely completed his strenuous provincial tour in the autumn of 1897 when the Liberals announced the calling of a fall session for 30 November. The government's explanation of this unusual decision to have a second session within the year was directly related to the American imposition of a tariff on Canadian sawn lumber. Ontario's pine lumber industry was affected by this action: American holders of Ontario logging permits began to export uncut logs in order to avoid payment of the new tariff and this, in turn, dislocated certain Ontario sawmill operations and created unemployment. Consequently, the government decided to seek 'the advice of the Legislature as to the advisability of adopting new regulations with respect to the getting out of logs.' Conscious of Ontario's barely hidden anti-Americanism, the Liberals sensed that any counter-action, designed to protect the province's interests, would make an excellent spring board from which to plunge into an election campaign.[60]

Whitney, too, thought retaliatory action necessary, but was unconvinced that the solitary reason for this hastily called assembly was the need for a debate on the matter. Noting that he had perceived general dissatisfaction with the government during his 'successful' provincial tour, he argued that the Grits had called the session to calm unease and strengthen their position. In the debate on the address in reply to the speech from the throne, Whitney was quick to restate his party's position on the lumber question. What was needed was a proviso, attached to any logging permit, stating that logs must be sawn in Ontario. Charging the government with failure to protect the province's interest, he argued that the exportation of uncut logs was ruinous to Ontarians and beneficial to Americans. Then, beating the drums of anti-Americanism, he accused the United States, 'this foreign country,' of 'the most utter disregard for anything like international feeling or generosity,' and 'actually gloating over the wrong which the imposition of a high tariff would bring upon the people of this Province.' He concluded by darkly hinting that the Hardy administration was pro-American, a clear attempt to score points with the electorate. In the end the government announced that, after 30 April 1898, most licences would contain a condition insisting that logs cut in the province must be manufactured into sawn lumber in Canada. Whitney had, in effect, secured his goal, although he failed to get immediate imposition of the regulation as 'a patriotic measure.'[61]

Although Whitney's chief concern of this session was the need to respond to the American tariff, he did direct attention to the educational field, and once more made a plea for additional money for the public school system so that its spheres of instruction might be widened 'to make them more useful to the agricultural and industrial community.' He regarded the elementary school as of prime importance in the 'education of the children of the poorer classes' who had to be given 'an opportunity for attaining sufficient education to fit them for their future lot in life.'

In Whitney's opinion, the government was not providing this service and the public school had become 'the forcing-house of higher education.' There was, in such talk, the idea that people should be fitted out for their respective stations in life, and not encouraged to reach for something which others judged was beyond their grasp or class.

His demands for the lower schools, he declared, did not make him inimical to higher education. He suggested that the University of Toronto should be separated from government control, an idea 'urged upon him by men' who occupied 'high positions' in that institution. Whitney had earlier hinted that, in the event of separation, government funds would cease to flow into the university because endowments would come in from people who would not 'go down into their pockets as long as the institution' remained under the government. Despite the length of this statement on the state and needs of education in Ontario, he said not a word about separate schools.[62]

As was soon revealed, the relatively quiet session of 1897–8 was but a prelude to a provincial election campaign. The Liberal government's decision to set 1 March as the voting day little altered the pace of Whitney's life. There was no need for him to accelerate because he had been running in high gear, with this election in sight, almost from the moment he had assumed the leadership. As a result, his speeches went over ground which he had already covered inside and outside the legislature, although they were delivered in the more exciting atmosphere of an election campaign, with its moments of high heartiness when 'For He's a Jolly Good Fellow' rang out, or its times of hushed appeal to the memory of Macdonald. He scored the Liberals for their unseemly extravagance and their creation of 'an army of fat, sleek, lazy officials, the majority of whom did nothing for the money they drew,' although he wisely did not pledge to end patronage if he became premier. He argued for the remodelling of the public school system and for the creation of an advisory board of educational experts. He pleaded for the careful conservation and development of Ontario's natural resources and an open investigation of the prices of school texts. He accused the Liberals of stealing the timber policy of his party and their leader of lowering the tone of political morality in the province. Whitney was in fighting trim and, of course, in a position to attack because being in the opposition ranks afforded him that advantage.[63]

During the campaign, the Conservative leader attended to another matter which was to be of prime importance to the party's future in Ontario: the selection of a candidate for Toronto South. Oliver Howland, a possible provincial leadership candidate in 1894, had sat for this riding. In 1897, however, the federal seat of Toronto Centre had become vacant, and Howland had been persuaded to contest the by-election. The ensuing campaign had had unpleasant religious overtones, produced largely by the Globe, which reminded its readers that Howland had stood for the coercion of Manitoba in the schools question and against Crawford's motion that had asked for Ontario's condemnation of the proposed remedial legislation. Howland went down to defeat before his Liberal opponent and, having resigned his provincial seat to contest the federal one, left the riding of Toronto South vacant, a condition that still existed when the provincial election was called.[64]

These circumstances set the stage for some intricate Conservative manoeuvring when it was time to choose a candidate for the provincial constituency. Obviously, Howland was available and, evidently, wanted the nomination; but he was not the man for Whitney, Marter, and other party lights. They wanted James J. Foy, a prominent Toronto Tory lawyer and, more important, a staunch Roman Catholic. Such a choice was not without its problems: Howland proved 'hard to handle,' while Crawford declared that Foy's nomination would 'defeat all the Conservative candidates in Toronto.' Such opposition to Foy caused a postponement of the Toronto South Conservative nominating convention while, presumably, attempts were made to soothe ruffled feelings. Finally, this potentially divisive meeting was held on 5 February. The crowd that gathered in full knowledge that Foy would seek the nomination was neither altogether friendly nor orderly. On stage, with other prominent party members, sat Whitney. He had broken a cardinal rule for his conduct as party leader to be present, because he had frequently asserted that he never attended nomination contests out of fear of being trapped in a nasty constituency association squabble. But there he was, and the chances of a verbal donnybrook lay everywhere. He gave no reasons for his presence, but was surely there to lend silent support to Foy and to dampen any spirit of rebellion.[65]

The list of nominees was long and 'Foy's nomination was made not half a minute before the nominations closed, and was received with but scant applause.' Then, one after another, the various nominees got up and announced their withdrawals in favour of Foy. Some in the crowd could not contain their annoyance with this show of party management and cries of 'shame,' 'never,' and 'run yourself' greeted some who begged out. When one retreating nominee commented that he could not believe that Conservatives would fail to unite behind Foy because he was Catholic, there were shouts indicating that such a development was well within the realm of possibility. The Tory party in Toronto – and, for that matter, in the province – was clearly heading in a new direction. A few could not bear to witness the spectacle and left; but most remained to make Foy the unanimous choice of the convention, although some sulked in their seats when a standing vote was ordered. It had been quite a night for the party: troublesome spirits were exorcised and Whitney was partner to the process.[66]

The wisdom of this move was heartily applauded by many Catholics: 'For ten years I have supported the Mowat government,' wrote one to Whitney. 'I feel confident that this time you will receive a large Catholic vote which you deserve. Catholics should not be forced into a corner by attacks upon their religion or schools and thus obliged to vote as a solid body for one Party. ... The nomination of J.J. Foy ... was a good stroke.' The Globe, however, was much less impressed by this 'good stroke' and argued that the opposition was cynically refusing to disavow its earlier policies on separate schools, while demanding that 'the 6,000 electors of South Toronto repent of it at the polls. Whom they persecuted, now shall they anoint; whom they cursed, now shall they bless.' But Whitney and many Conservatives could remain impervious to such acidic comments. The provincial party had finally acquired the services of a prominent Catholic who could well prove invaluable. Now, all that remained to be done was to parade Foy, who hitherto had been an important federal backroom figure – and get him elected.[67]

The Liberals, equally active, were generally confident about the outcome of the election, although a few were a little concerned about the first province-wide contest to be held since Mowat's departure. David Mills, who had replaced Mowat as minister of justice when the latter became Ontario's lieutenant-governor, was worried because the party had failed to take adequate measures to bolster its organization; he was sure that this neglect was bound to have unfortunate consequences, particularly in eastern Ontario. He saw Whitney's tours as giving a distinct advantage to the Tories because Grit ministers, before the campaign, had not trailed the opposition leader across the province refuting his statements, and had been content to answer his criticisms in the legislature. Mills, however, did not hold Whitney and his following in high regard and was convinced that the Liberals' success would 'depend more upon the weakness of their opponents than upon their own personal popularity.' To his mind, the charge of a school-book publication monopoly was just one of the 'little questions [raised] by little men.' He advised Hardy to conduct the campaign on large issues, such as the development of northern Ontario and the financial condition of the province, and to avoid being dragged down by the Conservatives into petty squabbles and semantic debates.[68]

Despite Mills's gloominess over organization, the Liberals were sure they were in good shape everywhere, including eastern Ontario, and were even convinced that Whitney was in serious trouble in Dundas. They sought, and obtained, Laurier's assistance in healing wounds created by disappointment over patronage appointments; he also helped them secure French-Canadian speakers for bilingual ridings like Russell. Inevitably, it seemed, the fortunes of the federal and provincial Liberals were becoming still more tightly bound. Hardy intervened in Frontenac constituency to force the withdrawal of the Liberal candidate, so that Patron leader Joseph Haycock would only face a Conservative, thus enhancing his chances of re-election. The premier also urged Willison of the *Globe* to 'blow a little' in an effort to undercut the confidence displayed by Conservative papers in their election predictions; and he confessed to difficulty in grappling with the Tories because, to his mind, they were saying nothing new and providing no concrete issues. Obviously the absence of the separate school question made for a duller, but shrewder, Conservative campaign.[69]

As the results began to come in, following the closing of the polls on 1 March,

1898 Election Results			
Popular vote			Seats
Liberal	207,044	(48.40%)	51[70]
Conservative	204,307	(47.76%)	43[71]
Patron	10,743	(2.51%)	0
Other	5,679	(1.33%)	0
Total	427,773	(100.00%)	94

the Liberal party soon discovered that it had 'nearly met its Waterloo in Ontario.' The Liberals took fifty seats – the figure became fifty-one in three weeks – and lost two cabinet ministers in the process; the Conservatives under Whitney captured forty-three seats. The Patrons failed to secure the election of a solitary candidate and, of the sixteen seats which they had formerly held, eleven went to the Conservatives and five to the Grits. Calling the results 'disastrous' for the Patrons, Goldwin Smith argued that 'lack of organization, want of money, want of general knowledge & leadership were noticeably fatal to the Patrons.' The growth of department stores was also cited by Archibald Currie, the Patrons' secretary, as a factor in the evaporation of this farmers' protest party: 'Many farmers, he says, joined the movement from motives of economy, thinking they would be able to save money by means of patron stores, but competition [from department stores] became so strong patron stores were of no advantage and membership declined very rapidly.' Whitney could take pleasure from the eradication of this movement, which he still suspected of having an American taint, and perhaps his attacks upon it had also taken their toll.[72]

The Liberals were quick to conduct inquests of their 'close call,' and forwarded a variety of reports. Several suggested that the party was out of touch with public opinion, advancing 'worn out' policies that lacked any imaginative spark. John Cameron of the Liberal *London Advertiser* thought that the Grits had failed to appreciate the quickly changing circumstances of the last decade of the nineteenth century:

Things have changed. A new electorate has grown up. The middle-class ruler has gone out to a great extent. The crowd are in it as never before. What is needed both as to Province and Dominion is such re-arrangement of work as would give time for one or two capable ministers and assistants to keep track of public opinion, strike out policies, keep in touch with the little and big magnates in every section. You need departmentalists. You need statesmen. But you also need those who may be better described as politicians.

David Mills echoed the criticism that the party was in need of new and impressive policies, while John Charlton judged the party leaders to be inefficient.[73]

Lack of adequate Grit organization was also given by some as a reason for the narrow escape from defeat. Catholics, however, were quick to point out that Liberals were losing their vote because of 'unfairness' by Hardy and Laurier in dealing with them. Others charged that the Tories were aided by the judicious distribution of 'large sums of money,' while the *Globe* suggested the opposite and was accused of 'whitewashing' the enemy. Perhaps, in this matter of vote-buying, Principal G.M. Grant of Queen's was most accurate when he wrote that 'on polling day in cities like Kingston, Toronto, London and Hamilton. ... A Seedy-looking lot loafed round the booths, and it was evident to the most careless observer that they were waiting to get their two dollars apiece before entering. Hundreds got what they waited for. Both sides bought.'[74]

The apparently insoluble temperance question was put forward as a factor in the loss of government support. 'The liquor men,' complained a successful Liberal, '... pretended to pledge to me their support. That was for the eye. Secretly they hurt me all they could in the interest of my Tory opponent.' It was David Mills, however, who shrewdly noted what had prevented disaster from overwhelming the party. 'I was pleased,' he wrote to a provincial cabinet minister, 'at what western Ontario did for you; in fact the district between Oxford and the Detroit River has practically saved you.' Old Clear Grit country had been largely responsible for the Liberal success. If he was ever to attain the premier's office, Whitney was going to have to shatter the loyalty of that region.[75]

On balance, the Liberals could not take much comfort from the election results. They had lost seats in the legislature and, beyond that, although their percentage of the total vote had risen because of the death of the Patrons, it was not as sharp an increase as was the Conservative one. Hardy wanted to underline the positive side of the total vote gain, but he was not anxious to show the Tories in a better light. 'I send you herewith,' he wrote to Willison,

a memorandum ... as to the number of votes cast for the different parties, the object being principally to rebut the assumption of the Conservative newpapers [sic] that the Liberals *had to some extent deserted the Government.* Instead ... we received ... more votes than the Liberal party received in 1894 ... True it is that the Conservatives received a greater accession to their vote of 1894 ... I referred to it somewhat reluctantly ... of the Patron and Independent vote of 1894, more of it went in 1898 to the Conservatives than to the Reformers. That is but the one drawback. What percentage of their vote was new vote, and what percentage was Patron or Independent, there is of course no way of even guessing; but I incline to think that the dregs of the cities and country towns in the new vote went largely in their direction, the liquor vote pretty largely, and that the Patrons and Independents of 1894 were pretty well divided. ...[76]

Trust those dregs and drinkers to vote Tory!

Although missing the premiership by a narrow margin, Whitney was buoyed by the election results, viewing them as a severe check to the Hardy administration.

He thought that 'the final defeat of the Government' would be 'only a matter of a short time.' He reasoned thus because he envisioned several by-elections resulting from contested election cases, and anticipated that these new battles would produce Conservative victories. Although his own majority in Dundas was reduced, possibly because he spent little time in the riding, he must have been pleased by Foy's triumph in Toronto South. That success, however, was slightly marred by the fact that a body of Protestant Conservatives had sulked at home on 1 March. Nevertheless, the Tory chief had acquired a Catholic right-hand man, something Meredith had never had.[77]

Whitney could be elated, then, even if he still was leader of the opposition. He had led Ontario's Tories to heights which they had not gained since Confederation. And his relative success had been achieved in a short span of time. Less than four years before, he had simply been one of Meredith's lieutenants in an anemic band. Just two years before, he had taken over the leadership of the Conservatives when they were short of men, money, organization, and friends. Now he was head of a revived and strengthened group whose base had been considerably enlarged by the election results. Whitney could thank himself, and the Liberals, for much of this. He had worked tirelessly, travelled endlessly, and attacked vigorously. Now, the overturn of the Liberals in just five ridings would give him the premier's office. Perhaps it had been worth the hard work, the trying irritations, the diligent letter-writing, and the personal financial strain.

3

'Ridding the Province of the Worst Government': 1898–1905

I

When the dust had settled after the election battle of 1898, Whitney had only two complaints: the absence of a Conservative victory and the presence of a severe cold. As it turned out, the defeat and illness were symptomatic of political and personal problems which were to plague him over the next three years. These developing difficulties sapped his strength, frayed his nerves, sharpened his tongue, and coloured his judgment. Thus, when at the end of the period he faced rebellion within the ranks of his party, he lashed out with biting phrases and bitter recriminations.[1]

Following the provincial contest, the Tory chief found his life full of contested elections, corruption trials, and wearing by-elections for the next twenty months; but his attention was initially directed to the government's decision to call the legislature into session on 3 August. The Liberal administration's increasingly precarious position lay back of this move because, as petitions seeking to unseat members mounted in the weeks following the election, it seemed possible that court verdicts could strip the Grits of their majority, at least temporarily. Moreover, the Conservatives had discovered a section in the election act which, given one interpretation, might overturn the election results.

The vital section stated that any person who was employed in connection with an election 'by a candidate or other person as counsel, agent, solicitor or clerk, or in any other capacity' and who expected to receive payment for his labours, was not entitled to vote. The question posed by the Tories was whether or not this clause included the special constables, largely Grit appointees, who served at polling booths for one dollar. The point was of consequence because 'several thousand' voters were involved. The Liberals conceded that the wording of this section was vague and referred the question to the Ontario Court of Appeal for a ruling. But, by sending the problem to the court, the Liberals applied the brakes to the legal machinery dealing with contested elections, and the Tories soon cried foul.

Further, the government discovered that the court was going to be slow even in deciding whether or not it would hear arguments on the troublesome section. Consequently, Hardy chose to call the legislative session to deal with the right of the special constables to vote. Although he offered other reasons to the public for his decision, he really wanted passage of retroactive legislation that would remove all doubts about the legality of the constables' votes.[2]

Whitney immediately saw the 'true reason' for the session and viewed it as the act of 'desperate men,' while Liberals argued that it was an honest attempt, supported by precedent, to clear away confusion. To one standing on middle ground, it was a rare and 'striking example of Legislative sharp practice.' The Tory chief, sensing a fine opportunity of showing the Grits in a bad light, intended to lose no time in 'driving home to the Government their misconduct in relation to the calling of the present Session.' Nor did he because, using his speech on the motion to re-elect Evanturel as speaker, he launched his attack. Charging the administration with perverting 'the system of responsible government,' he particularly noted that 'two of the most important departments of the Government [agriculture and crown lands]' were 'unrepresented in this House,' and that 'nearly two-thirds ... of the members' were sitting 'with the right to their seats attacked by protests.' The following day he returned to this theme, adding the broad hint that the Grits missed the stabilizing influence of Mowat and were adrift in a sea of troubles largely of their own creation.[3]

In the next three weeks of the short session, the Conservative leader gave no quarter and sought none as he raked the Liberals over the constable question and the failure of the two defeated ministers, John Dryden and John M. Gibson, to resign. The throne speech debate lasted for nine days and only concluded at two-thirty of a Saturday morning, when the Tories fell back exhausted. The Liberals passed their constable legislation, but Whitney was convinced that his side had had much the better of the fight. He was cheered not only by this feeling but also by the showing which the many new Conservative members had made; even the Liberal speaker acknowledged this fact. The opposition ranks had begun to harden into a formidable unit in just three weeks, thanks in part to Liberal error, but thanks also to Whitney's spirited leadership.[4]

With the legislative session out of the way, Whitney turned his full energies to the problems related to election trials and by-elections. He had never been one to shirk such work, but now there was the added incentive of possibly overthrowing the government, if enough Liberal winners could be upset and enough by-elections won. The tantalizing prize of the premier's office seemed to lie just beyond the next contested election trial. Small wonder, then, that he became irritated and sensitive when, after all his work, he was no closer to his goal. Not that all this exacting labour was wasted; it was not. It maintained a constant pressure on the government and forced enthusiastic Liberal supporters into committing blunders for all to see. It provided Whitney with a growing list of Grit electoral sins. And it kept many Tories in fighting shape. Indeed, not until December of 1899 could the Liberals regard their victory of twenty-two months before as secure.[5]

In the months between, Whitney attended meetings of the inner council of the party in order to map out strategy; spoke at dozens of meetings in the course of by-election contests; urged party workers on to fresh efforts; and advised local party managers on the conduct of campaigns. He was adamant that 'saw-offs' – the dropping of a Liberal protest in one constituency in exchange for a Tory pledge not to go to court in another riding – should not be arranged by his provincial aides. 'I have ... taken the ground,' he wrote, 'that local men, who have been responsible for a Petition, should decide whether such petition should be pursued.'[6]

The legal proceedings placed a severe strain on the party's limited financial resources. Entering protests and making deposits, arguing before the courts, and conducting by-election campaigns all cost money and, as early as May of 1898, there was concern over the red figures in the Tory budget. Consequently, Whitney undertook to encourage constituency associations to bear as much of the burden as possible. On other occasions, when Conservative prospects looked bright and the Tory leader did not want the chances of judicial victory placed in jeopardy for want of funds, he rummaged for money. 'It is impossible for me to put my hand on another dollar,' he wrote to one legal adviser, 'but I am ready ... to go on a note with 3 or 4 or 5 others to raise $400^x or $500^x more. ... if we do this & fail to get funds to meet it ... I think I can count on our Members in the House to be good for at least one half of it ...' Throughout these endeavours he maintained a cheerful face and pen for the benefit of party morale; but, privately, he sometimes found himself sapped of enthusiasm and energy, declaring himself to be 'used up.'[7]

Aside from the obvious main objective of upsetting the Liberal government, the motives for Whitney's diligence were mixed. When a Grit death created a vacancy in Wellington East in September of 1898, he wanted the defeated Tory candidate, Coughlin, to run again. His reason for pressing had little to do with turning out the Liberals, at least in the short run. Coughlin was a Catholic and, although Whitney foresaw a 'certain defeat,' the party leader did not want to 'chase after success in a Grit hive at the risk of annoying Dr C[oughlin]'s co-religionists.' 'Defeat there,' he observed with a measure of practical cynicism, 'with him as our Candidate can do us no harm.' Coughlin did run and lost to J.M. Gibson, the commissioner of crown lands; but the point had been made again that Catholics were fully welcome, and comfortable, in the Conservative camp.[8]

In Ontario South, Whitney pushed local workers to greater efforts because another cabinet minister's seat was at stake. John Dryden, minister of agriculture, had lost in the general election but had swiftly protested and successfully unseated Tory Charles Calder. Whitney urged Calder to contest the by-election and he did, only to lose to Dryden. But, pushed on by the party leader, supporters gathered evidence of corrupt Grit electoral practices, and Dryden was unseated in May of 1899. Rejecting all Liberal offers designed to avoid a contested by-election,

Calder ran against Dryden for a third time in December of 1899, only to witness a Liberal victory. Whitney, however, was quick to request his Ontario South followers to search again for evidence of illegal Grit activities. A protest against Dryden's re-election was duly entered, but time and expense were wearing down the resources of the constituency's Tories. Whitney begged them not to drop the protest but, in the end, they gave up and accepted an arrangement whereby they took Grit money to cover their expenses and called off the protest in August of 1900. There were, however, benefits for Whitney and the party from this protracted and unsuccessful struggle. 'There is a decided drift [of independent opinion] ... against the Provincial Government' W.D. Gregory wrote to Laurier. 'This drift has been increased by the disclosure of bribery in South Ontario. What most impressed ... was the evidence than [sic] an organized gang of bribers is employed in the interest of the Liberal party to carry constituencies by corrupt and improper means.'9

Whitney also devoted some attention to Elgin West, which, after initial confusion, had been declared a Conservative seat in the election of 1898, by the razor-thin margin of one vote. Subsequently, the Tory member was unseated and a Liberal triumph followed. Local Conservatives protested this outcome and, although they thought of dropping the matter, Whitney pushed them on to a trial. At that trial, the confession of corruption by Grit member Donald Macnish not only cost him his legislative seat but had reverberations beyond Elgin's borders. One observer thought the revelations could topple the government because some Liberal members were increasingly uneasy with the dimensions of proven corruption within their ranks. Whitney, immensely pleased by this turn of events, offered advice to the local Tories on the conduct of the by-election and toured the riding on behalf of his man. In December of 1899, the Conservatives captured the constituency, thus taking a significant step into Grit western Ontario.10

Wellington East, Ontario South, and Elgin West were only three of several ridings in which Whitney took a deep and active interest in the months following the general election. His efforts in them were typical of his hard work as he chased the Liberals through protest trials and by-elections. In the end he was not much closer to his goal than he had been at the beginning, but he had been making the headlines by putting the Grits on the defensive. There was, however, a flaw: perhaps Whitney's vigorous and partisan pursuit after Liberal corruption was an inadequate means of gaining power; perhaps he was earning a reputation as a destructive partisan, rather than as a constructive statesman. There was, about him, too much of the negative, too little of the positive.11

II

The Conservative chief's heavy involvement in election protests and related matters took the edge off his work in the legislative session of 1899, which was a comparatively quiet one. He did take advantage of the accumulating evidence of electoral corruption to advance a bill that called for the punishment of bribery by 'six months at hard labour,' and then castigated the Liberals for failing to accept it. Near the session's end his colleagues demonstrated their feelings for him with the presentation of a gold watch and chain, and a seal ring. Whitney, although obviously touched, took the opportunity to salute George Marter, his supporters, his party, and his long-suffering family. The rank and file seemed solidly behind his leadership.[12]

While Whitney had cause to be gratified with this show of solidarity, there were rumours that matters were not the same within the Liberal camp. Hardy had not enjoyed good health for almost a year and, by the summer of 1899, there were many stories which hinted broadly at his likely resignation. Whitney noted, however, that with fresh revelations of Liberal guilt in election cases at hand, Hardy's resignation at this point would result in his departure 'under a cloud.' The Liberal leader was not implicated in any of the corruption, but a sudden retirement might create the wrong impression. Thus, arguing that 'circumstances practically prevented decisive action earlier,' he retained office until October 1899, when some problems associated with the election trials had dimmed. And lying ahead were four critical by-elections in December; Hardy, surely if grudgingly, realized he had little energy left for active campaigning.[13]

The Liberals selected fifty-eight-year-old George William Ross as his replacement. Ross, a Presbyterian and strong temperance advocate, had been minister of education for almost sixteen years. To Goldwin Smith, who intensely disliked Ross's imperialist tendencies, he was an 'arrant knave.' To David Mills, he was 'shrewd and active' and just the man to give strong leadership to Ontario's Liberals. The new leader probably best described himself when he wrote to Laurier: 'The Ontario Liberal is not a radical in the English sense of the term. He is a cross between the radical and the conservative.' Ross was very much that hybrid.[14]

Upon assuming his new office, Ross administered a mild shake-up to the cabinet which he inherited. He took for himself the portfolio of provincial treasurer, and moved Richard Harcourt from that post to education. He dropped the only Catholic in Hardy's cabinet, William Harty, from public works to minister without portfolio; and then introduced a second Catholic, Francis Latchford, who took Harty's former post. Another newcomer was James R. Stratton, member for Peterborough West for thirteen years, who became provincial secretary and registrar, while Elihu Davis shifted from that position to crown lands and John M. Gibson moved up to attorney-general, following Hardy into that office. James Garrow was added as another minister without portfolio, and the currently unseated John Dryden was left in agriculture. Whitney surveyed this shuffling of chairs and then observed: 'The Government is thoroughly discredited and I think Mr Ross will find it uphill work to give it even an appearance of purity.' His grudging, partisan attitude did not prevent a kindly gesture towards Hardy. He urged the new attorney-general to consider an increase in the former premier's salary for a small patronage post at Osgoode Hall. And, after publicly saluting Hardy, Whitney privately acknowledged: 'I am indeed glad that my recollections of the time when I was ... brought ... into collision with you will not be of an unpleasant or disagreeable nature.'[15]

While prepared to show concern for an old opponent, Whitney was not so inclined towards Ross as they headed for their first joint test of strength: four by-elections in December of 1899. The seats at stake were Elgin East and West, Brant South, and Ontario South. Whitney thought a Conservative sweep was a distinct possibility, a development which would place the government in jeopardy. This did not occur, however, the Tories taking the first two ridings – a net gain of one – and the Grits capturing the latter pair. Ross had hoped for better, but most observers saw the premier as out of danger for the balance of this legislature's life. They also reasoned that Whitney had 'fallen below his opportunities,' but the Tory chief insisted, despite the failure of his forecast, that it was '*a growing time* for the Conservative party.' Ross, secure in the premier's chair, encouraged the *Globe* to pursue a line which masked the Liberals' occupancy of office for twenty-eight years: 'Calling our Government "the *New* Government" seems to take well and annoys Whitney's friends very much,' he wrote to Willison. 'Keep it up; it is helping us.'[16]

In a stronger position at the start of the legislative session of 1900 than Hardy had been a year earlier, the premier was determined to advance fresh policies in an effort to maintain the image of a new regime. There were several pieces of legislation designed to further development of resources in northern Ontario, then referred to as New Ontario. Minor amendments in the election law were proposed in order to take the sting out of Whitney's yearly criticism. And there was also legislation to improve factory sanitation and to establish a labour bureau for the collection of industrial statistics. But some of the impact of these new thrusts was lost in the furore created by the work of a commission which Ross had appointed to investigate the Elgin West by-election frauds committed early in 1899. Ross had named this commission to save his government 'from a crash in Ontario,' although he bitterly remarked: 'Had it not been for McNish's [sic] confession [that the Liberals were guilty of fraud] there never would have been a West Elgin scandal.' When the commission convened and took up the particular charge of ballot-box stuffing, it was revealed that the ballots, somewhat pertinent to such an inquiry, had been burned in April of 1899 at the legislative building. To Conservative eyes, 'incontrovertible evidence' had thus been destroyed, rendering the purpose of the investigation largely meaningless. Whitney, stripped of evidence, could only insinuate that the ballot-burning had not been an accident, and the Grits were convinced the issue would fade with time. The episode did give Whitney new ammunition, and it did damage to the Ross government but, more important, it detracted from the Grit legislation of 1900.[17]

III

In the latter part of 1900, it was federal politics which absorbed Whitney's time and energy. In expectation of an election, Charles Tupper decided to tour Ontario in advance of the event and swept through the province in the early fall, with Whitney in tow delivering speeches that concentrated on the Elgin West affair. Then, when Laurier did call an election for early November, Whitney resumed work in Tupper's interest, but this time concentrated on the eastern end of Ontario. Tupper lost the election of 1900, but he did take fifty-six of the ninety-two Ontario seats. This latter aspect of the contest provided Conservatives with the consolation that the handwriting was on the wall for the 'firm of G.W. Ross and Co.' Part of the Tory success in the province was attributable to the return of wandering followers who had angrily left the fold in 1896, part to Whitney's labours and qualified success as leader, and part to Tupper's organization of Ontario for the battle. This last point was of importance to the provincial chief because he was to use some of Tupper's organization.[18]

Tupper first gave serious thought to reorganizing Ontario in May of 1898, but a trip to England intervened and he took no definite action until February 1899. Tupper intended to have three organizers for the eastern, central, and western sections of the province respectively, but did not propose to make these critical appointments until the Conservatives had an organization fund of ten thousand dollars. J.J. Foy was placed in charge of this fund, and despite occasional difficulties the necessary money was evidently raised. Thus, in late July of 1899, Tupper could name A.W. Wright, T.W.H. Leavitt, and Whitney's old friend Andrew Broder to the western, central, and eastern districts. Wright and Leavitt were to receive one hundred dollars a month and travelling expenses, and the trio was to effect 'as promptly as ... possible a thorough and complete organization of the Province of Ontario.' The immediate supervisor of their work would be Samuel Barker, a wealthy Hamilton lawyer who gave freely of his time and services. This was the shape of the federal Tory organization in Ontario by summer 1899.[19]

This new structure was erected outside of the framework of the Liberal-Conservative Union of Ontario, which had long been the basic provincial organization and the domain of its secretary-treasurer, Robert Birmingham. Birmingham, undoubtedly provoked by this relegation which denied him money and men, had a bitter argument with Tupper in which he insisted that the party owed him funds while Tupper retorted that such was not the case. This heated exchange brought the secretary-treasurer's departure from the party in the spring of 1900, and the Liberal-Conservative Union died with his exit. Consequently, the Tories, although possessing some elements of an organization after the federal campaign, were without an overall body, a shortcoming of which Whitney was to be made acutely aware.[20]

Other ripples from that election also struck Whitney, one of them caused by the provincial Liberals' inquest into the results which, they thought, did not augur well for Ross. They soon concluded that restlessness among Ontario's English-speaking Catholics was caused by the dimensions of Laurier's Protestant appointments and suspicions about his motives. In an effort to calm this group, and assist Ross, the prime minister attempted to elevate Jim Foy into the chief justiceship of Ontario. But the manoeuvre to remove 'the strongest member of the Ontario opposition' failed because Foy refused the post; and, to compound the Liberals' embarrassment, the abortive attempt to weaken Whitney was exposed to public gaze. The Ontario Tory leader was delighted and, having kept Foy within the ranks, he moved to take advantage of this strength. With the Toronto lawyer frequently at his side, Whitney attended non-partisan Catholic parish picnics where he usually saluted the British Empire, the memory of John A., and the virtues of his own party. Further, he quietly cut any remaining links with the decaying Protestant Protective Association. The Protestant horse was being put out to pasture or, possibly, consigned to the glue factory.[21]

Whitney went beyond courting English-speaking Catholics and turned his attention to Franco-Ontarians. Convinced that it was Laurier, and not the Conservatives, who had resorted to racial and religious cries for political ends, the Tory leader exhibited Foy as proof that he was not similarly motivated; although one could use Foy as evidence of just the reverse. Consequently, when F.D. Monk, in company with the new federal leader Robert Borden, made his first foray into Ontario, Whitney beat the drum of national unity. 'There is no ill-feeling in the Province of Ontario toward the people of Quebec,' he informed a Toronto audience, which must have been slightly nonplussed at this assessment. He then turned to his favourite place in Canadian history, the war of 1812, to salute the French-Canadian contribution at Chateauguay and, closer to his heart, at Crysler's Farm where 'a company of French under a French officer stood shoulder to shoulder with the Canadian militia in defence of Canada.' Such talk could now be judged as patronizing, if not offensive, but Whitney was not that; he was looking to seize any pieces that fell from the Ontario Liberal structure with a clear eye on the next election. His actions, however, did not rest solely on political expediency or represent a compromise of principle. He was not anti-Catholic, a point best illustrated by the quiet enrolment of his younger daughter, Norah, in the bilingual Our Lady of the Sacred Heart Convent in Ottawa – scarcely the action of a racial and religious bigot.[22]

Whitney also prepared for the next election by seeking the nomination of strong, capable candidates. By the spring of 1901, he had begun a flow of correspondence to key men in constituencies, urging them to select their standard-bearers with care; to potential candidates, asking them to accept the nomination if offered it; and to nominees, requesting them to take pains with organization. *'Let nothing interfere with your being a Candidate again,'* he emphasized to a likely contestant and increased the pressure of responsibility by adding that *'the result as a whole may rest on your decision.' 'If we are to succeed in the Province,'* he exhorted another, *'it will only be by each of us shewing that we are ready to make sacrifices.'* There was no room for slackers.[23]

Beyond these written pleas, there was the endless round of speeches: here, a constituency's annual meeting; there, a Tory club's smoker; and between, a soggy picnic on a leaden afternoon. Whitney's remarks on such occasions verged on the repetitious. He flayed the government over electoral misdeeds, nearly wearing out the whip of Elgin West. He accused Ross of cowardice in fleeing from education because he feared the gathering storm created by his inept administration of the school system. On the positive side, Whitney began to sketch out Conservative policies, sometimes in vague terms reflecting fear of theft by Ross. By early 1901, he had touched on a future plank in the Conservative platform. Speaking in Niagara Falls, he indicated surprise upon discovering that the power for the electric lights of a hotel came from the United States. He suggested that hydroelectric power developed on the Ontario side should be produced by and for Canadians, and he hinted at a wariness of the monopolistic control of a resource that properly belong to the people of the province. Clearly, his mind was going to be open to suggestions about a power policy.[24]

IV

Impatient with the enforced rest of winter and eager to be at the Liberals in person, Whitney anxiously awaited the legislative session of 1901, although he did agree to a non-partisan throne speech debate out of respect for the late queen. But, following that respectful pause, he hotly pursued the Grits in the budget debate. The Tory leader waded into the Liberals, charging them with stealing Conservative policies, with suggesting there were 'masses and classes' in Canada, with lowering political morality, with recklessly spending public money, with too freely disposing of natural resources to 'corporations,' and with neglect in the educational field. The intensely partisan nature of the onslaught prodded an irritated George Ross to his feet on a variety of points of order. Impervious, Whitney pressed on to meet a frequent Liberal charge that he possessed no policy. He advanced the Conservative position on a range of issues, though in some instances vagueness was apparent. He was precise, however, on four points: a Tory administration would reduce the cost of appeals by cutting the steps from lower to higher courts; all requests for timber and mineral grants would be carefully considered, regardless of political pressure; severe punishment would be meted out to those guilty of election corruption; and increased aid would be given to the University of Toronto, thus ending that institution's suspension 'between heaven and earth, like the coffin of Mohammed.'[25]

Whitney returned to the university question with a more explicit statement later in the session. He argued that the province had to take 'a forward position ... or else consent to be left hopelessly in the rear with disastrous results, one of which will inevitably be that our young men will go elsewhere for higher education.' Then, shifting from an earlier position, the Tory chieftain stated that the institution's finances had to 'be put on a sound, stable, and permanent footing' by means of annual payments sufficient to meet its needs; these funds, he suggested, should come out of provincial succession duties. Beyond that important consideration, he urged the government to ease its control so that the 'governing body of the university' would have real powers in policy and appointments. Lastly, Whitney called for a sliding scale of fees so that poverty would not bar the entry of any man or woman. Close behind Whitney's speech, a group of university alumni met with Ross and his cabinet; they described this meeting as unsatisfactory, but did lavish praise on the Conservative leader and his policies. And, when the government did produce a measure of aid for the institution, Whitney emphatically pronounced the amount to be quite inadequate, and then rehearsed his earlier demands; but to no avail.[26]

Whitney's current stand on the university question represented a new position for him and a display of greater understanding and generosity. The explanation of this growth seems to lie, in part, with his mentor W.R. Meredith, who, by 1901, was chancellor of the University of Toronto. The relationship between former leader and lieutenant had remained and continued to be close; consequently, it is logical to assume that Meredith had pulled Whitney from rural wariness to fresh thinking about the institution. On the day the Morrisburg member had made his most recent demands for the university, Meredith, with senate members, had argued with the government for an annual allotment from Ontario's succession duties. Whitney was not one to be led blindly into a new policy, but, if convinced of its merits, he could become its staunch champion, even if it represented few votes. He thus began to shape a second substantial plank – to go with that of hydroelectric development – for the Ontario Conservative platform of the twentieth century.[27]

George Ross, convinced he could not give more aid to the university, sourly watched Whitney getting 'infinitely more credit than he deserved.' Ross had had trouble even getting his supporters to line up at his position on the subject and thought that the Conservative chief, 'very much under Meredith's influence,' was endeavouring to outbid the Grits 'for the support of the Alumni of Toronto University.' 'The effect at the ballot-box, however,' he snorted, 'will be of no consequence to him if he does.' Ross presented the appearance of a man who protested too much to disguise a genuine concern about the consequences of the Tory leader's new position.[28]

The detailing of his University of Toronto policy was Whitney's major contribution to the 1901 session, but he did concern himself with other matters. He again called for the drastic revision of the elementary and secondary school systems and the creation of an educational consultative council composed of experts. The Liberals also provided him with two subjects for assault. Ross introduced a bill extending the life of the current legislature should it expire while in session during 1902. Led by Whitney and Foy, the Conservatives attacked the measure, arguing against its dictatorial implications and discussing the possibility of a gerrymander bill being introduced in the extra time provided. But the opposition's motion for a six months' hoist was lost. Then, as the session wound down, Whitney unveiled further evidence of Liberal skulduggery: dominion census enumerators had been directed to complete additional forms indicating the politics and religion of every male over sixteen in Ontario's ridings, and to forward such useful information to the Liberal member or defeated candidate in each riding. The Conservative leader emphasized the value of such a record for provincial election purposes and observed that, because census-takers took an oath of secrecy, this directive was an order to violate a trust. Ross, the *Mail and Empire* reported, 'admitted that the Liberal party had fathered these circulars, and made light of the matter.' Ottawa Grits saw the affair in a different light, and, shortly after the conclusion of the provincial session, Sydney Fisher, the responsible federal minister, ordered the practice stopped. 'It is quite evident,' Whitney informed a supporter, 'that the Govt lost ground during the Session.'[29]

v

Any sense of satisfaction from that session must have been sharply limited by personal and party problems which bore in upon Whitney in 1901. His family produced the most immediate difficulty, which, although causing him deep distress, provoked him to little comment. In the summer of 1899, Whitney's elder daughter, Muriel, married Ernest Thompson. For almost a year she evidently hid the marriage from her father who, upon uncovering the secret, initially reacted with anger and even questioned the solemnization of the union. Within a day, however, he regretted his hasty temper and decided to accept the situation. The marriage, unfortunately, was not a happy one. By September of 1900, Whitney was desperately trying to find employment for his son-in-law, and soon after he was explaining the plight of the unfortunate pair to young Thompson's uncle. 'They have nothing to live upon,' he revealed, 'and since their marriage have been supported by me.' Consequently, he was beset by 'anxiety' because of their situation. Nor was there ever a positive solution to the problem because Thompson, after fathering a son and daughter, quietly drifted away, leaving Muriel to raise the children with crucial assistance from her parents.[30]

A regrettably familiar problem also plagued Whitney at the century's turn: continuing financial embarrassment. Upon facing his first critical shortage of funds in 1897, he had been promised twenty-five hundred dollars by party supporters. But as the election of 1898 and the subsequent session and by-elections came and went, the sum never exceeded seven hundred dollars: five hundred from

Ottawa and two hundred from a pair of Toronto Tories. By early autumn of 1899, the Morrisburg lawyer described himself as 'financially stranded' with 'his practice ... practically ruined.' Constant worry had impaired 'his ability to give his best for the benefit of the party.' What he now wanted, to set his books in order, was not the balance of eighteen hundred dollars, but twenty-five hundred. He maintained that, in light of his work since the original figure was set, his request for an additional seven hundred was 'not unreasonable.' He squirmed with embarrass-ment but resolved that 'when one finds onesself [sic] in a *corner* the only thing to do is to face the difficulty no matter how much it may hurt.' It was unpleasant; it was distasteful; and it mirrored a problem for the provincial party of thirty years' standing. But, and this was a mark of the man, it was not enough to drive him out of the leadership and politics.[31]

Nevertheless, the spectre of debt chased him into 1900: he deliberately postponed a Toronto trip until his complimentary Grand Trunk pass arrived. The much-needed money barely trickled in and, through gritted teeth, he emptily threatened resignation. After staggering through the session of 1900, he had to face more expenses that materialized with Tupper's tour and the subsequent federal election campaign. Whitney desperately needed money for electioneering through Ontario and he finally found it, but just five hundred dollars, and not a gift but a loan which had to be repaid. In the months that followed, a draft for this amount bounced around the province's banks as party officials juggled it in order to avoid a payment demand. Finally, the draft fell onto Whitney's doorstep. 'On Saturday [January] 26th [1901]' he complained to one of the jugglers,

I was in our Bank here when I was told that the draft had been returned unpaid a Couple of days before. Of this I had no warning from you. Then I wired you the same day – Saturday – but received no reply. I wired you again yesterday but could get no reply and have none yet.

What you mean by treating me in this way is, I am bound to say, beyond me. I am ashamed to wire you again and, to say nothing of the annoyance and worry, the open humiliation you have put upon me is pretty hard to bear as I am placed before our Bank people in the position of a liar.

These were the words of a proud man struck low, but they were more than that: they were a sign of high agitation and even a growing mistrust of friends. Whitney soon recuperated, but his finances did not, and in the summer of 1901, when George Foster proposed a business venture, he sadly replied: 'I have practically no business left and have no time to look after any.'[32]

But Whitney pressed along the path of politics, and consequently one must ask how his financial woes were eased. Morrisburg residents, recalling those days, offered the only answer in view: Edwin, Whitney's lumber baron brother, must have bailed him out when the flood of debts threatened to swamp him. And a positive aspect shines through all these troubles: Whitney remained relatively free of ties, ties that might have been reinforced by the bond of money, to people who might have used his indebtedness to them to squeeze out political favours. His straitened circumstances, in fact, left him a legacy: room for manoeuvre and flexibility at a later date. He did not owe, and he was not owned.[33]

Problems of family and finances would have sufficed to fill Whitney's plate of troubles, but he also was served large helpings of political difficulties, and the combination was cause for violent indigestion. His relationship with the Ottawa Tories became strained during the 1900 election period, when Tupper sought to have two provincial members contest federal seats. Dr Elisha Jessop, member for Lincoln, was approached without the courtesy of consulting Whitney who, in turn, refused to approve such a 'foolish' move. 'I think,' he lectured Tupper, 'it is clearly more important to hold our own in the Legislature than to take any step the result of which may be uncertain.' Reprimanded, Tupper temporarily retreated, muttering assurances that, in future, similar approaches would only be made with Whitney's 'hearty approval.' The episode triggered the rumour that federal and provincial chiefs were 'not entirely in accord.'[34]

Far more critical, however, was the attempt to recruit Foy as the federal candidate for Toronto Centre, then Liberal property. Whitney, adamant in opposition to the proposal, knew he would face intense pressure from the party federal hierarchy in Ottawa and Toronto, and so he opted to demonstrate dramatically that he had support for his position. By letter he asked every provincial Conservative member for his opinion, and, as anticipated, each backed his leader. Whitney then virtually dictated the public statement his Catholic lieutenant should make, and Foy, less than eager for the federal post, largely complied. Informed of these provincial developments, Tupper accepted the decision with grace. Some Toronto Tories did not, however, and continued to lobby Foy. This pressure produced warm words between the federal and provincial wings in Toronto, until Whitney intervened to protect Foy from federal overtures and retain his prize possession. After the Laurier triumph over Tupper, Whitney told Hugh John Macdonald: 'It was indeed fortunate that I did not let Foy go. A great many people see that now.' The whole affair undoubtedly heightened the Ontario leader's dark suspicions about the motives of some Toronto Tories, if that was possible, and it vexed him to think that such people should have so little regard for the provincial party and its prospects.[35]

On occasion, the lack of adequate coverage of Conservative events in the *Mail and Empire* only served to convince Whitney further that there was indeed a peculiar deficiency in some supposed supporters in Toronto. During the 1899 session he bitterly complained about the failure of the paper to employ a shorthand man in the press gallery, and, embarrassingly, he had to refer at least two correspondents to the *Globe*'s accounts of his remarks. Finally, in desperation, he detailed for the *Mail and Empire* three areas of dissatisfaction: inaccurate reporting of his speeches, failure to cover some Conservative meetings, and periodic silences on certain issues, thus allowing the *News* wrongly to portray itself as the voice of Ontario Conservatism. Whitney's criticisms were heard, but the newspaper scarcely rushed to address them; nor did his decision to avoid the paper's annual staff banquet repair the shaky relationship.[36]

The opposition leader, however, received his worst beating in printed form from C.R. Mabee, a pamphleteer who sold Whitney and A.W. Wright on the production of a Tory tract early in 1901. But a preview of its contents revealed an exceedingly scurrilous booklet, and the Conservative chief dropped the author and his work. Angered, Mabee turned to the Liberals and fashioned an equally abusive anti-Whitney campaign pamphlet which Alexander Smith, secretary of the Ontario Liberal Association, found 'an attractive document' and recommended be purchased by local organizations. The work, which Mabee claimed rested on the opinions of Conservatives, was an extraordinary document. The essence of the pamphlet was that, as a leader, Whitney was excessively vain, recklessly spendthrift, hopelessly disorganized, utterly lazy, and disastrously immature. Under normal circumstances the sight of an obvious chameleon altering his political pigmentation for money would have been amusing; but, unhappily for Whitney, the episode peaked just as he was suppressing a minor party revolt and did little for his humour.[37]

George Marter also gave Whitney trouble in this period and, because of Marter's former position, this was of concern to him. Difficulties began early in 1899 when Tupper was engaged in his reorganization of the federal party in Ontario. An immediate by-product of that work had been Foy's appointment as treasurer of the organization fund. The ex-leader was dismayed by this development because he had received no invitation to the organizational meeting and he had once been named provincial party treasurer, a post he had never formally relinquished. Hurt by being ignored, Marter was not soothed by a letter of apology from Tupper, written at Whitney's behest, and he next erupted after the 1900 session with the charge that the party 'had alienated the Corporations' while failing to secure the support of 'the people.' The party failures, he argued, would likely prevent his re-election. Later that year, Marter deliberately absented himself from a special caucus of Tory legislators, peevishly claiming that 'he had no special invitation or even intimation of the meeting' from Whitney. Complaining of poor treatment at his leader's hands, he hinted at an imminent retirement, convinced that such action would have a 'damaging effect' on Whitney at the next election. The party leader anxiously inquired if Marter had been sent a notice of the caucus and was informed that he had. What Marter wanted, however, was a personal invitation from Whitney, and there had been none. For whatever reason – Whitney's secretary thought the ex-leader was 'doting' – Marter was clearly looking for trouble and, not surprisingly, he found it. Consequently his querulousness continued and by the end of February 1901 he had publicly indicated that he would not contest Toronto North at the next election, making the point in the process that it was not his business interests alone that were shoving him out of politics. Now well launched on his rebellious course, he twice voted with the Liberals during the 1901 session and defended this action on the grounds that, by not attending the Tory caucus, he was free of its decisions. And he talked of running as an independent in the next contest because he could not 'run as a Conservative, and support the leader.' This truculence was embarrassing for Whitney, particularly so because he and Marter shared the same desk throughout the session of 1901.[38]

Whitney had always held Marter at arm's length and so his words were not that hurtful; but he was definitely wounded when Dr R.A. Pyne and Foy, whom he trusted, began to make critical noises. The difficulty stemmed from Whitney's stubborn and persistent refusal to take up permanent residence in Toronto and direct the party from that central location. The move had been proposed before, but the idea was advanced for urgent consideration in 1901. Initially, Whitney had calmly put the suggestion aside, commenting that, although others might see advantages in such a shift, he could see none. Pyne pressed the issue and, unwisely, contended that he should be willing to make sacrifices. Whitney found that admonition 'astonishing,' especially in light of his intensive labour. Unabashed, Pyne – with Foy's blessing – put forward the advice once more: 'I may tell you,' he wrote to his leader, 'that if you were with me or Foy day after day in Toronto, and had it "dinged" into your ears every time the matter was spoken of, that *you* should be in Toronto just *now*, and during the *whole campaign*, you would not wonder how impressed we are with the importance of your arranging to come and live here.' Whitney refused to budge and Pyne temporarily fell silent, only to return to the subject later and receive precisely the same negative response. Clearly, there was unhappiness with Whitney's maintenance of a permanent Morrisburg address, and some Toronto party lights saw weaknesses in long-distance direction, weaknesses that the leader would not acknowledge.[39]

These troubles with Tupper, Mabee, Marter, and Pyne were of a minor scale compared with those precipitated by some Toronto Tories of whom Whitney was so wary. During the last months of 1900 and early into 1901, they began to rock the boat; from Whitney's viewpoint, their labours were at least an effort at severe restriction of his power as leader and at most an attempted ouster. The key figures among the plotters were William F. Maclean, Conservative MP for East York and publisher of the Toronto *World*; Dr Beattie Nesbitt, a sharp and self-seeking politician; and organizers T.W.H. Leavitt and A.W. Wright, apparent disciples of Maclean. The publisher had grumbled at Whitney through the *World*'s columns, but his mutterings about the need for strong leadership had been muffled, and he had been hard pressed to produce concrete suggestions for improvement. His criticisms had provoked some Tories to anger, but Whitney had remained unmoved. After Tupper's defeat, however, Maclean made louder noises, calling for 'a caucus of all the Conservatives of Ontario,' and a 'regenerated' legislature that would send 'the Ross Government ... to the crematory.' This was possible, he argued, because the federal election results demonstrated that the party's fortunes were on the rise in the province. This was the moment for Ontario Conservatives 'to blaze out a new and straight road.' A convention, he later contended, 'would do a power of good,' because '... Whitney stands equally in need of the advice of the rank-and-file.'[40]

Whitney apparently took little notice of this gratuitous advice, although he began to toy with the idea of gathering all Tory legislators and defeated candidates of 1898 for consultation on party policies. He was thus completely taken aback when the *Mail and Empire* announced, on 24 November, not that he should call a convention but that he was calling one. Beyond that, the newspaper was precise in its description of the proposed meeting's shape and nature, indicating that it would be 'of a purely provincial character,' and consist of 'Conservative candidates in the elections of 1898, together with representatives chosen by the various Conservative organizations of the province.' Privately, Whitney angrily denied the report, which had been written by the *Mail*'s Hector Charlesworth and relied on information fed him by Wright and Leavitt. Initially, the Tory leader wanted a correction which would make it plain that he was only contemplating a caucus, augmented by defeated candidates, and that he was still in control of the party. Cooler heads prevailed, however, and he took no public notice of the convention announcement in order to avoid making 'a fool of both the paper and the party.'[41]

The agitation for a larger meeting temporarily subsided, but not before Whitney got a danger signal which he chose to ignore. He received a 'Lithographed Circular addressed to the President of the Conservative Association of the County of Dundas proposing that a Convention of the party be held' from R. Shaw Wood, who represented himself as president of the Middlesex County Conservative Association. Whitney wrote him a polite letter in which he implied that Shaw Wood must have been misled by the *Mail and Empire* announcement. 'In all probability,' he told the association president, 'the Opposition Members of the Legislature and the defeated Candidates of the Conservative party at the Elections of 1898 will be summoned or requested to meet me for the purpose of Consultation at an early date, but that is all for the present at any rate.' What the Tory chief failed to observe was that copies of the circular must have been run off prior to the *Mail and Empire*'s report. Only two days had elapsed between the newspaper story and Whitney's reply to Shaw Wood; this provided insufficient time for the printing, distribution, and receipt of copies of the circular. The eager Mr Wood was not taking his lead from the *Mail and Empire*; Whitney missed the point.[42]

Early in December there was finally a modest announcement of a meeting of Conservative members and defeated candidates called by Whitney. These men gathered and an 'enthusiastic' conclave was held, but there was a peculiar development: a number of uninvited guests, 'friends and well-wishers of the party,' put in an appearance. Whitney delivered a short speech, but a discussion of organization absorbed much of the time. A report described the affair as 'more in the nature of a caucus than anything else'; presumably it was not a convention, despite the presence of those 'well-wishers.' Maclean's *World* assessed the meeting as demonstrating 'a gratifying state of affairs,' and opined that Whitney has 'a united party.'[43]

Matters did not rest there, however, because in January of 1901, Shaw Wood distributed a second circular calling 'a meeting of the presidents of the Conservative Associations of all the Ontario ridings.' The date set was 22 January; the place, the *Mail and Empire* building. Whitney, recalling the earlier circular, dismissed Shaw Wood as a 'Crank.' He took the precaution, nevertheless, of requesting his friends to inquire about the proposed convention. Replies soon indicated that Pyne, Foy, and Scott Griffin – Toronto men whom he trusted – knew nothing about the meeting. But there were people who did know something about the convention: Leavitt wrote to Clarke Wallace, telling of the gathering and explaining its purpose. He wanted someone 'to take a strong stand in favour of some decisive action' with respect to the anticipated provincial election. He and Wright were united 'in the opinion that the present policy of drifting' would lead to defeat; and thus far, they had failed 'to induce Mr Whitney to make any advance along the necessary lines.' Leavitt and Wright may not have intended a palace revolution, but they certainly were attempting to wrest the lead from the party chief.[44]

The meeting was held, as scheduled, but Whitney and his associates remained ignorant of its sponsors and implications until after the event. With Shaw Wood in the chair, and Wright and Leavitt serving as secretaries, birth was given to the Ontario Liberal-Conservative Association, a body designed to foster party organization. Although membership was open to a wide range of officers from local Tory bodies, the only legislators invited to join the ranks were 'the whips of the party for the province in the Dominion and Provincial Parliaments.' Wood became president; Wright and Leavitt took the posts of joint secretaries; and Beattie Nesbitt was named chairman of the executive committee. The blocking of members of parliament and the provincial legislature from admission did not prevent Maclean and Wallace from delivering 'stirring addresses.'[45]

After the delegates had departed, Whitney and his allies pieced together the inside story of the convention. At first it was suspected that the assembly had been 'the product of Mr Maclean's genius,' but this was not quite the case. 'It was suggested originally,' Griffin informed Whitney, '... by Beattie Nesbitt who, no doubt, in consultation with Maclean, drafted a constitution which was produced, *typewritten*, at the meeting and adopted by those present.' 'The whole thing,' he continued, was 'a palpable effort by these men to further their own interests in the party and override the influence of the leaders.' Shaw Wood was 'entirely conscientious,' but merely a cat's-paw. 'The *best* men,' Whitney was assured, '... are content with you.'[46]

Despite advice to disregard this development, Whitney was in no position to do so. He had been seriously challenged as party leader, and there was now in place a provincial organization which virtually excluded elected Tory representatives. Shrewd as it might be to pay scant attention to Nesbitt's grab for power, because interference might enable the doctor to charge obstruction in his effort to assist the party, Whitney could not permit statements in the *World* that indicated his support for the convention to go unrepudiated. Further, the bumptiousness of the two organizers had to be checked, and the necessity of such action became more pressing when Leavitt, in a speech approving of the organization, indicated that it would 'relegate back to the rank and file the direction of affairs of the Conservative party.' Whitney immediately demanded that the organizer reveal his authorization for this statement and the body for whom he was speaking. Leavitt failed to answer the questions, although he did patiently explain the operation of the new association to his leader. When Whitney pressed him, Leavitt's response was edged in surliness as he pointed out that his statements were in full accordance with the organization's constitution and he referred the party chief to Nesbitt or Shaw Wood for confirmation of that fact.[47]

At this point, Whitney evidently decided against a public brawl with any of the rebels and quietly moved to reassert his hold on the entire party. With this shift to backroom manoeuvring, descriptions of developments disappear, but one fact is obvious: Whitney fought hard to place himself in control of the situation and, by late February, he was gaining the upper hand. 'As a result of a conference between Mr. J.P. Whitney and the Conservative members of the Legislature,' the *Mail and Empire* reported, 'the list of those eligible for membership of the Ontario Liberal-Conservative Association' had been lengthened to include senators, members of Parliament and the legislature, and defeated candidates for both houses. It was also decided to hold a meeting of the organization on 20 March. On the evening prior to that date, the key men of the Ontario Conservative party attended a dinner at which Whitney, in rebuttal of the Liberal charge that the Tories were adrift without policies, detailed the New Ontario plank of his platform which focused on increased control of timber tract grants. Nesbitt, Wright, and Shaw Wood sat through this talk and digested their meals while their leader undertook this thinly veiled attack upon them.[48]

At the convention the next day, a revised constitution allowing for the membership of legislators and candidates was quietly adopted, and a new executive council was created with room for representatives from the Senate, the House of Commons, and the Ontario legislature. Lastly, a slate of officers was elected: Bowell, Borden, and Whitney were named honorary presidents, and so was R. Shaw Wood; the new president of the association was J.J. Foy. No resolutions on policy were adopted and Whitney, surely secretly smiling, moved votes of thanks to Beattie Nesbitt and Shaw Wood. These manoeuvrings did not completely end friction within the party, but the problem was eased. And

Whitney, in a stronger position, placed Wright and Leavitt, now organizers for the new provincial body, directly under his control: they could not initiate projects or make public statements until they had cleared with the leader or, failing him, with Foy or E.B. Osler, another loyal party stalwart. Whitney did not punish the two organizers for their past actions, because he thought they could be 'of great service,' but he did relegate Nesbitt to a lesser post in the party structure. The Morrisburg lawyer was very much master of his party, no mean feat for someone leading a political body that had not tasted power for thirty years.[49]

None of this, however, prevented Maclean's continual sniping from ambush. Nor was the Toronto publisher averse to using Wright and Leavitt as conduits for periodic leaks of his plots and plans. In the long, hot summer of 1901, Whitney finally exploded in the face of this harassment. 'This sort of thing,' he complained to Foy, 'shews the hidden Volcano on which I have to walk all the time and what a lot of d—d unspeakable scoundrels the party in Toronto has in the membership.' He contemplated, then rejected, the revelation of the petty plotting to the Liberal-Conservative Association to let it glimpse the life he led 'surrounded by men compared to whom Judas Iscariot was a gentleman.' 'A nice life I have,' he fumed to Colquhoun, 'expecting some trap every step I take & surrounded by a set of d—d traitors whom no language can be found fitly to describe.'[50]

Some of Whitney's attitudes were hardened by what he perceived as this deliberate and malicious rocking of the Ontario Conservative boat. His conviction that he should not move to Toronto, despite the pleadings of Pyne and Foy, was likely reinforced by the petty in-fighting he witnessed in that centre of intrigue. And he had confirmation of his view that many Toronto Tories were men of small minds and even smaller consciences. There were exceptions, of course, such as Foy, Pyne, Osler, and Colquhoun, but their loyalty simply underlined the absence of that quality in others. He was also made more wary of conventions. He had always viewed their value with an anti-American scepticism but, having witnessed one in which his leadership was challenged, he was firmly convinced that they were not just worthless, but potentially dangerous to the leader, the party, and its policies.

Running parallel to Whitney's mounting personal and political troubles, which reached a climax in 1901, were periodic bouts of ill health that did nothing to ease his mind or improve his temper. In the spring of 1899, his ailments had been limited to 'a touch of lumbago,' but by year's end he complained of feeling 'pretty nearly used up.' During much of the following spring, he was not 'up to par' and regretfully concluded he was 'not a boy any longer.' 'I have,' he lamented in midsummer of 1900, 'a strong tendency to sleeplessness. Of course my nervous system is not what it was three years ago and I have had no real rest – that is my mind has never been free from something which caused worry.' And, in December, 'a combination of Cold, indigestion, and nervousness' forced cancellation of an engagement. As the Conservative party seethed in early 1901,

W.D. Gregory commented on the Tory leader's obvious irascibility: 'I hear,' he reported to a Conservative legislator, 'that Whitney has gone to pieces and that a new leader is talked of.' If such scuttlebutt reached Whitney, it probably did little for his peace of mind. Although he had beaten back a potential rebellion, he still had to endure periodic birchings from Maclean throughout the summer of 1901. And the temperature of that season did little for his mental attitude: 'I find it very difficult to do anything,' he confessed to Pyne in July. 'I dont [sic] know why unless it is that my nervous system is beginning to weaken. I worry all the time and about everything. I find it very difficult to be civil to people at all.'[51]

By mid-1901, Whitney was thoroughly dejected: little had gone right in the previous three years. Hopes that by-election results might overturn the electoral verdict of 1898 were dashed, and he remained leader of the opposition. Financial troubles and his daughter's ill-fated marriage had plagued his personal life. Toronto Tories, seeking federal success, had tried to pry Foy away from him; and then, craving for that elusive provincial triumph, had turned on him. And his health was dragged down by this constant drain on his energies. Small wonder he was harsh of judgment, sharp of tongue, and irritable of temperament.

VI

Whitney could not afford the luxury of prolonged depression, however, if he was to remain the effective leader of the Ontario Conservative party. He would simply have to live with Toronto intrigues which, in any event, diminished because of the tightening rein of Foy and Pyne and the more compelling smell of Liberal blood. Consequently, he was able to give his full attention to the proper goal, defeat of the Grits, which proved to be four tough years away. Henceforth, when angered by difficulties and frustrations, he generally vented his spleen on Liberals, not Tories, because he could look ahead and not over his shoulder.[52]

In his efforts to oust Ross, the opposition leader had the new tools of the Ontario Liberal-Conservative Association and assiduous organizers Wright and Leavitt. The old Liberal-Conservative Union, which had died with Robert Birmingham's angry departure, had never been of much help to provincial Tories, save for the labours of its secretary-treasurer; and so the new organization, with its distinctly provincial orientation, held out greater promise of usefulness, despite its troublesome birth. Consequently, Whitney was quite prepared to use this fresh machinery and its diligent operatives, provided he and his friends held ownership.

Wright proved to be particularly industrious. In July of 1901, he began a meticulous canvass of those ridings which might turn Conservative in the next election. He queried local Tories, proposed logical candidates, assessed financial and organizational needs, estimated Conservative chances, and advised on Whitney's tactics when in the constituencies. In Lambton East, where the Tory aspirant was a former PPA supporter, he urged that Foy accompany Whitney in order to test the candidate's loyalty and allay Catholic fears. Wright oozed confidence about the prospects in Lambton West, thanks to the 'almost perfect' organizational work of the candidate, W.J. Hanna. No money needed be found for this constituency, but 'a number of good speakers' would have to be recruited. Such campaigners should be aware that the Standard Oil Company was 'very influential in this riding and ... not a little popular with the people.' 'Mr. Hanna,' the organizer appended, 'is the Canadian legal agent of the Standard.' The Tories of Northumberland West had yet to select a nominee, but Wright uncovered the man who, in his opinion, was the best, Thomas Spence. The latter, however, needed guarantees of 'substantial assistance towards the expenses of the election,' before entering the contest. Four hundred dollars, Wright thought, would have to come from outside the riding; the amount equalled that locally pledged. This tidy sum was required because 'owing to the absence of railway communication, the livery bills of candidates' were high. The local organization also wanted repair but, with that remedied and Spence conscripted, Northumberland West could fall. These services by Wright had never before been provided to provincial Tories, even in Birmingham's palmiest days, and Whitney knew he possessed a resourceful political animal for probing and reporting on party strengths and weaknesses, particularly in critical ridings. Thus, he was disinclined to any vendetta against his sometime brazen organizers.[53]

In addition to these benefits of fresh and sound organization, another soon developed: money materialized for the party's coffers in larger amounts. Some funds resulted from a concerted drive for money, possibly made easier by the growing conviction that Whitney could topple Ross – not that the party was awash in contributions, but the trickle was regular. Consequently, Whitney no longer had to perform financial juggling acts or engage personally in demeaning begging exercises. With a central association, able organizers, and small but growing funds, the party was constructing a political machine with which to destroy that of the Liberals.[54]

Supported in this fashion for the first time in five years of party leadership, Whitney in concert with others was able to plot a provincial political tour, starting off with a speech to the Association's annual meeting in Toronto on 3 September, designed to catch Tories in town for the CNE. At that gathering, which re-elected Foy as president, the party chief had the podium to himself for a three-hour address that laid out the main points of the Conservative platform and refuted the charge of lack of policy. Little was new in his remarks, the majority of items having been covered on previous occasions. He returned to his calls for public school curriculum reform, a cheaper arrangement for textbook publication, and a sound financial footing for the University of Toronto. He demanded the proper development of New Ontario's unsettled areas and government aid for a railway in the Temiskaming region. He wanted 'substantial encouragement' given to the refining of Ontario's ores within the provincial boundaries and argued for adequate administration and conservation of Ontario's timber resources. The party leader urged that great care be taken in dispensing grants to railways and favoured aid only to those lines that would further provincial development and colonization. 'In every case,' he continued, 'stock on security should be taken for the amount advanced, and freight and passenger rates should be controlled by the Legislature.'

Showing no signs of fatigue, he pressed on to argue for law reform that would 'lessen the expense and expedite the results of litigation.' There had to be greater control of provincial expenditures in order to provide additional funds for agriculture and education. He envisaged the new aid for farmers as taking the form of agricultural schools and facilities designed to speed farm products to their markets. Whitney wanted a halt to all legislation which unduly favoured the corporations at the expense of municipal ratepayers. And, of course, he asked for tough laws to end ballot manipulation and electoral crimes. 'We believe,' he concluded, sounding a familiar theme, 'that the people of Ontario desire honest and clean government, and therefore we ask the assistance and co-operation of all those who are ready to defend the public honor and public decency.' Once the delegates were gone, Whitney judged the meeting 'a decided success in every way.' For a politician, he had advanced policy in a reasonably precise way, and had disproved the charge that he had nothing to offer but negative criticism. Naturally, he had also 'put on the *Hob nail boots* and kicked' the Liberals 'all over the field.'[55]

Having fired this opening shot in Toronto, the Tory chief began an unhurried provincial tour which lasted into late autumn, with occasional opportunities for retreat to Morrisburg for rest and refreshment. As Whitney visited London or New Hamburg or Port Colborne, his speeches were virtual duplicates of his Toronto remarks; but, speaking to local groups, he did close by emphasizing one point: the absolute necessity of thorough organization for the next provincial campaign. Since 'the back of the Ontario Government was broken,' only deficiency in this matter could prevent a Conservative victory.[56]

In a September speech at Caledon, Whitney did turn to a fresh subject: the relationship between Canada and Great Britain. Although the day was chilly, an impressive crowd gathered behind the Presbyterian church to hear Whitney criticize Ross for the latter's stand on imperial preference while visiting England. Ross had argued for a 5 per cent duty throughout the Empire on foreign imports, over and above any existing tariffs. The income so derived would be used for imperial defence, and the effect would be to create imperial preference. Whitney countered that the overburdened British working class would not accept such an imposition, citing in his argument an earlier Ross statement to much the same effect. This was the wrong basis, in the Conservative leader's opinion, on which to erect either imperial federation or preference. Canadians, he asserted, required 'no bribe to induce' them 'to take up willingly' their 'share of the burdens of the Empire.' Canada would stand by Britain 'in the spirit in which Ruth showed her devotion to Naomi.' He hoped, as he insisted that Macdonald had hoped, that this country would in the near future 'take her place as one of those outlying and auxiliary kingdoms which would ... become the buttresses and bulwarks of the British Empire all round the world.' That was how Canada should mature, and certainly not through monetary considerations or independence.[57]

Whitney's speech-making and organizational activities throughout the fall were, in part, dictated by his ignorance of the government's intentions with respect to an election. A surprise autumn test of strength was rumoured, and the Tory chief was unwilling to accept Ross's declarations to the contrary. He did think, however, that the government's position was so weak – his assessment rested on poor attendance at Liberal gatherings – that Ross could scarcely issue an election call, because disaster would undoubtedly befall the Grits. Nevertheless, the Conservative leader remained prepared, and warily watched for the sure signs of an impending contest. When these failed to materialize, he vigorously turned to the session of 1902, knowing that it would be the last before Ontario went to the polls.[58]

VII

The sharpest exchanges during that legislative session centred on liquor legislation, the proper use of Ontario's water power resources, and the customary Conservative recitation of Liberal electoral corruption. George Ross, a longtime temperance man, had to face squarely the extremely difficult question of prohibition in 1902. This was necessary, not because the problem had suddenly arisen but, rather, because the final barrier to governmental action had been removed and the premier had little choice but to act. The inaccurately named temperance movement had long pressed governments in Ontario for highly restrictive liquor legislation. In response to this lobbying there had been referenda on the prohibition question in 1894 and 1898, but Grit governments had deferred action, pleading the unsolved problem of jurisdiction under the constitution. In November of 1901, however, that legalistic cover was shredded when the Judicial Committee of the Privy Council declared as constitutional Manitoban legislation which would establish prohibition, with certain exceptions made for the fields of medicine, religion, industry, and science. Temperance warriors immediately besieged Ross and reminded him of his earlier pledge that 'the Government would no doubt go as far as the definition of constitutional limitations would allow.' These tough-minded reformers certainly thought that promise could now be translated into virtual prohibition, and they would brook no delay.[59]

Ross was no political illiterate: he well knew that many temperance supporters, especially among Methodists and Presbyterians, were staunch Liberals, but he was similarly aware that they did not represent his only source of strength. He had to attempt to formulate a policy, in the face of the judicial decision, which would pacify prohibition proponents, while not significantly antagonizing those less zealous in the population. His shrewd solution came very close to meeting such difficult requirements. On 12 February, with the province buzzing on the issue, Ross produced his answer. His bill provided for prohibition along the lines of Manitoba's act, and a referendum to confirm it. After some rethinking it was determined that 4 December 1902 would be referendum day, and that prohibition would be enacted if a majority, based on the total votes cast in the 1898 election, favoured it. Temperance advocates argued that the referendum, with its attached conditions, was an evasion of responsibility by the supposedly prohibition-minded Ross, while Whitney charged him with retreating from his previous position and with presenting a complicated measure designed to placate temperance champions while ensuring the defeat of prohibition. The Tory leader argued that the referendum was 'unconstitutional' and, instead of it, advocated a reduction in licensed establishments, strict supervision and enforcement of existing regulations, and complete freedom from political pressure for license inspectors. Whitney's position did not endear him to the temperance forces, but he was convinced that it was the only practical and honest policy any government could pursue. Nevertheless, the Ross bill passed into law and prohibitionist stalwarts, grumbling about the unfairness of the referendum, set to work for the December test of strength.[60]

Prohibition was an exceedingly divisive subject at the century's turn – sometimes as troublesome as questions of race, religion, or education – and, in this instance, the Tory party did not escape unscathed. George Marter, a consistent prohibitionist, broke party ranks on one critical vote and also sponsored three amendments that were crushed by Liberals and Conservatives. This maverick behaviour moved Marter to the outer edges of the party and Whitney, while surely regretting the split in party unity, undoubtedly saw trouble packing to leave. But the Tory leader's problems on this contentious issue were small compared to those of Ross, who feared that, after 'all the fireworks of the last five or six weeks,' the Ontario branch of the Dominion Alliance might request the bill's withdrawal, presumably out of concern that the referendum might fail. Ross confessed that, should this happen (it did not), he would have no idea what to do. The question of alcohol befuddled all.[61]

In this same session the subject of public ownership of hydroelectric development in Ontario reached the floor of the legislature. Who first suggested such a policy remains unidentified: a number of people have either claimed paternity or been awarded fatherhood. It is clear, however, that at the century's turn a variety of factors and forces came together to produce a growing sentiment in favour of governmental action. Ontario was most obviously blessed with a portion of the falls at Niagara, dramatic visual evidence of great energy potential, and the problem of long-distance transmission of hydroelectricity had been solved by use of the alternating current. Ontario, and especially Toronto, were becoming increasingly industrialized, with larger factories ever more evident, while they remained coal-poor. Thus the possibilities of hydroelectricity, particularly if cheap and readily available, dazzled both manufacturer and merchant, as well as the public at large. Further, Ontario's history possessed its share of precedents for governmental involvement with, or intervention in, business. By this time nearly one hundred municipalities operated a variety of municipally owned utilities: waterworks, electric street-lighting services, or gas works.[62]

In 1902, two American-owned companies, the Canadian Niagara Power Company and the Ontario Power Company, had contracts with the Queen Victoria Niagara Falls Park Commission for the development of hydroelectricity from the falls. Additionally, backers of an embryonic third company were preparing to knock on the commission's door in search of a contract. This Canadian organization, to be named the Electrical Development Company, was put together by William Mackenzie, Henry M. Pellatt, and Frederic Nicholls. These three companies quite unintentionally strengthened the feeling for public ownership. In the case of the first two, there was Ontarian annoyance at American control of a provincial resource. The Mackenzie combination had already aroused hostility, notably in Toronto, where it controlled the Toronto Street Railway and the Toronto Electric Light Company. By 1902, the Toronto City Council, led by Methodist prohibitionist alderman F.S. Spence, was making its third unsuccessful application to the legislature 'for authority to establish a municipally owned public utility to supply the city with electricity for light and power.' This failure produced significant public animosity toward the Mackenzie syndicate in particular, and large grey corporations in general; it also strengthened the forces which favoured government intervention or ownership in the field of hydroelectric production and transmission.[63]

Whitney had touched on this subject when, over a year earlier, he had sounded an anti-American note in suggesting that the development of Niagara's power potential should be in Ontarian hands. And he sensed the rising anti-corporation sentiment in the province and had already begun to play to that feelng. On the other hand, when Ross renewed the agreement with the faltering Canadian Niagara Power Company early in 1902, the *Mail and Empire* attacked him for his action, which, it argued, confounded his pledge never to 'be found on the side of the corporations as against the people.' Clearly, the word 'corporation' had acquired negative connotations; Whitney was prepared to accommodate the new definition.[64]

The Conservative policy statement on hydroelectric development came on 5 February, when Andrew Miscampbell (Simcoe East) and Henry Carscallen (Hamilton East) advanced the following amendment:

In all future agreements made between the Commissioners of the Queen Victoria Niagara Falls Park and any other person, or persons, power shall be reserved to the Provincial

Government to, at any time, put a stop to the transmission of electricity and pneumatic power beyond the Canadian boundary; and that in the opinion of this House, the waters of the Niagara River and its tributaries, as well as the waters of other streams, where necessary, should, at the earliest moment and subject to existing agreement, be utilized directly by the Provincial Government, in order that the latter may generate and develop electricity and pneumatic power for the purpose of light, heat and power, and furnish the same to municipalites in this Province at cost.

The amendment was lost on a straight party vote, but the, Tories had firmly announced their policy. This resolution was evidently drafted by Dr T.E. Kaiser of Oshawa, A.W. Wright, T.W.H. Leavitt, and Beattie Nesbitt, although major credit apparently should go to the first-named, who had earlier been informed: 'Mr Whitney has consented to adopt your power policy. We have converted most of the [Conservative] Members.' Some who had previously pushed Whitney on provincial organization and policy statements were now shoving the party down the path to public power.[65]

If Whitney was a reluctant convert to the cause of public ownership of the means of production and transmission of hydroelectric power, as he has sometimes been portrayed,[66] he gave little indication of it in this instance or a few days later at a banquet in his honour when he returned to the subject. The path to municipal 'ownership of public utilities' should be cleared of all obstacles, he told the gathering; and then insisted that 'it would be possible in the near future' 'for the Government to utilize' the unharnessed power of Ontario's waterways 'for the purpose of selling it to individuals and municipalities at cost.' This was scarcely the talk of someone dragooned into position.[67]

VIII

The political strife over prohibition and power policy formed the prelude to the election campaign of 1902. Although Ross did not announce the election date, 29 May, until late April, common knowledge favoured a spring contest. Consequently, Whitney readied for battle once the session concluded in late March, resting briefly in Morrisburg and then starting a seven-week round of speech-making. The party chief, accompanied by Foy, began campaigning in Port Hope, with a speech cast from a mould which he used repeatedly. As frequently happened, Whitney's assault on the Liberals overshadowed the positive points in his own programme. The Grits were arraigned on a variety of counts: financial policy, New Ontario's development, electoral corruption, educational matters, conservation of natural resources, temperance legislation, and the damaging Ottawa-Toronto axis. Near the end of his speech, the Tory leader offered a ringing sentence which was to become, for many, the epitome of Whitney. After raking the Liberals for ballot-stealing, stuffing, and burning, he declared: 'We are bold enough to be honest, we are honest enough to be bold.' Happily, the neat phrasing stuck to him like glue for the balance of his career.[68]

As Whitney swept through Ontario, Foy's constant presence on the platform marked a significant change in the Conservative party. Just four years earlier, serious obstacles stood in the way of this Catholic's nomination for Toronto South; now he was generally regarded and accepted as Whitney's right-hand man. The tie between the two was more than political; over these years, a bond of friendship developed which hardened into an enduring association during the 1902 campaign. Gone were the days of public battles with the Catholic hierarchy, and nothing made this clearer than when, in northern Ontario, Whitney and Foy were joined on a North Bay platform by F.D. Monk, Robert Borden's aide from Quebec. Usually speaking French, Monk enlightened New Ontario audiences about the 'grand history of the Conservative party,' and attacked those who portrayed Whitney as an anti-Catholic Francophobe. When Liberals replied, bilingually, that the portrayal was accurate, Monk rebuked them, arguing he would not be on the platform with Whitney if that was the case. This warm support illustrated one of the few benefits of being in opposition ranks federally and provincially: neither branch of the party had to take action that might strain unity, although, admittedly, either side could enunciate troublesome policies. For the moment, all was harmony as a federal French-Canadian Tory laboured to boost the fortunes of a provincial leader.[69]

Other developments affected the Conservative party during the campaign. Citing his dislike of the tyranny of caucus and demands for strict adherence to party lines, Marter finally made a complete break, running as an independent in Toronto North where the Liberals chose not to promote a candidate and offered the former party chief modest assistance. In his stead, the Tories of the constituency selected Beattie Nesbitt who, in 1901, had given thought to challenging Marter for the Conservative nomination, only to have Whitney quash the idea. The choice of the bumptious and self-seeking doctor probably did not sit too well with the Morrisburg man, but the Grits were decidedly dismayed.[70]

It was Nesbitt, however, who succinctly stated the Tory policy on hydroelectric development as being 'the Government at the switch, not the corporations.' This catchy phrasing was typical of a tack which Whitney and others took throughout the campaign: hostility to corporations and friendship for labour. Pyne observed that Liberal cabinet minister J.M. Gibson 'was president of electrical companies.' Foy followed suit in referring to Whitney as 'a leader in whom poor men could place confidence.' And Whitney took the same line in talking of 'the poor settler' in northern Ontario forced to sell his timber to a Liberal lumber baron, or referring to the forgotten and 'unfortunate insane people huddled together in the prisons of Ontario,' or twitting Ross about being president of a life insurance company. But he was in his best form when discussing the high price of school texts. He could not take the time, he informed a Simcoe audience, 'to expose the workings of the school-book ring,' but, he charged, 'every member ... was an extremely wealthy man, able to build the most expensive houses in Toronto,' thanks to the 'determination' of George Ross 'that the people of Ontario, whose children used text-books, should be taxed to support these school-book barons of Toronto.' His pitch to the electorate neatly combined an attack on the classes, particularly those resident in the provincial capital, with a promise of help for the masses.[71]

Another feature of the campaign was the action of some clergymen, made unhappy by the temperance referendum and the hard evidence of electoral corruption. Consequently, some supported the running of prohibitionist candidates in six ridings, and others took their places on Whitney's platform in protest against Grit election practices. In Guelph, a leading Methodist prohibitionist, Dr S.D. Chown, denounced the Liberal temperance policy as 'steeped in duplicity' and charged the premier with 'a moral collapse.'[72]

Whitney, then, had good cause to believe the campaign song, 'Whitney Will Win,' that greeted him at stop after stop. But, as the electioneering drew to a close and the *Mail and Empire* confidently predicted a ten- or fifteen-seat majority for the Tories, Ross was confiding to a correspondent: 'our prospects are fairly good. I cannot see just how the Government can be defeated.' On the other side, the Conservative leader said 'he would never believe that the people of Ontario were willing to condone acts which would cause their children to blush for this province.' Whitney was due for a surprise.[73]

1902 Election Results			
Popular vote			Seats
Liberal	206,825	(47.54%)	50[74]
Conservative	217,573	(50.02%)	48[75]
Independent	5,222	(1.20%)[76]	0
Prohibitionist	3,126	(0.72%)	0
Socialist	1,993	(0.46%)	0
Socialist-Labour	277	(0.06%)	0
Total	435,016	(100.00%)	98[77]

The Liberals triumphed for the ninth successive time in a provincial general election. There was little consolation for the Tories in the popular vote majority; nevertheless, they now held both Ottawa ridings and had regained London, in addition to retaining the two Hamilton seats and the four in Toronto. Clearly, they were in control of the major cities. Further, the Conservatives had made inroads into Grit country, southwestern Ontario, capturing Oxford South for the first time since Confederation, briefly holding Norfolk North, and gaining a fresh hold on Essex North, Lambton West, and Waterloo North. The Tories now had one French-Canadian, Joseph O. Reaume, of the four elected; could claim three of the four labelled as Irish-Catholics; and demonstrated a firm grip on the German-

Canadian vote. All of this represented strength, but not power; the latter still belonged to Ross.[78]

The premier was probably the most significant factor in the narrow victory. The Liberals had been on a downhill run under Hardy and, through vigorous leadership, Ross applied the brakes. Willison accurately observed that 'the party are thoroughly united upon Ross, and he is distinctly stronger personally than Hardy was four years ago.' Ross had given the Liberal party, now three decades in power, a sufficiently fresh appearance to negate arguments centring on its longevity in office. Temperance voters, it is true, were 'a disturbing element' in the Grit campaign – and may have cost the Liberals a seat or two – but the bulk of prohibitionists were apparently willing to continue their support of the government, at least until the December referendum had been held: better the devil one knew than the devil one did not. Considering the policies and assaults of Whitney, the developing Conservative organization, and the high quality of a number of Tory candidates, George Ross had not done badly at all.[79]

His Conservative rival, undoubtedly hurting, put on a brave face. He had gained seats, secured an increase in Catholic support, and captured all of Ontario's significant urban centres but Kingston. 'Public opinion,' he informed reporters, was 'distinctly favorable to the attitude of the Opposition on ... particular matters,' thus emphasizing the popular vote majority. Whitney also noted that Liberals had come to his side in this election, citing the particular case of Samuel Blake, Edward's brother, who had abandoned the Grits because of the government's inadequate funding of the University of Toronto. And, of course, Whitney remained convinced, in public and private, that corruption had aided and abetted the Liberals; but he anticipated that justice would be done through recounts, election petitions, and by-elections. These views fired a smouldering resentment within the Tory chief at having been, as he saw it, cheated of office, a resentment that occasionally flashed to the surface in bursts of bitter anger and intemperate language.[80]

IX

During the next six months, Ontario's political picture remained clouded. By the end of July, the Liberal majority stood at one as death claimed a Grit member and judicial decisions upset legislators from both parties. Many delighted Tories became convinced that they were on the edge of backing into office. Some excitedly suggested that Conservatives petition the lieutenant-governor to call the legislature into session in the hope that a few unnerved Liberal members would support the move. This did not occur, but Whitney was given an opportunity to secure a foothold on power: a cabinet minister approached him with the suggestion that they explore the possibilities of a coalition. The Conservative leader examined the proposition and then rejected it out of hand. 'It would be simply absurd,' he informed the public, 'to expect that the Opposition should, in defiance of public decency, allow themselves to be absorbed by a Government, the acts of the members of which they have denounced in the strongest terms.' Despite the fears of some Tories that Whitney would take the Grit bait, their chieftain had resisted temptation and left the Liberals to sustain their government.[81]

Consequently, the business of protests and election trials proceeded, although the impoverished Conservatives did agree to some 'saw-offs' to avoid fruitless expense. This display of financial weakness also suggests that potential contributors were not convinced of the party's proximity to power. By December, legislative party standings were forty-eight Grits and forty-six Tories, with four seats open – Grey North, Norfolk North, Perth North, and Renfrew North. The government decided against an immediate contest in the latter constituency, but did set 7 January 1903 as the date for by-elections in the first three. 'If we win two of these,' Whitney wrote in appealing for assistance in the contests, 'the Government cannot go on, if we win them all the Government must collapse at once.' The premier's office appeared tantalizingly within reach, particularly because the Tories had narrowly captured two of the ridings in the general election. But it was a mirage: the Grits took all three, and Ross, 'feeling much more comfortable,' could now face the legislature with a majority of five. 'You are now firm in the saddle,' Laurier told the premier, 'and it seems to me to be beyond doubt that the back of the Opposition is absolutely broken.' Not broken, but certainly badly bruised, Whitney could only repeat his pledge to continue the fight against corruption; and that theme, resting on fast-aging evidence, possibly was proving tiresome to the electorate.[82]

One more blow struck Whitney before the legislature opened on 10 March 1903: Robert Roswell Gamey, Conservative member for Manitoulin, announced through the *Globe* that he intended to support the Ross government out of concern for the development of northern Ontario and, in particular, his own constituency. Caught without warning, the shaken leader and party reacted angrily: 'I hope,' one Tory legislator wrote to Whitney, 'the people of Manitoulin will tar & feather him.' What else could go wrong? The answer, as it turned out, was nothing; lacking prescience, the Conservatives could not know that their fortunes had just struck bottom.[83]

The session opened quietly enough, with Chief Justice Charles Moss reading the Speech from the Throne in the absence of a seriously ailing Oliver Mowat. Whitney was there, of course, and attentive as he prepared his opening shot for the following day; but whatever his plans, they were scattered on the second day by the largest bombshell ever dropped in Ontario political history. As Whitney rose to commence his attack, Gamey sought and secured recognition from the Speaker. The Tory leader was obviously vexed by the apparent rudeness of the Manitoulin turncoat, but his attitude of bristling irritation soon changed to one of entranced amazement as he listened to Gamey's hour-long speech. The essence of the latter's remarks was that he had been approached in August 1902 about the possibility of giving his support to the government in exchange for financial reward and patronage privileges; that he had decided to pursue the matter in hope of securing evidence against the Liberals; that, on 10 September, in the outer office of provincial secretary James R. Stratton, he had received the first instalment of the money – fifteen hundred dollars – given in return for his pledged support; and that Stratton had, in effect, dictated Gamey's statement for the *Globe* of 30 January, a statement which was purchased with an additional five hundred dollars provided on the preceding day. Gamey then calmly crossed the floor to Whitney and presented him with the documents from which he had read and a package containing some of the pay-off money, nine fifties, two twenties, and a ten-dollar bill.

'I have never witnessed a more astonishing scene than the transformation in feeling which ensued on both sides of the House,' an eyewitness to the event later recounted.

Stratton paled and was like a man of stone. The Prime Minister sat with bowed head, his beard on his chest, almost a stricken man. Their followers were dumbfounded. On the other hand the Conservatives whose hostility towards Gamey had not been concealed, became a noisy, enthusiastic mob. The Premier rose and in hardly audible tones moved the adjournment of the House, and the reporters knocked one another over to get to the telephones. The bulletins were up on the downtown newspaper offices almost as soon as they could get the messages through, and going back a few minutes later into the press gallery, whose broad windows looked southward through Queen's Park down University Avenue, I presently saw a most remarkable sight. Hundreds and hundreds of people were running towards the Parliament Buildings. The news had spread magically and everyone wished to be on the scene.

Thus began the Gamey affair.[84]

When the legislature resumed sitting the next day, Ross announced the means of investigating the charges: a royal commission of two judges. This course immediately put the premier at odds with Whitney, who wanted a legislative select committee to examine the accusations, thus ensuring Conservative representation on the investigating body. The Tory chief also deplored Ross's decision to adjourn the legislature until the commission reported because, he argued, this move gave unfettered power to a government in want of public confidence. The respective positions of the partisan debaters who followed their leaders were thus established. Meanwhile, Ross secured the services of Sir J.A. Boyd, president of the High Court of Justice of Ontario, and W.G. Falconbridge, Chief Justice of the King's Bench, and drafted the commission's terms of instruction. The judges were asked to decide whether or not Stratton had obtained Gamey's support by either gift of money or promise of patronage. The Whitney-led Conservatives immediately charged that the terms were too narrow and that the scope of investigation should include Ross and other cabinet ministers. The debate on the form and dimensions of the inquiry rolled on until 27 March, when the two leaders made their final statements. Such was the intensity of feeling on the subject that there was no pairing during the votes on Conservative amendments which followed; the government turned these back, and the legislature finally adjourned on 31 March. Ross, who found the situation 'a very trying one and very unfortunate under the circumstances,' reflected on developments: 'What our opponents want,' he told Clifford Sifton, 'is to spread out all sorts of fanciful remarks and gossip [by means of a select committee] with a view to exploiting their case on the platform in bye-elections and otherwise.' He was confident that Stratton would 'pass through the ordeal' unblemished but, he added, it would require a like opinion from the judges to 'dispose of the charge.'[85]

The commission began its labours on 3 April, and, with interruptions, continued through to 23 May, sitting for twenty-seven days and hearing from one hundred and nineteen witnesses who poured forth about thirty-two hundred pages of testimony. In the course of the hearings Gamey was proven to be a devious person of doubtful memory and dubious action who weakened his case by temporarily fleeing to Buffalo when he apparently thought he might be prosecuted for forgery. But Stratton did not escape unscathed, because it was established that Gamey did receive control over some patronage matters in his constituency and that the provincial secretary had had a large hand in drafting the Gamey letter to the *Globe*. Whether Gamey went to the government and freely offered his support or was bought out by sums of money and promises of patronage remained an unanswered question. When the commissioners presented their report to the legislature on 4 June, they cleared Stratton and, in effect, labelled Gamey a liar.

The acrimonious debate on the report began on 17 June, and lasted until the 26th. Ross took the position that there was 'no stain upon' the Liberal 'escutcheon.' Whitney would have none of this and cited the patronage granted to Gamey as evidence; then, he went further and questioned the impartiality of Justice Boyd, noting that the judge had three sons in the provincial government's employ and that he had received money from the Grits for work done outside of his judicial office. It was an extremely low blow, but Whitney, smelling blood and convinced of Liberal corruption, was simply not prepared to abide by the rules. His intemperate language established the quality of debate which followed; immoderation ruled the Ontario legislature. Only the fact of a Liberal majority ensured the report's acceptance and Gamey's censure.

Legislative votes, however, did not end the Gamey affair. The issue was endlessly debated throughout the province. Despite the verdict of the judges, a number of level-headed and influential men remained sceptical of Grit innocence. J.S. Willison, who had recently departed the Liberal *Globe* for the neutral *News*, told Laurier that the Ross administration had 'outlived its usefulness and that the methods revealed in the Gamey inquiry seriously discredit[ed] the whole Government.' Another newspaperman, Hector Charlesworth, was convinced that Stratton had given Gamey money in exchange for his support, but had not informed the premier. Then, the Manitoulin legislator found life in his constituency uncomfortable once his switch of allegiance was known. Consequently, he suggested to Stratton that he resign his seat, confident that he could retain it in the ensuing by-election. The provincial secretary, according to Charlesworth, faked agreement with this proposal, and then attempted to unearth a candidate who would challenge Gamey once the latter had resigned. But the Manitoulin maverick uncovered this plot and decided to tell, not everything, just that part implicating Stratton. Much later, yet another reporter of that day, W.R. Plewman, insisted that Stratton was a 'slippery eel,' quite capable of bribing Gamey. He thought that the Manitoulin member, once bought, could see a double-cross that would redound to his advantage; hence his revelations in the legislature. The charges of Grit corruption made during this affair strengthened the Conservative attack, swayed many neutral observers, and shook some Liberal supporters. As for Whitney, to him they represented the ultimate evidence needed to convince the Ontario electorate. And the affair occurred at a most fortunate time, just when Ontarians were tiring of the Tory leader's continual recitation of increasingly hoary Grit misdeeds.[86]

In light of the Gamey episode, it was remarkable that anything of consequence was accomplished during the legislative session of 1903, when the atmosphere was made close and uncomfortable by vitriolic word and partisan statement. Ross, however, did manage to get some legislation of note onto the statute books. Pressed by developing public opinion and the declared Conservative policy, he finally took limited action on the question of hydroelectric development in the province. In 1902, an eager group of manufacturers, principally from the Grand River valley, had begun an examination of the subject of cheap transmission of hydroelectric power. As their discussions proceeded, they came out in favour of a government commission that would arrange for the construction of power lines to participating municipalities. Given such thinking, it was inevitable that they would be distressed when, early in January 1903, the Queen Victoria Niagara Falls Park Commission granted a franchise for power development to the Mackenzie-Pellatt-Nicholls group, which then received a provincial charter as the Electrical Development Company. In the ensuing protest, directed against the government and the park commission, it was not difficult to portray Mackenzie, Pellatt, and Nicholls as robber barons; for those with a suspicious turn of mind, it was possible to see a conspiracy in this new arrangement, if they looked at the officers and directors of the Manufacturers' Life Insurance Company. In 1903, George Ross was president of the company, a position he had held for nearly two years. In itself such a situation was not particularly noteworthy in that era, but Henry Pellatt, president of the Toronto Electric Light Company, was first vice-president of the insurance company, and William Mackenzie, president of the Toronto Street Railway, was on Manufacturers' board of directors. Further, it was later revealed that the insurance firm had dabbled in Electrical Development Company stock. It would be difficult to describe the premier of Ontario as hostile to the 'corporations.'[87]

Against this background the Liberal government took its first steps to relieve pressure applied by public ownership proponents. The park commission, when granting the franchise to the Electrical Development Company, announced that the three concerns with franchises – the other two were the Canadian Niagara Power Company and the Ontario Power Company – would produce so much electric power that competition, and presumably cheap prices, would result. Ross followed this statement with a letter to the commission 'requesting an estimate of the cost of transporting power within a practicable distance of the Falls.' But such action did little to mollify western Ontario businessmen who met in convention at Berlin in February 1903. This gathering heard a report which favoured municipal co-operation in the development, transmission, and distribution of hydroelectric power. The document went on to recommend that the provincial government be asked for the necessary enabling legislation. And a stiff amendment was appended which urged upon 'the Ontario Government the advisability of the government building and operating as a government work, a line for the transmission of electricity from Niagara Falls to the towns and cities.' One sponsor of this resolution was London's mayor and new Tory legislator, Adam Beck, attending his first meeting of the public ownership movement.[88]

When convention delegates met with Ross to state their views, he took the position of the park commission: the three companies would produce a surplus of hydroelectric power, and fair rates through competition would follow. The premier, however, did promise enabling legislation that would permit interested municipalities to co-operate along the lines recommended in the Berlin report. The Liberal chief later defended his position, arguing he had no intention of putting Ontario into debt for the sake of a handful of municipalities in close proximity to the Falls; if the concerned cities and towns wanted to take action, they would be freed to do so. On the same occasion, Whitney attacked the granting of a third franchise to private interests and the possibility of unrestricted export of Ontario-developed power to the United States. He requested the government to 'investigate the problem of supplying power to all places within 150 miles of Niagara,' or to create a commission that might provide the means of transmission. The Conservative chief, increasingly sensitive to the demands of urban Ontario, which provided him with much of his political strength, was moving well past Ross, whose diminishing potency was drawn from rural Ontario and whose ties were so obviously with private power interests.[89]

Moved by this lobbying, Ross introduced power legislation, in May of 1903, which was passed into law a month later. W.R. Plewman, Adam Beck's biographer, has summed up the measure:

It gave municipalities the right to acquire or construct the necessary works for the supply and distribution of electrical or other power and energy. It empowered the municipalities to appoint a commission consisting of one electrical engineer, and not less than two nor more than four other persons, business or professional men, to determine the feasibility and desirability of securing the establishment and operation of municipal power, heat and light works. If the municipalities, after the report of the advisory commission was received, favoured by a vote of its taxpayers the construction of such works, this Act gave the municipalities concerned the right to set up a Board of Commissioners of not less than three nor more than five persons, who would undertake on their behalf the construction and operation of such works. Thus the municipalities obtained the machinery for proceeding with a co-operative power project. The Act did not require the government to accept any responsibility or financial obligations for the proposed co-operative municipal power projects.

Eager municipalities soon began to appoint advisory commissions as provided under the act.[90]

The Ross act was scarcely innovative legislation, particularly because the province assumed no real responsibility in matters of financing or guidance. The municipalities were left to their own devices and, should they choose not to develop their own power but, rather, purchase it from one of the three companies, they would be at the mercy of these corporations when it came to price. Ross was leaving this field of public ownership to interested communities. In view of his political sagacity and the numbers of influential people clamouring for government intervention, it is difficult to understand the premier's decision. Possibly he was enmeshed by free enterprise, or honestly fearful of potential costs, or astigmatic in his perception of the public ownership movement. Whitney, on the other hand, had long sensed the ingredients of a political issue in this subject and assumed a position considerably to the left of Ross, despite fears that the premier would steal any policy which the Tory enunciated.

Ross did move on the hydroelectric issue; on the liquor question he remained inert. The referendum of the preceding December had resulted in a two-to-one vote for prohibition, but the total of favourable ballots had failed to achieve the mark of half the votes cast in the election of 1898. Ross thus had his reason for not instituting prohibition, but he was pledged to some action, as restless temperance forces constantly reminded him. After the Gamey story broke, the premier argued that this factor, plus the need for careful scrutiny of any measure, meant that liquor legislation could not be introduced until 1904. He insisted that this was not dereliction of duty, merely postponement. Nevertheless, when the Ontario board of the Dominion Alliance met late in May, the Liberal leader was unceremoniously dropped from its list of vice-presidents. Despite being in deep trouble with the temperance movement, Ross would not be pushed to prohibition, convinced as he was that 'public sentiment' was 'not ripe' for it and never would be in his lifetime. 'Any attempt to enforce such a law,' he told a confidant, 'would be a failure and would be injurious to the administration of all laws. Especially would it be injurious to the cause of total abstinence which I preached in my youth and have practised all my life.' While Ross wrestled with this most persistent problem, Whitney was free to proclaim his own policy: tough enforcement of tight regulations, with favouritism to none.[91]

In light of his mounting woes, it is not surprising that the premier again contemplated a possible coalition with Whitney. 'Something must be done,' he wrote Laurier, 'to relieve the stress of the present situation ... I have no fear of my own friends nor of the approval of the Province.' But he was anxious to have the federal leader's views, and Laurier responded with reservations. Nevertheless, the Ontario premier permitted talks with Whitney to proceed through an unnamed provincial cabinet minister, and the Tory chief again rejected such overtures. Consequently, there was little the Grits could do but struggle on under a constant Conservative barrage.[92]

While Whitney and Ross trod divergent paths within the confines of Ontario politics, one followed closely upon the other's heels in the larger domain of the British empire. In 1903, when colonial secretary Joseph Chamberlain's pronouncements on tariff reform and imperial preference provoked great debate within and without Great Britain, both leaders quickly lauded his proposals which, if adopted, would lead to greater imperial unity. Ross was extremely anxious that the Toronto branch of the British Empire League should salute Chamberlain for his efforts and he unsuccessfully urged that the Canadian House of Commons should assist the Britisher in his campaign with a supportive resolution. Whitney, for his part, sent to Chamberlain a stirring statement on imperial trade from the Ontario Liberal-Conservative Association and assured him that Ontarians were 'practically unanimous in support' of the position which he had 'assumed & championed.' On this subject, the two provincial parties were Tweedledum and Tweedledee. Consequently, one Canadian imperialist could assure another that, where their cause was concerned, it mattered little whether Whitney or Ross ruled Ontario.[93]

Partisan politics, however, prevented Ross from joining the Chamberlain campaign in England for 'three or four weeks of platform work,' and thrust him into another confrontation with Whitney, in three by-elections during the fall and early winter of 1903. In the first two, the parties exchanged seats, the Tories winning Muskoka and losing Sault Ste Marie. But the real battle was in Renfrew North where the Liberals called an election for late December, after the seat had been vacant for almost nineteen months. The campaign there approximated a little general election with leading lights from both sides holding an impressive number of meetings. Whitney's course was simply to attack the Liberals on all fronts and virtually ignore his own policies. Convinced that he was fighting a 'dying Government,' he did not intend to provide it with any weapons. The premier, nevertheless, remained confident of victory, and some shared his perception because the Tories were not 'strong enough morally to put Gamey out of business as an advocate of their side.' But the Conservatives thoroughly trounced the Liberals and turned a deficit of nearly five hundred votes in 1902 into a majority of almost six hundred. Some commentators began measuring the Grits for a coffin. What cheered Whitney, aside from the addition of a vital seat, were Liberal defections caused by the Gamey affair or the liquor question. Then, just three days after the by-election, Liberal Andrew Pattullo died and the government found itself with a majority of two, exclusive of the speaker. In addition, there were still protests lodged against some Liberal members, and these had yet to come to trial. For Whitney, the year was ending on a hopeful note.[94]

X

The announcement that the legislature would meet on 14 January 1904 elicited howls of protest from the Conservatives, who argued that the move was designed to postpone election trials whose outcome might upset the government. Rejecting Tory charges, the Grits patiently explained that an early session was necessary in order to vote fresh appropriations and pass legislation enabling a start on the Temiskaming railway. That was for public consumption, however, and privately Ross acknowledged that the opposition had reasoned rightly. 'We are doing right in calling the House,' he informed Laurier, 'otherwise it would not be possible for us probably to call the Session before April or ... May, and in the meantime we would have the expense and worry of protests, with possibly the worry of bye-elections in addition.' The premier then gazed into the future:

It is hard to tell how we may fare during the Session. My followers are as devoted as I could wish, and nothing but the accident of sickness or some unexpected catastrophe would alienate a single one of them. We have to start with a majority of two, but we hope [Pattullo's riding of] North Oxford will go right and that will help us a little. My purpose is to keep control of the House during the Session, then afterwards possibly re-construct the Government in some respects. Whether there should be a dissolution as well as a re-construction is a question that can only be settled after the session and on a more careful survey of the situation. I have some idea that it would be well to have a Convention of the Liberals of Ontario in order to interest them more particularly in the fate of the Government. Everything, however, depends upon our success during the Session.[95]

The session of 1904 began in comparatively quiet fashion, although there was a trace of ominous sultriness in the air. Whitney, of course, denounced the government for stalling the election trials, and he offered to rush through supplies if the house could then adjourn to let the trials proceed. He condemned the Grits on University of Toronto grants and textbook prices, but his words lacked fire. Ross, for his part, could take comfort from victory in the Oxford North by-election and be puzzled by the 'exceedingly mild' Tory attacks. Then the storm broke.[96]

The renewal of partisan strife stemmed from a report on Sault Ste Marie's Consolidated Lake Superior Company (ancestor of Algoma Steel), which had collapsed in late summer 1903, throwing thirty-five hundred men into unemployment. The failed company had pledged that it would pay off these men on 28 September, but when this failed to occur a riot had erupted necessitating militia intervention. The Ontario government then guaranteed wage payment to the unfortunate employees. About nine hundred workers, including the company's chief officials, were paid the full amount due them; the government held as security for the company's repayment of these funds an earned but unconveyed land subsidy to the Algoma Central Railway, a subsidiary of Consolidated. While these wage settlements were being distributed, the Sault Ste Marie by-election was in progress and the Tories charged that, although payments to dislocated workers were justified, they had the look of a massive bribe to the riding.[97]

A return of the payments made was laid before the legislature in 1904, and that sparked the heated debate. The Conservatives were quick to note that large sums had been paid to company officers: $6,693.45 to the president; $2,645.16 to the superintendent; $1,606.45 to the vice-president; and $1,455.77 to the comptroller. The opposition argued that only the 'foreman, mechanics, workmen, clerks and labourers' should have been assisted and that there should not have been financial salvation for those who had mismanaged the company. The argument spilled over into the public accounts committee, and it was renewed in the legislature when a company reorganization was announced which involved the province in guaranteeing two million dollars of Algoma Central bonds. Whitney doubted a two-million-dollar guarantee could save the corporation and he questioned the wisdom of accepting an unprofitable railway as security. He further observed that two Liberal members, C.M. Bowman and James Conmee, were personally involved in the fortunes of Algoma Central as creditors. These criticisms provided the focus for a three-week debate, but company reorganization proceeded and the Tories were forced to concede a narrow defeat. Whitney and his followers, however, had once more played the role of corporation foe.[98]

The session was also noteworthy for what it failed to produce: liquor legislation did not materialize. And when it seemed as if the religious cry might be raised – over the issue of apportioning an extremely modest sum of public school money to the separate school board of Sturgeon Falls – Whitney and Ross fell strangely silent and carried the bulk of their supporters with them. The question caused barely a ripple in the legislature and most of the press made no comment. The Protestant horse went back to the barn for want of a rider. Under Whitney's leadership the Conservative party had apparently hung up its spurs.[99]

Once the session ended, the election trials could proceed, but summer intervened and a start could not be made until late in that season. Conservatives faced petitions in three ridings, but, when these came to trial, each was dismissed, much to the opposition's smug delight. The election trials for five Liberal members had an equally happy ending, for the Tories. Short trials unseated the members in Norfolk North, Perth North, and York North. In the first two cases, the Conservatives charged that the Grits had admitted guilt early to avoid further revelations of corruption; in the latter riding, the Liberal member appeared to have made an honest, although technically illegal, error in judgment. In Grey North, the trial of A.G. MacKay's election became a prolonged affair and was terminated late in the year by the legislature's dissolution.

It was, however, in the fifth Liberal riding of Sault Ste Marie that the sensational nature of the testimony severely shook the government. In the course of four days, it was proven that voters had been bribed with money and whisky, that fraudulent voters were sworn in on bogus Bibles, that the Algoma Central Railway had taken an active part on the government's behalf, and that twenty impersonators were carried from the Michigan side to ballot in Ontario on board the *Minnie M.* where they were freely plied with whisky, beer, and cigars. Nor was that the end of the story: attorney-general Gibson had been publicly warned before the election of the use intended for the *Minnie M.*, and he had failed to act. Needless to say, the Liberal member was unseated. Whitney's list of proven cases of Grit corruption had now grown to almost unmanageable proportions; the cumulative effect of this fresh evidence was to shake the convictions and loyalty of some Ontario Liberals, persuading them that their party did, indeed, possess a crooked political machine. Some smaller, longtime Liberal newspapers began to falter badly in their support and to ask awkward questions of their party. The Tory leader, who had so long expounded on Grit political immorality, could now nose the tantalizing aroma of success.[100]

XI

Even before the dismal results of the election trials arrived to haunt Ross, he had been contemplating the possibility of a January election, preceded, of course, by major party surgery. Now, in light of the recent disclosures, leading Liberals were pressing him to hold a convention in an effort to breathe fresh life into the organization. To this the premier agreed and, immediately before that meeting, he took a carving knife to the cabinet. Stratton stepped down and out of provincial politics and Gibson departed the attorney-general's office, while E.J. Davis, the commissioner of crown lands who had been unseated in York North, announced his retirement. Ross retained the post of provincial treasurer and left Richard Harcourt and John Dryden in their respective departments of education and agriculture; Frank Latchford, the former commissioner of public works, became attorney-general and Gibson was lowered to minister without portfolio. Four new faces were added to the cabinet picture: commissioner of public works W.A. Charlton; commissioner of crown lands A.G. MacKay; provincial secretary G.P. Graham; and minister without portfolio F.A.E. Evanturel. The last-named was the first French-Canadian appointed to any cabinet in the post-Confederation history of the province. The day after the swearing-in, the Ontario Liberal Association convention began. [101]

Ross did not relish the prospect of a convention – questions would be raised which were 'very embarrassing to the Government' – but he required a 'mandate from the Party' before acting on them. He viewed prohibition as 'the most difficult,' relegating matters pertaining to 'public ownership and administration' to positions 'of minor importance.' The premier surely must have made this assessment only in light of the composition of the Liberal party and its obvious rural strength; such an ordering of questions facing his government could not have been made with knowledge of Ontario's increasingly urban complexion. Ross and his fellow conventioneers were surveying and representing a province that was disappearing. [102]

Although Laurier adamantly refused to bless the convention with his presence, possibly fearing contamination by association or even thinking that Ross's downfall might redound to the federal advantage, many prominent Ontario Liberals gathered in Toronto on 23 November for the first meeting of this kind in eleven years. Ross, of course, was a key speaker and he dwelt on accomplishments, avoided the corruption issue, and detailed his prohibition position. Before a policy statement was hammered out, there were vigorous attacks on Stratton and the Sault organizer, and it was decided to organize a new provincial Liberal association. The final product of these deliberations was a document which approved of the current educational policy, the Temiskaming Railway development, and Liberal hydroelectric power legislation. Ross was duly congratulated and corruption condemned. On the contentious liquor question the party stood for local option in municipalities, rigid enforcement of existing laws, and severe limitations on the number of new licences; this policy was nearly identical with that of Whitney. Grits rated the meeting as successful, while Tories judged it arrogant and machine-managed. [103]

Close behind this gathering came the second of the year for the Liberal-Conservative Association, evidently inspired by the need for election preparations and the hope of attracting anyone desirous of 'clean, honest and decent government.' Whitney even asked Goldwin Smith to attend, but the aging scholar, while he offered encouragement to the Tory leader, declined after considerable thought. Foy set the tone of the meeting when he charged that the province was in 'the hands of grafters, heelers, rake-off men, thimble-riggers, robbers and thieves.' Whitney then moved to the spotlight and detailed Conservative policy and Liberal crime. He again pressed for law reform that would ease the cost of litigation to the poor, and demanded a comprehensive plan of development for northern Ontario. He insisted on 'public sale in open competition of pulp-wood rights and timber limits' and he opposed, with a few exceptions, grants to railways. A commission of teachers should advise the minister of education, and agricultural instruction should be extended. Municipalities had to be the beneficiaries of legislation that would give them an unimpeded road to public ownership. Prohibition, he argued, could not be achieved 'in a Province'; therefore, it was 'idle to discuss that remedy.' The answer lay in 'wholesome restriction' – decrease the licences, free administrators from political interference, and enforce the law honestly. The Tory chief then reviewed the long list of proven Grit electoral misdeeds and went on to startle his audience with the revelation that a fresh coalition offer had been made within the past fortnight, with the rider that he would become premier inside a year. In conclusion, he raised the old, but urgent, appeal for renewed efforts at organization.[104]

Speaker after speaker then took up the corruption cry and the call for clean government, much to the apparent satisfaction of the audience. The resolutions adopted were generally broad in scope and left Whitney with room for interpretation and manoeuvre. They supported him and his policies, as enunciated at the convention, on the platform, and in the legislature, including Tory statements on public ownership of utilities. They backed his stand against the coalition offers, and called for better factory legislation and measures that would lead to swifter settlements of labour disputes. Lastly, they expressed sympathy – a relatively inexpensive item – with the efforts to promote temperance and moral reform. Whitney had the party behind him, the premier's office before him, and few specific pledges to burden him in his race.

That race entered the stretch drive on 13 December, with Ross's announcement of a general election for 25 January 1905. Whitney exuded confidence, going into the campaign as he did with the support of a hungry, organized party, disgruntled Liberals, and irritated temperance workers. Beyond that, a lengthy list of newspapers offered editorial encouragement. Nevertheless, there remained those who questioned Whitney's abilities and, consequently, the likelihood of his winning. 'I don't think much of Whitney,' wrote one sceptic, 'but I would take a dose of bad medicine if I thought I could drive a tape-worm out of my interior.' Adam Shortt, surveying the political scene from Kingston, judged that no one was 'satisfied with the Liberal record' and that the Grits 'would be the better of a term in opposition.' But, he continued, there was 'a very general lack of faith in Whitney's capacity to withstand the evil element in his own party and to give a reasonably efficient and honest administration.' The Tories, he admitted, had 'plenty of good material,' but it would have to be 'brought into service' in the event of victory.[105]

Whitney did not look far for the focal point of his campaign: the desperate need for clean and honest government. He lectured crowds across the province on the subject and, of course, on Liberal practices. In the interests of party purity and the proper operation of the British political system he urged independents and Grits to pause, think, and join his cause. During a Guelph speech his comments were typical of those made throughout the campaign, as he charged that 'almost every crime that might result in benefit to the Government' had 'been committed with impunity.' 'No person,' he noted, 'has been punished. No person has even been sent to trial.' And these crimes had been committed 'to keep in power a Government' which had 'lost the confidence of the people.'[106]

Only after a ringing denunciation of Grit political immorality did the Tory chief turn to other matters, frequently citing the coalition offers as proof of the government's desperate condition. Then he would restate his position on the liquor and education questions and re-emphasize the need for cheap textbooks. Finally, he pledged again to reform the assessment law and to tax railways in equitable fashion.[107]

The premier, in his campaign, placed emphasis on the development of the province under Grit rule, with the promise of more to come. Occasionally he attacked the Conservatives on the subject of corruption and attempted to produce a list of Tory crimes, but probably he should have avoided the exercise. He questioned the competence of inexperienced Conservatives to run the province and he raised the spectre of Gamey in a cabinet post, but that was the language of a man in trouble. He denied that he had personally made coalition overtures to the opposition leader, and J.M. Gibson came forward to name himself as the cabinet minister who had inaugurated these fruitless discussions. Unhappily for Ross, such talk was of a defensive – even negative – nature. Saddled with the responsibilities of government and forced to make a case for a party some thirty-three years in office, he could not establish himself as a front runner.

1905 Election Results			
Popular vote			Seats
Conservative	237,559	(53.36%)	69
Liberal	201,865	(45.35%)	29[108]
Other	5,760	(1.29%)[109]	0
Total	445,184	(100.00%)	98

That fact was confirmed on 25 January, when Whitney led his party to a resounding triumph over the Grits. The Tories captured the lion's share of legislative seats, while Ross lost the ridings of four cabinet ministers, Dryden, Gibson, Charlton, and Latchford. And F.A.E. Evanturel lost his constituency to another Liberal. Brant North, Bruce South, and Kent East, all Liberal since Confederation, fell to the Tories. Among the cities and towns of the province, only Ottawa, Kingston, Owen Sound, Brockville, Welland, Napanee, Cobourg, and Sarnia stood out as rejecting Conservative rule. Prominent Tories like Foy, Pyne, and Reaume were returned with handsome majorities.[110]

The forty-seat majority was more than even the most optimistic Tory had dreamed possible. Whitney found it a little staggering, as he conceded in a note to Borden: 'It is difficult to express my appreciation of the situation, but I am glad that large numbers of Liberals joined with us in ridding the Province of the worst Government which ever existed in British America.' Others were less modest about the meaning of the victory – 'the cause of Truth and Righteousness triumphed in Ontario,' crowed one Conservative, '... a Clean, Uncorrupt, and Incorruptible Government was elected' – and less calm about its dimensions: 'the Ross Gov^t was shattered, snowed under, and busted-up by an overwhelming avalanche of public indignation,' wrote another Tory. Since Confederation, provincial Conservatives had never really had occasion for uninhibited jubilation and so they cared little that, as the victory celebrations finally concluded, they had to trudge home through the snow with the temperature below zero.[111]

George Ross expressed a sense of relief at finally being pushed off the slippery slope into defeat. 'I was taxed far beyond my strength,' he informed G.M. Wrong, 'and had to deny myself almost everything like pleasure or even recreation.' In writing Laurier, he analysed his defeat, placing blame 'almost entirely' on 'the combination of the liquor dealers with the temperance men.' 'We lost very few Liberals,' he protested, 'except those who were extreme in these two respects.' And, he argued, 'the cry of "Corruption" was pretty well shattered during the campaign.' The Tories, however, were also assisted by 'an enormous election fund.' 'The most our opponents expected was to win by 10 or 12 of a majority,' Ross concluded; 'they had not even fully appreciated the strength of their own artillery.'[112]

Ross's analysis of the Conservative victory was imperfect. Undoubtedly, temperance people annoyed at Liberal vacillation on prohibition supported Whitney, and so did members of the liquor trade, probably with financial contributions. But such an explanation of the Tory triumph is inadequate, particularly in light of the dimensions of the sweep. Ross lost Liberals who were not 'extreme': for example, S.H. Blake, brother of the sometime party leader, J.S. Willison, ex-editor of the *Globe*, and Walter Mills, son of a former Liberal minister of justice. This trio defected because of proven Grit corruption, and uncounted others followed their lead.

Liberal organization by the time of the 1905 campaign was wanting, and the creation of the General Reform Association for Ontario to replace the tainted Ontario Liberal Association failed to meet the deficiency. Further, tensions had developed over the years between Ottawa and Toronto that hurt the cause of Liberal unity. On the other hand, the Ontario Liberal-Conservative Association, which had been created, in part, to challenge Whitney's leadership, soon provided him with a strong and loyal basis of organization under Foy's presidency. And, free of the burden of his party's being the Ottawa government, the Tory leader faced few problems from that quarter. Foy also proved useful in dampening down religious fires within the party's ranks. Roman Catholics, driven off in Meredith's day, began a return to the fold once the party leadership fell silent on separate schools and Roman Catholic domination.

Thirty-three years of governmental responsibility had deadened the reform urge within the Liberal party. The spark of Clear Grittism was very faint indeed by 1905. Not that Ross had been particularly remiss in this matter: he had attempted to present the image of a new, progressive, and energetic government when he assumed command, but he could not really break down the inertia, a fact which troubled serious Liberals. Whitney sounded much more the imaginative reformer when he talked of a public power policy, educational change, aid to the University of Toronto, honest administration, and protection of the little man from injustice – and the corporations.

Yet another factor may have played a part in Whitney's success. The province of Ontario had undergone a notable change during the period from Whitney's first election to his assumption of office. In that interval, the rural population found itself yielding the majority position to the urban. As manufacturing continued to develop, there had been an increase in the rate of urban growth. Some rural, Grit constituencies faced depopulation, which gradually gave power to the Tories in such areas, particularly if the riding's urban centre continued to grow. By 1905, then, Ontario was not at all the province it had been in 1888. The provincial population was growing and shifting; and many of its needs had been altered. The Liberals apparently failed to meet those needs. In Whitney the province found a man who sensed the transformation and, accordingly, made his appeal. The province responded by finally taking a chance on him.[113]

4

'A New Order': 1905

Whitney waited for the election returns on 25 January in the Morrisburg Music Hall. By nine-thirty p.m., the large and boisterous crowd knew he was the premier-elect of Ontario, and a round of congratulatory speech-making began, with old friends, like Andy Broder, standing up to salute the victorious party leader. Finally, these necessary preliminaries disposed of, it was Whitney's turn and he rose to the sound of deafening and sustained cheering. When the sounds of triumph had subsided sufficiently, he thanked his constituents, praised his party, and, already consciously moving to cement campaign alliances, acknowledged Liberal assistance. Nearly seventeen years before – it had been 31 January 1888 – he had stood in the same place to say a few words of appreciation to those who had laboured successfully for his first election to the Ontario legislature.[1]

The triumphant party chief did not then catch the next train to Toronto. Next day he busied himself with greeting well-wishers who flocked to his substantial two-storied red brick home. Some undoubtedly came believing that the perpetual mirage of a ripe patronage plum had at last been transformed into a reality that dangled tantalizingly before them: the years in the desert were over. All day long they trekked to the house, had a word or two with the premier-designate, reminded him of their Tory credentials, enjoyed a warming cup of coffee, and, mercifully, departed. Newspapermen, anxious for a different story, invaded the house and, failing to glean significant news, resorted to reports on Whitney's well-stocked library and his two grandchildren.[2]

The Conservative leader did more than chat with his constituents and provide reporters with thin copy while he remained in Morrisburg. Retreating to the seclusion of his law office, he worked out the composition of his cabinet. That done, he placed the completed list in his pocket with the silent vow not to alter one name when he reached Toronto with all its attendant political pressures. And on 30 January, when he was in Toronto for a round of conferences with party associates, he made no public disclosures about the ingredients of his cabinet. Still tight-lipped two days later, he returned to Morrisburg for a giant demonstration in his honour. He chose that occasion to re-emphasize the bipartisan nature of the support which had produced his triumph, a theme which he sounded constantly during these heady post-election days. Having garnered significant backing from wavering Liberals during the recent contest, he was most anxious to retain it. For the moment flattering phrases would have to be the glue; in the future, deeds could replace words.[3]

Whitney's exasperating silence did not prevent the newspapers from making cabinets and proffering advice. It was generally agreed that Jim Foy was the logical choice for the post of attorney-general and that Arthur J. Matheson of Perth was likely to be provincial treasurer. John S. Hendrie of Hamilton, a railway contractor, engineer, industrialist, and financier, was seen as destined for public works. And William J. Hanna, the bright, ambitious, and witty member for Lambton West, was regarded as an inevitable nominee for place. But, after advancing this quartet as safe bets for position, the newspapers lost their unanimity. Thomas Crawford was touted as a possible minister of agriculture, but, then, so was Finlay Macdiarmid from Elgin West. Confident predictions suggested that lawyer Isaac B. Lucas of Grey Centre would be given some post. And the openly ambitious – notably Beattie Nesbitt and J.W. St John, both physical, if not political, heavyweights – were not overlooked, although their eagerness for office was seen in some quarters as a potential liability.[4]

In light of such speculation, naturally enough, there was surprise, delight, and dismay when Whitney finally made his cabinet choices public on 8 February, the day when the new ministers were sworn into office. The new premier took for himself the office of attorney-general, but produced confusion and criticism by announcing that his hold on the latter post was but temporary. Foy became commissioner of crown lands – again not a permanent arrangement – and Pyne was named minister of education. Samuel Nelson Monteith, graduate of the Ontario Agricultural College and member for Perth South, was given the ministry of agriculture. Matheson, MPP for Lanark South since 1894 and the party's financial critic, took the position of provincial treasurer, as had been forecast. W.J. Hanna, an exceptionally able debater, became provincial secretary, while Joseph Olivier Reaume, from Essex North, secured the post of commissioner of public works. Three men were named ministers without portfolio: Adam Beck of London, fast moving to the fore in the movement seeking strong government intervention in the field of hydroelectric development; William A. Willoughby, member for Northumberland East and Whitney's longtime friend; and, oddly to many minds, John Hendrie. Save for the north, the cabinet contained someone from each significant provincial region. Whitney had almost met one criterion for sound cabinet-making.

The surprises in the cabinet were the medical doctors, Reaume and Pyne.

Inclusion of the member from Essex North marked the first time in Ontario's history that a French-Canadian had been given cabinet rank with departmental responsibilities. In selecting Reaume, Whitney – ever desirous of building bridges for the party – probably reasoned like F.D. Monk, who had urged him to place a Franco-Ontarian in the cabinet: 'the effect of such a policy,' Monk had written, '... would silence, in Quebec, voices that have been uplifted against us since over twenty years and if the minister named by you knew how to utilize his position it would give you the Ontario counties in which there is a French vote, solid for a long time.' So the doctor who spoke English with a 'marked but pleasing accent' was in, despite his obvious lack of experience for the office he held.[5]

The appointment of the other doctor, Pyne, to the ministry of education, particularly when he had spoken so little on the subject, proved a puzzle to some and an 'awful disappointment' to others. But he had been chairman of the Toronto school board and the free library board, and that meant he was not without some experience. More important, however, he was a loyal Whitney man and a stalwart of the party organization. Amiable and mild-mannered, he was a nice balance for his blunt and aloof leader, while his Orange credentials must have eased the worries of militant Protestants who anxiously noted the presence of Foy and Reaume in the cabinet.[6]

The other surprise was Whitney's announced intention of retaining the post of attorney-general briefly, before moving Foy into that office from crown lands. The Liberal press was both quizzical and querulous. The reason for such an arrangement later became apparent: the Conservative leader wanted to hold the crown lands portfolio open for an appointee from northern Ontario. He had virtually pledged such an appointment in 1902, as well as the creation of a department more specifically concerned with that section of the province. But, obviously, the election results of 1905 had not given him the man for the job. Clearly, recruitment outside of the legislature would be necessary and then the premier could shuffle his cabinet.[7]

There undoubtedly was delight in Catholic circles at witnessing the appointment of Reaume and Foy. In giving portfolios to this pair, Whitney had broken fresh ground. For brief periods earlier in Ontario's political history, there had been two Catholics in the inner circle, but at no time had both been responsible for departments. Pyne might be an Orangeman, as was speaker-to-be J.W. St John, but the days of equal rights and the PPA were, it was to be hoped, dead and gone. Surely separate schools would not now come under assault with Foy and Reaume serving as Catholic guardians. Of course, it should also have been remembered that Jim Foy, with his unruffled appearance and manner, was every bit as loyal to party as he was faithful to his church. That, after all, was one reason for his presence in the cabinet.

Business interests, which might have been made slightly uneasy by some of Whitney's earlier anti-corporation statements, could now rest content in the knowledge that Hendrie and Hanna were in the cabinet. Hendrie's business connections were well known: among his interests were the Bank of Hamilton, the Great West Life Assurance Company, and the Hamilton Bridge Works Company. And Hanna had links with the Standard Oil Company.

Dismay settled on those who, having expected office, were left on the outside. Gamey and Nesbitt were conspicuous by their absence. The Conservative leader fully appreciated that the former could be an erratic liability, and the latter a devious plotter of uncertain loyalty. He probably reasoned like a supportive Liberal who argued that, should this pair 'exercise a strong power in ... Provincial affairs ... the last state might be as bad, if not worse, than the first.' Thomas Crawford, sitting for Toronto West since 1894, was also ignored; Whitney had no room for the militant Protestant wing of the party. Crawford bitterly noted that, although he had province-wide support for his elevation and had sat in the legislature four years longer than either Foy or Pyne, the premier had not even consulted him about cabinet composition. Rumour soon had it that the dis-appointed were not going to accept the role of back-benchers. Nesbitt, Crawford, and other malcontents were reported to be seeking to organize a bloc that would not necessarily support the government in order to point up – and protest – the weakness of the cabinet, a cabinet presumably made weak by their lack of membership. An alliance of the neglected failed to materialize, although there was audible muttering. Beattie Nesbitt and the others soon realized, despite their peevishness, that the premier was 'not the man to be bullied or driven.'[8]

At sixty-two, Whitney was the oldest member of his cabinet; Hanna, at forty-two, was cast in the role of baby. Every member had been born in Ontario. Six – Beck, Matheson, Monteith, Pyne, Willoughby, and Whitney – were Anglicans; Hanna was the solitary Methodist, and Hendrie the lone Presbyterian. Like their leader, Foy, Hanna, and Matheson were lawyers. Willoughby was the third doctor on the team, and, not surprisingly, Monteith was a farmer. Hendrie, whose militia background may have provided him with the appearance of a tough sergeant-major, had a variety of business interests, while Beck was a modest cigar-box manufacturer. With one notable deficiency, these were Ontario's new political masters.

The deficiency was, of course, a representative of northern Ontario, and Whitney remedied it when the legislative session was completed late in May. At that time the premier vacated the attorney-general's office in favour of Foy and assumed the presidency of the council. And Frank Cochrane, a wealthy fifty-two-year-old Sudbury hardware merchant and Methodist, moved into the position of minister of lands and mines. Cochrane, who also maintained a Toronto residence, had been the unsuccessful Tory candidate in Nipissing West in the provincial election of 1902, but had not sought office in 1905. Nevertheless, there is some evidence to suggest that tentative arrangements had been made prior to the latter contest to open a riding for Cochrane should the Tories be victorious. Charles

Lamarche, the successful Conservative in Nipissing East, appeared only too willing to stand aside for the Sudbury retailer and, quite conceivably, he only contested the riding in order to nail down Catholic Franco-Ontarian support for the Tory party. If there was a script calling for Cochrane to replace Lamarche, then, clearly, Whitney had early determined on the strong man from the north whom he wanted in any cabinet he might form. The four-month delay in executing this manoeuvre is easily explained by noting a freak accident on 2 February, when Cochrane lost his lower right leg in slipping under a moving railway car. This injury would have caused Whitney to shelve any plans involving Cochrane and a cabinet position. By the end of May, the tough northerner, now equipped with an artificial limb, had recovered sufficiently to enter the Tory inner circle. Cochrane took the Nipissing East seat by acclamation when the Liberals backed away from a contest.[9]

The smoothness of this political operation – it was just a shade too smooth – produced grumbling from within Conservative ranks. Undoubtedly Gamey was disappointed, but for once he remained silent. W.R. Smyth, member for Algoma since 1902, was not so inclined: hopeful of securing the lands and mines portfolio, he expressed incredulity at this turn of events, although Whitney's delay in making the appointment must surely have dulled his expectations. The Conservative leader rejected Smyth's complaint, noting that 'in this country it has been quite common for men to be taken into the Cabinet from private life.' 'It was my duty,' he informed the Algoma member in language that did nothing for Smyth's ego, 'to try to get a man from New Ontario at once able and capable and who had also had the necessary knowledge and experience for such a position. I believe I have succeeded ... I have no doubt whatever that I have acted wisely.' Clearly, there would be no further discussion of the matter. The cabinet was set.[10]

II

The province, now firmly held by the Tories for the first time since Confederation, was well launched along the route of industrialization: the hammering noise of production and the dark belching of smoke-stacks were now rivals to quiet fields of grain and the intense autumnal colours of the countryside. Ontario was 'by far the most industrialized province in Canada' when Whitney assumed office. It possessed almost one-half of all capital invested in the nation's manufacturing, and much of that capital lay in larger enterprises that, contrary to the generalizations of some historians, had grown to their present size during the last third of the nineteenth century. Ahead lay larger leaps in capital invested and smaller jumps in gross value of production. And that productivity was in a diversity of areas: clothing, iron and steel, food processing, wood products including paper, shoes, textiles, and farm implements, to name some of the more prominent. The centre of much of this activity, but by no means the sole location, was Toronto; the productivity of Hamilton, Berlin, Brantford, Windsor, Guelph, Peterborough, and a score of other cities and towns cannot be ignored.[11]

There was a darker side to this picture of economic buoyancy. The families of many breadwinners in the work force lived at or under the poverty line, unless a second member contributed to the family income. Compounding these economic difficulties was the fact that, for many workers, real wages declined during the first two decades of the twentieth century. In addition, dismissals and temporary lay-offs, made more likely by periodic recessions, were two stark realities that many in the blue-collar class faced; and relief under such unhappy circumstances was afforded by municipalities and private charities in irregular and parsimonious fashion.[12]

Conditions of work were often harsh: the worker laboured for nine or ten hours a day, six days a week, frequently on a piece-rate basis which heightened not only productivity but also injury; and he, or she, sweated in surroundings that were noisy, dirty, poorly ventilated, and lacking in adequate sanitation facilities. There was legislation on the books designed to curb the worst abuses suffered by workers, but its effectiveness was severely curtailed by a shortage of inspectors, who invariably sought the persuasion – and not prosecution – route with truculent employers. When improvement occurred it came, frequently, not because of legislation or conscience but because the employer had finally been convinced that a healthy worker in a clean environment was a better producer.[13]

For many, the home circumstances were scarcely any better than those of the work-place, and this was particularly true in Toronto, an exceedingly unhealthy place as is evidenced by high death and infant mortality rates. Matters were frequently made worse by inadequate systems of water supply and sewage disposal, with the result that typhoid outbreaks were not uncommon. And Toronto also suffered from an unclean milk supply. Disease, thus readily started, easily ran its course in the capital city through the crowded families of the working class, many of whom shared accommodation in order to make payments on the homes they were buying; home ownership statistics, read in a vacuum, covered the poverty, the filth, and the overcrowding. Despite the best efforts of well-intentioned reformers, improvement was slight because, at bottom, insufficient earnings prevented advance. Conditions were not as grim in many smaller Ontario manufacturing centres, but a shortage of income remained a constant demeaning characteristic of the working class.[14]

One means of bettering this low standard of living might have been trade unionism; but, as industrialization spread, unions simply did not stand a chance of changing the situation, let alone seizing control of it. Aggressive employers, aided by periodic recessions and a large labour pool, were able to refuse recognition; if faced by a strike, they were frequently in a position to break it and, in the process, shatter the union. In any event, unions were generally for the skilled; beyond their pale, as a rule, the unskilled laboured with the threat of instant dismissal poised over their heads. Docility was inevitable. There were strikes, to be sure; and there

Ontario's rural/urban population distribution, 1901–11[15]

Population 1901		Population 1911		Decrease/Increase	
2,182,947		2,523,274		+340,327 (15.59%)	
Rural	Urban	Rural	Urban	Rural	Urban
1,246,969 (57.12%)	935,978 (42.88%)	1,194,785 (47.35%)	1,328,489 (52.65%)	−52,184 (−4.18%)	+392,511 (+41.94%)

was angry violence; but, for the most part, the poor, ill-housed, undernourished urban worker quietly went to his daily labours, six days a week – when there was work.[16]

Rapid and grubby industrial growth further accelerated the movement from country to town in the first decade of the twentieth century. And immigrants to Ontario, except for the occasional well-funded one, had little choice but to seek urban employment, thus swelling the labour pool, intensifying the poverty, and dramatically increasing city populations. One urban centre after another suffered intense growing pains in the first ten years of the new century. Some of this was due to the expansion of boundaries, but much of it was due to the numbers that crowded inside the existing limits.

Population growth in Ontario's cities and towns of over 10,000 inhabitants, 1901–11[17]

Cities and towns	Population 1901	Increase 1901–11		Population 1911
Toronto	208,040	168,498	(80.99%)	376,538
Ottawa	59,928	27,134	(45.28%)	87,062
Hamilton	52,634	29,335	(55.73%)	81,969
London	37,976	8,324	(21.92%)	46,300
Brantford	16,619	6,513	(39.19%)	23,132
Kingston	17,961	913	(5.08%)	18,874
Peterborough	11,239	7,121	(63.36%)	18,360
Windsor	12,153	5,676	(46.70%)	17,829
Fort William	3,633	12,866	(354.14%)	16,499
Berlin	9,747	5,439	(55.80%)	15,186
Guelph	11,496	3,679	(32.00%)	15,175
St Thomas	11,485	2,569	(22.37%)	14,054
Stratford	9,959	2,987	(29.99%)	12,946
Owen Sound	8,776	3,783	(43.11%)	12,559
St Catharines	9,946	2,538	(25.52%)	12,484
Port Arthur	3,214	8,006	(249.10%)	11,220
Sault Ste Marie	7,169	3,815	(53.22%)	10,984
Chatham	9,068	1,702	(18.77%)	10,770
Galt	7,866	2,363	(30.04%)	10,229

The other side of this coin of urban growth was rural depopulation: virtually every county in Ontario lost people to the cities and towns; some yielded a few hundred and some several thousands. In Whitney's Dundas bailiwick, the decline was as evident as elsewhere: the four rural townships witnessed a drop of more than thirteen hundred people between 1901 and 1911. And village centres did not escape unscathed: Iroquois lost nearly a quarter of its population in those years, and Morrisburg's total grew by a scanty three.[18]

This evident flight from the land was caused by Ontario's lack of additional good farm acreage; the superficial attractiveness of town work to the farm labourer; the ongoing acceptance of primogeniture in matters of inheritance; the economic desirability of increased farm size; the ever-broader use of machinery; and weary capitulation to the hard fact that some land was not sufficiently productive. But in the face of all of this, it must be borne in mind that nearly one-quarter of the entire Canadian population lived in rural Ontario in 1901; and, even in 1911, after tens of thousands of immigrants had arrived, almost one out of every six people in the dominion still lived in the province's countryside. Farming remained quite consequential in the Ontario economic and social picture.

Just as industrialization had altered and was altering the urban centre, so the products of industrialization were changing the face of farming. By the turn of the century, many Ontario farms were thoroughly mechanized by means of binders, threshing mills, seed drills, hay mowers, manure spreaders, potato diggers, disc harrowers, and cream separators. These time-saving devices not only enabled the farmer to do much more with much less labour, and thus contend with the city-ward drift, but also allowed him to cut his costs per acre of produce, a desirable result in light of the drop in the value of farm produce, which did not return to its 1882 level until 1910. Mechanization, at relatively cheap prices, gave the farmer time, reduced his labour requirements, and, fortunately, saved him money.[19]

By 1900, many successful Ontario farmers had turned away from wheat as the basis of their income; low and/or extremely uncertain prices had dictated this move to these canny men, who wanted greater consistency in their cash returns. Feed grains, such as oats, and fodder crops – corn, hay, and roots – had taken up the lands once given over to wheat. And these new crops were needed for the ever-increasing numbers of livestock as the farmers turned to mixed farming that yielded products for the growing home and diminishing export markets. Ontario's bulging urban centres greedily ate up provincially produced beef, ham, bacon, milk, cheese, and butter. These demands meant, in turn, that increasingly better and more suitable breeds of livestock, especially cattle and swine, replaced the mongrel foragers of field and forest and dramatically raised the standards of animal husbandry. Some of these changes were responsible for spawning, just before the century's turn, hundreds of cheese factories and scores of creameries which reflected consumer demand, quality control, new specialization, and technological advance. By the time Whitney came to power, the Ontario farmer had advanced 'from the rank of strenuous toiler to the more complex status of a business proprietor.' He had to be so transformed in order to be successful; if he failed to change, then he was doomed to scratch a livelihood from the soil.[20]

These were some of the urban and rural aspects of Ontario which faced the new premier and they certainly suggest a heterogeneous society. But there were other factors which gave this society the appearance, and the reality, of significant homogeneity. Better than three-quarters of Ontario's residents claimed either British background or birth. Less than a tenth were of French origin, and about the same number claimed German background. Obviously, persons of any other origin were not numerically significant.

Origins of Ontario's population, 1901–11[21]

Origins	1901		Increase/Decrease		1911	
British	1,732,144	(79.35%)	194,955	(11.26%)	1,927,099	(76.37%)
English	701,413	(32.13%)	183,019	(26.09%)	884,432	(35.05%)
Irish	624,332	(28.60%)	−16,195	(−2.59%)	608,137	(24.10%)
Scottish	399,530	(18.30%)	25,343	(6.34%)	424,873	(16.84%)
Others	6,869	(0.32%)	2,788	(40.59%)	9,657	(0.38%)
French	158,671	(7.27%)	43,771	(27.59%)	202,442	(8.02%)
German	203,319	(9.31%)	−10,999	(−5.41%)	192,320	(7.62%)
Dutch	23,280	(1.07%)	11,732	(50.40%)	35,012	(1.39%)
Jewish	5,337	(0.24%)	21,678	(406.18%)	27,015	(1.07%)
Indian	24,674	(1.13%)	−1,630	(−6.61%)	23,044	(0.92%)
Others	35,522	(1.63%)	80,820	(227.52%)	116,342	(4.61%)
Total	2,182,947	(100.00%)	340,327	(15.59%)	2,523,274	(100.00%)

If an analysis of the origins of Ontarians produced figures that indicated a large degree of homogeneity, an examination of their places of birth yielded even stronger evidence of uniformity. When the Tories gained power, over 80 per cent of the province's residents could claim birth in Canada, and an overwhelming preponderance of that group was Ontario-born, a fact which the Whitney cabinet accurately reflected. Only those born in Quebec were of sufficient numbers to avoid categorization as negligible. Persons of British birth amounted to over 10 per cent of the population and this figure more than kept pace with provincial growth between 1901 and 1911, thanks to very large English, and much smaller Scottish, immigration; while those of Irish birth dropped in absolute numbers by over 25 per cent. In these years there was also significant growth in the ranks of those born in the Austro-Hungarian and Russian empires, Italy, and Finland; they provided the brawn in mines and forests, and on railroad construction. But, despite a rapid increase over their 1901 base numbers, their totals in 1911 were relatively puny in comparison to those of British or United States birth. By the yardstick of origins,

Place of birth of Ontario's population, 1901–11[22]

Place of Birth	1901		Increase/Decrease		1911	
Canada	1,858,787	(85.15%)	156,658	(8.43%)	2,015,445	(79.88%)
Ontario	1,784,760	(81.76%)	146,966	(8.23%)	1,931,726	(76.56%)
Quebec	61,776	(2.83%)	3,007	(4.87%)	64,783	(2.57%)
Elsewhere	9,791	(0.45%)	2,925	(29.87%)	12,716	(0.50%)
Not Given	2,460	(0.11%)	3,760	(152.85%)	6,220	(0.25%)
British Isles	239,873	(10.99%)	108,808	(45.36%)	348,681	(13.82%)
England	120,600	(5.52%)	109,637	(90.91%)	230,237	(9.12%)
Ireland	68,094	(3.12%)	−17,959	(−26.37%)	50,135	(1.99%)
Scotland	49,881	(2.29%)	15,095	(30.26%)	64,976	(2.58%)
Wales	906	(0.04%)	1,460	(161.15%)	2,366	(0.09%)
Lesser Isles	392	(0.02%)	575	(146.68%)	967	(0.04%)
British Possessions	2,530	(0.12%)	2,554	(100.95%)	5,084	(0.20%)
British Unknown	–		4,903		4,903	(0.19%)
'Foreign' born	76,913	(3.52%)	71,851	(93.42%)	148,764	(5.89%)
Austria-Hungary	1,241	(0.06%)	14,314	(1,153.42%)	15,555	(0.62%)
Finland	–		6,871		6,871	(0.27%)
France	1,254	(0.06%)	625	(49.84%)	1,879	(0.07%)
Germany	18,699	(0.86%)	−3,689	(−19.73%)	15,010	(0.59%)
Italy	3,301	(0.15%)	13,110	(397.15%)	16,411	(0.65%)
Norway and	1,506	(0.07%)	3,757	(249.47%)	1,603	(0.06%)
Sweden					3,660	(0.15%)
Russia	3,373	(0.15%)	16,045	(475.69%)	19,418	(0.77%)
United States	44,175	(2.02%)	11,499	(26.03%)	55,674	(2.21%)
Other	3,364	(0.15%)	9,319	(277.02%)	12,683	(0.50%)
At sea	178	(0.01%)	219	(123.03%)	397	(0.02%)
Not given	4,666	(0.21%)	−4,666		–	
Total	2,182,947	(100.00%)	340,327	(15.59%)	2,523,274	(100.00%)

Ontario was very much a British province throughout the Whitney era; by the yardstick of birth, Ontario was possessed by its own.[23]

One final form of measurement, religious affiliation, produces – at one level – arguments favouring a mosaic interpretation of Ontario's society in Whitney's day; but, examined another way, the province can be seen as strongly Protestant. The Methodists, although the largest denomination, failed to grow with the province between 1901 and 1911, and their numbers were nearly frozen, a fact which gave them cause for concern. Similarly, the second-place Presbyterians, although growing in adherents, could not match the provincial pace. But the Anglicans, aided by immigration, narrowly leapfrogged over the Roman Catholics and into third place by the end of this decade. Despite the loss of position, however, Catholic growth was at a faster pace than that of the provincial populace. Lutherans, Jews, and Salvationists had, relative to their own ranks, dramatic increases, but they still remained diminutive on an Ontario-wide scale. In sum,

Denominational Strengths in Ontario, 1901–11[24]

Denomination	1901		Increase/Decrease		1911	
Methodist	666,388	(30.53%)	5,339	(0.80%)	671,727	(26.62%)
Presbyterian	477,386	(21.87%)	47,217	(9.89%)	524,603	(20.79%)
Anglican	367,937	(16.85%)	121,767	(33.09%)	489,704	(19.41%)
Roman Catholic	390,304	(17.88%)	94,693	(24.26%)	484,997	(19.22%)
Baptist	116,281	(5.33%)	16,528	(14.21%)	132,809	(5.27%)
Lutheran	48,052	(2.20%)	18,656	(38.82%)	66,708	(2.64%)
Jewish	5,321	(0.24%)	21,446	(403.04%)	26,767	(1.06%)
Congregationalist	15,289	(0.70%)	−597	(−3.90%)	14,692	(0.58%)
Mennonite	12,208	(0.56%)	620	(5.08%)	12,828	(0.51%)
Salvation Army	6,479	(0.30%)	4,926	(76.03%)	11,405	(0.45%)
Other	77,302	(3.54%)	9,732	(2.86%)	87,034	(3.45%)
Total	2,182,947	(100.00%)	340,327	(15.59%)	2,523,274	(100.00%)

four out of five Ontarians professed some version of Protestantism, while Roman Catholics, some thousands of Jews, and a few dozens of brave agnostics and atheists were not, obviously, in this main stream. Whitney's cabinet accurately reflected the proportions of the provincial Protestant-Catholic division; but the Anglicans, with six council posts, were vastly over-represented, and Presbyterian Hendrie and Methodists Cochrane and Hanna under-represented their denominations.

III

That cabinet, with the Tory caucus in tow, now turned its attention to the new legislative session, scheduled to open on 22 March. But, even before that event, Whitney had to face the first waves of delegations which were to roll in upon him in his years as premier. He was compelled to listen to the pitch of representatives of the Dominion Grange, who seemed to forget where they were and largely discussed federal matters, save for a call for a provincial secret ballot – an issue dear to the Conservative leader's heart – and a demand for an end to subsidies of land and money to railways. The veterans of 1866, 1870, and South Africa appeared before him to complain about problems arising from their land grants of one hundred and sixty acres each; and the vigilant Lord's Day Alliance pressed him to halt the running of Sunday streetcars and to limit Sunday labour, issues which he carefully skirted in reply by pointing out the need to wait for a Privy Council decision on sabbatarian questions. Whitney was thus quickly thrust into some of the tasks of government; his position allowed for no gradual easing into place.

The premier had predicted that the new session would 'not be long' and might be 'a little slow' because, as yet, the cabinet had formulated no large plans and, being new, would move 'with due care.' This forecast, however, was surely hedged with modesty, for Whitney intended taking strong action, within and without the assembly, on the University of Toronto question and hydroelectric power development. When the Morrisburg lawyer came to the premiership, James Loudon had been the well-meaning but unconciliatory president of the University of Toronto for a dozen trouble-filled years. Loudon had continually found himself at odds with William Mulock, the vice-chancellor, until the latter had retired from the academic scene in 1900. The president had faced student rebellion in 1895 and harsh and unfounded undergraduate criticism in 1904; in the first case the government had had to appoint a commission to investigate the troubles, and in the second a select committee of the university's senate had examined the state of affairs. Loudon had seemed to go out of his way to antagonize Victoria College – notably over its acquisition of university land – and his intransigence had brought him into open conflict with the University of Toronto's board of trustees. He had been responsible for the creation of the University of Toronto Alumni Association, but had failed to claim credit for it and allowed the glory to pass to others. Unhappily, Loudon seems to have been a man who carried his own black cloud with him.[25]

In actual fact, the difficulties of Loudon's presidency were symptomatic of deeper and enduring problems which were not of his creation. During his time in office the University of Toronto was constantly in the shadow of the legislative buildings just to the east. The assembly hamstrung the university financially and troubled it administratively. W.R. Meredith described one aspect of this unfortunate situation to Whitney:

I want to tell you of a very bad practice which prevailed under the last administration and which I hope will not be followed by yours. I refer to the practice of members of the [university] staff urging upon ministers appointments to the staff[,] promotions and increases of salary for themselves & others. I venture to suggest that this is all wrong and that all communications should come through the President or the Principal of University College according as they relate to the University or University College.

Loudon was not the man to stand up to Ross in the face of such political intervention and, as a historian of the university, W.S. Wallace, has noted, 'appointments were made to the staff without consulting the wishes of the president, and even against his express recommendation.'[26]

On the financial side, the attitude of the Liberals under Ross, again according to Wallace, was 'niggardly and cheese-paring.' It is true that, in 1901, the province had undertaken the financial maintenance of the departments of chemistry, physics, and mineralogy and geology, but the deficits of the university had continued to mount thereafter until Whitney estimated the 1905 shortage to be over forty-five thousand dollars. The institution was obviously in need of generous financial assistance if it was to rise above a cap-in-hand existence.

The Conservative premier, not his minister of education, unveiled the first portion of his remedies for the university in the legislature in mid-May. His initial concern was to give the institution greater strength and independence through adequate grants. There would be government money to aid in the construction of men's residences, a new physics building, a science building addition, Convocation Hall, and a new hospital to be used jointly by the city of Toronto and the university medical faculty; there would also be a thirty-year grant of thirty thousand dollars per annum for building purposes. 'The total proposed expenditures dealt with by the Bill,' Whitney told the legislature, 'would be $1,600,000, and of this sum the direct grants by the Government would amount to $465,000. While this was a large sum, it would at once put the University beyond the danger of embarrassment.'[27]

There was little for the Liberal opposition to say. Harcourt had the temerity to suggest that the Conservatives were following lines laid down by the former administration. Ross repeated this observation and also argued 'that residences were not an essential feature of University life.' Outside of the legislature, there was broad acceptance and rich praise of the government's action. Sam Blake, a longtime friend of the institution, was nothing less than ecstatic: he had to write Whitney and thank him 'most heartily' for the 'splendid work for the University.' 'In your first Session,' he continued, 'you have done more than has been done at least in ten years past by the former Government. We have received pauper doles and promises, depending upon political exigencies, and our University has been almost run to the ground.' Ross, he charged, was 'pitiful' and 'utterly misleading' in his remarks. Blake concluded with his blessing on the premier: 'may you long be spared in strength to build up on true and honest lines our Province, which has run so much to seed during the past twenty years.' And, more remarkable, that secular invocation had come from the pen of a most substantial Grit! Blake's immense pleasure arose from Whitney's speed in dealing completely with a long list of university problems enumerated for him by a committee of concerned citizens. These interested supporters of the institution could not have asked for more. And Whitney, in addition to demonstrating a breadth of mind which some of his detractors had not anticipated, secured more tightly to his side an element in that bipartisan support which had given him his electoral triumph.[28]

With such legislation, Whitney began the work of placing the University of Toronto on a sound foundation. The financial woes of the institution had been largely eased by the generous action of the new Conservative government. This action left the administrative side of the university untouched but, although the Tory leader took no steps on this matter in the 1905 session, he had privately made clear his intention to appoint a commission 'to enquire into all matters pertaining to the University.'

The government's position on hydroelectric development received a thorough airing during the session, although the Conservatives did not produce any legislation on the subject. They indicated, however, that this would be forthcoming after study. One reason for the discussion was the government's decision not to seek legislative ratification of a fresh contract signed by the Electrical Development Company and the Queen Victoria Niagara Falls Park Commission to permit the corporation to develop another one hundred thousand horsepower, over and above the one hundred and twenty-five thousand permitted under the initial contract. Using stiff language, the premier announced that his government was not going to give away the province's resources: 'the water power all over this country shall not in future be made the sport and prey of capitalists, and shall not be treated as anything else but as a valuable asset of the people of Ontario, whose trustees the Government of this Province are.' Adam Beck elaborated upon the government's attitude later in the session. The former London mayor argued that the rentals charged the contracting companies at Niagara Falls were too low; that Ontario would soon require all the power that these corporations could produce; that the public was left unprotected by current arrangements; that the companies were financed by bonds while a handful of men retained the capital stock, and the control. He then singled out the Electrical Development Company and charged that its contracts were scarcely drawn in the public interest.[29]

Beck's assault produced a reply from Ross, who repeated an old argument: the presence of three companies at the Falls precluded the possibility of monopoly or extravagant charges. The government also drew a response from the Electrical Development Company, which, in injured tones, insisted that as a Canadian corporation spending funds in Ontario it deserved better treatment at the hands of the Conservatives. That curt exchange indicated that the young adminstration had fallen afoul of three important entrepreneurs, Henry Pellatt, William Mackenzie, and Frederic Nicholls; or, just possibly, it was the other way around, which would be a new experience for this trio.

Had the new government done nothing more in its first session than provide some financial stability for the University of Toronto and spell out its concern for future hydroelectric development in the province, it would have deserved praise. But Whitney also directed it along lesser avenues. The numbered ballot, which the premier had long regarded as a means of violating the secrecy of the polling booth, was abolished. The Succession Duties Act was altered to exempt estates of less than ten thousand dollars, a modest measure of relief for families of smaller means. Legislation changed the designation of the commissioner of crown lands to that of minister of lands and mines, indicating an awareness of the need to devote more attention to one aspect of Ontario's resource development. The commissioner of public works became the minister of public works; and a new portfolio, to be held by the premier, was created: president of the council.

The Conservative leader also moved to block a frequent occurrence in the legislature: the late consideration of private bills by committee, followed by their hasty passage through the assembly at session's end. Whitney appeared at a meeting of the railway committee, which was considering some controversial legislation centring on electrically operated railway lines in York County, and read it a lecture. 'For a dozen years,' he charged, 'the practice has been in operation for men to come to the Legislature with measures of far-reaching importance, near the end of the Session.' This procedure would stop with this bill, which the government had not had an opportunity to study and, consequently, could not endorse. One further thing was certain: if the bill contained 'a provision for a perpetual franchise,' his government would 'never consent to it.' And, if the promoters refused 'to let the Bill stand till next year,' then the government would 'move in the House to strike out the Bill.' While the press, including the Liberal *Toronto Star*, cheered this display of domineering bluntness, the Conservative majority on the committee – except for Beattie Nesbitt – ran for cover and opted not to proceed with consideration of the matter. Clearly, the premier thought that the assembly should be supreme in all areas of its rightful jurisdiction. Equally important, the episode demonstrated that Whitney was in charge of that assembly.[30]

The session did not conclude without one obviously partisan act by the Conservatives. Robert Gamey was given his head to review the affair which bore his name. In a bombastic address, he denounced the commissioners' report of 1903 as an error-filled document and judged his revelations as having had a decisive effect in the 1905 election. He then moved a resolution which, if carried, would rescind the legislature's adoption of the report, withdraw the thanks extended to the commissioners, and remove the censure of his conduct. The opposition protested that such moves would constitute a rank insult to the judges concerned, but Whitney stood by Gamey and contended that 'the late Government ... had degraded the Judiciary by employing its members in a partisan issue instead of leaving the whole matter to a Legislative Committee ...' Gamey's resolution carried along party lines; the premier and the Manitoulin maverick were satisfied.[31]

The session was also noteworthy for what did not happen. Apparently Beattie Nesbitt had it in mind to present a resolution in the legislature condemning the arrangements made for separate schools in Laurier's initial autonomy legislation for the new provinces of Saskatchewan and Alberta. Roman Catholic Conservatives who had applauded Whitney's decision to elevate Foy and Reaume were appalled by such a prospect, which would be a 'bomb shell ... unnecessarily thrown into the ranks of the Party.' The Conservative leader swiftly allayed Catholic fears with a clear enunciation of his position: he was 'strongly convinced' that it was 'unwise, injudicious and improper to bring this matter before the Legislature of any of the Provinces.' Leaders of his party, he continued, had consistently opposed the introduction of questions that lay beyond the assembly's competence. 'We ... assume the same attitude now, no matter what the consequence may be,' he concluded. His administration would not trespass in fields belonging to other jurisdictions. It was a sound principle and, like many sound principles, it had political advantages.[32]

Nevertheless, the Tory chief had strong personal convictions about the matter before the federal body: were he in the House of Commons, he 'would vote against the Bill without any hesitation.' Whitney argued that in 1896 the Conservatives had been rejected by the voters – including Catholics – when they had attempted to protect the Manitoba minority and fulfil the obligations of a compact. Now, in the premier's reading of history and current events, Laurier had reversed his 1896 position – an interpretation the Liberal leader would have bitterly disputed – and was insisting upon a compact when none existed. 'So far as my knowledge goes,' he averred, 'the history of this country affords no other such instance of stupid and asinine determination to embroil our people in a racial and religious conflict than this one.' Laurier should have 'held his hand' and, in all likelihood, the new provinces would have done voluntarily what Laurier was going to legislate. And compulsion in the matter of separate schools was, Whitney contended, exactly what the Liberal chief had denounced a decade earlier. So much for Laurier's reputation as a skilful compromiser and unifier – at least in the provincial leader's eyes. The commentary, however, was private opinion. The premier had no intention of providing a public forum for any exchange of opinions, and so he closed the door through which religious bigotry could slither onto the floor of Ontario's legislature. His decision permitted him the luxury of being high-minded and pragmatic at the same time.[33]

There were also lesser matters than the treacherous question of religion and education to occupy the new premier's attention. Hundreds of patronage-seekers pressed their cases with Whitney from all sides; of course all were party stalwarts, and they only sought a position that would 'bring say about $100 per month with increases.' For most there was nothing: the Tory leader, possibly with a touch of exaggeration for effect, informed one applicant that he received five hundred applications for every vacancy in the civil service. But when a position did open, such as that of night watchman in the legislative buildings at '$650 per year,' he was quick to fill it with an old and trusted acquaintance from Morrisburg. In the midst of such pleading, begging, and whining, he usually retained his sense of humour; beset by a particularly determined female from his home town, he appealed to Andy Broder: 'What are we to do with this woman? There are no vacancies, and if there were and she was appointed to one, I might naturally expect to receive a coat of tar and feathers the next time I come home. You had better see if you cannot get some place for her outside of a Government position, and if it comes to the worst, you might pay for a divorce from her husband and marry her yourself.'[34]

Whitney's fellow Tory legislators and defeated Conservative candidates were similarly besieged by those who envisaged plentiful jobs and contracts now that decades of Grit rule had ended, and who demanded the instant dismissal of Grit appointments, ranging from justices of the peace to asylum officials, on the grounds of partisan political activity in the recent election. Then there were the proponents of temperance and moral reform who refrained from demanding immediate action on their causes but who, nevertheless, announced their watchful presence and indicated a willingness to offer free advice. The premier, for his part, was prepared to meet with them, but that was all.[35]

IV

With the legislative session behind him and his cabinet-building completed, the premier turned his attention to the questions of the direction of hydroelectric development and the composition of the commission of inquiry into the subject which had earlier been promised. Beck, now the established and single-minded leader of the public power movement, was the choice for commission chairman, a selection that made an impartial report unlikely. Whitney decided that George Pattinson, the manufacturer-member from Waterloo South, and P.W. Ellis, a Toronto wholesale jeweller, would complement him. This trio met with the cabinet in late June to discuss the scope of the commission, which the premier wanted to make as broad as possible. Early in July, the make-up of the group – the Hydro-Electric Power Commission – was announced, as were its terms of reference.[36]

The inquiry was to discover 'the present and probable demand for hydraulic and electric power in the Province of Ontario'; 'the location, capacity and capital cost of development of the various water-powers within Provincial jurisdiction and which might be required to supply present and probable needs'; 'the rates or prices that would require to be charged to various classes of consumers of hydraulic or electrical power'; 'the possible saving to consumers by rates or prices applied as the result of this investigation'; and 'the cash capital cost of hydraulic and electrical power undertakings of existing Ontario Companies.' These instructions represented a fairly tall order but, if followed, the provincial government would have the information necessary for the formulation of a comprehensive power policy. The first move made by the commission seemed to be a wise one: it appointed Cecil B. Smith, an acknowledged authority, as its engineering expert. Adam Beck, taking the bit in his mouth, was off and running.[37]

With this second inquiry into the hydroelectric power question begun – the municipally appointed commission of 1903 was continuing its labours – the premier could devote more thought to another problem before his government: the administrative tangle at the University of Toronto. This difficulty had been placed before the public as a consequence of a senate investigation – headed by Meredith – into charges that Loudon was guilty of favouritism in awarding fellowships. The senate report, in May 1905, had strongly recommended that the overburdened president be relieved of some lesser responsibilities and that his office be strengthened by a clear definition of his powers. In June, an Alumni Association committee suggested greater centralization of university government and increased freedom from political interference for the institution. Adoption of the latter point was constantly pushed by the *Globe*,which also argued for higher faculty salaries and a stronger administration.[38]

Clearly, there was a call for action on the matter and, throughout the summer of 1905, the Conservative leader gave more thought to the constitution of the commission that would thoroughly investigate the University of Toronto. He discussed the subject with Goldwin Smith, while Meredith kept prodding the premier for action. By late September, Whitney had reached some conclusions: 'I have delayed a little about the composition of the University Commission,' he wrote to Meredith. 'After a good deal of fussing on my part, because nobody has interfered with me, I have decided tentatively on the names. Perhaps I might have done better, but ... I will have the satisfaction of knowing that they were chosen by myself.' He hoped that Joseph W. Flavelle would serve as chairman, and the rest of the group would consist of Meredith, Byron E. Walker of the Bank of Commerce, Goldwin Smith, Canon H.J. Cody, the Reverend D.B. Macdonald, and A.H.U. Colquhoun who would serve as secretary. All agreed to participate and, on 2 October, the make-up of the commission was made public.[39]

The terms defining the scope of the inquiry were broad; the committee was to report on:

(a) A scheme for the management and government of the University of Toronto in the room and stead of the one under which the said University is now managed and governed.

(b) A scheme for the management and government of University College, including its relation to and connection with the said University of Toronto.

(c) The advisability of the incorporation of the School of Practical Science with the University of Toronto.

(d) Such changes as in the opinion of the Commissioners should be brought about in the relations between the said University of Toronto and the several Colleges affiliated or federated therewith, having regard to the provisions of the Federation Act.

(e) Such suggestions and recommendations in connection with or arising out of any of the subjects thus indicated as in the opinion of the said Commissioners may be desirable.

Although there was wide approval of the Tory leader's action, not everyone was pleased. Only hours before the public announcement of the commission's creation, President Loudon had suggested that the time seemed 'opportune for the re-organization of the University.' Failing to see – or acknowledge – that matters were now out of his hands, he proposed striking 'a small committee' to examine the problem and make recommendations; his group would have consisted of himself, Meredith, and Smith. Loudon's desire for reform was too little too late: he would have to sit on the sidelines, watching the commission tackle the job.[40]

The vice-president of the Alumni Association cast a critical eye over the members of the new body and suggested that the academic element might have been strengthened by the inclusion of educational experts from Harvard or Cambridge; and, while content with the business representatives on the investigating team, he was not happy with the choice of Cody and Macdonald as alumni representatives. Definitely miffed by such criticism, Whitney counter-attacked:

the Commission is instructed to enquire into the merits of other systems and report a new system, having regard to the conditions that prevail here. In doing this the Commission will necessarily avail itself of the knowledge of various gentlemen such as those whose names you mention. But I am bound to say it would never occur to me to suggest that men from Oxford, or Cambridge, or perhaps even Harvard, should lay down a scheme for the management of our University. So far from agreeing with you I am afraid that I should consider their presence on the Commission a decided weakness.

Pride in province, inherent in those place-of-birth figures, dictated that Ontarians would shape their own university! As for his selection of those two clergymen 'to represent the graduates,' the premier noted: 'Considering the present atmosphere which surrounds University matters I apprehend any choice made by even an angel from Heaven, for instance, would not be considered suitable by many graduates.' And Whitney was sufficiently humble to know he lacked angelic inspiration in his decisions.[41]

Methodist president Nathanael Burwash of Victoria College was distressed by the prospect of products of Wycliffe and Knox Colleges – Cody and Macdonald respectively – sitting on the commission; in his view, those two institutions were 'not deeply interested in the federation policy' under which Victoria had moved to Toronto. The premier tried to reassure Victoria's worried head that the government would do nothing 'which would interfere in the slightest degree with the situation or the rights of any College under the Federation Act.' He continued by criticizing Burwash for raising the question of religious representation on the commission, observing that the pair in question were not appointed because of their denominational affiliations. After all, commission members would belong to some church, but that was not the basis of selection; otherwise the Tory leader would have had to 'choose a representative of every Church in this Province.' This argument, however, may have been designed to draw Burwash away from hic chief complaint – and put him on the defensive – because the Methodist really had raised the question not of religious representation but rather of college representation.[42]

In any event, Burwash remained unhappy, and delivered a short lecture to Whitney on the attempt which had been made to 'force' Victoria 'into the position of a federated theological college like Knox and Wycliffe,' and on the manner in which Victoria had battled to remain above this level. He insisted that Cody and Macdonald, because of their backgrounds, might well take a negative attitude towards the system of federated colleges. The premier finally resorted to a private interview in an effort to calm Burwash's fears. But the Methodist's concerns may have been rooted in factors other than those to which he gave expression. J.P. Sheraton of Wycliffe, writing to Cody, threw a rather different light on Burwash's behaviour, noting that he had reversed field in the matter of government appointments to the university's governing bodies. Burwash had argued, in defence of his shift of position, that much had changed in the last four years, but Sheraton cuttingly noted that one of those changes meant that Burwash 'no longer has the influence with the Government that he had with the Ross Government.' The Methodist leader had lost his friends at court, and was genuinely fearful of what the Tories might do. Nevertheless, Burwash did have the makings of a point: J.W. Flavelle, who was named chairman when Smith refused, was the only Methodist on the commission; the rest, save for the godless Smith, were either Anglicans or Presbyterians. In terms of denominational affiliation, the commission looked more like the cabinet than the population of Ontario. Clearly, Whitney was not very close to the province's large Methodist constituency; but, then, many of its members had never been very close to the Tory chieftain.[43]

Given that the criticism of the commission thus far had centred on its composition – indeed, there was nothing else to criticize at this juncture – it was obvious that this body had its work cut out for it, and that work could not begin until Walker returned in late November from a trip to England.[44]

v

While Whitney attended to the hydro and university commissions, the liquor question continued to pop up at almost every turn – like a spook in a midway fun-house – in part because it was necessary to administer existing legislation and to appoint local inspectors. From the day he set foot in the premier's office, Whitney was troubled – he might have said tormented – by temperance deputations and showered with gratuitous advice. Thus confronted, he made his position plain from the start: the existing licence law, whatever its defects, would 'be properly enforced.' He was convinced that the Conservative party owed little to either the 'machine temperance men' or 'the liquor men' for its January triumph, but it did have a duty to provide 'efficient administration of the law.' The premier also hinted that, after due consideration, it might be necessary to alter or replace the existing liquor legislation.[45]

Provincial secretary W.J. Hanna outlined government policy in a letter to all licence commissioners and inspectors. They were bluntly told that political considerations were not to influence their decisions about applications for licences, and they were informed that the best managed hotels should be given preference. 'In many Counties,' Hanna remarked, 'there are places called hotels which are merely drinking places, the bar being the first consideration and accommodation for man and beast but secondary. Make the licensees of such places live up to the requirements or refuse their licenses. Make them keep hotel!' These instructions were followed by legislation which absolutely prohibited the sale of liquor to minors; which increased the cost of a licence transfer to 50 per cent of the licence's cost; and which provided that the fines received as a result of any prosecution initiated by the licence department should go to that bureau and not to the licensee's municipality. The new administration, although scarcely prohibitionist, was definitely moving to tighten up the enforcement and administration of Ontario's liquor laws.[46]

The appointment of licence commissioners and inspectors provided more grist for debate than did the administration of legislation. The board of licence commissioners in each electoral district was appointed for a year and, although the posts were without remuneration, appointments to them were a means of distributing 'prestige' patronage. The office of licence inspector was another matter, because its holder received a salary of about five hundred dollars per annum and, in Whitney's view, had to be reappointed annually.[47]

When the Conservatives came to power they discovered that it was necessary to appoint two hundred and seventy-five commissioners. This they proceeded to do, and while Whitney took pains to be sure that the new appointees were honest and reliable men, it was also evident that most were Conservatives. Thus the administration was open to charges of partisan conduct, but the premier's policy was best described by himself as he faced the problem of naming men for his own constituency: 'My sole endeavour,' he said, 'has been to choose men the mere mention of whose names will be a guarantee to the community that they will do their duty.' He did not want 'liquor or temperance men,' rather he sought 'good honest citizens' who would 'enforce the law without reference either to private opinions or political views.' 'One of the men you suggest as Commissioner is a good man,' he informed a Dundas County supporter, 'but hardly up to the required standard.' And the premier insisted upon the 'required standard' when his supporters put forward names for their respective constituencies. The Conservative leader lectured one man to whom he offered a commissionership: 'No license should be granted, and no license refused for political reasons. No matter what the Commissioner's individual opinion may be of the License Law he should endeavor faithfully to carry out the law.' 'Once the commissioners take office,' he continued, 'they are practically supreme, and cannot be interfered with either by the Government or by any other influence.'[48]

The Conservatives also moved on the licence inspectors and the initial removal of those who had been active Liberal partisans was followed by the dismissal of most of the others. It could not be disputed that this was top-to-bottom Tory housecleaning, but Whitney stoutly defended the action: 'The Government will be held responsible for the acts of these officials. Therefore, it must be expected that the Government will appoint men in whom it has confidence.' In the past, he argued, with some exceptions commissioners and inspectors had used the law 'openly and undisguisedly as a political weapon.' That, he contended, was 'a greater evil than the inefficient enforcement of the law.' The appointment of new inspectors meant that the government would 'know whether it was being properly served or not.'[49]

There were complaints about the government's dismissals, but most accepted the decision, some with grumbling, until the trio of Toronto commissioners – newly appointed in April and headed by Methodist Joseph Flavelle – suddenly resigned in late November, amidst a barrage of charges. The cause of the storm had been the government's firing of Toronto's chief inspector and his assistants without bothering to consult the commissioners. That trio claimed that the inspector had been efficient in his duties and that his dismissal was nothing but a rank grab for patronage by the Conservatives. The *News*, owned by Flavelle and edited by Willison since 1903 and thus far a supporter of Whitney, flayed the Conservatives, while the premier blustered that his government did not have to consult the commissioners before taking such action. But his critics insisted that he had yielded to pressure from that patronage-minded politician, Beattie Nesbitt; that he had been forced to throw the party's old-style politicians something, and he had thrown them the inspector. The new government could no longer be regarded as virginal.[50]

The Conservative leader was not particularly alarmed by the hubbub that had arisen, except for a concern that Flavelle might also take his leave of the university commission. After a ninety-minute interview with the premier, however, the Toronto meat-packing entrepreneur remained in the more important post. Whitney offered the opinion that the whole affair had occurred because the government had lifted Flavelle 'up so high that the lighter atmosphere may possibly have affected him.' The moralizing tone of the *News* did give the premier some offence and he remarked that the 'row ... would be laughable were it not for the rascally manner in which the "News" ... treated the Government and the falsehoods it ... publish[ed].' But the battle of words raged on, and Whitney grew annoyed. 'The funny part of the trouble over the dismissals,' he told one correspondent, '... is that these thin-skinned Commissioners were ready to take the place of men who were dismissed without any reason whatever; and also the fact that the dismissals of Inspectors all over the Province without any reason given had no effect upon their sensibilities until the Toronto ones were reached.' The high-minded Methodist had just run into the pragmatic Anglican.[51]

Whitney maintained a public silence on the issue, trusting that it was better 'to let the matter alone,' but in a letter to his brother Albert he vigorously denied that Beattie Nesbitt had been behind the affair, as charged by the *News*. He also noted a fringe benefit from the uproar: 'You can understand that the mere dismisal of these men here has acted as a tonic on all our friends in the Province who were growling because we did not dismiss officials.' Willison of the *News* had 'simply lost his head,' because the 'Chief License Inspector ... was an intimate friend and chum of his.'[52]

This brouhaha raised the matter of patronage as administered by the new Tory government. After thirty-four years in the wilderness, many party stalwarts were convinced that they had arrived in the promised land and that occupation of the territory could be expedited by throwing out all the Grits. The government, however, was not so vindictive and, generally speaking, maintained its balance while under a good deal of highly partisan pressure. Office-holders did change, with Liberals departing and Conservatives arriving, but the turnovers were seldom excessive. 'I ... note what you say with regard to some of our friends who object to appoint[ing] Grits to the Magistracy,' Whitney told a supporter, 'I am sorry to hear of this, because the position is undignified and unfair, and without going further it is a proof of ignorance of our British system of Government on the part of those who object. In my opinion at least one third of the Magistrates should be chosen from our political opponents.' In adopting such a course, the premier was not going to be influenced by earlier Liberal actions, because he was not in power 'to follow in their footsteps.' Any Conservative legislator who disliked the policy simply lacked 'the requisite backbone.'[53]

When a whining letter arrived from a disappointed patronage-seeker, the premier would reply telling the malcontent that if he had worked for the party in hopes of 'material reward' and not something of 'a higher nature,' then his leader was sorely disillusioned. Whitney did not intend to make room for Tories by dismissing someone 'from an important position without some good reason.' He even tried, with mixed effect, to shame some office-seekers into an embarrassed retreat. In the face of this barrage of requests, Whitney's patience with supplicants soon wore thin. 'It is impossible to describe the rush for office,' he complained to a Morrisburg doctor, '... I am bound to say that half the satisfaction which I have taken in the splendid record we have been able to make has been taken away by my realization of the craze which has taken possession of our people on this subject.'[54]

Irritated, the Conservative leader soon vented his annoyance, first on Beattie Nesbitt and then on Sam Hughes. The representative for Toronto North prepared a long list of officials whom he wanted discharged and an equally long list of proposed successors, and then paid a visit to the premier. Whitney, after a few congenial words with Nesbitt, discovered the purpose of the doctor's appointment. The ensuing eruption rattled the office door as he roared at a startled Nesbitt: 'Get to hell out of this office! Never come to me with such a proposal again.'[55]

Sam Hughes had twice suggested to Whitney during the first six months of the administration's life that Conservatives were not happy with the premier's control of patronage and distribution of jobs, but Whitney had brushed aside the complaints. In mid-September, however, the two men staged a public verbal brawl on the subject when Hughes, with his customary egocentricity and prejudice, bluntly informed the premier that he was appointing 'many micks' to public office. Whitney exploded, labelling Hughes a religious bigot, and the two parted, the Tory chief in a state of high anger and Hughes sorely wounded. Hughes was not vanquished, however, and pursued his point by letter in which he cleared himself (to his satisfaction) of the charge of being anti-Catholic. 'I have never objected to any man of any religious belief – being placed in a position,' he wrote, 'provided he were *qualified* over others. I have a record which you would do well to imitate ... The first appointment I ever made was a Roman Catholic. Not thank goodness because of so called *religion*, but because ... of fitness and party loyalty.' Whitney, he charged, was handing important positions to Catholics of dubious political fidelity and thus depriving hard-working – and Protestant – Conservatives of jobs. The premier replied that Hughes was talking 'childish nonsense,' and invited the egotistical Tory to drop by, when he was next in Toronto, and 'have it out.' Patronage, or the expectation of it, might be the glue of party unity, but the new premier was discovering that it could be extremely sticky in other ways. Only occasionally could Whitney take comfort in a letter which saluted him for 'resisting the spoils system.'[56]

VI

While subjects ranging from the University of Toronto to patronage demanded Whitney's time in his early months in office, yet another matter required urgent attention: resolution of the problem resulting from the blanket claims made by greedy speculators in the silver-rich Cobalt region in 1904, which prevented legitimate prospectors from having access to the region by the time the Tories had assumed office. In this task the premier now had the assistance of his new minister of lands and mines, Frank Cochrane, and action followed:

Pending an overall examination of policy, the Whitney government revived a hitherto ignored section of the Mines Act first introduced in 1897 which forbade anyone staking a claim unless he had actually discovered a vein, lode, or other deposit of mineral. By another order-in-council, on July 14, 1905, the government appointed a corps of competent mining engineers to inspect every claim. Rigorous examination quickly dissolved the Cobalt monopoly. Unless the licensee could prove his discovery to the satisfaction of an inspector, the mining recorder refused to grant a patent and threw open the property once again to legitimate prospectors.

As Whitney noted, the government had moved to protect 'the ordinary prospector ... as against the speculator or syndicate.' But this action only met a particular problem; still ahead lay the formulation of a permanent mining policy, including the method of taxing the industry.[57]

The Morrisburg lawyer's elevation to the premiership naturally brought him into closer contact with other provincial leaders, and with Sir Wilfrid Laurier and Robert Borden. He soon found himself engaged in correspondence with Lomer Gouin, premier of Quebec, on the subject of the federal subsidies paid to Ontario. Although expressing some reservations about upsetting the original financial 'arrangements between the Federal Government and the Provinces,' Whitney thought that a 'rearrangement' was now necessary in light of post-Confederation settlements with other provinces. The Ontario premier then turned to Laurier, requesting that he set 'a reasonably early date' for a dominion-provincial conference in order to discuss financial and related matters. The dominion prime minister did not choose to rush a reply.[58]

The question of the extension of provincial boundaries through the Territory of Keewatin to Hudson Bay was raised during 1905, when newborn Saskatchewan made an appeal for an outlet on that body of water. This prompted Manitoba to ask for a piece of any land that was going to be divided and Whitney, in turn, made it plain that Ontario also wanted its share, although the province already owned seashore on James Bay. Faced by the domino effect of Saskatchewan's request, the federal government temporarily shelved these petitions by incorporating the District of Keewatin into the Northwest Territories and removing it from the governance of the lieutenant-governor of Manitoba. Before the matter was thus concluded for the moment, Whitney was made more wary of Laurier, thanks to Borden's information that the federal Liberals had in mind a narrow grant of the Hudson Bay shore to Ontario.[59]

The federal and provincial leaders of the Conservative party had been on good terms ever since the former's acceptance of his position as national chief; but Whitney's triumph in Ontario provided Borden with a loyal supporter who could now bring a large measure of strength and influence with him. When Borden had been personally defeated in the 1904 federal election, he had seriously contemplated quitting his position, and had even gone the length of offering an informal resignation to some caucus members at a Montreal meeting. But, urged on by his compatriots and shaking himself free of a defeatist mentality, he had decided to continue as leader of the opposition. Borden had informed Whitney that the Ontario chieftain was largely responsible for his fresh resolution: he had been persuaded that his 'retirement at this juncture would result in a condition which would not improve and might materially prejudice [Whitney's] prospects of success.' That, surely, was a misleading distillation of the complex factors which had kept Borden at his post, but it was flattering to Whitney and a mark of the federal chief's respect for his provincial counterpart.[60]

Despite that apparent vote of confidence in Borden, elements in the party continued to be restless, and it was suggested that there might be a Conservative convention in order to get 'the party leadership into proper hands.' Failing this, one observer thought the party might best be served by 'four or five first-class funerals.' The ongoing unease meant that, in late July, Whitney found his name being bandied about as a possible federal leader; he immediately denied any intention of entering national politics and testified to Borden's abilities. Nevertheless, the Ontario premier's performance still drew admiring glances from those unhappy with Borden, and Whitney once more had to battle for the federal leader. The occasion was an October banquet given in Whitney's honour by the Jacques Cartier Club of Montreal, ostensibly because, true to his word, he had appointed a French-Canadian to his cabinet. To his dismay the premier discovered that the invitation had deeper implications. Early in 1905, the club's officers had quarrelled with Borden over a grant which they had sought from party funds and which he had blocked. Angered by this action, they had discussed the desirability of new blood at the top, and finally had arranged the Whitney banquet, possibly to scrutinize the Ontarian's potential for the federal leadership. Whitney had agreed to attend the dinner, under the impression that Borden would be present, but shortly before the set date he discovered that the national chief had not been invited. Whitney then refused to come. 'There were alarums & excursions & in the end Borden interposed and induced Whitney to accept. Whitney, however, made an entirely unreported and exceedingly forcible speech to them in private. Borden was formally invited & sent a telegram of regrets.' Word leaked out, however, that in addition to reviewing Ontario politics and saluting the Conservative party, the premier had paid particular tribute to the national leader. Borden indeed had a faithful supporter in Whitney.[61]

Following this firm demonstration of loyalty, Whitney began the arduous chore of preparing for the coming year's session and, as a consequence, tried to avoid banquets and receptions like the plague. There was much to be done but, as his first year in office drew to a close, he could take pride in what had been accomplished. He was never in danger of being too satisfied, however, because Meredith was always at hand to prick the bubble of contentment: 'Dont you think some of your departments require waking up? There is in some of them as much red tape and delay as at Ottawa or under the old regime in this Province. I thought that a new order of things had come in with the Millenium [sic] ushered in a few months ago.' Humility and common sense would not allow Whitney to have his young era portrayed as 'the Millennium'; he could be content with 'a new order of things.'[62]

5

'Bold Enough to Be Honest': 1906

I

When the exhausting legislative session of 1906 was drawing to a close, Whitney looked back over its weeks of work and boasted to his old friend Andy Broder: 'In the history of the Province there has been no Session in which there has been half as much important legislation proposed and enacted and we all naturally feel more or less comfortable on that score.' Such a proud assessment was neither inappropriate nor inaccurate: in three months, the government had cut a wide swath through the social fields of education and liquor control, and the economic areas of transportation, mining, and hydroelectric power.[1]

'I told the people upwards of two hundred times on the platform,' wrote the premier in defending changes in the public school act, 'that the reform and improvement of the educational system would be the first question to which we would turn our attention.' So it was that Pyne, with Whitney at his elbow, began the legislative moves designed to refurbish the quality and restructure the organization of Ontario's educational system. Rural schools in particular, the minister contended, had fallen below expected standards of excellence in terms of teachers and equipment. The decline had been precipitated by rural depopulation and urban growth, the unattractiveness of country teachers' salaries, and the beckoning prospects and money offered in the rapidly growing prairie provinces. The net result had been a proliferation of rural teachers holding temporary certificates, far more 'than concern for the welfare of the schools could justify.' And penny-pinching rural school boards frequently compounded the problem. Salaries 'in some places in Ontario,' the ministry observed,

are now actually lower than they were ten or fifteen years ago, notwithstanding the increased cost of living. To-day we must pay the man who splits our wood at least $1.50 a day; we can get a teacher – a poor one, indeed – at less than a dollar a day. The cause is not far to seek; many sections market their schools and take the cheapest (and generally the poorest) applicant. Some years ago, when there were forty or fifty applicants for nearly every vcancy, the standard was not at once raised. Under-bidding lowered salaries, and this inevitable result has in turn become the cause of our present distress.[2]

Not surprisingly, money formed part of the government's answer to these difficulties. A special grant was made to rural schools in order to improve salaries. But, conscious of the fact that a miserly board might grab the grant and add nothing – or, worse still, cut its contribution – the government ordered that the special grant had to be matched by the counties, and the township levy was increased by law. A sliding salary scale that rested on assessment values was devised, enabling the minister to state that this would mean a minimum salary of five hundred dollars where there was but one teacher, with at least three hundred dollars for assistants. All this arithmetic resulted in an average increase of about one hundred dollars for country pedagogues. The new rules were designed to prevent school sections – 'a very large number' in the opinion of the department – from 'spending far less than they are able,' and, of course, to attract and keep good teachers in rural settings. The legislation left little to chance or good will; compulsion was the order of the day in an effort to raise teaching standards and improve school accommodation and equipment. Should a teacher opt to sign for less than the minimum, the school inspector was free to lift the miscreant's certificate. And the inspectors themselves found their salaries increased and their job security better protected.[3]

To meet the need for improved teaching qualifications and standards, additional normal schools – the number was not specified in the legislation but became four by year's end – were to be created; these, with the three already in existence, would become the chief producers of elementary school teachers holding second-class certificates. This meant the gradual abolition of county and city model schools, which Whitney judged werc 'utterly incapable of doing the work which they ought to do.' Only a handful of district model schools in poorer areas would be retained and 'made thoroughly efficient'; but the expectation here was that they, too, would ultimately disappear. And so would the holders of third-class certificates. In this scheme of things, possessors of first-class certificates and high school assistants would emerge from the new faculty of education at the University of Toronto.[4]

The administrative side of the department was also revamped in a second piece of legislation. Pyne already had a new deputy minister in the shape of A.H.U. Colquhoun, the secretary of the University of Toronto commission who had been an editor with the Toronto *News*. But now there would be a superintendent of education possessed of sweeping powers: he would have 'the general supervision and direction of all classes of provincial, high, public and separate schools, the professional training schools and examinations for teachers of said schools, the art schools, the public libraries and the inspectors of said schools and libraries.' When the legislation had become law, John Seath, the inspector of high schools since 1884, assumed the new post; started by that move, a game of educational musical chairs then ensued at lower levels in the department. The second major administrative change came in the form of a new advisory council, consisting of seventeen members to be elected by university senates; public, high, and separate school teachers; and public school inspectors. This body would form a consultative committee to advise, but not direct, the minister. Further, the council would 'also exercise such executive powers in connection with the university and departmental examinations as may be conferred upon it by the senate of the University of Toronto and the department of education, respectively.' The goal in these administrative changes was improved departmental organization and productivity, as well as higher educational standards throughout the province.[5]

Finally, under this legislation the government secured the power to create commissions of inquiry into educational matters, the first item on this list being, as everyone knew, the issue of contracts, character, and prices of textbooks. This body was soon given form with T.W. Crothers of St Thomas serving as chairman, John A. Cooper of the *Canadian Magazine* as commissioner, and A.C. Casselman as secretary. G. Lynch Staunton and J.A. Macdonald would act as government counsels. The textbook commission began its labours in mid-September, hearing witnesses and burrowing through the prices and contracts of the Canada Publishing Company, W.J. Gage and Company, and the Copp, Clark Company; this trio composed what an irritated G.N. Morang had once termed the schoolbook 'ring.'[6]

Although these bills were converted into law under Pyne's stewardship, Whitney was far from silent during the ensuing debates. He was quick to point out that the new consultative council was not just the 'development of an old idea,' as Richard Harcourt insisted: the old committee, Whitney asserted, had been 'appointed by government, whereas the new body would now be elective,' giving the teachers a much stronger voice in their field of endeavour. The public was expecting 'great things' of his government, which was going to meet those expectations with, among other items, a textbook commission. 'We propose,' the premier said, 'to find out what will be a proper, reasonable price for school books in this province, and, when we find that out, we propose to see to it, that the people of the province shall receive text books at that price.' It was a little difficult to tell whether this legislation was the property of the minister or his leader.[7]

Behind the scenes, however, Whitney took an even tougher stand in dealing with some of his rural members who, reflecting the views of their farming constituents, grumbled about the compulsory features of the legislation and its accompanying price tag and argued that a 'moral suasion' campaign would have produced positive results. 'Every law means coercion and compulsion,' he lectured one Tory representative. There would always be a 'certain amount of objection' whenever any law asked the public to pay, he continued, but 'with proper explanations' there would be 'no perceptible opposition' to the education legislation. Anyway, the government would 'not recede from its position.' If Ontarians had changed their minds and did not desire an improved educational system, and Tory supporters in the house refused to stand by them, 'the result will of course be that the Government will resign and our opponents will come in. The responsibility will then rest on the proper shoulders.' As often was the case, once Whitney had turned aside specific criticism with warm argument and blunt threat, he then proceeded to generalization. On this occasion he reminded his complaining follower of a legislator's responsibilities – as he saw them: 'The Members of the Legislature must not imagine that their duty is simply that of delegates to repeat what they hear in their own localities and nothing more, because if that were so, any man could be sent up to the Government from time to time with messages. The duty of the Legislature is to help to show the people what it is right to do in the interests of the people themselves.' 'Evidence of slight dissatisfaction' should not cause a member to run for cover; rather, it should push him 'to show the facts to the people.' Implicit in this firm stance, of course, was the assumption that the premier and his government were right.[8]

II

If Whitney had had to play second fiddle to Pyne in public school affairs, save for the vital chore of whipping recalcitrant members into line, he was not obliged to accept a junior role when it came to the fate of the University of Toronto. The commission which he had appointed in the previous autumn to examine that institution had its report completed in remarkably short time – about six months – and the document was ready for presentation to the legislature. 'The labours of the Commission,' its members explained,

... have been directed not to the severing of the connection between the University and the State ... but to submit such changes of administrative machinery as may tend to harmonize and unify its somewhat disjointed parts and lend new vitality to the whole system. A method has been sought by which the Province might adapt from the experience of other State institutions. ... We have been mindful of the fact that the University of Toronto, although faulty in its scheme of government, has a history and tradition peculiarly its own. ...

Nor should it be overlooked that the future expansion of the University, not less than its present needs, is a consideration of vital moment. We have a right to assume that in the years to come the University of Toronto will more and more assert its influence in the national life of Canada ... A scheme of government created to-day must keep in view the gradual but certain enlargement of half a century hence.[9]

After an examination of the history of the institution and a review of its present circumstances, the report advanced the recommendations over which the commissioners had laboured. They concluded that 'the powers of the Crown in respect to the control and management of the University should be vested in a Board of Governors, chosen by the Lieutenant-Governor-in-Council'; 'the Senate

... based upon the principle of representation of the federated and affiliated institutions and the faculties and graduates, should direct the academic interests of the University'; 'the School of Practical Science should be united with the University as its Faculty of Applied Science and Engineering, and the same ... connection should, as far as practicable, apply to the relations of the Faculty of Medicine to the University'; 'University College should continue as ... constituted, with a Principal, Faculty Council and Registrar of its own'; 'there should be created, a Council of the Faculty of Arts composed of the Faculties of all the Arts Colleges and representatives of the federated Colleges, and a Council for each Faculty'; 'there should be created a Caput or advisory committee, having authority in certain matters of University discipline'; 'the Office of Chancellor should be retained'; 'the office of Vice-Chancellor should no longer exist'; and 'the office of President should be clothed with additional powers.' Other suggestions were also advanced, including recommendations for the creation of law, forestry, art, and music schools. Security of tenure for full professors and higher salaries for all teaching staff were also proposed.[10]

The report did not ignore the necessity of financing the operation of the institution and, after projecting what demands would be made of the provincial legislature over the next three years, the commissioners thought that a percentage of the succession duties should be set aside for the use of the university. Since the revenue from these duties had risen steadily in recent years, with the exception of 1902, the commission obviously had an increasing yearly grant in mind. It suggested two hundred and seventy-five thousand dollars as the amount of the initial annual allotment.[11]

Within a month, the government had legislation based almost entirely on the report ready for presentation to the legislature. Whitney introduced the new measure, which incorporated all the major recommendations of the commission except the proposal for an endowment of a million acres of northern Ontario lands. In moving the house into committee to consider the bill, the premier constantly referred – for almost an hour – to the commission's report, noting 'he had no apology to make for quoting so extensively ... because the government endorsed practically all its conclusions.' The premier did cut the amount of the initial grant to two hundred and fifty thousand dollars, to be taken from succession duties, and indicated that future allowances from this source would be equal to a set percentage of these duties, with that quarter of a million dollars used as the base to fix the percentage. The university could thus reasonably expect a growing yearly subsidy.[12]

Although the board of governors was to be selected by the government of the day, Whitney insisted that political interference was now impossible under the new arrangement, that the university was finally out from under the shadow of Queen's Park and 'on a sure and firm basis.' He also made it perfectly clear that Loudon would be replaced as president and that the search for his successor had virtually begun. There was little for the opposition to say. It muttered about state benevolence drying up private assistance and defended the Liberal treatment of the institution, but voted with the government at every major step. There was but one matter to mar the evening on which the new legislation was first fully discussed: a large number of empty chairs in the legislative chamber. George Ross had a reasonable excuse – he was ill – but many others, Tories and Liberals, were wining and dining at a banquet tendered to lawmaker residents by a grateful Walker House. The university was not quite a burning issue with some of the premier's followers. The absentees also illustrated the problem of keeping legislators in their seats when the government possessed a forty-seat majority. For someone consigned to the back benches under these circumstances, a convivial dinner was much more attractive than academic fare.[13]

But despite this revealing lack of interest, the University of Toronto legislation must be ranked as one of the major achievements of the Whitney era. It provided the institution with a foundation for growth in the twentieth century and it represented a complete break with almost every aspect of Liberal policy towards the University of Toronto. By accepting most of the recommendations of an exceptional group of public-spirited commissioners, Whitney may well have been the greatest friend the institution has ever had. And he took this action when it counted for little in terms of popular support – witness the members of his own caucus – although a number of prominent Liberals discovered that their usual words about Conservatives were severely tempered by the premier's legislation. From Whitney's standpoint, of course, there was nothing wrong in so blunting Liberal criticism and weakening Grit resolve: it was always better to fight a foe who found himself off-balance and hesitant with his punches.

As the lavish praise rolled in, the premier showed understandable pride in his achievement, a major progressive act. 'I shall always feel,' he observed to G.M. Wrong, 'that nothing can come to me in the future which will equal my satisfaction … in having been permitted to put upon the Statute book very important legislation intended to make permanent the position of our University and to secure its usefulness.' He undoubtedly also felt a debt of gratitude to the man who had helped him grow to this position on the university question: W.R. Meredith. And the former party leader assisted Whitney with the measure by carefully checking the bill for errors and by suggesting alterations.[14]

The premier was not quite finished with the university, however, because he had to wrestle with the selection of those to be named to the new board of governors. Working on his own, he had made his choices when the new university legislation took effect on 15 June 1906, and it was a bright and powerful group of men: J.W. Flavelle, B.E. Walker, W.T. White, E.B. Osler, Chester Massey, and J.A. Macdonald, the *Globe* editor, whose selection was nothing if not shrewd. It was now the responsibility of this board to find a new president; Loudon's tenure, of course, would only last until his successor was secured. As it turned out, Loudon resigned in peremptory fashion in July, when he failed to secure the dismissal of the registrar with whom he had battled over the years. Principal Maurice Hutton of University College was named as acting president to fill the gap.[15]

Now at a good arm's length from the university, Whitney nevertheless took a keen interest in – and was kept posted on – the search for a president. And names for the office were suggested to him almost as soon as the university legislation was law. Howard Ferguson, a new and relatively young legislator from eastern Ontario, was one of those with recommendations, and he offered the name of Canon Cody, late of the university commission. Whitney replied, detailing his views on the qualities required for the position. 'My idea of the man who should be President,' he told the Kemptville lawyer, 'is that he be fairly well educated, very level-headed, a man who understands human nature thoroughly and who knows something of Collegiate management. In addition, he should be a man of great force of Will, not hasty in his decisions, but firm as a rock when he has come to a decision. In fact, the man whom [sic] I think is necessary might fairly be called an intellectual tyrant. If you take away any offensive meaning of the word "tyrant" you will have my exact view.' The premier had, quite unintentionally, just applied for the job: his description was largely a self-portrait. And, when Ferguson mistakenly thought Whitney meant a 'tyrannical' attitude towards the students, the Conservative chief replied: 'I had in view his dealings with the nineteen Governors. ... I mean that the President shall be a man of force of character enough to meet the opposition or antagonism of the Governors when necessary.' Not unlike a premier curbing and controlling the forceful personalities of a robust cabinet, a strong-willed Beck or a hard-headed Hendrie or a firm-minded Hanna.[16]

The board of governors pursued the hunt for a new president throughout the rest of 1906. W.R. Meredith and S.H. Blake temporarily had high hopes that they could secure the services of Dr William Osler, but Whitney was justifiably never so sanguine. Goldwin Smith became annoyed because of the delay in finding the right man and the barriers in the way: 'There is an objection to a stranger, an objection to a clergyman, an objection to one of the present staff on account of connection with cliques and quarrels. What is left?' Whitney, anxious that the best choice be made, counselled patience: 'Having regard to the difficulties which are admittedly in the way is not delay the only course to adopt?' Finally, in April of 1907, all agreed on Robert Falconer, a clergyman, a stranger, and principal of Pine Hill Presbyterian College in Halifax.[17]

III

Changes in public education produced ripples of opposition from parsimonious farmers and agitation on the part of a few nervous Tory legislators; university reform created scarcely a breath of negative comment. But alcohol regulation whipped the Whitney government into its first real political storm, from which it emerged intact but bruised. The premier approached the subject of new liquor legislation with little of the verve that marked his performance in educational matters. He disliked the whole question, not because he had any serious doubts about the changes which his provincial secretary W.J. Hanna introduced, but because entry into the field produced a spate of moralizing letters, petitions, and speeches which implied that he was in league with the devil. He wearily explained that he was 'tired of trying to establish a reasonable medium between two unreasonable extremes': absolute aridity and an alcoholic flood. He could have added that, although he never heard from drunkards and sometimes was approached by the liquor interests, the prohibitionists were always shouting in his ear. The politically and socially impossible position of the temperance people, as he saw it, and their irritating assumption that they were on the side of the angels forced the blunt premier to address them through gritted teeth. He generally kept his temper in check whether writing or talking to prohibitionists, but it is easy to sense the tension in pen or speech as he strove to remain civil.[18]

The Conservative leader was convinced that he had 'given more thought to the subject than the majority' of his fellow citizens. He had brought his 'common sense' to bear upon the problem and was of the opinion that his consequent position was the correct one. Whitney conceded that drink could produce 'evil' in a social sense, but he was not at all prepared to make a moral judgment about those who drank – of which he was one – or those who produced alcohol in its various potable forms – of which his brother, Albert, was one. He was quite willing to attempt to lessen the social evils that stemmed from liquor abuse, just as he would move 'to lessen the sufferings from poverty,' but he did not believe these evils could ever be eradicated. He was convinced that, because of legal and social factors, prohibition could not be achieved, and he had no intention of butting his head against a stone wall 'simply because a certain thing which cannot be carried out would be desirable if it could be carried out.'[19]

To Whitney's eyes, the prohibitionists carried on their campaign in total ignorance – or, worse still, deliberate neglect – of other matters that were just as pressing as alcohol regulation, if not more so. These people had incorrectly placed their objective in an exclusively prime position and, in the premier's opinion, had seriously injured their own cause as a consequence. A host of problems had to be worked out for the 'general welfare' and to see only one problem was to be wrong, dead wrong. The Conservative chief argued that, in urban centres at least, there was more drink caused by poverty than poverty by drink. This being so, he would worry about poverty first, but the prohibitionists always wanted it the other way around. He believed that the implementation of local prohibition should have obvious majority support to indicate that 'public opinion [was] behind it unmistakably.' These ideas represented the essence of Whitney's thinking on a very tricky subject, and he was confident in the knowledge that he had produced them by 'abandoning sentiment and looking at this matter in the cold light of surrounding conditions and probable results.' To his mind, to do anything else was to be unreasonable. Whitney may have been able to abandon sentiment in reaching his conclusion, but he could not discard his background. He himself had been a drinker from a fairly early age, and he was of a church which, although it had prohibitionists within its ranks (such as his own caucus member W.K. Mc-Naught), had never made a clear statement on prohibition. His views might have been differently coloured had he been raised a staunch Presbyterian or a devout Methodist. And, to be fair to the prohibitionists, it must be noted that numbers of them laboured for other reforms – female suffrage and urban improvement, for example – but the premier chose to see them as single-minded since temperance was the subject with which they constantly belaboured him.[20]

Thus, although the Methodist provincial secretary, W.J. Hanna, introduced the new liquor legislation during the 1906 session, much of its content directly reflected Whitney's thinking on the subject. Under this proposed measure licence fees for taverns and shops were dramatically increased on a graduated scale that was tied to population. In cities over one hundred thousand – Toronto being the sole member of this group – tavern licences would cost twelve hundred dollars and shop licences one thousand; in cities over thirty thousand, the tavern and shop permits were each seven hundred dollars. And so it went down to the township level where the owner of a tavern paid one hundred and twenty dollars, while the shopkeeper had to produce two hundred dollars. Any municipality, except a city, could increase the licence fees by any amount, provided the electors approved the appropriate by-law. One-half of all monies collected for licence fees would go to the province, one-half to the municipality concerned. It was estimated that, under the previous arrangements, licensees had paid nearly four hundred thousand dollars a year for the privilege of dispensing alcohol; now they would have to pay eight hundred thousand dollars.[21]

Large changes were made in the local option clause: if 25 per cent of the electors of a municipality indicated by petition their desire for a vote on a local option by-law then one had to occur on the same date as the municipal elections. Sixty per cent of those voting had to indicate approval – or a desire for repeal – of such a by-law before the local council could act; then the council had to legislate, unlike earlier times when it could afford the luxury of deliberate procrastination. Votes on repeal could occur every second year and, should the vote on approval fall short of the 60 per cent mark, then temperances forces had to wait two years before petitioning for another vote.

These were the major changes proposed in the liquor control legislation, but there were a host of minor ones. In cities and towns, the closing hour for taverns would be eleven p.m., except on Saturday when the set time was seven p.m.; in villages, townships, and unorganized territories, the end of service had to be at ten p.m. No bar sales could occur on Sunday. Licences would be cancelled for varying periods of time – a year was the minimum – for offences on a long list that included selling during prohibited hours, keeping a disorderly house, supplying liquor to minors, and selling to named alcoholics. Permits would be available for the sale of liquor on sailing vessels and railway dining cars. In the cities and towns of southern Ontario, bartenders had to be licensed – for a two-dollar fee – and be 'of good character.' Women were forbidden to tend bar. Finally, 'licensees ... [could not] enter into contracts restricting purchase of liquor'; in effect all taverns were to be 'free houses.'[22]

The legislation, designed to tighten control of alcohol sales and allow for prohibition in communities where such feeling was sufficiently strong, was met with a barrage of criticism from temperance and liquor interests. Both groups were only too eager to meet with government representatives and plead their particular cases. As it happened, the prohibitionists were first through the Queen's Park doors to meet with Hanna, Whitney, and three cabinet colleagues, because the Ontario branch of the Dominion Alliance met in convention in Toronto about a week after the legislation's introduction. The temperance workers were particularly upset by the so-called three-fifths clause, which required 60 per cent of the vote to send a municipality into the dry category. This arrangement was not, in the opinion of teetotallers' representatives, 'fair, British or honourable,' because it placed temperance forces at a distinct disadvantage, permitting the votes of two possibly wicked men to equal the ballots of three presumably good men. One 'dry' supporter put the argument to the premier:

I want to make it plain so you cannot misunderstand it. We will say you are an Episcopalian, I am a Methodist, and our first cousin is a Presbyterian. There is a certain case to be tried in court. We three are witnesses on one side, and we all swear that such and such a thing took place in a certain house, at a certain time.

Now for the defence, a hotel-keeper and a customer of his swear that this did not happen.

Now the magistrate on the bench dismisses the case, from the fact that the Ontario Government has passed a law, that the evidence of two men, that would scarcely be considered reliable, is equal to the evidence of three reliable men.

That is what I understand the three-fifths vote for Local Option in the New License Act means. ...

Would it not be wiser to withdraw the bill altogether for this year, than to pass it with that three fifths clause in it[?]

The prohibitionists were also opposed to that section which allowed a vote on repeal of local option in two years, 'an unreasonably short period.' The clauses permitting the peddling of alcoholic drinks on steamboats and railway diners were judged 'entirely retrogressive features that public opinion had not asked for, and does not approve.' These complaints, but particularly the injustice wrought by the three-fifths clause, were the heart of the letters and petitions which soon covered Whitney's desk.[23]

The hotel-keepers and liquor vendors soon had their turn, and about six hundred of them crowded into the main corridor of the legislative buildings to hear their advocates plead for a one-third reduction in the proposed licence fees, an extension of the weekday closing hour to midnight, compensation for licensees who lost their businesses through the initiation of local option, and an easing of the severity implicit in punishment by licence cancellation. They also sought the right to serve alcoholic beverages to hotel guests on Sunday. Despite the fact that some licensees undoubtedly saw their investments at stake in the new legislation, a note of levity was injected into the proceedings when the question of knowing a named alcoholic in a large centre was raised. This problem permitted the chief spokesman for the liquor dealers to offer a poetic definition of a drunk:

He is not drunk who from the floor
Can rise and drink and ask for more;
But he is drunk who prostrate lies
And who can neither drink nor rise.

Hanna, who again was present with the premier and a trio of cabinet members to meet the appellants and who possessed the fastest wit in the cabinet, could not resist a come-back, and so he provided his definition:

Someone had told his friend, 'When you've had enough whiskey, why don't you call for sarsaparilla.' 'The trouble is,' returned the other, 'when I've had enough whiskey I can't say sarsaparilla.'

There had been no room for such vaudeville humour when the prohibitionists had met with the provincial secretary; temperance and drunkenness had no lighter sides for the sober teetotallers. Whitney undoubtedly preferred Hanna to a roomful of Rechabites.[24]

The administration had heard, and would continue to hear, from both sides in the alcohol debate. Whitney concluded that, since prohibitionist F.S. Spence had accused the government of 'having for its motive the pleasing of the liquor people,' and since the licensees were anything but pleased, the Conservatives must be acting fairly. 'Our duty,' he had told the hotel-keepers, 'is to hold the balance as evenly as possible, and trust to the commendation of the people to tell us we are right.' It helped, of course, if the premier told that same public that the government's course was correct, something he frequently did. He insisted that this liquor control measure, 'the best legislation ever offered to the country on this question,' was 'neither unfair nor un-British.' He further noted that a vote favourable to local prohibition meant immediate enactment of an appropriate by-law and that opponents of temperance faced the 60 per cent barrier in any attempt to return a dry municipality to a wet condition.[25]

The furore was sufficient, however, to make the Tories pause and reconsider what they had proposed. After all, some irritated temperance workers at their

Toronto convention had unsuccessfully tried to secure support for a motion calling for the 'defeat of every member favorable to the three-fifths clause,' and an angry Dundas hotel-keeper, although a Conservative, had vowed to work for a trouncing of Whitney at the polls unless the government produced a compensation measure that would apply where local option succeeded. A few timid legislators suggested a retreat on the local option clause to a percentage more pleasing to the prohibition element. The premier, however, convinced that the arrangement produced a 'settled expression of public opinion,' decided that the government's position was 'unassailable' and that any change would be 'a blunder.' When the measure came up for full consideration in the legislature, a couple of Tory back-benchers criticized the size of the new licence fees, but their words were ignored, as were those of the opposition on the 60 per cent clause. Hanna made only one change of consequence in the legislation: local option could not be tested at the polls until three years, instead of two, had elapsed since its inception. There was also a crumb or two for licensees; but the three-fifths clause remained intact, as did the higher licence fees.[26]

Although Whitney and Hanna had certainly listened to the critics of this measure – indeed, the accessibility of the premier and provincial secretary to complainants is noteworthy – they had virtually not been moved, largely because the Tory chief was convinced that while tight regulation was possible, complete elimination was not. He also thought that the public approved of the general thrust of this legislation. But, in this judgment, he chose to ignore two inevitable developments: an increase in tavern and shop prices, and the consequent grumbling of imbibers. Toronto tavern-keepers, banded together under the rather impressive heading of the Toronto License Holders' Protective Association, were the first to act, boosting the amount charged for every form of alcohol they dispensed. For instance, the price of a shot of bottled Scotch or gin or Canadian whisky jumped from ten to fifteen cents. And they agreed to standardize beer glasses at the twelve-ounce size. Liquor-shopkeepers made the next move, adding a nickel or dime to the price of bottled Canadian whiskies – Seagram's Star rose from seventy-five to eighty cents, while Gooderham's Special went from ninety cents to a dollar – and ten cents to a bottle of Scotch. There were comparable increases for ales and lagers. Naturally, the dealers pointed to the rise in their licence fees, from four hundred and fifty dollars to a thousand, as being the villain of the piece, and they noted 'that the advances made were very moderate, by comparison with those of the hotelmen,' which amounted 'to about 50 per cent.' The drinking public muttered, but found solace in the bar where they assuredly discussed this matter at greater length than educational reform.[27]

IV

In addition to positive moves in the fields of education and liquor control, the Whitney administration also saw to it that the Toronto General Hospital, helped by a quarter of a million government dollars, secured a new constitution and the power to acquire land for a new building, and that improved sanitary conditions existed in Ontario's cheese factories and creameries. But, while encouraging progress in these areas, Whitney absolutely refused to countenance the grant of a provincial vote to some female Ontarians. John Smith, the member for Peel, attempted to get the legislature to contemplate, in a serious manner, giving the franchise to 'widows and spinsters qualified to vote in municipal elections.' Smith, in moving his motion, argued that 'women paid taxes, and that 90 per cent. of the public school teachers looking after child tuition were women.' The premier, in turn, accused the unfortunate Smith of 'making a football of women's status in a way discreditable to himself ... and a direct insult to women.' But he was less than clear in explaining the thinking that lay back of such remarks. Nevertheless, the Tory chief took the lead in giving the proposed measure short shrift, as his words to end the debate indicate: 'Now, if five members will stand up we can have a vote on it. Let us play the farce out.' In fact, nine stood for the measure, but sixty-six rose against it. Whitney, who thought women should not be exposed to 'the unlovely influence of party politics,' could be satisfied. Votes for women was simply not a reform issue to be considered: politics were meant for men, and vice versa.[28]

'Honest Enough to Be Bold': 1906

While the attraction and retention of competent teachers in rural schools or the virtual recreation of the University of Toronto were measures that generally evoked significant and laudatory comment about Whitney's government during the 1906 session, the administration's ventures into economic fields provoked louder responses from larger voices, not so much because more people were affected, but because more money was at stake. Thus the government's moves in the areas of transportation, mining, and hydroelectric power development were examined more critically within and without the legislature – and by later historians.

Early in the session, J.S. Hendrie introduced two pieces of legislation designed to regulate railways, especially electric railways, within the province, and to create the Ontario Railway and Municipal Board. In tackling aspects of the provincial transportation question, Hendrie was not engaged in curbing competition or aiding entrepreneurs, as was the case with some contemporary American regulatory legislation which, it has been argued, was not in the public interest but that of private capital. Rather, the measures grew, in part, out of an ongoing and acrimonious dispute between the city of Toronto and outlying radial lines, whose owners sought easy access to the provincial capital. As well, the intent was to remove from the legislature the burden of dealing with nearly every railway question by means of a separate bill, a time-consuming and inefficient method of government. And, it was hoped, the developing expertise of a board would enable it to make sound decisions, unlike those frequently reached in haste by ill-informed or heavily biased legislators.

Many Torontonians had long been suspicious, if not decidedly hateful, of the Toronto Railway Company and its principal owner, William Mackenzie. Over the years there had been numerous battles between the city and the company in the matter of fares, Sunday cars, service, roadbeds, and rental fees. Consequently, even in 1905, many politicians and people, urged on by the press, looked forward to that great day in 1921 when the thirty-year franchise possessed by Mackenzie would give up the ghost. The city would then acquire the company, it was assumed, and operate it as a municipal enterprise, undoing the harm wrought by its avaricious owners. Occasionally, someone even debated the merits of purchasing the company long before that third decade of the century arrived. Thus, in 1905, when the Toronto and York Radial Railway Company sought entrance to the city over three sets of tracks that would be laid down by the Toronto Street Railway Company, in order to meet and serve the Mimico (west), Metropolitan (north), and Scarboro' (east) lines which the Toronto and York either owned or projected, the city of Toronto balked. And for a very good reason: the Toronto and York was owned by the Toronto Railway Company. Mayor Thomas Urquhart, in meeting with representatives from York, Peel, and Ontario counties, all of whom wanted radial access to Toronto, made his city's position plain: 'the city was ready,' he declared, '... to allow the radial lines to reach the center of the city, but the [Toronto and York] Radial Company desired to have a franchise for Toronto extending beyond the time when the Toronto Railway franchise expired, and to this the city could not consent.'[1]

The city and its citizens were decidedly fearful that anything less than an ironclad guarantee with the Toronto and York would lead to 'conversion of a strictly limited franchise [for the Toronto Railway Company] into a virtually perpetual one.' The companies tried to reassure nervous Torontonians by explaining that 'the Toronto Railway Company is not asking for an arrangement which will give the company a franchise that overlaps its present franchise.' The Toronto and York, it was argued with sweet reasonableness, was simply requesting 'that the Toronto Railway Company should, on streets not now used by the Toronto Railway Company, lay down three lines of railway suited to the gauge of the radial roads, which, by the way, is standard all over the Dominion; and that the Toronto Railway Company shall take possession of the radial cars when they connect with these lines, carry them into the centre of the city and, after discharging their passengers and goods, return them to the Radial Companies at the city boundaries.' So far so good, but then came the sticking point: should Toronto acquire the Toronto Railway Company, the city would be expected 'to continue this arrangement with the Radial Companies.' There was the trap, at least in the minds of Toronto's politicians: the city would not escape Mackenzie's clutches even after the death of his city franchise, or, worse still, his monopoly might be resurrected by some unearthly means. Consequently, when York and Toronto lawyers, together with representatives from neighbouring municipalities, descended on Toronto's board of control, 'they found the [board] members ... decidedly averse to making any stipulation which would give the radial railways running rights in the city after the Toronto Railway system passes into the hands of the municipality.' 'The conference ... concluded,' the *Globe* observed, 'without one step towards a settlement of the question being made.'[2]

The impasse between city and company soon arrived on Whitney's doorstep when, on 10 May, T.H. Lennox, the Tory MPP for York North, introduced a deputation from York, Halton, and Peel counties to the premier, and argued the need for 'legislation securing the entrance of the radial roads to the city, so that persons need not transfer or produce be changed from radial to city lines in order to reach the market, the waterfront or the Union Station.' In response Toronto's legal representative rehearsed a familiar argument: the city would not make agreements binding it beyond the year 1921. The premier listened and then elaborated on a clue dropped by a talkative Adam Beck the day before: possibly 'the question might be found to be one that could be settled by the commission which the Government propose to create.'[3]

Outside the narrow confines of the dispute between Toronto and the railways, there were other factors which had moved Whitney to contemplate a railway commission. Practical political considerations dictated the need for a way out of the radial stalemate. Beyond the four Toronto legislative seats which the Tories held in a hammerlock, there were seven seats in York, Ontario, Peel, and Halton counties, of which the Conservatives claimed six. Some of these were recent acquisitions where disappointment in the radial matter might augur trouble for the government at the next election. The premier was not about to place these seats in jeopardy by ignoring the demands of these regions. Further, Toronto's fight with the Mackenzie interests was not the only railway problem to demand the attention of the legislators. In the same week that Lennox and the suburbanites attempted to squeeze legislation out of Whitney, Hendrie had to insist that an Ontario Electric Railway Bill be altered 'to protect the municipalities, which without it might find their streets turned into freight yards.' And, the next day, a measure was being considered by the private bills committee which would, if enacted, 'compel the Hamilton Street Railway Company to live up to specific agreements with the city.' It seemed that in the lobby, committee, or legislature, railways – notably electric railways – were making inordinate demands on the time of members. Just a week later, on 19 May, Whitney blocked the Toronto and York Radial Railway bill in committee when he denounced its late appearance for consideration. In cowing the railway committee into a rejection of the proposed legislation, he halted the effort of the Toronto and York to secure a perpetual franchise for its Scarboro' line – something neither the premier nor Hendrie could accept, although committee member Beattie Nesbitt had pushed hard for inclusion of this particular clause. Clearly, in the matter of railway franchises, municipalities did need protection, sometimes from themselves.[4]

The Ross government, of course, had not been free of electric railway problems and, in 1902, had created a special cabinet committee of three to deal with them. But the difficulty here was that each railway was still dealt with individually, and comprehensive guidelines were absent, except for the consistency and continuity provided by the committee's membership. When Whitney assumed office, Hendrie was given the chairmanship of the legislature's railway committee and the cabinet body did not function. But, in light of subsequent developments, this was obviously a stopgap arrangement. The premier and his cabinet not only began to develop the idea of a railway commission under the pressures which have been described; there were also other factors. The federal Board of Railway Commissioners had come into existence in 1904, and it quickly achieved a relatively high profile through public hearings as it listened to criticisms and disputes that focused on lines with national charters. As it happened, in April of 1905, just as the current quarrel between Toronto and the radials was emerging, the federal commissioners were in the city to hear the 'complaints of several shippers.' The *Globe* was quick to praise this federal Liberal creation and salute it for work accomplished by men whose 'constant thought and occupation' centred on railway difficulties. It is not surprising, therefore, that just a few days later, when Toronto and the Mackenzie interests became deadlocked, the newspaper should recommend a provincial railway commission when commenting on Hendrie's action with respect to the Ontario Electric Railway. Citing the federal example, the *Globe* called for a provincial regulatory agency that would make 'its own laws' and decide 'cases in accordance with them.' There might be, it continued, 'some reluctance toward passing under a comparatively despotic authority in such matters, but there is no other practical plan in sight for the regulation of electric railway operations or the adjustment of disputes in railway development.'[5]

In view of all these circumstances, it is scarcely remarkable that, shortly after Whitney's encounter with the Lennox-led group, York County's solicitor C.C. Robinson, Hendrie, and law officers of the legislature should commence drafting provincial railway legislation. But Whitney could not have been that pleased with their progress or satisfied with their results because, in late October of 1905, he wrote to his old leader, W.R. Meredith:

I [wish] ... some person ... would furnish me with a memo ... showing the object and purpose of a permanent Commission to be created to deal with disputes and questions affecting Railway, Telegraph and Telephone Companies etc. such as has been incidentally mentioned in conversation between you and me.

I would like such a memo. to point out clearly the scope of the authority of such a body, also the difference, if any, between the powers to be entrusted to it and those entrusted to the Dominion Railway Commission. Practically what I would like to get would be material out of which to frame a Statute creating such a Commission, and which would make me feel that success would attend the operation of it.

The fine hand of Meredith was thus likely present in the two railway measures which Hendrie unveiled before the legislature in mid-March 1906.[6]

The first of these, the so-called railway bill, represented both innovation and consolidation, and presumed the creation of the board. This legislation directly tackled the vexing dispute between Toronto and the radial companies:

The clause touching the entrance of radial railways provides that where there is now a street railway in a city or town, and there is no provision for the admission of radial roads, and if either the company or the municipality wants the radials to have an entrance, then the radials shall have the right. The right is to be subject to such terms as may be agreed upon between the two companies and the municipalities. If they cannot agree, the board settles the terms of entrance, subject to the following restrictions:

There shall not, without the consent of the municipality, be any alteration or variation of any agreement between the municipality and the existing street railway. No franchise shall be given to radials for a longer period than the unexpired term of any existing street railway franchise. At the expiration of that time the municipality and the radials may enter into an agreement for a further term not exceeding 25 years. If they cannot agree the board will make the terms. This provision as to renewal shall not interfere with any agreement or order of the board giving the city the right to take over the roadbed, etc., within the limits of the municipality.

Hendrie observed that this clause guarded 'the rights of municipalities without checking radial extension.' And the *Globe* noted that, 'from Toronto's point of view,' this was 'the most important clause of the bill,' and it largely met the city's nervous concerns about the possible extension of the Toronto Railway Company's franchise beyond 1921.[7]

The legislation, however, was not for the capital city alone, and it spoke to other important matters in its coverage of all railways, of any description, under provincial jurisdiction. All street railway franchises were limited to a maximum of twenty-five years, and municipalities could acquire them at expiration 'on payment of the actual value, to be determined by the board.' This time limitation on franchises, Hendrie argued, was intended to check the 'extraordinary agreements entered into by municipalities with railways which they desired to have upon their highways.' 'Councillors,' he continued, 'who were elected for only twelve months were often led into making contracts with roads for forty or fifty years,' and those covenants 'were often loosely and carelessly drawn.' Fares on electric railways were to be closely regulated: five cents was the maximum charge 'for any distance not exceeding three miles,' with a maximum of two cents a mile for any distance over those first three. Cheaper charges were established for children under ten and school pupils under seventeen. And, by no means least important, the government bowed to constant pressure from the Ontario Lord's Day Alliance and denied the privilege of Sunday operation to any company under provincial charter which did not already possess that right.[8]

There were fresh rules and regulations designed to standardize equipment and improve safety. The 'gauge of every railway and street railway under provincial jurisdiction' would 'be the standard gauge of 4 feet 8½ inches.' Electrically driven cars had to 'be fitted with such fenders or guards, brakes or other life-saving appliances as the board' might order. 'Summer cars built after Jan. 1, 1907' had to 'have seats facing forwards, with aisles down [the] centre.' Motormen were to have vestibules 'cut off from passengers entirely,' because as Hendrie explained with compelling logic, at 'a high speed, such as that of seventy miles an hour, ... it was necessary that the motorman should not be interfered with.' Employees had to pass tests for physical fitness and colour blindness, and were assured of 'a 12-hour stretch of rest' after any continuous duty of twenty-five hours, plus 'proper lavatories and conveniences.' Finally, it became 'unlawful for a company to contract itself out of liability for death or injury of an employe[e].'9

The decrees of the railway bill were to be enforced by the Ontario Railway and Municipal Board, the creation of Hendrie's second piece of legislation. This body, which replaced the railway committee of the executive council, would consist of three members, holding office during good behaviour and removeable only at the instance of the lieutenant-governor-in-council. Appointees to the board would thus be free from political interference unless judged guilty of serious misconduct or evident incompetence. At a later date, it was determined that the chairman should receive six thousand dollars per annum and his fellows four thousand, with the secretary not being paid more than two thousand. Commissioners were forbidden to act as officers or directors 'in any public utility or any company that has power to invest any portion of its funds in a railway company.'10

Although the board was created primarily to be the instrument for operation of the railway bill, it was given powers with respect to municipalities, aside from those directly connected to railway matters. The new agency could approve or deny municipal territorial changes which included annexations and boundary alterations, and it possessed confirmation rights with respect to municipal by-laws dealing with finance and public utilities. These provisions for jurisdiction over municipal affairs appear to have been afterthoughts, possibly drawn into the legislation by the board's powers to direct municipalities on railway subjects. The fact that members would be wearing two hats was noted by Liberal critic Thomas H. Preston of Brant South, who proposed 'the constituting of two boards, making the personnel ... the same.' Whitney, evidently recognizing that the municipal wing was less than a harmonious addition, thought Preston's notion was 'a good thing,' but for the moment the government would 'proceed along the lines suggested, and then broaden the idea.'11

The 'lines suggested' produced a powerful authority whose decision 'upon any question of fact was to be binding and conclusive upon all companies and persons in all municipalities and courts.' Only 'upon a question of jurisdiction or of law' could there be an appeal. Whitney's administration had erected a body, outside of the legislature, the likes of which had not been seen before in Ontario's history, and this marked a new step in the governance of the province: dawn on the day of the board or commission had arrived. And, to cap the agency's powers, it was given a task in the field of labour relations, serving as an arbitration board in any railway strike or lockout.12

Criticism of these two measures from the opposition benches was limited. George Ross questioned the propriety of abolishing the railway committee of the executive council and giving over its jurisdiction to a commission, thus relieving 'the government of its responsibility.' And he wondered if there would be sufficient work for a permanent board. Hendrie, in reply, cited the opinion of former attorney-general J.M. Gibson to the effect 'that the appointment of a strong board independent of the companies' was a wise move. Provincial secretary Hanna was confident that the new creation 'would find constant employment.' And George Graham weakened Liberal opposition by praising the death of the perpetual franchise. There was more unhappiness outside the legislature among 'promoters and financiers' who disliked the ban on the extension of Sunday car operations, and who were disturbed by the twenty-five-year limit on franchises. Whitney informed Hendrie that, while the minister from Hamilton was absent because of his father's illness, the government was 'badgered with attempts to amend the Bills up to the last moment.' 'And,' he continued, 'I have no doubt these attempts would have continued for a month if we had not shut down upon them on Monday.' The premier approvingly quoted a correspondent who thought they were 'good Bills' and, of greater importance, that much more would 'depend upon the way they are administered than upon the wording of them.'[13]

Administration being the key to the board's success, the selection of a chairman was not a matter to be taken lightly. But, even before the legislation was introduced, Whitney had his nominee in mind: James Leitch, a Cornwall barrister, an old crony of the party chief, and the premier's personal lawyer. The new chairman, although eight years younger than Whitney, was in large measure his contemporary. Because Whitney had broken his legal training, he was not called to the bar until 1876, the same year that Leitch was summoned. The pair, therefore, must have been law students at the same time in Cornwall. And Leitch, having served as mayor of that town from 1884 to 1886, made an unsuccessful attempt to capture the Cornwall and Stormont provincial seat for the Tories in the latter year when Whitney ran into defeat in Dundas. Leitch tried again to become an MPP in 1890, and repeated his failure. Undeterred, he attempted to retain the federal seat of Stormont and Glengarry for the Conservatives late in 1896, when the death of Catholic Dr Darby Bergin necessitated a by-election; once more the Presbyterian Leitch tasted loss. Nevertheless, he had most certainly established his Tory credentials, if not his abilities as a vote-getter, and his political activities roughly paralleled Whitney's more successful ones in the next county. Thus thwarted, Leitch turned his full attention to the law and developed a solid reputation in the field of municipal litigation. With Whitney's victory in 1905, he had certainly expected a reward, and had thought elevation to the bench might be the plum. But Whitney, seeking a man 'with backbone enough to protect the Municipal interests of the people against the monopolists,' chose the Cornwall lawyer for the chairmanship of the new board. Flattered, Leitch pledged all his energies, experience, and 'horse sense' to 'making a success of the Board.' But Whitney, while pleased to choose a man he knew and could trust, made it clear that not only was Leitch's reputation on the line, so also was the premier's: 'The chairmanship will be one of the most important positions in this Province and a great deal will be expected from him. I have taken it upon myself to use strong language as to your capacity and fitness and I have no doubt that the result will justify me.' There would be no room for pleading novelty of position as an excuse for errors.[14]

In addition to Leitch, the board consisted of Andrew B. Ingram, MP, as vice-chairman, and Henry N. Kittson. The former, from trade union ranks although he had also dabbled in real estate, was sometime president of the St Thomas Trades and Labour Council. He had been the Tory MPP for Elgin West, from 1886 to 1890, thus serving during Whitney's first appearance in the legislature; then, in 1891, he had secured election to the House of Commons for Elgin East. He was still in Ottawa when offered the board position. Kittson represented the business component of the tribunal, being president of the Central Ontario Power Company and the Victoria Mutual Fire Insurance Company. A Hamilton resident, he had once served as president of that city's board of trade and was, in all likelihood, Hendrie's nominee. Thus the board consisted of three Conservatives, two of whom had been active in politics when the premier had begun his career. Together, they represented law, labour, and business, and they came from the east, west, and centre of southern Ontario. Save for its obvious Toryism, the agency had a fine balance to it.[15]

During the first few months of its existence, the board exercised its mandate in a variety of directions, from allowing Belleville to extend its municipal gas works to ordering the London, Hamilton, and Toronto street railway companies to halt the deterioration of their respective systems through large expenditures on repairs, track construction, and new cars. The tribunal also had to intervene in labour disputes. In the instance of the July 1906 London street railway strike, one historian has judged the agency as less than effective, from labour's standpoint, because the union gained nothing from the subsequent board settlement. And only Ingram argued, in vain, that men who had been fired should be reinstated.[16]

This affair, however, was but a tempest in a teapot compared to the violent Hamilton street railway strike of November 1906, which began amidst charges of bad faith in contract matters, but which undoubtedly was bred of foul labour relations made worse by company attempts to eliminate the union. Although management attempted to keep the cars running with the use of 'scab' workers, the strikers, numbering only about one hundred and eighty men, drew large public support. Cars were damaged, sympathy processions organized, and, on one occasion, shots fired. The mayor, anxious to avoid an escalation of violence and determined not to call upon the military, urged the railway board to intercede. He need not have pressed so hard; Whitney, concerned about the deteriorating situation, had virtually ordered the tribunal to the Hamilton scene with some serious advice: 'when you meet tomorrow morning in Hamilton ... state that you are going to finish up the investigation, that you will make an order, which you hope will be obeyed, and that if it is not, you will then proceed, under the provisions of the Act, to take possession of the Railway and run it. This need not be said as a threat, but as a *mere recital* of what the proceedings will be.' The premier, sure that the public wanted results from the board under such circumstances, was pointedly calling for swift action – but he did not get it. The commissioners, possibly cowed by the poisonous atmosphere of the city, chose to withdraw from the battle when confronted by intransigence on both sides.[17]

Riots grew on this failure, with cars being destroyed – and the troops ordered in. Two major disturbances followed on 23 and 24 November, when thousands of Hamiltonians were involved. In these running street fights, the police wielded batons in 'wild' fashion, hammering 'innocent people,' while the troops employed cold steel to disperse crowds that refused to accede to the Riot Act, which was read on both occasions. Scores were injured, but the frightening dimensions of the violence pushed both sides back to the bargaining table, and an armistice was reached. Negotiations were thus resumed and, on 30 November, the contending parties agreed to arbitration by the railway tribunal while employees grudgingly returned to work.[18]

The board quickly got down to cases and heard the disputants' representatives. John M. Gibson, sometime member of the Mowat, Hardy, and Ross cabinets, put in an appearance on behalf of the Cataract Power Company, which owned the street railway operations. As an investor in the power producer, he argued that the union had taken the company 'by the throat,' and he called for an end to this 'intolerable' 'interference of the union in the affairs of the ... company.' But the commission was not significantly swayed by his appeals and, on 6 December, ordered company recognition of the union, while accepting the street railway's position on wages and hours. The imposed agreement was binding on both parties for three years.[19]

In this labour dispute, the board initially had been ineffective, although this failure was not entirely of its own making; in the end, it had been the means of resolving the dispute. Whitney, in all likelihood, was less than completely satisfied with his government's creation in this instance, even if the beleaguered mayor of Hamilton waxed enthusiastic about the commission's performance. 'Had it not been for the tactful and patient handling ... by all the members of the Board,' he informed the premier, '... no settlement would have been brought about in such a peaceful way.' But a Tory supporter threw cold water on this warm gratitude by complaining to his leader that the agency 'did not act just right,' delaying intervention 'until the riot took place.' The agency's slow performance tarnished its ultimate success. And the premier had clearly been pushed to interfere with the commission in order to secure a resolution of the Hamilton troubles. True, his motive was a desire for labour peace, but he had not allowed the board the freedom which he had earlier insisted was its inviolate property.[20]

There was, from Whitney's standpoint, another negative aspect to the Hamilton difficulties. On 4 December – after the railway workers had returned to their jobs, but before the board rendered its judgment – a by-election was held in Hamilton East to produce a successor to Tory MPP Henry Carscallen, who had died in late summer. The labour dispute combined with lesser factors to create a startling outcome in the shape of a victory by labour candidate Allan Studholme. An 'astonished' premier put the result down to the strike, Hamilton East's large working-class population, the absence of a Liberal candidate, and remarkably light voter turn-out. The government, a Hamilton Conservative argued, could have nominated 'the angel Gabriel,' and even he 'would have been defeated by a tramp.' Many 'sore and sullen' Hamiltonians had either voted labour or not at all. And Studholme's victory raised a question: was this the shape of things to come or merely some local aberration?[21]

II

The creation of a regulatory agency for urban and suburban carriers was not the only railway matter to concern Whitney and his council. They also had to attend to an inheritance from the Ross administration, the Temiskaming and Northern Ontario Railway, which carried the new government into yet another area of management in another region of Ontario. The publicly owned T&NO came into being because of Ross's desire to nail down firmly Ontario's ownership of land awarded to it in 1884 by decision of the Judicial Committee of the Privy Council, and to impress the electorate with the 'courage and initiative' still possessed by his party. There were also annual appeals from settlers in the isolated areas around Haileybury and New Liskeard for a year-round link with the south, which would, in addition, serve to strengthen these essentially Anglo-Protestant settlements against incursions from French-Canadian Catholics who were a mere border away. Fusing neatly with such ambitions and requests was the wish of Toronto businessmen to possess a colonial frontier of their own that need not be shared with Montreal entrepreneurs. And, of course, there were forests to be exploited and, just possibly, minerals – in addition to those hard-working settlers. Finally, because no railway builder would seriously contemplate a north-south line in this region, it was left to the Ontario government to construct its own railway.

Legislation creating the T&NO was introduced – and passed – in the session of 1902; at that time, Whitney had argued for leaving the project to such private interests as the Canadian Northern Railway (then being built) which, presumably, could garner lavish federal subsidies from which the province could benefit. But the Tory leader's plans foundered on the hard rock of entrepreneurial indifference.

Consequently, proceeding on its own, the government named North Bay as the line's southern terminus, turned the necessary sod during the 1902 election campaign, named a commission to oversee the railway, and announced that the T&NO would run on standard gauge to New Liskeard, a distance of one hundred and thirteen miles.[22]

E.A. Ames, the thirty-six-year-old head of a Toronto stock brokerage company – and son-in-law of George A. Cox, a prominent financier of strong Liberal persuasion – was appointed chairman of the T&NO commission. He was joined by four others with manufacturing, financial, mining, and railway interests, plus warm devotion to the Grit cause. This body soon faced the chore of route selection and, following the advice of experts, chose one that, on leaving North Bay, went around Trout Lake and then through the North River valley. A second decision meant that construction would be on the contract system, as opposed to commission-managed building, and the appropriate documents were signed with the lowest bidder in the fall of 1902.[23]

'Construction out of North Bay began in earnest during the summer of 1903, with grading and laying of track going to the 57th mile by fall, more than half the distance to New Liskeard.' While this work proceeded, two items of news began to have a further impact on the railway. The Laurier government made clear its intention to build the National Transcontinental Railway, and this development spurred the commission to undertake surveys beyond New Liskeard with a view to a possible junction with the new line. And, even more important, the first silver discoveries along the route of the T&NO were made in 1903, in the vicinity of what became Cobalt. The provincial government's railway had swiftly gained two fresh points in its rationale: it could tap the trade of the booming Canadian prairies, and it could serve the needs of prospectors, miners, and financiers sucked into the vortex of the Cobalt silver rush. Consequently:

When the first stage to New Liskeard opened in January 1905, the T&NO was already more than a colonization road to settlers in the Haileybury district; it constituted a major carrier of supplies and equipment for the mining industry, together with prospectors and their gear, heading north. Trains returning south pulled cars loaded with silver ore. Ten per cent of the freight by 1913 consisted of ore, while cars going north were filled with the coal, food and manufactured goods needed by the mining communities. The bulk of freight and passenger traffic came from agricultural and urban settlement, but revenue after 1905 was augmented decisively by rates on ore shipments and by royalties on leased property in the mining area.[24]

With the railway creeping towards New Liskeard, the commission found itself beset by problems of financing and leadership. Bonds offered by the T&NO in 1903 did not enjoy brisk sales, thanks partly to a money scarcity where railway securities were concerned, and a short-term bank loan proved insufficient to cover the reprojected costs of the line, now estimated at thirty thousand dollars a mile. Frustrated by these difficulties and more concerned with the future of his closer interests in brokerage and trust companies, Ames quit as chairman at the end of 1903. Robert Jaffray, the financier-publisher of the Toronto *Globe*, replaced the young entrepreneur and was the beneficiary of an adequate loan from British banking houses, engineered by Ross and his government. But sound financing for the railway was scarcely in place when the Grits fell before the Tory onslaught in 1905.

The Whitney triumph prompted the swift resignation of the entire commission as the Liberal appointees quietly accepted the implications of a lost battle. The T&NO was now Tory property and the new government was free, presumably, to do with the line as it saw fit. Despite the new premier's opinions of the project delivered just three years before, however, the Conservatives were not about to auction off the road. Several hard facts prompted retention. The T&NO was popular with Toronto businessmen who had imperial designs on northern Ontario, and there was little reason to give offence in that quarter. Excitement generated in the larger Ontario community by the silver strikes had focused attention on the government-owned line and, more important, produced approval of it. And, lastly, none of the major railway entrepreneurs put in even an informal bid for the operation. The Tories would stay with public ownership.

Whitney thus moved to replace the five former commissioners with three of his choosing. Cecil B. Smith, a Toronto engineer, became the temporary chairman; he was to resign 'in October 1906, to become consulting engineer for the Commission.' Jacob L. Englehart from Petrolia was the second member; he was destined to follow Smith into the chairmanship, a post he would hold for the next thirteen years. Englehart, one of the creators of Imperial Oil, was a wealthy man at the time of his appointment, with strong Conservative ties created, in part, by his support of tariffs against American oil. His party affiliation led him to electoral support of his friend and business colleague W.J. Hanna, who undoubtedly had a hand in his appointment. Denis Murphy, a defeated Tory member of the legislature in the 1905 election, filled out the reshaped commission. The former legislator was another wealthy entrepreneur with interests in the Ottawa Transportation Company, an insurance company, and a lucrative silver mine at Cobalt.[25]

'With the issue of the chairman resolved, the construction of the T&NO continued to progress, first towards the Height of Land, and then towards the junction with the National Transcontinental at the place eventually to be called Cochrane.' By the end of 1906, the railway had reached a point that would be named Englehart, some twenty-five miles north of New Liskeard; the line was now in full operation over one hundred and thirty-eight miles of track. And nearly every foot of that track had been put in place and ballasted – as much of the remainder would be – by tough, unskilled European immigrants who dug, hauled, blasted, and sweated for a dollar a day. Canadians and British held down the clerical and lighter construction positions of the work, which ultimately reached Cochrane in the middle of 1909. Two hundred and fifty-two miles of government-owned track now lay between that location and North Bay.[26]

In the meantime, Whitney and his treasurer, A.J. Matheson, had been busy with the problem of financing the T&NO. Late in 1905, with help from Lord Strathcona, Matheson renewed the Ross government's loan, but this time through the Bank of Montreal.

Subsequently the Whitney government removed dependence of the Commission on bank loans and debentures, and made it possible instead for the T&NO to draw on the Consolidated Revenue Fund of the province. In 1907 an Act of consolidation which synthesized and repealed all previous legislation, established a separate account in the Treasury Department, called 'The Temiskaming and Northern Ontario Railway Account.' All previous loans were now centralized in this one account, to which the Lieutenant Governor in Council – namely the cabinet – could advance money from the Consolidated Revenue Fund. It followed that 'all expenditures on account of construction ... shall be charged against the said account.' The purpose of this legislation was to stabilize and secure the financing of the railway. It committed the Whitney government to a large public liability, more clearly defining responsibility for public ownership.[27]

While wrestling with the large question of T&NO financing, Matheson found time to turn his attention to railway taxation during the 1906 session, and significantly increased the amounts charged to steam and electric railways within the province. Formerly, railways over one hundred and fifty miles in length had been taxed at rates of thirty dollars a mile 'for single track,' and ten dollars a mile 'for each additional track.' The new rates would be double these figures, which had applied in organized districts; in unorganized districts, where assessments had been twenty dollars a mile single track and five dollars each additional track, the tax was also doubled. For railways under one hundred and fifty miles, the tax would be fifteen dollars a mile single track and five dollars each additional track. It was estimated that these increases would produce close to two hundred thousand dollars in additional revenue for the province. Out of the total sum collected – about three hundred and seventy-five thousand dollars – thirty thousand would be set aside to meet the expenses of the ORMB and to cover collection costs. One-half of the remainder would be allotted to municipalities in proportion to population, and would form a credit against which a portion of asylum costs would be charged. While the railway companies, not unexpectedly, strongly protested this fresh taxation, the bulk of the press supported the government in its decision, as the premier said, 'to take more money from the railways.'[28]

III

Dealing with the T&NO was not the only matter which drew the Whitney administration into the faraway field of northern Ontario. Because of the rapid rise of mineral production in that area, especially in the silver-rich Cobalt region, it became necessary for the government to articulate and legislate a mining policy. In approaching this subject, the Tories took a spectacular step which may well have been accidental: they decided to have the government engage directly in mining. The background to this move lay in recent developments in the province's north.

In August of 1905, the government had withdrawn the Gillies timber limit, close to the rich finds at Cobalt, from prospecting. In law there should have been no such activity on any land under timber licence, but prospectors, drawn by visions of wealth and impatient of legal niceties, had secretly staked claims on the limit in anticipation of the expiration of the licence. The government's action had halted all such furtive labour, but the question remained of the policy to be pursued when the timber licence ran out on 1 October 1906. It was to meet this problem that Whitney announced government intentions in the legislature on 3 April: 'The Government, after considering the circumstances and conditions up there, have decided that after the timber is removed on Oct. 1st they will not dispose of this valuable area, it being our property. We will keep it, and we will use it, develop and mine it, for the benefit of the people of the Province of Ontario.'[29]

On the surface the statement read as a policy of government ownership of future mining operations inside the limit. But H.V. Nelles has argued that Whitney had intended 'to say the government had not yet decided what to do with the property, whether to parcel it up and sell it to individual miners as the mining community requested or to auction it off to large companies.' Certainly Andy Broder thought the premier was debating these alternatives, because the Dundas MP wrote to his old friend: 'Since seeing you I have thought the best way to deal with the Gill[i]es Limit Mining property would be to parcel it out in Lots of 10 to 20 acres and put it up at auction.' Clearly, Whitney had discussed the options before him with Broder and had remained undecided. Noting the 'unanimous expression of approbation of our course with regard to the Gillies limit,' while writing to brother Ned, the premier talked of having 'plenty of time to decide on the best methods of running it.' And, when Borden saluted his general policy 'with regard to the mineral wealth of the Province' as being 'a splendid departure from the traditions of the past,' Whitney was quick to reply: 'We are not adopting what is called Government ownership. We are simply utilizing something that is already ours in the best interests of the people and we have no idea as yet just how we will do it. It is too soon to come to any conclusion as to the possible results of this policy.'[30]

If Whitney thought he still had time in which to choose a course with respect to the Gillies tract, the watching public – reading his rhetoric literally – soon indicated that they thought he had already selected the public ownership path. 'Let me congratulate you upon taking power to keep the Cobalt and Silver wealth of the north in the hands of the people,' S.D. Chown, general secretary of the Methodist department of temperance and moral reform, told him; 'It is a master stroke of policy.' 'Your [hydroelectric] Power and Gillies limit legislation are the first big things done in many years for the whole people of Ontario,' wrote one admirer; 'the "Man-in-the-street" is with you.' An avowed Grit assured him that his decision was 'a move in the right direction,' and then, undoubtedly, startled the premier by suggesting that it was 'only a beginning.' With so many thinking that Whitney intended 'to operate the mines within the Gillies limits for the benefit of the people at large,' the premier quietly conceded that 'a new line of thought' had been opened for him. When it came to suggestions on public questions, Whitney insisted that his pores were 'always open,' and the Gillies limit would be no exception: the government would operate a mine on the tract. And this it did until 1909. Of course, there was also political advantage in such a move.[31]

In addition to his Gillies limit announcement on 3 April, the premier set out the regulations that would govern mining development in a three-and-a-half-mile stretch of the T&NO right of way which cut a swath through the richest Cobalt claims. Tenders would be invited for mining concessions under specific conditions: payment of a fifty-thousand-dollar annual bonus for the concession itself; 'a yearly rental of $500 for site of mining buildings'; and a royalty based on the quality of the extracted ore. Obviously, the government had just dealt itself in for a share of the rich stakes in northern Ontario.[32]

New mining legislation, introduced by Cochrane, followed Whitney's pronouncements – both the intentional and the inadvertent – of policy. The bill, containing over two hundred and twenty clauses, repealed most of the previous legislation on the subject and provided a uniform law for the entire province. A mining commissioner, possessed of wide powers, would be appointed, although George Ross 'questioned the need' for such an official. The machinery of administration was to be decentralized in the interests of both prospector and government because it meant fairer treatment and closer supervision. And it was necessary to discover valuable minerals in order to secure a title to the land claimed. Lastly, fresh regulations provided miners with better conditions with respect to health and safety. Cochrane, in guiding the measure through the legislature, 'showed a familarity with every feature of the bill, justifying the predictions of his friends that his appointment would prove one of the best Premier Whitney has made.'[33]

IV

While the new government's transportation and mining policies generally drew praise even from grudging admirers and political opponents, the proponents of public ownership – or, at the least, tough supervision – of the production, transmission, and distribution of hydroelectric power grumbled about the Tory delay in producing the appropriate legislation on this subject. When it was rumoured, in March of 1906, that the legislature might rise without passing such a measure, the *World* barked: 'This ought to be the power session of Ontario's legislature. There is no need to prorogue in haste. Let some well defined policy be immediately outlined.' And, once the cabinet had turned to consider the matter and was slow to resolve differences of opinion, the same newspaper was quick to suggest that the government was 'all at sea as to its electric policy.' 'It is being said,' the *World* continued, 'that the Hon. Adam Beck is too far ahead of the rest of the team to be comfortable; that he is preparing too radical a bill for his colleagues, and that the government supporters want the government to go farther than the government itself seems to desire.'[34]

That there were troubles within the cabinet in seeking agreement on a provincial power policy was not a surprising development. After all, the members were, for the most part, strong individuals with firmly held convictions of varying hues, and not the least of these was Adam Beck. As well, as the *World* noted, there was 'no precedent to go upon'; consequently, precedent would be set by government action. Lastly, there was a numerically small but financially powerful opposition which stood against popular demands – often orchestrated by Beck – for government intrusion into the field. Whitney, therefore, had to be very much the sensitive politician as he walked the dangerous ground between the various camps. Before the session of 1906 was ended, however, there was sweeping legislation on the statute books that directed the government into a field held only by private enterprise at the provincial level. Such an entry could not be made without a stiff struggle.

The bases for public discussion and agitation on the question, prior to government action, were the report of the Ontario Power Commission – appointed under 1903 legislation to investigate the feasibility of municipal cooperation for the transmission and distribution of hydroelectric power, and having Beck as a member – and three reports from the Beck-directed Hydro-Electric Power Commission, which had looked into nearly every aspect of source, production, cost, transmission, and distribution of hydroelectric power in Ontario. The reports of both commissions looked favourably upon some form of public ownership of the means of distribution and transmission and, in the case of the Ontario Power Commission, production; but Beck's committee took a stand distinctly more hostile to the private corporations, particularly on the grounds that they failed to compete and, consequently, to lower prices to consumers.

The private power companies also generated ill will during the Hydro-Electric Power Commission's investigations when the Electrical Development Company and the Ontario Power Company refused to provide all the information on production costs requested of them by Beck and his fellow commissioners.

Whitney had supported Beck in his demand for such figures and signed an order-in-council requiring compliance with the request. Nicholls, of the Electrical Development Company, finally provided the premier with some prices for power, but these were only for Whitney's eyes. And, just before the first Beck report was made public, the Ontario Power Company scrambled to give Whitney its prices for delivered horsepower per annum.[35]

The private power interests, especially Pellatt and Nicholls of the Electrical Development, felt that they had cause for annoyance, if not justification for imperious surliness. More than once it had been broadly hinted by those in authority that the government intended to take legislative action on hydroelectric power development during the 1906 session; on each occasion, one or other of this pair asked for an opportunity to explain his position, before the government was 'stampeded ... by popular clamour.' Each time Whitney put them off with statements to the effect that all reports had not yet been received or that the government was not bound by the findings of any report. Finally, when it was evident that the Whitney government intended to act on the basis of the Beck commission report, Pellatt pleaded with the premier:

I understand that you are being pressed very hard for power legislation before the close of the present session, and before the matter has been fully investigated, and I take the liberty of reminding you of your promise made to us, that there would be no such legislation until the many different parties interested could be heard from, in order to show the true facts of this matter.

The financial interests are very large, and in the case of the Electrical Development Company, some of the largest financial interests in Canada, as well as *in England*, are affected.

If the conclusions of the Hydro Electric Commission were correct, I would have nothing to say, but they are *incorrect*, and can easily be proved to be so.

Clearly, in addition to stating his case, the entrepreneur was implicitly threatening Whitney with damage to Ontario's position in the British money market if the government acted without due regard for private interests.[36]

Whitney's reply to Pellatt was a deliberate insult. He informed the Electrical Development Company's president that the cabinet intended to consider the power question on that day, Saturday 5 May, and he suggested Pellatt phone him on the morning of Monday 7 May. Then, later on that Saturday, Whitney had his secretary telephone Pellatt's home and leave the message that the government would hear any of his representations on the power question 'on Monday the 7th instant from 12.30 noon to one p.m.' There were two cutting aspects to this proposition. Pellatt was supposed to accumulate materials for the defence on Sunday and present them – inside half an hour – on Monday; and more insulting still, the cabinet was evidently considering the power legislation when these messages were sent, with the intention of introducing it on Monday. Thus, an angry Henry Pellatt wrote Whitney on Monday morning: 'In the absence of a proper hearing upon reasonable notice, it was believed by the Companies that legislation would not be brought down this Session, and yet reliable information has reached us that a Bill is now ready to be brought before the House this afternoon – such being the case ... it would I think be useless for us to take up the time of the Council at the hour named to-day.' The premier replied, regretting 'to observe the tone' of Pellatt's note and wondering if the matter might fail of a reasonable conclusion because the entrepreneur was being unreasonable. Pellatt did not respond.[37]

Whitney, as usual, had used a battleaxe on an opponent when a smaller blade would have served the purpose. But he had given Pellatt, Nicholls, and their company a particularly severe beating when, as he knew only too well, there would be no benefit to anyone should the Electrical Development Company collapse. Undoubtedly he resented the conduct of these entrepreneurs in the matter of the revelation of cost figures, and he was probably being punitive for that sin. Yet, there was more to his conduct than that. The hydro question was carrying the government into unmapped regions, and the venture was undoubtedly creating questions, debate, and division within the cabinet. The premier was probably apprehensive, if not downright nervous, about such an exercise in trail-blazing and, in all likelihood, he was on edge – the more so because this matter was being handled at the end of an innovative but wearing legislative session. In such circumstances, bald brusqueness might be explained as a case of nerves or even as a cover for serious doubts. Finally, it should be noted that this tough small-town lawyer was not the man to knuckle under to those accustomed to deference and preference. He had already battled Flavelle on the question of the dismissal of the Toronto liquor inspectors, and he seemed to relish such challenges. Whitney apparently had no intention of yielding to monied men of power and influence, especially when he saw them as bullies. After all, he was the premier, and that, in his eyes, was the prime position in the province. There was a touch of arrogance in all of this; but it was not without its justification, particularly if one believed in the supremacy of an elected legislature.[38]

While Whitney tilted with the entrepreneurs, there were other developments in the hydroelectric power question. Adam Beck was here, there, and everywhere, preaching the gospel of cheap power to enthusiastic audiences and suggesting rates considerably lower than those which the private concerns had in mind. As a consequence, petitions and delegations arrived at the premier's door and the message was almost always the same: legislate to ensure, at the least, government transmission of power and, at the most, government ownership of the means of power production. Ontario's citizens, whether on boards of trade, township councils, or labour bodies, were unashamedly excited about the possibilities of cheap hydroelectric power.[39]

Beck introduced the proposed power legislation, which Meredith had supposedly helped to draft. The bill provided for the creation of the Hydro-Electric Power Commission of Ontario, a body having three members, one of which had to be a cabinet minister (and two of which might be). This body could appoint its own staff and was given the power to acquire 'any needed lands, waters, water power and installations.' It was given a free hand in arriving at satisfactory contracts for the supply of power.

Any municipality requesting power would be told by the Commission the maximum price per horsepower at which it could be supplied. Plans and specifications, estimated cost of transmission lines, and distribution works would also be provided.

The municipality might then make a provisional contract with the Commission to supply its power needs, but this contract would not become permanent and binding until it received the approval of the ratepayers.

The commission would also exercise control over the rates to manufacturers and the rates of generating and distributing companies. The government would provide support for loans raised for purposes of implementing the act. Should any company refuse to supply required information to the commission, it could be fined one hundred dollars a day. And it required the consent of the attorney-general in order to commence a suit against the commission or its members.[40]

The entire measure was distressing to the private power interests, but there was one clause which they found particularly alarming: that giving the commission broad powers of expropriation. Nor did Whitney relieve anxious minds when he informed the legislature that expropriation would only be used in the face of intransigence over commission-fixed rates and that he believed such a step would not be necessary. Reaction was immediate because, on 8 May, opportunity was afforded at the cornerstone laying ceremony of the Electrical Development Company's powerhouse at Niagara Falls. B.E. Walker of the Canadian Bank of Commerce, Whitney's ally in university matters, commented directly when he observed that 'public ownership, applied to a problem so intricate [as hydroelectric development], is as useless as the breath of the politicians who advocate it.'[41]

Clearly, the forces of private power enterprise were mustering for a battle which Whitney would have preferred to avoid, but whose outcome he never doubted because of the strong public support which he already possessed. And, from the judicial bench, Meredith urged him to stand firm. 'I sincerely hope,' wrote the former party leader,

that you will not be, shall I say, stampeded into withdrawing or emasculating your power bill.

It is a safe & conservative measure. Nothing can be done without the action of the

Commission on which the Government will be represented if it has not a majority of the members.

If the right to expropriate is exercised which is not likely to happen full compensation will be paid to the property owners & no bondholders [sic] rights need be disturbed.

...

It is I think more than probable that the main purpose the bill will serve will be to compel those who have a monopoly of the power to supply it at reasonable rates.

Whitney held to the original bill, which became law one week after its introduction. In the interval the Liberals asserted that they had taken as much action on the subject as was proper while in office; Richard Harcourt, the former education minister, stood staunchly opposed to public ownership. In the same period the price of public utility stocks plunged downward on the market, despite statements by the premier that no precipitate action would be taken against capital and that no investors in power companies had any cause for alarm. Whitney then undertook to allay the fears of English bondholders by letter and sent copies to two persons who were hostile to the expropriation clause: Sir Wilfrid Laurier and Earl Grey.[42]

On 7 June, the members of the Hydro-Electric Power Commission were appointed: Beck would be chairman; John Hendrie, minister without portfolio, and Cecil Smith, the engineering expert, would fill out its ranks. Hendrie undertook the task with some reservations, fearing 'friction' with Beck, who might resent his presence. Whitney persuaded Hendrie, who could be a useful restraining influence on Beck, to serve: 'I have no fear of friction,' the premier wrote. 'The Government will be so close to the work which may have to be done that the Commission must practically [be] a Committee of the Cabinet with certain statutory powers.' The Conservative leader had every intention of keeping control of Beck, the commission, and hydroelectric policy. Thus, the commission had its birth in 1906, created by legislation which must rank as of major significance in Ontario's history.[43]

The creation of the tribunal did not, of course, dispose of the hydroelectric question. The premier had to hold to his plan and keep a vigilant eye on Beck, his new organization, and his opponents. And, when a weary Whitney fled the confines of his office, in company with Pyne, for the freedom of a summer trip to Great Britain and Europe, he found he could not shake the cares of Ontario hydroelectric development. He had to take time 'to communicate ... with some' of the Electrical Development Company's bondholders in England in order to make the government's side of the power debate clear to them. He hoped to demonstrate that the attacks upon the Conservative legislation were unjustified. But, while he renewed his strength abroad and moved to shore up confidence in Ontario as a sound place for investment, a variety of Ontario papers published letters from assorted *noms de plume* who argued that Beck's estimates for transmission and distribution costs were deceitfully inaccurate. The pernicious part of this attack was that, although the letters were paid for, they did not appear in the newspapers as advertisements. There was simply no escaping the hydro question.[44]

V

Whitney was justifiably proud of what had been accomplished during the legislative session of 1906. Although somewhat 'worn out' by his labours – not a surprising condition in light of his close association with much of the major legislation – he boasted to Borden: 'I think that I may say that the work of no two previous Sessions in the Ontario Legislature will compare with that done by us during the one just closed.' Tired or not, he was now possessed of a confident sureness that came from the knowledge of jobs having been well done or well begun. The bulk of commentators, save for highly partisan Liberals, agreed with his view. Assessing the major pieces of legislation, the *News* judged the session without 'parallel since Confederation.' Sam Blake, verbose as usual, offered a similar opinion:

For the first time in a good many years we have had a display of statesmanship in dealing with the affairs of the Province. In place of doling out such a petty measure of relief as might for the time satisfy grafters and keep alive in them the necessity for working the machine for all it was worth in order to retain a Government in power in the hopes of obtaining another dole at an ensuing Session, we have had a full measure of relief given on a large well digested plan in many matters that have to do intimately with our welfare.

'What a ruthless thoroughness in the rush the Whitney people made at these problems,' the Ottawa correspondent of the *News* wrote privately. 'Of course, they had special advantages. They had been out of power so long that the capitalistic crowd had taken no pains to conciliate them in advance.'[45]

Yet, behind the premier's exuberant confidence and the public's lavish praise, there was a nagging question in Whitney's mind: 'how long will this last?' Could the progressive wave roll on indefinitely? Was it not bound to expend itself? His worrying of these queries was, in part, a consequence of the overwhelming success of his actions and legislation in terms of public approbation. The nature and pace of the reforms had not only secured widespread approval; they had undoubtedly raised expectations that there was more of the same to come. Knowledge of such a popular feeling was the source of Whitney's doubts. Before Ontarians, however, he provided no clue about his sobering thoughts. 'Whatever we may think ourselves,' he told Borden, 'we have no hesitation in saying to the public that it will last as long as we are in power.' And, as if to prove this point, he named his textbook commission once the session was finished. Whitney was now ready – as ready as he ever would be – for that trip to Great Britain where, among other engagements, would be a dinner given in the premier's honour at the Athenaeum Club by Lord Strathcona, the Canadian high commissioner.[46]

On his return from overseas in mid-September, Whitney's first major involvement with the federal government was on his calendar: a dominion-provincial conference on the problem of federal subsidies to the provinces had been set to begin in Ottawa on 8 October 1906. Behind this meeting was a growing restlessness on the part of the provinces over the current fiscal arrangements with the central government. The interprovincial conferences of 1887 and 1902 had served as witnesses to this developing unease; the provinces wanted a larger share of growing federal revenues in order to meet the rising costs of government.

The Ontario premier's approach to the conference was scarcely bloodthirsty. While arguing in his brief that the arrangements of 1867 should not be regarded as sacrosanct, he made little in the way of a demand for more money for his province. The reason for his moderation was obvious: Ontario contributed largely to the federal coffers and, consequently, any significant increase in provincial subsidies would ultimately be felt by the Ontario resident. The premier's memorandum did state that if subsidies were to be raised, then Ontario's contribution to federal revenues should be taken into consideration. And Whitney did favour 'some definite and permanent arrangement regarding the Subsidy question; one which ... [would] render unnecessary and ... impossible periodical applications for re-arrangement of the Subsidies.' 'In the future no special grant ... should be made to any one Province.' He was evidently more concerned with securing fiscal order than obtaining more monies for his home province. Thus, in comparison with the hectoring words of British Columbia's Richard McBride, the Ontario premier's remarks seemed general and even anemic. Criticism followed comparison: 'The impression here [in Ottawa],' C.F. Hamilton of the *News* informed Willison, 'is that Whitney has done very badly. It seems to me well-grounded. His memorandum is a singularly inept production, leading nowhere. He receded from it.' But Ontario gained the 'biggest increase in dollars.' Perhaps Whitney could walk quietly – of course it helped to have the big stick of representing the largest province.[47]

The question of the possible disposition of the District of Keewatin produced a further conference at Ottawa in November, at which Ontario, Manitoba, and Saskatchewan, as well as the federal government, were represented. Whitney argued that Manitoba's eastern boundary should be run to the Churchill River and then down it to Hudson Bay; Ontario would willingly take up the area to the east of such a line. Manitoba countered with its standard arguments for the entire territory, while Saskatchewan sought some corridor to the salt sea. Whitney's position again irritated Hamilton, who observed: 'Laurier is simply using this conference to egg Whitney on to hurt Manitoba: thus (1) punishing Manitoba, (2) setting the two Provinces at variance.' 'Whitney is confirming my judgment,' he further told Willison, 'that his sole qualifications are his probity, his obstinacy and a certain instinct for what the people want – and that he is far from being clever. Laurier has played him beautifully on this boundary question – got him to do his dirty work for him.' Leaving aside the fact that the qualifications attributed to Whitney by Hamilton were far from useless to any good politician, it may have been that Laurier was playing a game of divide-and-conquer with the provinces. No doubt Whitney's demands were extreme but, only too conscious of his electorate, he could scarcely have stood aside for Manitoba and cheerfully sacrificed Ontario's claims, however nebulous they were. And he may well have regarded his position as merely an opening one, to be followed by some concessions.[48]

Bargaining did not ensue, however, and the brief conference held in the prime minister's office accomplished nothing. Possibly, Laurier's refusal to negotiate and mediate had its source in special pleadings from George Ross: 'The reason why I do not want an immediate settlement of the Western boundaries of Ontario is because, if done just now it might strengthen the Whitney Gov[t] in New & perhaps in old Ontario. Kindly remember that I do not want Ontario not to get her rights or to be deprived of any advantage that might properly come to her in a readjustment of Provincial boundaries, but if her case would not be prejudiced by delay, then delay would be expedient.' Ross's partisan urgings, it could be argued, would neatly fit in with possible Laurier strategy: thwart Ontario Tories, divide two Conservative provincial administrations, and leave the federal government holding Keewatin. In any event, delay most certainly ensued. It was not until 1912, when Robert Borden was prime minister – and in Whitney's debt – that the present boundary line was drawn to Hudson Bay between Manitoba and Ontario.[49]

Failure to resolve the Keewatin dispute, however, scarcely marked a setback for the Ontario premier; after all, other parties were involved and they had to be in some measure of accord. Nevertheless, the year did end on a slightly sour note for Whitney, with that triumph by Allan Studholme in Hamilton East. Otherwise, 1906 had been close to perfect for the premier who had grown in his position, and in his confidence in himself, his party, and his province. Ontario was on the move, and he and the Tories were in the van. Whitney had captured this feeling when earlier he had written, only half in jest, to a legislative supporter: 'Dr. Pyne and I returned yesterday from our visit to mediaeval and effete Europe. What we saw has resulted in strengthening the conviction, already ours, that Ontario is the most favoured country in the World, especially under its present Government.'[50]

7

'Practically Unanimous Approval by the People': 1907–1909

At the outset of 1907, the provincial Liberal party changed leaders. Laurier, always looking since Mowat's day for an Ontario strong man – but not too strong – reached down and lifted a very willing George Ross into the Senate. Although the former premier thought his elevation met 'with general approval' and even hoped a cabinet post might be his, there were Liberals with reservations because of his well-known imperialist and protectionist sentiments. Nevertheless, he was gone and the provincial party had to find a successor – even a temporary one – because the legislative session was fast approaching.[1]

Two names were most frequently mentioned in the ensuing speculation: George P. Graham, member for Brockville and managing director of that town's *Recorder*, and Alexander G. MacKay, member for Grey North and a lawyer. Graham was not an eager candidate, because he did not want to disqualify himself from advancement to the federal cabinet and because of the financial strain the leadership would impose. Laurier, however, chose to ignore this willing volunteer for national politics, and Graham accepted the provincial leadership when the caucus unanimously elected him. But he continued to keep a watchful eye on Ottawa and insisted that his appointment was only a stopgap measure. Such an attitude was not likely to produce dedicated and aggressive stewardship, a fact that scarcely held terror for the Tories.[2]

Whitney naturally stood outside of these manoeuvrings, but he made observations and offered grossly inaccurate predictions – privileges reserved for the leader of the other party. Having informed his brother Ned that he had 'no idea who will be the Opposition leader,' he willingly guessed it would be Richard Harcourt, Ross's former minister of education. MacKay, he judged, had 'more brains' than 'all the rest of them,' but was not vigorously promoting his candidacy, while Graham, he commented, was actively seeking the job. The premier was quietly hoping the choice would be Harcourt because of the latter's long and strong tie to the discredited Ross administration and his vocal opposition to anything that smacked of public ownership. Whitney reasoned that such an opponent, caught in an unpopular and weak position, could only help the Conservative party. Such wishful thinking was to remain just that, however, and it was Graham who faced Whitney when the assembly reopened for business, following the Liberal shuffle.[3]

The legislation presented at the ensuing session lacked the sparkle of that of the previous year. But this did not mean that the government front benches were now filled with sputtering volcanoes. It was just that the administration was now more concerned with loose ends, and the major enactments of 1906 were still keeping Whitney and his cabinet occupied, but generally outside of the legislature.

As has been noted, during the preceding session the Conservatives had dictated a floor salary of three hundred dollars for teachers, and this compulsory minimum had produced a hostile reaction from some of Ontario's miserly trustees. In response, the premier now announced a sizeable increase in grants to rural schools, in order to ensure firm adherence to government wishes with respect to the minimum and a more generous increment policy on the part of country boards. Whitney followed this pronouncement with a measure that authorized 'the Board of Governors of the University to borrow up to a limit of $2,000,000; all loans to be approved by the Governor-in-Council before becoming effective.' He pointed out that new and enlarged buildings were needed, and added that the university's rising revenue would ultimately wipe out any debts that were incurred.[4]

This fresh university legislation provoked an opposition statement, from Graham and MacKay, that university funds should come out of general revenue and thus be subject to yearly scrutiny by the legislature. Whitney, annoyed, charged that the Liberals, while pretending to interest the public in university affairs by such an approach, were actually aiming at creating public suspicion of the institution. He reasoned that the Grit proposition had the earmarks of potential political interference, that very objectionable feature which he was determined to eliminate. He was resolved to provide the freedom, both academic and financial, which the University of Toronto required in order to develop into 'the central educational institution of this Country.'[5]

Early in the session the government made public the report of the textbook commission which had been appointed in the previous year 'to investigate the price of school books ... in order to see whether the cost of school books in ... [Ontario could] be lowered.' The report of this body indicated that textbook prices were too high, a consequence of awarding contracts without calling for tenders; that Gage and Company, Copp, Clark and Company, and the Canada Publishing Company had a virtual monopoly of publication; and that the end products were 'markedly inferior' to either British or American textbooks. The commission recommended a variety of means for procuring the manuscripts of texts, and firmly argued for the use of the tendering system when a publisher was sought. As Whitney had anticipated, all that was needed to rectify the existing situation and implement the commission's recommendations was a change in policy by the education department. This shift was now executed, with the government calling tenders for the publication of the Ontario readers – a set of five books. The longtime producer of these, the Canada Publishing Company, secured the contract on a tender of forty-nine cents per set, as against a charge of a dollar and fifteen cents under the previous system. This arrangement was but temporary, because Pyne announced that a new set of readers would be prepared for use by Ontario's school children, and that would mean a call for fresh publishing tenders once preparation was complete.[6]

Honouring a pledge made earlier, Frank Cochrane rounded off his labours of the year before by introducing legislation which provided a new and permanent formula for taxing the mining industry. The measure 'imposed a 3 per cent tax on mining profits over $10,000, a two-cent acreage tax on mineral lands, and a modest tax upon the production of natural gas' and 'represented a major departure from former policy.' Not unexpectedly, there were noisy protests from interested parties, but the government, after making minor alterations, persisted with the legislation, despite cries from the Toronto Standard Stock Exchange of 'partial confiscation.' Whitney willingly stood by the Cochrane bill, convinced – as he so often disarmingly remarked in defence of his government's actions – that 'public opinion' demanded it. In addition, the mines minister provided for bonuses in order to encourage the refining of metals in Ontario.[7]

Joint stock companies were also affected by government measures in 1907, when W.J. Hanna's department, reflecting the fine analytical mind of its chief, boiled nineteen long, involved, and repetitious regulating acts down to one. The distilled product named the provincial secretary's office as the sole one through which incorporation might be sought; protected shareholders by demanding detailed financial statements of companies; prohibited bonuses to directors unless a two-third vote of shareholders approved such an arrangement at a special meeting; ensured that there could be a compulsory yearly audit on the application of any shareholder; and named directors as being directly responsible for any prospectus statements. As often is the case with such legislation, these regulations mirrored abuses that the law had previously, and generally inadvertently, allowed.[8]

Provincial rights were twice debated during this session of the legislature, once in regard to actual legislation and once in an angry exchange of words with the federal government. Early in the assembly debates, Whitney indicated a growing annoyance with the tendency of companies to seek federal incorporation and thus remove their subholdings from provincial jurisdiction. For example, the federal incorporation of a holding company owning a railway line in Ontario would remove that line from the regulatory control of the Ontario Railway and Municipal Board. 'For the last few years a perfect stream of applications has been going to Ottawa from local [rail]roads to take them out of our jurisdiction,' the premier informed the legislature; '... our Government will not submit to this unless it is compelled.'9

This strong language was followed by equally strong action in the shape of a 'Bill respecting certain Railway and other Corporations.' This measure declared that any company operating a public utility incorporated in Ontario would lose all 'powers, rights, privileges and franchises,' if it obtained federal incorporation or was absorbed by a company of federal creation. In addition, any agreements between companies so affected and municipalities would become null and void. And, unless the lieutenant-governor-in-council approved, there could be no agreements between municipalities and companies that lacked Ontario incorporation. Whitney agreed that this was 'serious,' even 'drastic,' legislation; but he continued:

It is designed to ... put a stop to the insuperable barriers and obstacles with which officious legislators at Ottawa seek to embarrass the Province. It is aimed against the trend of affairs at Ottawa to trample upon Provincial rights. When a Department of the Dominion arrogates to itself the power to break contracts between man and man, it is time to call a halt and, as far as it is humanly possible, this Government intends by this Bill and other efforts which will be evident later on, to stop the recklessness – the collective recklessness – of the Parliament of Canada in dealing with Provincial rights.

To George Graham, who witnessed this foray by the Conservatives into the old Mowat territory of provincial rights, the act was both a 'big club' and a dangerous one.10

This assertive legislation was followed by harsh words over the manner in which the federal government acquired land for the Petawawa military base. Negotiations for the dominion government's lease or purchase of about fifty-five thousand acres of land near Pembroke had become tangled and protracted because of Ontario's insistence upon adequate protection of the rights of provincial timber licensees on the land. Angered by the delay and Whitney's demands, Sir F.W. Borden, Laurier's minister of militia and defence, took action late in March of 1907, and moved to acquire the acreage 'for defence purposes under the British North America Act.'11

The provincial premier, provoked by this turn of events, relished the prospect of a fight. He informed brother Ned that the land had been 'confiscated' 'under cover of a doubtful clause in the Confederation Act.' 'I think,' he wrote, 'that by the time we get through with him, Sir Wilfrid Laurier will have his doubts about the value of his Minister of Militia.' The Tory-dominated legislature responded with a strong resolution of protest against the proposed federal action, and Whitney charged the Laurier government with riding roughshod over provincial rights. Sitting on the sidelines, W.R. Meredith cheered the premier's actions and noted that 'the ground taken should prove splendid fighting ground for your Government at the next election.' Throughout the uproar the provincial Liberals sat unprotesting and unopposing the Tories' words and action, while the federal Liberals, still insisting upon their rights under the BNA Act, backed off and stated that they would 'deal justly with the licensees.' Then, they retreated, allowing that the province did have some rights in the matter. Somewhat smugly, Whitney examined his victory: 'Without notice or warning, (Frederick) Borden reached out and took our property. He took occasion to say in the House of Commons that we were not entitled to compensation and that he did not intend to give compensation. Now, after weeks have elapsed, Aylesworth and Fielding say of course they will pay the lumbermen and they are ready to settle the question of the ownership of the Province. This is exactly what Borden should have done and then there would have been no trouble.' The premier could enjoy being the champion of provincial rights against the Liberal government, and the local Liberals, trapped by the heritage of Mowat's stand – as well as by some of Laurier's own words – could do or say little. The fact that the Grits were in power in Ottawa, while the Tories held sway in Toronto, meant that federal-provincial tensions could be politically profitable to Whitney. There was no such benefit in the situation for the provincial Grits.[12]

II

The work of the 1907 legislative session did demand a significant amount of Whitney's attention, particularly when Foy's temporary illness threw a greater load on the premier; but, away from the assembly floor, the hydroelectric development question ravenously consumed much of the Tory leader's time. The imposing demands of this subject began with the new year because the citizens of Toronto and eighteen other western Ontario municipalities approved a standard by-law which empowered their respective councils to negotiate contracts with the Hydro-Electric Power Commission for delivery of hydroelectricity. That positive development meant that the government or the commission – one could not act without the support of the other – had to start the search for the required power at a low price, and also had to decide what agency would assume the responsibility for transmission. Now the government and the commission were very much into uncharted waters with virtually no guides, save common sense; and Whitney's cautious behaviour in the ensuing months largely reflected his awareness of this significant fact. The situation would have taxed the ingenuity and patience of most men, but Whitney had additional problems: on the one hand, there was Adam Beck, preaching the gospel of cheap power and gaining converts who displayed all the enthusiasm generally associated with rebirth; and, on the other hand, there was the financially troubled Electrical Development Company, directed by Nicholls and Pellatt who laboured, like zealous counter-reformationists, to protect their interests, meanwhile antagonizing Beck's righteous supporters. The prospects were surely exhausting for the premier to contemplate.

The Electrical Development Company was a particularly unattractive organization, fouled by fiscal irresponsibility and the foolish arrogance of its few supporters. Clifford Sifton, no enemy of capitalism, savagely analysed the company early in 1907:

First That the Electrical Development Company secured a very wide charter from the Dominion Parliament, a charter which, by the way, the Dominion Parliament never should have passed.

Second That the same Company secured wide privileges respecting the development of power at Niagara Falls.

Third That this Company contemplated an electrical monopoly of Western Ontario including Toronto.

Fourth That this scheme has been knocked to pieces by the Power policy of Beck, which has been made effective by the vote on the Power By-law in Toronto, to be followed, no doubt, by similar votes in other Municipalities. The Electrical Development Company made desperate efforts to secure the defeat of the Power By-law. Having failed, they have apparently now entered upon a campaign to compel the City [of Toronto] or the Government [of Ontario] to buy them out, at a price which will provide liberally for the holders of the stock, which is absolutely, as I understand, all water.

Reading the 'Toronto News' regularly it has become evident to me that that newspaper is absolutely the organ of the Electrical Development Company, and I should imagine from the columns of 'the Globe', that the person influential with the 'Toronto Globe', also has some of the watered stock. Apparently the only newspaper that sees clearly is 'The World'[;] Billy McLean [sic] has the other fellows thoroughly sized up, and for once has them right.

...

As I understand it, the case is absolutely clear. The Company got a Charter to get power to develope [sic]. They have no exclusive rights, they are open to competition by anybody, and the suggestion that before competing with them for development, or hiring power at a lower rate themselves than they (the Company) are willing to give it, the City or the Province is morally bound [to] buy them out is the most colossal piece of assurance that I ever heard of. That is what the News is everyday laboring to establish on high moral grounds, and apparently what the Globe is quite willing should be established. The proposition will not stand argument for half a minute ...

Whitney would undoubtedly have murmured an amen to Sifton's angry, if inelegant, phrasing. That being so, it is necessary to offer some explanation for his protracted efforts to find some accommodation for the company in Beck's plans for provincial hydroelectric development. The premier simply could not dispassionately watch the collapse of this Canadian corporation; whatever his personal feelings, the company had to be kept alive, if possible. Otherwise, there would not only be damage done in Toronto financial circles, but more important, the province of Ontario would assuredly suffer in the London money market. Already, in that location, there was 'a want of confidence which has been gradually growing up as a result of State Socialism and intereference [sic] by Municipal and Government bodies in trade and against Capital.' Hydroelectric legislation had 'left a nasty taste' in London mouths. 'One big Co. refused to look at ... bonds guaranteed by Ontario, because it has set a black mark against that the richest Province in Canada!' Such a perception of Ontario's legislation might anger the premier, but he had to be aware of it.[13]

The first fresh difficulty with the Electrical Development Company arose out of the Commission's call for tenders for the delivery of power at Niagara. Only two firms made proposals: the American-owned Ontario Power Company and the Electrical Development Company. The tender of the first was $10.40 per horsepower per annum (up to twenty-five horsepower), while that of the second was $12.00. When this became known, the Electrical Development Company pleaded that its figure was not a real tender; that failure to secure a contract would bring financial ruination; and that an American company was being favoured over a Canadian one. Faced by these arguments, the premier bit his tongue and responded in a notably fair manner. Without consulting his colleagues, he inquired of Sam Blake, Ontario Power's counsel, if his corporation was prepared to share the contract for the first twenty-five thousand horsepower with the Electrical Development Company. Blake's reply underscored the reasonableness of his company and the lack of a similar quality in its opponent: he observed that the representatives of the Electrical Development Company were prepared 'to make themselves millionaires no matter at what cost it might be to all others, and they naturally are disappointed when they fail in accomplishing this object.' In any event, the Electrical Development Company could not be moved in the matter of price and the government had to act: on 30 April 1907, the Hydro-Electric Power Commission and the Ontario Power Company signed a contract.[14]

This did not end the premier's problems with Pellatt, Nicholls, and company; he once more had to take them into account when planning a holiday trip to Great Britain in the summer of 1907. He informed F.W. Taylor of the London branch of the Bank of Montreal that he 'would like, while in England, to take some step to lay the truth before men of standing in a financial way there.' He also rehearsed with Taylor what he would try to make clear before such an audience:

A year and a half ago, we passed an Act relating to Hydro-Electric matters, which in effect gave Government [the] power to assume or expropriate electric power at Niagara Falls.

...

As we have had on the Statute Book for fifty years, powers of expropriation of Gas and Water Companies, there was nothing unusual in applying the same principle to the Niagara situation. It was done simply with the object of assuring the cities and towns of the Province power at reasonable rate. We neither had, nor have any idea of expropriating any of these properties, and would feel very much disappointed if we were compelled to do so.

The result of it all has been that the Government received propositions or tenders of power at certain rates – I may say reasonable rates. The proposition of the Ontario Power Company was so much lower than that of the Electrical Development Company, the other one that tendered, that we were bound to accept the former. We did so, however, only partially, and as a result of our efforts, the successful Company consented to confine their operations to a line running North and South, which leaves Toronto, and practically the rest of the Province North and East from that City, to be served by the Electrical Development Company, if they chose to do so at the same rates. We went out of our way, to an unreasonable extent, in putting pressure on the Ontario Power Company in this way.

Now, ever since the passage of this Legislation, the Electrical Development Company has fought the action of the Government; it has endeavoured to get our legislation disallowed at Ottawa; it has spread rumours abroad, without a shadow of foundation, to the effect that our legislation was confiscation, and that we were interfering with vested rights, etc.

So far from this being the case, and in order to meet the situation the Speech from the Throne, at the close of the Session of 1906, ... declared that vested rights and the rights of investors would be protected.

While we have done everything in our power to counteract the efforts, which I have indicated above, the Electrical Development Company, or, at any rate, certain men connected with it have in season and out of it, tried to prejudice the public mind against our action.

Whitney had his desired meeting with these London money men in the offices of the Bank of Montreal and, as a result, 'alarmed not quieted the Bond holders.' Although they were pleased to hear that 'State ownership was completely outside the intention' of the provincial government, they were dismayed by the acceptance of the Ontario Power Company's tender to supply 'a very large zone embracing the most active centres of manufacture,' and by the province's decision to build its own lines for the transmission of Ontario Power's hydroelectricity. The effect of these actions, they argued, could only be detrimental to Ontario's interests, not to mention those of the Electrical Development Company which had 'done so much in the past towards building up the electrical supply industry in Canada.' The premier could only sigh in exasperation.[15]

Aside from his failure to make these bondholders and their representatives understand the position of the province in hydroelectric development, Whitney enjoyed his time in England. 'I took a great deal of comfort in walking about London,' he wrote a friend in Iroquois, 'and investigating the ten thousand or more objects and localities of great interest which are there.' Refreshed and relaxed, he came home – to the Electrical Development Company, which now chose to reject the opportunity, noted by Whitney in his letter to Taylor, to provide power to Toronto and municipalities to the east of that city at Ontario Power's rates. Disgusted, the Tory chief informed his brother: 'all prospects of an attempt to arrange so that the Pellatt Company would have a share of the territory have come to an end.'[16]

But the Electrical Development Company would not go away, and late in 1907, it turned to do battle in the upcoming votes on municipal by-laws 'to give definite approval to the signing of an exclusive power contract by the municipalities with the Hydro partnership.' The fight was particularly sharp in Toronto where a different by-law, in need of public approval, represented an even more serious threat to the prospects of the Electrical Development Company. On 1 January 1908, Toronto ratepayers would be 'asked to approve a $2,750,000 bond issue to build a municipal network which would distribute the Hydro-Electric Commission power that the electorate had committed the city to taking the previous year.' The creation of a municipally owned system would present a rival to the Toronto Electric Light Company, which was the Electrical Development Company in another guise. At the same time, it was most certainly in the interest of the Hydro-Electric Power Commission to have Toronto vote for a publicly owned operation: such a development would give the commission access to the large Toronto market, while freeing the city from the monopolistic grasp of Nicholls, Pellatt, and company. Clearly, the stakes were high; consequently, the brawl was fierce, with propaganda and innuendo marking the campaigns on both sides in the by-law struggle.[17]

In the midst of this fight, it was suggested that the government should take over the Electrical Development Company, and the Toronto Electric Light Company – at a good price – to 'do justice to British bondholders and uphold Provincial credit.' The premier rejected this proposition, and Frank Cochrane offered reasons for such a decision in a letter J.S. Willison: 'I do not like the idea of expropriation. One reason is that it is going to tie up so much of the money of the Province in one spot. As you will readily understand, the whole North country must be opened up in some way. We have only one-fifth of the Province yet disposed of, and the great wealth of our Northern country is practically unknown and will remain unknown and undeveloped until some way of opening it up is found.' Further, Whitney would not accept criticism from Willison, by way of columns in the *News*, to the effect that expropriation was the only honourable solution. 'It would be all right,' he remarked sarcastically to his brother, 'for us to repudiate our contract with the Ontario Power Company and then spend ten or twelve million dollars in expropriating the other people's property, in order that the pocket of Mr. Flavelle may not be injured.' Obviously, the premier was growing increasingly irritated with the campaign of the private power interests, interests that he had tried to assist. Finally, two days before the by-law vote in Toronto, an angry Whitney spoke out for the record: 'The combination has, during the last ten days, flooded the Province of Ontario with thousands of circulars filled with silly falsehoods directed against the Government and its policy on the Power question. ... The combination includes gentlemen of position in financial institutions here, as well as ... foreign worthies.' Consequently, the premier could take some satisfaction from the fact that, in the first week of January 1908, thirteen municipalities including Toronto approved their various by-laws; and all – except Galt – proceeded to make contracts with the Ontario Hydro-Electric Power Commission. 'The Power By-Law was carried ... [in Toronto],' the premier wrote to Ned.

Similar By-Laws will be voted on in other Cities and Towns next Monday and the effect of the Toronto vote will be very great. This result has made it quite clear that Pellatt, Nicholls, Flavelle and White and the others are out of it so far as public opinion is concerned. It is an advantage, too, that the Grits are in control of the City Council. This is an advantage because it puts the interests of the City with regard to power in Grit hands and they will have the responsibility. Altogether the situation is comfortable and pleasing.[18]

'Comfortable and pleasing' as the situation may have been when Whitney witnessed the battering of Pellatt and Nicholls, he still had to concern himself with the fate of their company. Consequently, he was partner to two further unsuccessful efforts to extricate the corporation from the corner into which its imperious and greedy supporters had painted it. In the first instance, he persuaded Sam Blake, acting for Ontario Power, to talk to Electrical Development representatives in the hope that a possible 'adjustment' might yield something to the Canadian company; but the discussions went nowhere, thanks to Blake's tough stand. Then, the premier agreed to listen while deputies of the English investors attempted to persuade him to take over the power plant and the transmission line of Electrical Development; but they met with no success. Whitney and his government were through with the Electrical Development Company.[19]

III

While the Electrical Development Company dogged the premier at every turn throughout 1907, the prohibitionists – with lighter footsteps – did likewise, continually complaining about the injustice of the three-fifths clause. Their protest was renewed at the start of the year when forty-four of a hundred and one municipalities voting on local option went dry. The temperance workers claimed that another forty-one places would have gone the same route had only a simple majority of votes been required. Whitney's legislation, they contended, wrongly kept a hundred and thirty bar-rooms in existence. Consequently, demands for repeal of the 60 per cent clause were made in petitions and delegations, and in the legislature where George Graham unsuccessfully attempted to meet the prohibitionists' wishes. But Whitney would not be moved, firmly convinced that the contentious clause provided a permanency to municipal decisions on temperance which a simple majority could not. And he increasingly resented the suggestion that only those who opposed the three-fifths clause were truly 'Christian men' and the 'Servants of God.' 'People will not be dragooned by this sort of abuse,' he told one correspondent, 'and, in my opinion, it is a survival or a revival of the same methods that burned men at the stake a few years ago.' Further, he remained convinced that the 'lessening of the drink evil has been put back for years, and is kept back steadily by the exclusive and peremptory insistence on the part of those who hold extreme views that their views shall be adopted to the utmost and that those who hold more moderate views are bad people and bad citizens.' There had to be, he reminded temperance workers in pointed fashion, some Christian charity in this matter.[20]

The premier paid for his firmness on the three-fifths clause: he was subjected to a 'torrent of denunciation' and threatened with defections from the unofficial coalition which had helped to put him into office in 1905. He could cope with the unwarranted abuse; he boasted: 'My skin is so thick now that I almost welcome unfair and untruthful criticism.' But the cry of 'Whitney must go,' which emanated from temperance Liberals who had earlier abandoned Ross, was of greater concern to the Tory leader. He would not be cowed by such talk; but he scarcely could have welcomed it.[21]

The possible return of unctuous turncoats was about the only bright spot for the provincial Liberals in 1907 because, after a legislative session in which they were thoroughly outclassed by the Tories, the Grits underwent another change of leadership. At the end of August, George Graham – after strongly urging his own elevation – went into Laurier's cabinet as minister of railways and canals: the prime minister was still casting about for that elusive strong man from Ontario. Whitney was convinced that the move indicated that the Liberals had given up, for the time being, on achieving success at the provincial level; that federal back-benchers would be humiliated by being ignored in this cabinet appointment; and that the Ontario Tories had been handed 'a distinct advantage.' To replace Graham, the Liberal caucus now turned to Alexander Grant MacKay, member for Grey North since 1902 and, briefly, cabinet minister under Ross. This shuffle necessitated a by-election in Graham's provincial riding of Brockville, and there the Conservative candidate, campaigning in quiet fashion, captured the Grit constituency despite strenuous efforts by the Liberals.[22]

It was a rock-bottom beginning for MacKay's new career as provincial leader, but Whitney was naturally delighted with the turnover in a Liberal riding. 'It is almost as important an event,' he noted, 'as the last general election. The people took up the record of the Government themselves and pronounced a very distinct verdict in its favor without any interference on the part of the Government.' MacKay was 'in a position deserving of pity.' Thoughtful Liberals were worried; some saw disaster at the next provincial election in the Brockville result, while others fretted about the implications for the federal party in Ontario. Certainly this turn of events must have had a demoralizing effect upon the provincial Liberal legislators, who also had to adjust to their third leader in as many years. The consequent condition of the Grits, combined with the fact that the Conservatives were content to be neat housekeepers, produced a lacklustre session of the legislature in 1908.[23]

IV

During that session and surely inspired by Whitney's intense dislike of election chicanery, Foy introduced a new measure which named as a corrupt act almost anything – save standard campaigning – that could influence the outcome of an election contest. Penalties for proven corruption were made considerably stiffer. It became illegal to promise a government position to an individual in the course of the campaign, or to provide vehicles for transportation to the polls. The attorney-general also offered a series of resolutions on law reform which were to provide the basis for discussion in the current session and legislation in the next. Enactments based on them would be designed 'to decrease appeals, expedite trials and lessen the cost of litigation.' Debate in the legislature followed and the law associations presented their views.[24]

The legislators were also made aware of the problems created by the existence of the automobile when farmers' organizations protested the presence and reckless handling of such machines in rural areas. The Ontario Motor League countered by arguing that this vehicle required just legislation because it was 'now a factor in business as well as in pleasure.' Whitney thought that any law would have to be based on the principle that the motor car was 'here for good.' 'Having regard to advances made in scientific matters within the last ten years,' he wrote to a young E.C. Drury in Crown Hill, 'it would be hard to set bounds to the possibilities of such vehicles in the future. Practically the situation has settled itself in the Cities. But in my opinion it can never be settled in the rural districts until the horses become as fairly accustomed to the motors as they are in the Cities. It seems to me, but of course I offer the suggestion with diffidence, that the longer we put off making the horses familiar with the cars, the longer we postpone the settlement of the difficulty.' A sound if somewhat light reply from the blacksmith's son. The Conservative leader did not bother to tell the future premier that, personally, he rode a bicycle to the legislative buildings, when the weather was good and when rheumatism was not sharply troubling his foot. In the end the legislature produced an act making it mandatory for a paid chauffeur to have a provincial licence; prohibiting anyone under seventeen from driving; requiring the stopping of a motor if a horse appeared to be frightened; and demanding that the vehicle operator provide his name and address – without being asked – to anyone injured by his car. The age of the automobile had been duly recognized in Ontario.[25]

Two matters particularly vexed the premier while the assembly was in session. He found it increasingly difficult to make his way from his office to the legislature without being set upon by lobbyists, 'all asking for something that should not be granted – some interference, some letting down, some getting around, or some crawling through.' He angrily announced that he found the situation 'intolerable' and would stand for it no longer. He was not in the business of creating loopholes; he resented the implications of such requests; and he was contemptuous of the Uriah Heeps who attempted to curry favour. Of course, the entire matter was also illustrative of how few buffers stood between public figures and the public in that day.

The Tory leader was further irritated by the introduction of a bill in the Senate for the incorporation of the Ontario and Michigan Power Company, and he charged that this legislation, if it became law, 'would give away valuable water-powers, and privileges, and exportation rights.' A lengthy resolution in the Ontario house roundly denounced the proposal, and the bill proceeded no further in the Senate. Whitney, in the best of the Mowat tradition, was vigilantly guarding his province's rights. Naturally, one had to be more alert because of that Liberal presence in Ottawa.[26]

The passage of a redistribution bill marked the end of the session. This measure increased the number of legislators from ninety-eight to one hundred and six, by doubling Toronto's representation to eight and adding four seats in northern Ontario. Minor alterations were made in other ridings, Conservatives explained, in order to make them adhere more closely to county boundaries and provide fairer representation. Of course, if such changes strengthened the Conservatives and weakened the Liberals that result would not make the Tories unhappy. The Grits, with some justification, charged that a gerrymander had been perpetrated and they attacked the creation of dual-member constituencies in the provincial capital. Toronto's growing population undoubtedly deserved greater representation, but the Liberals could rightly see that strong men like Foy and Pyne could now carry weaker Conservatives to victory with them. Eight separate constituencies might just have given the Grits a Toronto seat or two in the legislature. The premier coolly replied that justice was being done, but he did not say to whom. He knew only too well that there were advantages for his party in this new arrangement, despite the complaints of some Ontario Tories that even more favourable boundary lines could have been drawn. The Liberals, already tottering in advance of any election, had been struck a low blow by the Conservative leader, who had just taken out some unnecessary victory insurance. Unlikely as he was to admit it, Whitney was busily constructing an awesome political machine.[27]

v

Having further improved his party's position, the premier called a provincial election for 8 June, and no one expected that the Conservatives would face any real trouble in the upcoming contest. They possessed a popular leader who had grown immensely in his office and who presented a confident and trustworthy figure to the public. The former Morrisburg lawyer, now some distance from being an average country barrister, had proven himself more than equal to his job, a development recognized by most, including the premier. 'I have become accustomed,' he told a fellow legislator, 'during the past three years, to do[ing] many things, without hesitation, which at one time would have seemed to be impossible to tackle.' The Tories had also compiled an impressive legislative record in those three years. And Whitney made constant reference to that fact in his appeals to the Ontario electorate when he recounted the achievements of his administration: the implementation of a public power policy; the solution of the University of Toronto's problems; improvement of the elementary and secondary school systems; creation of the railway and municipal board; development of northern Ontario's assets; the production of precise and sound liquor legislation; the virtual elimination of electoral corruption; and firm resistance to federal encroachment. These subjects, considerably expanded, provided the bases for much of the Conservative campaign.[28]

The premier thus asked the province's voters to approve what had been done, but he promised nothing specific for the future and only hinted that the public might expect more of the same. In Hamilton, he resisted pressure to pledge a technical institution for that city: 'I am not here,' he told his audience, 'to promise anything to the City of Hamilton. Whatever will be said of me after I leave office, it will not be said that I stood up and did not disdain to bribe a Constituency.' He recognized that his government might 'lose votes' because of such a position, but he intended to 'stand fast to it': 'this Government,' he concluded, 'will do what is right and fair by the City of Hamilton and it will do it no matter whom you elect.' Such a remarkably blunt statement was not without its appeal to Ontarians. C.F. Hamilton of the *News*, and a reasonably level-headed observer of the provincial scene, remarked: 'I said ... that were I in doubt the Hamilton incident alone would make me vote for Whitney.'[29]

Beneath the talk, the Conservative organizational machinery ran smoothly. After a long exchange of correspondence with Robert Borden on the subject, the provincial Conservatives had hired an organizer for their own purposes late in 1906, and he proved to be a diligent worker. The premier, conscious of the racial and religious skeletons in the Conservative closet, moved to keep that door closed whenever he could. Thus he suggested to a party worker that it might be best for the Tories of Prescott County to select a French-Canadian standard-bearer, and they did. As the premier's party gathered a full head of steam, the only real question was whether or not over-confident party members, disappointed patronage-seekers, and angry temperance workers would cause a small reduction in the Tory majority.[30]

The Liberals did not have much in their favour. They had been weakened by rapid changes in leadership and suffered from a lack of money. Nor was there much help from the federal party: Laurier felt the province was 'in bad shape' and he had 'very little hope of improvement.' George Graham, now ensconced in the federal cabinet, confided that neither he nor the prime minister thought he should be 'too prominent in the Ontario campaign.' 'We are sure to be defeated both in Brockville and in the Province,' he gloomily continued, 'and it would weaken me considerably if I were to be prominent among the slain.' Thus left to his own devices and limited resources, MacKay proved to be, nevertheless, a game fighter and he tirelessly toured the province. But he could not mount a frontal attack on the Conservatives because his party was so weak and because the bulk of Conservative policies were too popular. Thus he did not come out for prohibition, but stayed with local option and pledged to support a simple majority clause, rather than the three-fifths one. He did not oppose the improvement in the University of Toronto's position, but only the way in which the money was provided: he wanted more direct government control. At no time did he indicate that he expected his party to win.[31]

Nor did it. The Tories captured eighty-six seats; the Liberals, nineteen; and Allan Studholme was still the Labour member for Hamilton East. Whitney was left nearly speechless: 'The situation here,' he wrote to Ned, 'can hardly be described. The result is so conclusive and so crushing that there is little left for discussion or comment. I will only say this: no man in my position could in his wildest dreams look forward to or expect such treatment as I have received from the people at the last Election, and more especially at this one.' The only dark spot on the whole Conservative picture was Perth South, where Nelson Monteith, the minister of agriculture, went down to defeat. The explanation of that upset may lie in local conditions or, possibly, in a rural perception that this government was not sufficiently alert to farmers' needs and complaints. But this was of little consequence to a jubilant Sam Blake, who termed the triumph a 'wonderful and unequivocal endorsement ... of honest progressive and helpful government.' Half in jest and half in earnest, W.D. Gregory sensed one of the factors in the sweep when he told the victorious Conservative in Brant South, the riding which had once been A.S. Hardy's fiefdom: 'A preAdamite Tory like yourself, however, will feel like a fish out of water when you get down among the radicals that make up the Government majority, and show how meaningless party names have become.' Was that government majority 'radical'? Even in the context of time and place, that judgment is extreme; but the government was progressive, responsive to the needs of a changing Ontario – and for that sensitivity the Tories had been amply rewarded.[32]

It was a time of introspection for the Liberals. MacKay thought that the two key factors in the defeat had been 'a solid liquor vote' for the Conservatives and their 'unlimited campaign fund,' but he also muttered about 'the nonsupport or luke-warm support given by several Dominion Members in their respective Ridings to local candidates.' Others cited the absence of organization and the presence of internal quarrels, while W.T.R. Preston, the old and unscrupulous

1908 Election Results			
Popular vote			Seats
Conservative	246,324	(54.68%)[33]	86
Liberal	178,739	(39.68%)	19
Labour-Socialist	11,102	(2.46%)[34]	1
Other	14,307	(3.1%)	0
Total	450,472	(100.00%)	106

Grit organizer, fell on the *Globe* and its Presbyterian minister editor, J.A. Macdonald. Apparently no Liberal was bold enough to suggest that Whitney's performance over the preceding three years just might have been a factor.[35]

Whitney's triumph of June 1908 was capped by a knighthood in July, when the Prince of Wales, visiting Quebec City for its tercentenary, conferred honours bestowed by his father, Edward VII. The new knight took the opportunity afforded by an imperial banquet, given on the occasion by Earl Grey, to salute both founding groups and the Empire: 'here, on this continent,' he informed the assembled diners, 'we men of French and English nationality, people of this great auxiliary kingdom within the Empire, are affording an object lesson of the benefits of free representative government under the British system ... we stand for the continuity of the Empire.' As he proceeded through his speech, the premier, searching for a means of reconciling the problems inherent in the presence of the two groups in Canada, found his answer in a common blooding which evoked memories, but no antipathy: the war of 1812. Obviously, the Plains of Abraham, the affairs at St Denis and Batoche, and the Boer War would not do, but Chateauguay and Crysler's Farm would. Having done this, Whitney then ran into a dilemma he shared with many like-minded imperialists: if the war of 1812 marked the beginning of a Canadian identity, then how was one to argue for the maintenance of the British connection? The premier's solution, like that of many others, was to introduce the imprecise 'auxiliary kingdom' theory, which allowed for Canadian development with the retention of the British connection. Such theorizing, however, was an attempt to ride two horses – nationalism and imperialism – and the result could be distressingly uncomfortable, although it has been argued that, in the Canadian context, the latter was an expression of the former.[36]

Such thoughts by the Conservative leader were not simply engendered by the tercentenary celebration: he frequently paused to consider the future of the empire and he was not particularly pleased by what he envisaged. He was annoyed by the apparent failure of the British people – as seen in their voting habits – to 'make up their minds' as to 'what steps' might be necessary 'to render permanent and lasting the bonds which connect[ed] ... the different parts of the Empire.' 'Rightly or wrongly,' he lectured a British member of Parliament,

Canadians feel that ever since the negotiation of the Ashburton Treaty at any rate, the Mother country has 'turned them down' from time to time, without any hesitation, in order to please the United States. Canadians are willing – to put it mildly – to make sacrifices in the direction of the continuity of the Empire, but knowing as they do, that no effort on the part of the Mother country will, for a long time at least, make of the United States a friendly Nation, and that giving way to them repeatedly in order to avoid friction, merely encourages them to insist on further sacrifices, Canadians may some time become tired of the situation, especially as the sacrifices they are willing to make for the continuity of the Empire have an effect entirely opposite to that intended.

On the Canadian scene Whitney was also irritated by Laurier's failure to press for 'a small general tariff on all foreign goods entering any British territory' because this Tory thought that implementation of such a policy 'would have been the first step towards free trade within the Empire.' The premier was 'disturbed' by the prime minister's 'deliberate policy of drift' on the subject because the Ontarian feared 'a fatal effect on the vitality of the Empire.'[37]

Thus, when Whitney made another trip to England late in the summer of 1908, he managed 'a half-hour's conversation' with Lord Milner, at the Rhodes Trust office, just before the latter sailed for Canada and an extensive tour. The Ontario Conservative leader 'suggested' to the viscount 'that if, in his speeches in Canada, he went into details & boldly advocated immediate action and tariff reform, Sir Wilfrid might possibly, at the present juncture, make use of it with the French Canadians for election purposes.' There were times when it was necessary to be discreet in the interests of imperial unity. The two men also debated Whitney's view that 'immigrants coming into Canada from the North Western States' made 'good British subjects'; Milner 'seemed to doubt it.' The premier was also concerned lest Milner's presence in Canada, on the eve of a federal election, might drive Liberals who were favourably disposed towards the Britisher's ideas in behind Laurier, out of a concern for party unity, and thus give the false impression of strong Canadian opposition to Milner's proposals and to the 'continuity of the Empire.' For Whitney, the problem of the empire's future remained a vexing one.[38]

VI

Because of his visit to England, the Ontario premier was not on the scene at the start of the federal election campaign of 1908. When he returned to Toronto on 28 September, however, he threw himself into the battle, speaking on Borden's behalf not only in Ontario but in Montreal and the Eastern Townships. In Quebec he emphasized 'the absence of any real racial feeling in Ontario' and charged the Liberals with deliberately raising the subject. In Ontario he attacked Laurier for his extravagant railway policies and informed the public that Foy 'would see that no electoral misdeeds occurred in the Northern part of the Province.' Despite his labours, Whitney expressed no surprise at Laurier's triumph or Borden's inability to improve his majority position in Ontario. 'I am,' he wrote, assuming a positive outlook, 'practically satisfied with the result. I believe it will be much better for the Liberal-Conservative party to postpone taking office for three or four years than to have come in with a small majority at the present time.' He had not been impressed by the calibre of some Conservative candidates, and he thought that the influence of the Grand Trunk and 'a silly little Orange pamphlet' had hurt the party in his province. Borden was 'practically certain to succeed at the next appeal to the Country.'[39]

Borden had failed in his bid for an electoral triumph in 1908, but Whitney had not: the premier had received a strong mandate for his policies and he had to turn to the task of fulfilling pledges implicit in those policies. In August, the construction company of F.H. McGuigan was awarded the contract for the building of the Hydro-Electric Power Commission's two-hundred-and-ninety-three-mile transmission line through south-western Ontario; and the first sod for this project was turned in November. Meanwhile the Commission, closely watched by Whitney, prepared to call for tenders for the equipment of the distributing and transformer stations that would line the transmission route. As the expenditures began to mount, there was hesitation on the part of some of the premier's colleagues. But Whitney now had no intention of calling a halt to public ownership of the transmission line; he had already exhaustively explored other possibilities without success. 'It seemed to me,' he reported to Foy after a meeting with the commission, 'that we cannot go back. We must go forward no matter what happens, and it is possible that circumstances may occur in addition to those which have occurred already which may justify some further legislation next Session. No matter how we look at it, it all comes back to this, that we must go on and not look back. There may be danger in the former, but there would be practical ruin and humiliation in the latter.[40]

'Circumstances' most certainly did develop and the premier was forced to take strong measures to prevent legal action from halting the drive to public power. The difficulty began with the mayor of Galt who, after the 1908 by-law was approved by voters, refused to sign a contract with the commission on the grounds that it differed substantially from that proposed when the municipality had sought public approval for entering into such a contract. Following the lead provided by the balky first citizen of Galt, private power interests supported legal challenges to the right of London and Toronto to enter into such agreements. This action was taken despite provincial legislation, passed in 1908, validating the by-laws of 1907 that approved of municipalities entering into contracts.

Whitney met the difficulty head on with the Power Commission Amendment Act of 1909, which stayed any legal action, validated all municipality-commission contracts, and ordered the mayor of Galt to sign the contract. This measure not only distressed the customary opponents of the Conservatives' hydroelectric power policy but also shook up the business community, angered British investors, and produced a spate of wild stories. Attempts were made to terrorize farmers along the route of the transmission line with tales of the dangers of high voltage passing overhead. Appeals were made to the federal government to disallow this 'highly improper' – or 'abominable' or 'monstrous' – legislation. 'Bankers, bondholders, and financial writers,' B.E. Walker told Laurier, 'all feel that part of the foundation on which they relied for safety in Canadian investments is being swept away.' Earl Grey, who was deeply disturbed by this episode, heartily approved of Goldwin Smith's dictum: 'They have opened the gates of confiscation & closed the doors of justice.'[41]

The federal government, as represented by Laurier and justice minister A.B. Aylesworth, did not act because, regardless of their personal feelings, they knew that the legislation was not *ultra vires*. Whitney held his ground, reasonably confident that disallowance would not be tried, irritated by the solid suspicion that 'British journals received payment' in a 'cold-blooded way' for carrying hostile articles, and angered by the effort 'to injure the financial credit of Ontario.' He was annoyed when anyone dared to suggest that his power policy and socialism could be equated. 'It is indeed a ghastly joke,' he informed a British newspaper editor, 'to charge the Ontario Government with being socialistic etc., when it is the bulwark in Canada by means of which such influences will be shattered.' This was the language of an Ontario progressive Conservative and it makes much clearer the purpose behind some of Whitney's legislation: orderly advance to avoid disorderly retreat. But caution had to be the keynote; otherwise chaos might result. 'There never was a time in the history of free Government,' he lectured one supporter, 'that it was so necessary that parties and people should move slowly with reference to public matters. There is a tendency to delirium in this respect all over the world which must be faced and dealt with carefully.'[42]

The power act which was passed during the 1909 session of the legislature overshadowed the other subjects which were considered in the course of those seven weeks. After entertaining briefs on the subject of the law reform resolutions of the previous session, Foy guided a measure through the legislature which was largely in line with the goals he had established twelve months before. Whitney produced a bill which gave a land grant of two million acres to the Canadian Northern Railway as aid in the construction of five hundred miles of line in northern Ontario. The provincial government retained the mineral and pine timber rights in the area, and could dictate the time and price of the sale of land; the company, in turn, had to run the road through the 'clay belt.' Whitney, in support of the measure, argued that the government had a duty to develop 'the Northern territory for both agriculture and mineral purposes,' and, he noted, the land was 'worthless without a railway.' As a clincher, he advanced the proposition that it was 'much better to give 2,000,000 acres subject to ... conditions than to spend $25,000,000' in government construction of a line. But there was more to this grant than this. Whitney was clearly signalling the restless residents of northern Ontario, some of whom had already called for creation of a separate province out of irritation with domination by imperial Toronto, that he had not forgotten them. (He could also have pointed out that the T&NO now stretched to Cochrane and a link with the National Transcontinental.) And he was telling entrepreneurs, such as William Mackenzie, that there were limits to public enterprise in the province and that his government was open to co-operation. Possibly flushed by this concession, Mackenzie pressed for either a cash bonus or a guarantee of his railway company's bonds, and blustered that he wanted the bill withdrawn. But when the government remained firm, the railway entrepreneur wilted and took what he was offered.[43]

Just after the 1909 session was prorogued, the Conservative government was able to make one further announcement which, in Whitney's view, marked 'the fulfilment of all the pledges given to the people – all in a little more than four years.' A ten-year contract for the printing of a new set of five public school readers had been awarded to the T. Eaton Company, the lowest of the tenderers. The retail price of the set would be only forty-nine cents; this compared most favourably with the price for the old set of one dollar and fifteen cents, from 1884 to 1907, and forty-nine cents from 1907 to 1909. By the end of the year the prices of other textbooks had been sharply reduced. A few Grits grumbled that John Eaton had no business, as a Liberal, in winning the contract at such a low price and thereby helping Whitney; but, on the whole, there was little but praise for the results of this particular policy.[44]

Despite the reforming tendencies displayed by Whitney in the legislation which he and his administration presented, there were subjects upon which he would not be moved. One of these continued to be female suffrage. The premier would have nothing to do with the matter and, when faced by the question, tended to be vague or facetious or both. He did not think that there were indications of 'anything like a woman's suffrage movement' in Ontario. 'Of course,' he wrote a female correspondent, 'there are people who insist that "women suffer" but these same people are willing to *suffer* her to continue in her present position.' It was all very amusing, except when the women got reasonably well organized and then it was annoying. 'This infernal Council of Women is here,' he wrote to Ned, 'with Lady Aberdeen bossing the job. I will have to preside at a meeting.'[45]

Nor was he particularly sympathetic to the plight of some unemployed in the booming first decade of the twentieth century. When a deputation representing Toronto's unemployed met with the premier, he advised them to abandon fruitless urban living and seek labour on the farm. He was of the opinion that part of this problem was created by bringing into Ontario immigrants who were neither needed nor wanted; the immigrant should have 'some means or ... be qualified to engage in farm work.' He told others looking for work to move west, declaring that 'there were ... many opportunities for active, intelligent young men between Fort William and the Pacific Ocean.' The premier was not without compassion in individual cases of hardship, and, at times, quickly pulled the necessary strings to provide a job for someone who was down on his luck. But he had no solution to the general problem of unemployment, nor did he regard the matter as being his government's particular responsibility. And his views undoubtedly reflected his own experience, which demonstrated that an Ontario-born blacksmith's son could rise, by dint of hard work – and a bit of luck – to the premier's chair.[46]

Generally, however, Whitney could reflect contentedly on what had been achieved since he came to that office, and the public largely approved of his actions, of that he was sure. Nor had the task really been that onerous because, as he wrote to a supporter, 'while the people desire straightforwardness, they do not ask for perfection.' That was just as well, he thought, for 'few men' were 'more convinced of their fallibility' than he. There were, of course, the bitter critics who could comment as follows: 'Capital seems to be safer in South American countries than here at the present time. With the disadvantages of our climatic conditions unless we call a halt in what you speak of as ultra-radical legislation, we are not likely to get much money from outside to develop ourselves.' But, then, Whitney did not think that he was 'bound to answer to charges of every Tom, Dick or Harry' who chose to attack him – because the people were with him.[47]

8

A Toast to Empire – 'The Greatest Secular Influence for Good': 1909–1911

I

Throughout his public career Whitney always kept a watchful eye on imperial developments, particularly anxious to ensure that the Canadian tie to the mother country was in no way threatened and eager, when possible, to strengthen it. He behaved in this manner out of conviction, but he was also confident that most of his fellow citizens shared his concern. 'I believe,' he informed a British correspondent, 'that at least eight men out of ten in the Dominion of Canada – except in Quebec where there are good reasons for a different view – are warmly interested in everything that pertains to the Empire and its future.' He was also convinced, by 1909, that events were 'pointing toward a recasting and rearrangement of the relations between the groups, including the Mother Country, which compose the Empire.' He thought that 'the action of the people of the Over-Seas Dominions at the time of the South African War' had clearly indicated 'what one aspect of the rearrangement would be': he obviously wanted an imperial defence pact. But, despite the positive notes which he sounded, the premier was also on record as deploring Canadians' insufficient gratitude for Britain's protection of them. And he worried the question of whether or not the empire could be continued by means of 'sane imperialism.' 'Sane imperialism,' he evidently hoped, would be the way 'by which the different groups or communities of British peoples all over the world' would 'join in and share the burdens of Empire, while retaining their autonomy.' Recognizing the nearly contradictory aspects of his hopes, the Ontario premier added: 'To bring this about may seem difficult, but difficulties are made to be overcome, and I have no doubt that the old British spirit will make itself felt, and that the result will be all that may be desired.'[1]

It is not surprising, therefore, that Whitney plunged headlong into the debate over imperial relations which began with the announcement in March 1909 by the First Lord of the Admiralty that Germany was closing the gap in a desperate naval race with Great Britain. Hard on the heels of this statement came the debate in the

Canadian House of Commons on a resolution, presented by George Foster, which called for Canada to assume 'her proper share of the responsibility and financial burden incident to the suitable protection of her exposed coast line and great sea-ports.' The vagueness of this phrasing was eliminated in a final resolution which was accepted by the house, without division, and which supported 'any necessary expenditure designed to promote the speedy organization of a Canadian naval service in co-operation with and in close relation to the Imperial Navy.' The premier's reaction was immediate: 'I think you did right,' he told Foster,

in agreeing to Laurier's Resolution which was passed, and which, of course, is of much more value than any action would have been which was not unanimous. I still think Laurier lost a great opportunity. Without really pledging himself or his party to anything more than he did, he could by declaring his intention to offer one or two Dreadnoughts at once to the Empire, have made the outside Nations sit up and take notice of what the Over-Seas Dominions are about, and in that way perhaps could have saved the Empire in the end the cost of half-a-dozen Dreadnoughts. More than that, by doing so he would have quieted perhaps forever all timidity and restlesness [sic] in the minds of French-Canadians as to what his opinion is as to Imperialism.

Whitney's obviously anglophone opinions make it perfectly evident that he neither appreciated Laurier's tightrope act nor understood the thinking of French-Canadians: the Toronto perspective on imperial affairs presented a picture that was crisp and clean – and it was a million miles from that offered in Ottawa. But the premier had unequivocally indicated what he personally wanted in the way of a Canadian naval policy.[2]

Consequently, Whitney was prepared to comment when the federal government hinted in October 1909, and announced through the Throne Speech in November, that it intended to introduce legislation that would lead to the creation of a Canadian navy. 'I would not oppose the Government's scheme,' he wrote to P.D. Ross of the Ottawa *Journal*, '... but I would strongly favour an immediate contribution of one or two Dreadnaughts [sic].' Those battleships – he most definitely wanted them presented as a gift but, conceding that all might not agree with him, he said he would willingly settle for one. For the moment, however, Whitney could live with Laurier's cautious first step because it demonstrated, finally, that Canada was prepared to assume its share of defence responsibility in the future. But, he argued, should war come 'within the next few years,' the naval struggle 'would take place in the North Sea,' and he doubted that any Canadian cruisers would be of 'much value then.' Nevertheless, the cruisers should be built and manned. His main quarrel was with men like O.D. Skelton – 'an out and out Little Englander' – and F.D. Monk – 'he should have received a good dressing down long ago' – who wanted to do nothing in return for the benefits of empire.[3]

When Borden asked for Whitney's advice on how to approach the Liberal naval policy, the Ontario leader repeated what he had said to Ross about the proposed Canadian navy and the dreadnought gift; then, he added a further opinion: 'As far as losing Parliamentary strength is concerned I would face it boldly, no matter how many men like Monk may be estranged, and I think they would be very few. To my mind this action is a patriotic duty which devolves upon us, and one which I am sure that few of us have the inclination to dodge.' He also advised the federal leader that it would be unwise 'to move the six months hoist to the Government Bill,' because it would be 'a tactical mistake' – 'having regard to the attitude assumed towards the resolution of last session' – and would 'create a wrong impression in the minds of many people.' The premier emphasized one more point with Borden: the dreadnoughts – or the money for their construction – should be a gift, and the ships should not belong to Canada; a few Tories wanted the reverse, but not Whitney. 'If in this attitude,' the provincial chief told the opposition leader, 'we do not receive the sympathy of our people that will mean that the majority of the people look forward with equanimity to the time when the connection between the Empire and Canada shall be dissolved and the sooner we know it the better.' In the lengthy debate which followed Laurier's introduction of his naval service bill early in 1910, Borden made every effort to hold his French-Canadian support, such as it was, but ultimately closely followed the suggestions by Whitney. The sentiments of Ontario's Conservative premier had become the policy of the federal Conservative party. Whitney, almost accidentaly, was moving into a national role, albeit one that usually confined him to the wings where, lacking any strong desire for greater attention, he was usually content to remain.[4]

II

The activities of the Ontario legislature in 1910 paled in comparison to the dimensions and implications of the debate on the imperial relationship which the naval question sparked inside and outside of Ottawa. Further, that session of the provincial house lacked any large issue which might have provoked widespread public comment, possibly because Whitney thought that all pledges made to the public by the Tories prior to 1905 had been fulfilled. There was also the fascinating diversion of national developments to catch the premier's eye, and he could afford the luxury of being diverted because he possessed a set of competent cabinet ministers to handle matters closer to home. MacKay, not surprisingly, deplored the 'paucity of prospective and progressive legislation.' Yet the critical suggestions of the Liberal leader were limited to proposals for further aid to technical education, an investigation of high prices, implementation of additional forest conservation measures, and consideration of the number of teachers in a school when grants were given. He was silent on the controversial three-fifths clause because he was not committed to temperance, although some of his followers did argue for a simple majority or prohibition. Whitney remained unmoved: his local-option regulation was more than satisfactory.

The Liberals were critical of the manner in which the Hydro-Electric Power Commission had acquired land easements from farmers for transmission lines, and they objected to the prices paid and the absence of appeal to the courts. The Grit stand on this matter was indicative of a general problem that the party faced: it continued to be the spokesman for the farming communities and not for the growing urban centres of Ontario. The latter were largely in Whitney's domain, and much of the legislation of this session, as others, showed a consciousness of the rise of cities and towns with their attendant problems. Thus, the government placed all telephone companies in the province under the authority of the Ontario Railway and Municipal Board, which could regulate rates. Municipalities were given the power 'to inspect the source of the local milk supply' and it became compulsory to provide 'clean and sanitary quarters for cows giving milk.' In a continuing policy of penal reform, the government was able to announce that, having acquired the land, prisoners would be set to work on the site of the proposed Guelph reformatory. None of this was very startling, but it was reformist, essential, and, largely, urban-oriented.[5]

Even normally reserved western Ontarians, however, were stirred by excitement in mid-autumn 1910, when the transmission line from Niagara Falls was sufficiently complete to permit a 'switching-on' ceremony in Berlin. The 12th of October was the day and many of the province's most prominent citizens found their way to the chief town of Waterloo county. Whitney and Beck were there, and so was the Waterloo North member of Parliament, Mackenzie King. The event was staged at the local hockey rink, and there Whitney took Beck's hand and guided it to the button. The arena was suddenly ablaze with light; the crowd roared its approval; the final pledge had been met.[6]

Yet there could be no rest for the premier, for now, as with most durable governments, he had to meet problems that arose, not pledges that had been made. Prominent among the former was the issue of bilingual schools, and there was an irony in this because, from the time that he had become leader of the Ontario Conservatives, Whitney had worked diligently to eradicate the reputation his party had for fostering appeals to race and religion. Taking cautious advantage of the work that had been so tentatively, if not accidentally, begun by Marter, he had encouraged the return of Roman Catholics to the party fold. The Tory chief had secured the services of J.J. Foy and dispensed with those of the Protestant Protective Association. On assuming office, he had placed Roman Catholics in two important portfolios, and this move evoked nothing but praise from people of that faith, who became convinced that a new day had dawned upon the Conservative party's relationship with them. And even in 1906 and 1907, when faced by the thorny question of provincial certification for teaching members of religious orders, the Whitney government had shown exceptional skill in producing an answer. The administration had awarded certificates – which were graded according to Ontario teaching experience – once teachers concerned had attended a specially devised summer school course. If this arrangement had not proven completely satisfactory to all, it had kept religion out of politics.[7]

After pressing J.O. Reaume quite hard, Whitney had finally persuaded him to run for office in 1902, and the Tory chieftain had received the active support of F.D. Monk during that same provincial campaign. Following his assumption of office and distribution of cabinet posts, the new premier had been saluted as a Conservative fully conscious of French-Canadians and their rights. This was all very flattering, and a misreading of the man, for Whitney firmly believed that Ontario was an English-speaking province and that the British connection was absolutely essential. Yet although the premier had never courted racial and religious troubles – rather, he had studiously avoided them – one of the most severe strains in Ontario-Quebec relations had its beginnings during his administration and, in the course of its growth, had serious implications for national politics and unity.

Open signs of difficulties for the government on the question of bilingual schools in Ontario first became apparent in 1910, but these troubles had their roots deep in the province's past and prejudices. French had been used as the language of instruction in a handful of Ontario schools prior to Confederation. The language was given no official recognition in the province under the BNA Act, but its use continued in comparatively few institutions where French-Canadians formed a sizeable proportion of the population. Thus, these schools served communities in Essex and Kent counties, where the first French-Canadian settlers had established themselves before the Loyalists arrived, and in Russell and Prescott counties where the westward drift of population paid little heed to the boundary between Ontario and Quebec.

For nearly two decades after confederation these French-English, or bilingual, schools were permitted by a seemingly uninterested provincial government to travel paths largely of their own choosing. Their numbers grew, particularly in the eastern end of the province, as the gentle flow of population across the border continued; and the majority of them were public – not separate – schools. This latter development possibly occurred because a number of them had been in existence before the old Province of Canada had made the basic arrangement for Canada West's separate school system in 1863. Others were public, undoubtedly, because incoming French-speaking Canadians had simply taken over schools which had been operated by departing English-speaking Canadians.

In 1885, the Ontario department of education, prompted to action by the growth of these bilingual schools, presented its first regulations on the subject of instruction in French – and German – in the public schools. Public schools, not separate, were singled out for attention because the bulk of bilingual schools fell into the former category. These regulations permitted instruction in French and

German, but also insisted that English be taught. The year of these initial rules was also the year in which Louis Riel was hanged and, in the controversy and bitter words that surrounded that event, the issue of Ontario's bilingual schools was raised. The *Mail* took up the question first, but it soon had support from some provincial Conservative legislators. By 1889 there had been sufficient questioning about these schools to prod George Ross, as minister of education, to order an examination of the institutions. Public bilingual schools in Prescott, Russell, Kent, Essex, and Simcoe counties were investigated, and the ensuing report indicated very uneven standards of English and French language instruction, but excused some deficiencies on the grounds that the 1885 regulations had not been operating long enough to produce satisfactory results.

The issue did not die with the presentation of the report. It was an aspect of the 1890 election campaign when the privileges of separate schools were subjected to sharp Conservative criticism. This storm produced important consequences: in that year the department of education issued new regulations which specifically required that English be the language of instruction in all public schools, except where the pupil's lack of comprehension made such a course impracticable; in that case, French (or German) could still be used. Evidently disturbed by the tone of the 1890 election campaign, a number of French-Canadian ratepayers converted their public schools into separate ones and, by 1893, the majority of bilingual schools were of the latter variety. The Franco-Ontarians who pursued such a course were not, however, actually escaping the regulations of 1890, even if they thought they were. In those regulations, as in the orders of 1885, public schools were specifically mentioned only because bilingual schools were then primarily of that group.

The issue of bilingual schools was peripheral to the 1894 election campaign in which a considerable amount of heat was generated by the subject of separate schools, heat intensified by the presence of the Protestant Protective Association. Thanks in part to the course pursued by the Conservative party after that election, this troublesome question then dropped out of general public view for better than a decade; but it lingered in sight for some Ontarians. Militant Protestants, particularly those of the Orange Order, continued to watch the westward movement of French-Canadians across the long Ontario border. And they had companions in their watchfulness, notably – but not exclusively – in the Ottawa area, where Irish Roman Catholics were gradually pushed into a minority position within their church and schools. Under these circumstances it is not surprising that some English-speaking Roman Catholics began to question the standards of instruction inside the growing number of bilingual separate schools. A few thought that nationalism, not religion, was being fostered and furthered within their walls. Archbishop Alexander Macdonell of Alexandria pointedly expressed the concerns of English-speaking Catholics when, in 1903, he wrote to Richard Harcourt, then Ross's minister of education:

Our French fellow Citizens in certain localities, have established Schools, which they call Separate Schools, but, in so doing, they are actuated, not from religious, but national motives, to propagate and perpetuate the French language. The Schools in question are conducted regardless of the requirements of the Ontario School law, in the matter of employing non-legally qualified teachers, and not pursuing the course of studies, prescribed by the Department of Education. ...

... The best remedy to cure them ... is to place their schools under the jurisdiction of the English Inspector, who should strictly enforce the provisions of the law.

Frank Latchford, the Catholic member of the cabinet, was moved to comment upon these remarks: 'I endorse with all my heart & soul the views expressed.' Obiously, if these sentiments of English-speaking Catholics were publicly stated, tough-minded Protestants would not be restrained from adding their own commentaries.[8]

In addition to the suspicions of English-speaking Catholics as to the real purpose of bilingual schools, there was also the problem of the standards in these institutions. There is little reason to doubt that they were frequently inefficient and substandard. Recruitment of competent and certified teachers for them was a perennial difficulty that was compounded by the decision in 1900 to end a four-year experiment of training teachers in the Ottawa bilingual model school 'on account of the small number of students in attendance.' Thus there was room for the legitimate critic who wanted to discuss the quality and nature of instruction in Ontario's bilingual schools, but such talk was bound to open the door to religious and racial bigotry.[9]

This situation was not helped by a short, sharp clash that erupted in 1906, between the minority English-speaking and the majority French-speaking members of the Ottawa separate school board over the decision to erect another bilingual school, and to spend a mere five thousand dollars on an English-speaking separate school. Not only did the English-speaking group object to this division of funds, but it went on to urge the government to action:

... the teaching of the English language in these Bi-Lingual Schools has been neglected ...

It is therefore very urgent that you should take immediate steps to have a proper English Inspector of these Bi-Lingual Schools, on which such an enormous sum of money is to be spent, with a view to having them properly organized so as to conform to the Regulations of your Department.

When the French-speaking members of the board made use of their numerical strength to censure the separate school inspector, Michael O'Brien, for his criticism of the proposed expenditures, the English-speaking group charged that bilingual schools had 'no legal existence in this Province.' The war of words had suddenly become very hot and militant Protestants had not even fired any shots.

But the battle did not get out of hand – a development which would have sent most politicians of that day either scurrying for cover or searching for a peace-keeping method – because both sides, likely recognizing the dangers of attracting too much attention, reconciled their differences before the end of 1906. For the next two years there was relative quiet on the bilingual schools question.[10]

In the interval, however, separate and public school inspectors in northern Ontario began to ask questions about the regulations governing bilingual schools; they sought clarification of the standing rules set down in 1890. How much time in the day should be devoted to instruction in English? How long should French remain the language of classroom communication? These queries grew with the expansion of the French-Canadian population in northern Ontario, the Ottawa region, and Russell and Prescott counties. In the 1890s, French-speaking Ontarians had represented about 5 per cent of the province's total population; by 1910, that percentage figure had nearly doubled.[11]

To the minds of some observers, there were an increasing number of unhappy consequences of the bilingual school question. Roman Catholic religious instruction was being given in at least one school that was nominally public in eastern Algoma, where new Canadians of Finnish background kept their children at home, fearing they would not learn English. In other cases, little English was being taught to French-Canadian students, with the result that French continued to be the language of instruction in the upper grades. In some separate schools in the Mattawa region, the two language groups were segregated upon entrance – a trend that was on the rise – and the creation of 'two schools in one school building' seemed imminent in a few cases. Such problems were simply not going to disappear and, consequently, the department of education was pushed to give some thought to 'reorganizing the Course of Study for the French Schools.'[12]

At the end of October 1908, education minister Pyne commissioned F.W. Merchant, chief inspector of public and separate schools, to investigate a limited number of bilingual schools in the Ottawa valley. His report, produced three months later, was a glum document which indicated that many pupils left these schools lacking any facility in English. These schools were also weak in other respects: the teachers were frequently poorly qualified and even French was inadequately taught. Few quarrelled with the criticisms contained in the report; concerned Franco-Ontarians were as conscious of the weaknesses of their schools as were Merchant, English-speaking Ontarians (both Protestant and Catholic), and the provincial government. The door to invective and bitterness was opened by the argument over how to remedy the situation.[13]

The first open proposals for solutions to the problem came from the French-Canadian side in the course of preparation for, and participation in, the Education Congress of the French-Canadians of Ontario held in January 1910. Although invited, Whitney did not attend this Ottawa meeting and, when asked, advised the governor-general to miss the proceedings. 'There are a number of reasons why I think you would not care to touch this matter,' he informed Earl Grey.

I believe the scheme or object had its origin in a bitter quarrel between the Irishmen and Frenchmen of Ottawa. I am led to believe that they propose to ask for changes in the law and practice of our educational system which cannot be considered for a moment. ...

Dr. Pyne the Minister of Education will not attend, but Dr. Reaume will go as we made up our minds it would be better for him to do so than to stay away. I think, you know, that it will turn out to be simply a tempest in a tea pot.

The premier was not about to embarrass himself politically through his attendance, which might readily be construed as countenancing significant concessions in the matter of bilingual schools, something he would never contemplate. Besides, he viewed the meeting, wrongly as it turned out, as just another round in an old Ottawa valley Roman Catholic family fight; one did well to avoid such feuds. Undeterred by Whitney's absence, the Congress aggressively pressed the Ontario government for official approval of a rational bilingual schools programme, bilingual normal schools, bilingual secondary institutions, and a redivision of taxes between separate and public schools.[14]

The Conservative administration observed these events and received these demands in silence, but scarcely anyone else was as taciturn. 'I would advise you,' wrote a small-town Tory to one of Whitney's cabinet, 'and your fellow Ministers to grant no concessions to the French Canadian residents of this Province in school matters. It should be sufficient if the French is permitted *only* in *primary classes* as a *means* of *instruction* in *English*. We do not want another Manitoba school agitation.' 'The Orange body as a whole,' threatened one writer, 'stand[s] ready to condemn you if your Government legalizes the Dual Language school, which would be an un-British act, as well as an act of folly; and in future generations would anathematize the name of Whitney, as the destroyer of the Public School system of Ontario.' Militant Protestants were unequivocal in their language: they would surely punish the Conservatives at the next provincial elections should the government produce 'accursed legislation' to meet the demands of the Education Congress of the French-Canadians of Ontario.[15]

English-speaking Roman Catholics were nearly as irritated by the stand of the Congress. Just when they thought that there was a possibility of legislation that might provide separate schools with improved revenues or extend their system to the secondary level, the bilingual issue cruelly shattered their rosy hopes. Some echoed those 1903 sentiments of Bishop Macdonell that Roman Catholicism was merely being used as a cover to strengthen French-Canadian nationalism. Some feared Protestants would not see the issue clearly – or would not want to see the issue clearly – and would simply launch an attack on Roman Catholicism and all separate schools. Others sided with an English-speaking priest who concluded that 'bilingualism lowers the standard of education, hampers us financially and militates against the English education of our children.'[16]

The chief Roman Catholic spokesman against any concessions to the Congress soon became Bishop Michael F. Fallon of London. A tireless fighter on behalf of separate schools, Fallon had had an unhappy experience with bilingualism as a professor at the University of Ottawa some nine years before and he never forgot the episode. The bishop first expressed his sentiments on the bilingual schools issue to the provincial secretary, Hanna, late in May 1910, while the cleric was visiting the Sarnia region of his diocese for the first time. Hanna reported the interview to Pyne – and to Whitney – in a lengthy letter, a copy of which was later stolen and published. In his talk with Hanna, Bishop Fallon called for an end to bilingual schools out of a concern, he said, for the future welfare of Franco-Ontarian students whom he did not wish to see become second-class citizens in an English-speaking province. Whatever the good bishop's concerns, stated or otherwise, this was no plea for containment; it was a strident call for destruction. On behalf of a number of English-speaking bishops and archbishops, Fallon personally pressed this same point upon Whitney in a midsummer interview. In the interval the premier had made it clear that, although the statutes of the province provided for two school systems, one of which was confessional, he had no intention of creating a third based on language. In the autumn of 1910, Fallon moved into the public eye with an open pronouncement of his attitude. That was the signal for the battle to be fully joined: newspapers, Orangemen, French-Canadians, and Fallon's supporters all shouted their opinions in a wild verbal donnybrook. Faced by this clamour, Whitney turned again to F.W. Merchant, appointing him 'to investigate and report upon the English-French Schools, Public and Separate, of the Province.'[17]

This action did not halt the debate; it simply slowed the pace. The subject of bilingual schools was heatedly discussed around the province and entered the debates of the 1911 session of the legislature. There Orangeman Howard Ferguson offered a resolution calling for the use of English only as the language of instruction in Ontario's schools. He did so, he said, 'to secure better facilities for teaching the English language' and did not intend 'anything derogatory of any class, or creed, or people.' Given the intent of his motion, others might question the sincerity of the latter part of his remarks. In any event, under pressure, Ferguson altered his resolution to allow the use of another language where, 'in the opinion of the Department of Education,' the use of English was 'impracticable.' Whitney took the opportunity afforded by discussion of this resolution to state that, in his opinion, there was 'no such thing in the Province as a bi-lingual school'; that is, such an institution had no foundation in law. That was his firmly held private, as well as public, view; but it must be noted that to have indicated otherwise in that atmosphere would likely have invited political disaster. By the time of the Ferguson resolution, however, something of graver importance to Whitney was taking the premier's attention. Bilingual schools could wait for the Merchant report.[18]

III

On 25 January 1911, on the eve of W.S. Fielding's speech in the House of Commons on the reciprocity proposals that had resulted from Canadian-American negotiations, Robert Borden wrote to Whitney asking him to present his views 'as soon as possible after the announcement.' And, on the day following the minister of finance's statement – when the Tory federal caucus was plunged into 'deepest dejection' by the apparent Liberal *coup* – the premier penned his initial reaction. His opinions reflected the thinking of many in Ontario – after all, he knew his province well – and pointed the way to the strategy for successful opposition to the measure. He implied, in grumbling fashion, that the agreement had occurred because of the British government's opposition to 'sane Imperialism' and the Canadian government's desire to weaken the ties with the mother country. 'Mr. Fielding,' he told the federal leader,

has never been loyal to Confederation, and from childhood up his political vision was apparently bounded by the New England States and the City of Boston. I heard an admirer of his say once that before he came into Federal politics he never considered anything of more importance than the desirability of getting a hake of fish and a bag of potatoes into the Boston market on the most favourable terms. ...

With these two Governments then in the attitude I have indicated we have the unmistakable desire – and I think I may say intention – of the United States to bring about political union. ... with the situation as it is here, with the cold shoulder turned to us by Great Britain, the making of commercial treaties with the United States, and other Nations, will soon together bring about a condition of affairs when the people of the British Dominions in North America will begin to entertain the idea that they may as well drop off the parent tree.[19]

Along with the anger and frustration in this letter were also embryonic arguments that could be developed and used against the reciprocity proposal, at least in Ontario: the disloyalty of the Grits; the threat to imperial unity; and the danger of annexation. Underneath Whitney's statements lay his constant concern for the future of the Empire and his ceaseless distrust of anything American. Superior British institutions in Canada were being threatened with ultimate replacement by inferior American counterparts. On one occasion, when arguing the merits of his three-fifths local-option clause with an opponent who wanted him to adopt simple majority rule as had been done in some American states, Whitney commented that Canadians would do much better to be guided by British example than American. Pursuing the subject, he offered an assessment of the United

States: 'There is no civilized country on the earth where morality of every description is at so low a level. Divorce, use of drugs, the revolver and the unwritten law are dominating forces there, and even the influences for good – and there are some – which come from there are generally tainted with some objectionable peculiarity. I hope the time will never come when our conditions "Must be nearer American conditions than Old World conditions." ' John Strachan could not have said it better. In another instance, the premier's anti-Americanism led him to ridicule events south of the border: 'It is only a short time ago that one Legislature passed a resolution permitting the eating of pea-nuts during debates by the members, and another that the sheets of all hotel beds should be nine feet long. There are numbers of other instances which I could give you showing clearly the abnormal mental condition of the people.' It would be well worth a fight to avoid such a fate for Canada, or at least Ontario.[20]

The fact that he was not on the proper battleground for such a struggle – the House of Commons – did not deter Whitney in the slightest: his government opened its assault on the reciprocity proposals in the course of the provincial budget debate and fed ammunition to the federal Conservatives. The premier personally entered the campaign in the legislature in mid-February, when he argued that Fielding and William Paterson, the minister of customs, had brought back 'dynamite in their suitcases.' 'The life of Canada,' he concluded, 'had begun through the death of Reciprocity in 1866.' The Tory chief was clearly convinced that the reverse of this proposition could now come true unless something was done, and he intended to act. 'Canadians,' he cabled the London *Daily Express*, 'will not submit tamely to being wiped off the map.' The veteran of the Fenian raids was on active duty again.[21]

Once he had publicly assumed his position, the provincial Conservative leader paused but once in his attack: he wanted to be certain that a further lowering of the American tariff on foodstuffs would not trap the party in an awkward position. Reassured on this point, he pressed on. In early March he moved a resolution strongly condemning the reciprocity proposals, citing the 'unionist' statements of President William Howard Taft and Champ Clark, speaker of the House of Representatives, as proof of the annexationist intensions of the American leadership. This action was a far cry from the premier's argument in 1896 – with party unity very much on his mind – that any provincial resolution on the subject of remedial legislation was 'an unwise and unwarranted intrusion upon the proper domain of the Parliament of Canada.' Of course, the issue and the times were entirely different; nevertheless, he was dealing with a matter which fell well within the federal jurisdiction. It was a mark of his personal convictions and his political sagacity that he should do so. And, after a prolonged debate, during which the provincial Liberals upheld the federal Grit position, the resolution was adopted and the legislators – at least the Tory ones – sang 'The Maple Leaf' and 'God Save the King.'[22]

Over the next three months the premier continued his unabated attack on the reciprocity proposals. The provincial leader was particularly incensed by Taft's statement that he was anxious 'to prevent the strengthening and consolidation of the British Empire,' and he urged Borden to protest these remarks in the House of Commons. In a state of high excitement, Whitney sent a telegram to the federal leader following Taft's May speech to the National Grange: 'Taft's speech to the Grangers that under reciprocity American farmers will sell more agricultural products to Canada than Canada will sell to the United States should be plastered on every barn and other available spot in the Dominion of Canada.' And he was upset when 'the representation of the Battle of Chateauguay' was 'struck out of the Pageant of Empire to be given during the Coronation season for fear the feelings of our American brethern [sic]' would be hurt. 'When our Federation was being put together,' he told Earl Grey, 'a weak-kneed Colonial-Secretary objected to the use of the word "Kingdom", and the word "Dominion" was used instead, for the same reason, namely that the feelings of our American cousins be not hurt.' The reciprocity proposals had clearly produced a bout of sustained anger in the premier which had no equal in his life, save in the days of the *Minnie M*. and Gamey affairs. Certainly he could become angry – explosively so – under other circumstances: sanctimonious prohibitionists, injudicious entrepreneurs, and foolish petitioners could all bear testimony to that fact. But seldom did the mood last. This was not the case now: he was genuinely convinced that the future of his province, his country, and his empire was at stake. It was just as well that his trip to England for the coronation gave him an opportunity for relaxation, although the occasion undoubtedly served to strengthen his convictions.[23]

The Ontario Conservative leader was back at his desk when the dissolution of the federal parliament was announced in late July. In the ensuing campaign, Whitney spared neither himself nor members of his cabinet as they sped around the province battling the Liberals almost exclusively on the issue of reciprocity, emphasizing the twin dangers of annexation to the United States and disruption of the British connection. The scheme was designed, the premier told his audiences, to make Canadians 'hewers of wood and drawers of water to the Americans.' But Whitney did more than talk: he was consulted by Borden at almost every turn in the campaign, and he freely offered his advice. Further, the premier grudgingly permitted provincial Conservative legislators to contest federal seats, and of the seven who succeeded in their efforts, six captured Liberal ridings.[24]

Just as important in fashioning the Tory triumph as the appeals to emotion, the strategy, and the candidates was the fact that the Ontario Conservative organization ran at full throttle throughout the campaign. Individual provincial Tory legislators worked diligently in support of the federal candidates in their regions. In Huron South, for example, Henry Eilber – one of Whitney's men who would not run federally – laboured long and hard in a riding that generally went to the Liberals in dominion contests. Jonathan Merner, the Tory candidate, and Eilber were both German-Canadians, and the provincial politician did most of the talking on behalf of his fellow Conservative, whose English left something to be desired. In marked contrast to this display of strength, unity, and vigour, the Grits were weak, factious, and weary. The provincial Liberal organization was more apparent than real, and was divided by petty quarrels. Laurier's decision to abandon the Ontario party in the 1908 provincial election campaign had not strengthened his position but, rather, done the reverse. Nevertheless, the prime minister remained optimistic about the state of affairs in Ontario, and sharp complaints to Liberal managers about evident weaknesses drew little response from Ottawa. One other difficulty plagued the party in Ontario: a number of Grits had crossed the line to vote for Whitney in two provincial elections and, by 1911, their party loyalty must have been weak indeed.[25]

These factors – the premier's personal campaign, the labours of his men, the strength of the Conservative organization, and the weaknesses in Liberal ranks – would appear to have been just as important in the Tory sweep of the province in 1911 as any discussion of reciprocity and naval defence, or whispers about Laurier's race and religion, or emotional appeals to imperial and anti-American sentiments. Whitney's personal feelings about the triumph were sharply summarized in a cablegram to an English friend: 'Rule Britannia.' 'No such good work was ever done in British America before,' he informed Borden, 'and having regard to its effect on the future of the Empire I doubt if any one day's work in England in modern times ever signified as much.' Even seven weeks after the Conservative federal victory, the premier was still euphoric: 'In my opinion,' he wrote the new finance minister, W.T. White, 'no event has occurred since the Battle of Waterloo fraught with such momentous results to the British peoples and the British Empire as our action with regard to this question.' It was the mark of the depth of his commitment to the imperial connection that Whitney should allow himself the luxury of such an extreme judgment. To his mind the way had now been opened to 'sane imperialism.' The gloomy prospects of the Empire now evaporated for him in the light of a truly new day.[26]

In explaining the disaster, many Liberals accepted Laurier's dictum that the people of Ontario were 'carried away by the open cry of loyalty and the secret canvas of "down with French domination."' Some cited anti-Americanism and some protectionist sentiment, but only a handful obliquely hinted that men and organization were the source of their defeat. Yet these latter were surely critical in Ontario, and none more so than Whitney and his machine.[27]

Once the election results were known, Borden wasted little time in arranging for a conference with Whitney about the composition of the new cabinet. The federal leader was anxious to discuss matters with the man who had been key to the triumph in Ontario and who had stood with him faithfully over the years when others had wavered: the national chief readily acknowledged a political debt. Borden and Whitney were closeted together in Ottawa on the evening of 28

September. At this meeting the Ontario leader strongly supported the suggestion that Toronto financier W.T. White – one of the 'Toronto eighteen' – should be given a cabinet position. Despite the fact that White had bitterly attacked the Ontario government's power policy, Whitney wanted him included because the provincial chieftain judged him to be 'the keystone of the arch.' The premier was more concerned with being a politician than a partisan in offering such advice: emasculation of the Liberals and the acquisition of a prominent financial figure was of far greater importance to him than continuation of any personal vendetta.[28]

The Ontario leader's views on the other men from his province who became members of Borden's cabinet – George Foster, Frank Cochrane, Sam Hughes, Thomas Crothers, John D. Reid, and A.E. Kemp – are not known, but it is safe to assume that he strongly supported the choice of Cochrane, a solid man from his own cabinet, and Crothers, who had served him well on the textbook commission. He probably had to hold his tongue on the subject of Sam Hughes. Whitney also wanted Andy Broder in the cabinet, but in this he failed. Borden apparently offered Broder the post of minister of agriculture but, faced by the facts that Reid and Broder came from back-to-back constituencies and that room had to be found on the Ontario slate for Hughes, the federal leader dropped the Dundas County man. Whitney was not consulted prior to the abandonment of his old Morrisburg friend and he was considerably puzzled and a little annoyed at this decision. Aside from this matter, the premier – who was rumoured to have rejected the justice portfolio – was fairly content with the final composition of the cabinet. But he did offer Borden one final piece of gratuitous advice: 'When your men [of the cabinet] are assembled together for the first time I think you should tell them plainly that your intention is to have a straight & clean Government in every respect – that you have every confidence in each one of them, but that you feel so strongly on this subject that you feel bound to make the statement in order that there can be no misunderstanding.' Characteristically blunt directions from the gruff Ontario leader.[29]

IV

The successful anti-reciprocity campaign and the ensuing general election had carried the premier – and with him, the province – onto another plane of activity for much of 1911, a fact which had led A.G. MacKay to observe to Mackenzie King as early as March: 'I find that strictly Provincial issues are decidedly at a discount now – with the farmers the Reciprocity question is about the only one, for the time being, they want to hear discussed.' In the legislature, the subjects which had sparked the sharpest exchanges had been Whitney's anti-reciprocity resolution and MacKay's counter-proposals. Legislation that provided for the creation of technical schools in Ontario or that gave the Hydro-Electric Power Commission jurisdiction over the transmission lines of private companies was unintentionally screened from the public view by the smoke of the reciprocity debate. Only a discussion of the three-fifths clause – a timeless topic, apparently – drew widespread attention, and then only from the temperance forces. The federal Liberal proposition of reciprocity overcame all, and it was only when this question was settled by the election that provincial politics ceased to be 'at a discount.'[30]

Whitney gradually drew the limelight back to his domain with the appointment of William Howard Hearst, a Sault Ste Marie lawyer, to replace Frank Cochrane in his cabinet; the premier now had a northerner with a portfolio and that would still some grumbling in the upper reaches of the province. He followed this bit of fence-mending with the announcement of a provincial election to be held on 11 December. Mackenzie King later argued that 'the Ontario Government took advantage of the Liberal defeat of Sept. 21, to hurry on an election a year ahead of time.' Publicly, the premier denied such charges, noting that the current legislature had had a longer life than either of its two predecessors. Further, by-elections had to be held in a number of constituencies and, should a general election be postponed, expenses in such ridings would be duplicated within a year. But privately Whitney must have known that victory would be relatively cheap and easy in the wake of the federal sweep; that the election would be more in the nature of a re-coronation than a contest.[31]

The Tories largely stood on their record before a numb Ontario electorate that had been emotionally drained by the September campaign. Whitney's confidence was most marked by the relaxed approach taken towards the opposition: he did not assault the Grits, as he had done on many previous occasions, but simply held them up to ridicule. When the Liberal leadership changed from A.G. MacKay to Newton W. Rowell early in the campaign, the Conservative leader welcomed the latter as 'a great moral reformer' who had supported the Ross government with all its alleged sins. Rowell's platform, he declared, was 'a skimpy chicken,' which was scarcely an accurate description – but it served the premier's purpose.[32]

The bilingual school question and the unity of the provincial Conservative party probably gave Whitney more cause for concern during the campaign than the Liberal opposition. He had to assist in stamping out a threat to Reaume's renomination in Essex North, which had been started by angry Franco-Ontarians and militant Orangemen. He announced that, as far as he was concerned, English was the language of the province, but a child would have to be brought to an understanding of it through his mother tongue; it was Dr Merchant's task to discover if this was being done. Foy, however, made matters awkward by going further than that and stating that 'no other language [than English] should be taught in these schools ... in the interest and for the benefit of each one of the rising generation.' The attorney-general may have been inspired to utter this comment out of a desire to protect the separate school system from attack; but there were Tories who questioned the wisdom of his outburst, and the problem troubled the party throughout the campaign.[33]

The Liberals faced internal difficulties that were far graver, however, because they were involved in a battle 'without any organization, funds, or even a leader.' When Whitney first indicated that there would be an election, MacKay was still the Grit leader and he roundly denounced the proposed dissolution. The Owen Sound lawyer was, however, under attack from some elements within the party either because of the rural flavour he imparted to the Liberals or because of his refusal to pick up temperance as a big stick. These noises were intensified when MacKay was falsely charged with personal indiscretions, and, despite a show of confidence in him, he resigned as leader at the end of October. In his place, the Grits selected Newton Wesley Rowell, a relatively young Toronto lawyer already prominent in party and temperance ranks. Rowell's appointment represented a move by the party to give itself a more urban appearance, but the new leader was forced to seek election in a rural constituency, Oxford North. Mackenzie King – striking a strong personal note – later described the trials of the campaign that followed:

at the meeting at which he [Rowell] was selected as leader, I was made President of the General Reform Association of Ontario ... We got to work at once, and in a day or two had the platform ready and part of the literature under way. Then we began the public speaking. Rowell took a certain number of ridings I took another lot, and with the aid of a few other speakers here and there, we kept the campaign going. Each of us spoke every night for over three weeks, doing a great deal of travelling in between. ... The party's defeat in Ontario in September was so great (only 13 Liberal seats left) that all the other men kept out of the fight, not to be identified with a second loss. We had no money, no anything, the outlook was hopeless and there was little to criticize in the Government save inaction, and indifference. ... The Liberal organizer tells me that the entire work of this campaign for the whole province did not more than equal the amount spent in some of the individual ridings of the Federal Campaign. Rowell and I are known to be utterly opposed to 'machine' methods in politics, the result was we got no help from machine men.[34]

No one could have been very surprised at the outcome, then, on 11 December, when the Conservatives took eighty-two seats – seventeen of them by acclamation – and the Liberals secured twenty-two; Allan Studholme persisted as the Labour member for Hamilton East. The Grits gained three seats over their 1908 total, but their portion of the total vote marginally declined. 'The result of the Elections,' a 'tired out' Whitney informed his brother, 'is quite satisfactory although we are about three seats short of our former position. There are good reasons for this condition of affairs. There is no doubt that the bad weather kept a lot of our voters away from the polls in the country, and local reasons and jealousies affected others. I think in the main all the Party workers did well and were not careless, but it was very difficult to stir the voters up and make them see the necessity for going to the polls.' Conscious that the bilingual issue probably caused the defeat of two French-speaking Conservative members in the constituencies of Prescott and

1911 Election Results			
Popular vote			Seats
Conservative	205,338	(55.59%)[35]	82[36]
Liberal	143,806	(38.93%)	22
Labour-Socialist	12,171	(3.29%)[37]	1
Other	8,093	(2.19%)	1
Total	369,408	(100.00%)	106

Sturgeon Falls, the premier could be moderately cheered by the victory of Napoleon Champagne in Ottawa East. These were minor setbacks, however, and the triumph – Whitney's third consecutive sweep – was both remarkable and easy. The Tory leader exuded a certain smugness: 'when one considers that there is no instance in our history of a Government with so strong a hold on the confidence of the people, there is no room for any other feeling but that of great satisfaction.' Reflecting on his victory, the premier observed: 'we are perfectly contented.'[38]

9

Keeping an Even Keel: 1912–1914

I

With his significant contribution to Borden's triumph and his own easy victory of 1911 behind him, Whitney entered the new year confirmed as the dominating political personality in Ontario. 'He was,' as the *Canadian Annual Review* insisted, 'first in the Government, first in the House, first in the Province.' His frankness of approach and bluntness of speech – once seen as potential handicaps – were now enshrined as admirable, maybe even lovable, traits. Stories illustrating these characteristics had become legion, some undoubtedly resting on fact while others bordered on fantasy. But, regardless of their accuracy, they mirrored the strong position of the premier, the esteem in which he was held, and the power he possessed. Master of much he surveyed, his rule had become a reign.[1]

Just as surely as he held the province in the palm of his political hand, he was also the unchallenged master of the provincial Conservative party. When, during the 1912 legislative session, three Toronto Tory members, eagerly and ably assisted by Newton Rowell, attempted to secure the abolition of separate ballots in municipal elections and their replacement with long ballots which would list all candidates for every post, the premier sent them scampering for cover when he scored the proposed legislation as being fraught with problems, late in arrival, and unannounced to the government. W.K. McNaught, Thomas Crawford, and W.D. McPherson quickly yielded to their leader and left an abandoned Rowell wearily shaking his head. The premier's dominance, however, was not confined to such minor displays of strength. It was he who announced that five million dollars would be set aside for the development of northern Ontario, and that another million was earmarked for highway improvement; these two major items of policy could have been revealed, just as readily, by his new minister of lands, forests, and mines, William H. Hearst from Sault Ste Marie, and public works minister Reaume. It was also the premier who took on single tax petitioners and wrote them off as promoters of 'fakes and fads,' and who tilted once more with the well-organized advocates of prohibition.[2]

This is not to suggest that one-man government had become the order of the day in Ontario. Rather, it was a mark of the fact that the premier was not – and never had been – buffered from the public by a coterie of ministers or a retinue of retainers. This meant that, should an organization or an individual be seeking support for a programme or desirous of a political plum, it was logical to approach the leader, and it was equally logical for him to respond, either explaining the government's position or defending its policies. But the process did focus a great deal of attention on the man, and he, in turn, did not shun the limelight. There is little doubt that he enjoyed his very secure position. Still, he let his ministers do their jobs, with occasional exceptions. Beck had to be watched, lest his zeal turn to extravagance; Reaume had to be nudged, lest caution become inertia; and Pyne had to be guided, occasionally, lest he miss the premier's path. But, generally, Whitney left his ministers alone, and he came to count on the advice, inventiveness, and administrative ability of Hanna. As the administration grew old – after all, Whitney would be seventy in 1912 – it was the relatively younger Hanna who frequently stood with the premier as they met this issue or that group.

That the provincial secretaryship was a grab-bag portfolio helps to explain the Lambton representative's presence here and there; for example, it was his department which administered liquor legislation. But that explanation alone detracts from his importance and accomplishments. It was he who revamped the provincial prison system and established the reformatory at Guelph. This reform had begun in 1907 when the process of land acquisition near Guelph had been set in motion. In 1910, the new institution had received its first prisoners, who surveyed the property, opened up quarries, cut fence posts, under-drained marshlands, and erected temporary buildings. In such labour, Hanna viewed rehabilitation as the mate of punishment. And, by 1912, two hundred and ninety prisoners at the reformatory were being given the opportunity of 'working toward better things personally while making their labour also productive and useful to the public.' In the same year, a similar development was begun near Fort William.[3]

Beyond this, Hanna could report that shop, tavern, and other liquor licences were on the decrease, as they had been since he first came to office, while regulations governing liquor were given yet another tightening turn. Such administration of a most contentious matter even earned him grudging praise from his fellow Methodists. It was also the provincial secretary who, in 1912, saw to the division of the province into seven districts, each with its own officer of health who was responsible for health and sanitary conditions in his region. In addition, he supervised the upgrading of training for nurses who were to work in hospitals for the insane, which, themselves, had been markedly improved. It would be no mistake to see Whitney's provincial secretary as the man who sustained the reform impulse of the administration when other ministers became increasingly contented with operation rather than innovation, a fact of life with an aging government. And this aging process was given concrete form in 1912, when A.J. Matheson, the treasurer, missed much of the session because of illness and was thus unable to present his budget.

The government, however, although moving more slowly in some instances, had not become inert, and it pressed ahead in matters other than those already noted. The hours of work for street railway motormen and conductors were more sharply regulated, despite the huffy complaints of the Toronto Street Railway Company. Legislation introduced by Pyne – who now leaned heavily on his deputy, A.H.U. Colquhoun – provided for the creation of the Royal Ontario Museum. Compulsory universal smallpox vaccination was firmly set in place by virtue of legislative amendments. Power was granted to municipalities to expropriate local telephone systems, and this was seen, not quite correctly, as a step in the direction of public ownership. Significant grants were made, as they had been in the previous years of the Whitney administration, to sanitaria to assist them in the care of tubercular patients. Meanwhile, Foy moved to check the nasty 'operations of loan "sharks" and extortionate money-lenders'; his legislation gave 'the courts the right, where money ... [had] been loaned at an excessive rate, ... to reopen the contract' and 'relieve the debtor from payment of any sum in excess of what' the courts deemed 'to be fairly due.' And the Ontario Hydro-Electric Power Commission added to the number of municipalities purchasing power from it.[4]

II

While the legislature was sitting in 1912, the long-standing issue of a northerly extension of Ontario's western boundary was finally resolved by federal government action that came, not surprisingly, with the Conservatives now ensconced in Ottawa. Since 1906, Whitney had contended that his province's western boundary with Manitoba should run straight north until it struck the Churchill River, and then it should proceed down the middle channel of that river until it entered Hudson Bay, with both provinces sharing the port of Fort Churchill. This proposal had gone nowhere with the Laurier government, and subsequently, in an effort to break the deadlock, the Ontario Tories had proposed a northward line that would stop at the Nelson River twenty-five miles from its mouth, and then proceed downriver to the Bay. This arrangement would have given the province not only the south shore of the river but also the site of York Factory. But this suggestion had a fate identical with that of the first proposition. There matters had rested, although charges had been made that the premier had not been aggressive enough in pushing Ontario's case; with Laurier's reluctance to act, however, there really was little that could be done.

When clear signs of impending Ottawa action could be seen in 1912, Newton

Rowell was quick to argue that Ontario's western boundary should follow the course urged by Whitney in 1906, and that the province should settle for nothing less; that, in fact, it was entitled to seeing its boundary run due north to the sixtieth parallel, but common decency to Manitoba prevented insistence on such a claim. To settle for less, the Liberal leader affirmed, was to be partner to the robbery from Ontario of a port for ocean-going vessels. Whitney responded by insisting that Manitoba had to have access to the sea, something Rowell had not denied, and by rehearsing the intransigence of the Laurier government.

Thus, when the present-day boundary was decreed by Ottawa late in February – and it produced less than Toronto had wanted – Whitney was quick to note that, in addition to the land that had been surrendered by the federal government, the province of Ontario could select, within five years, a five-mile strip of land through Manitoba to the Nelson River for purposes of a railway extension. And he saluted Ottawa and Toronto for ending the impasse deliberately created by Laurier in order to set Ontario and Manitoba against each other. The provincial Liberals countered by arguing that, had the province secured what it had demanded in 1906, it would have received an additional area of forty thousand square miles that was rightfully Ontario's. But such criticisms were brushed aside by a jubilant government, which undoubtedly had received its reward for faithful service in the 1911 federal election.

This small empire – it was larger than the land mass of the British Isles – acquired by Ontario and to be known as the District of Patricia, contained some 146,400 square miles and increased the area of the province by 56 per cent. Legislation 'provided for the appointment of a Commissioner to investigate conditions' in the new region; when R.R. Gamey turned down the position, J.W. Tyrrell was appointed to examine these large spoils of electoral battle.[5]

III

Even the news of this major settlement, however, had trouble holding public attention for long once Dr F.W. Merchant's report on bilingual schools was finally produced – at a safe distance from the provincial election campaign of the previous year. The results of the commissioner's investigations were made public early in March, about a month before the session was prorogued. The contents of the report – which was quite thorough – probably surprised no one. Merchant had discovered that conditions in many bilingual schools left much to be desired. Many teachers lacked departmental certificates and others, who possessed temporary certificates, had very elementary academic qualifications. Some teachers could not speak English and the quality of English instruction varied widely from school to school. In addition, in some of the public bilingual schools, Roman Catholic doctrine was imparted during school hours. Merchant's general conclusion was that many pupils left the majority of these schools educationally ill-equipped. To remedy this unhappy situation, he suggested that French should be the language of instruction only in the primary grades, with English being gradually introduced so as to replace French in the upper grades. He was also anxious to improve the quality of the bilingual teachers.[6]

Five weeks later, Whitney – who had received large amounts of unsolicited advice in the interval – announced the government's policy, which served as the basis for the order officially known as 'Circular of Instructions, 17.' 'The Government proposes,' he informed the legislature,

to provide additional inspection so that every school shall be visited by a Supervising Inspector to observe and test the progress made and enforce the carrying out of the Regulations; to make State aid conditional upon the employment of teachers capable of giving instruction in English and, where necessary, to give further financial aid towards the payment of such teachers; to insure that no text-books be used in any school other than those authorized by the Department of Education and that instruction in English shall commence at once upon a child entering school; to permit the use of French, as the language of instruction and communication, to vary according to local conditions upon the report of the Supervising Inspector but in no case to continue this beyond the end of the first form.

When 'Circular of Instructions, 17' – which was to be adhered to in the school year 1912–13 – was produced, it varied slightly from the Whitney pronouncement in that it made allowances for the pupil who was already in a bilingual school and whose knowledge of English was judged to be inadequate.[7]

This was the regulation upon which the battle was joined during the next decade. On the one side stood the Conservative government, most provincial Liberals, and the bulk of Ontario's English-speaking residents. On the other were many of Ontario's French-speaking minority and the press and populace of Quebec. Between was a handful of department of education officials who seriously doubted – on pedagogical grounds – if the goal of the regulation could be achieved within the three years of the first form. Vicar-General J.O. Routhier of Ottawa spoke for many French-Canadians when he protested to the Conservative premier: 'The Catholics and the French Canadians will not submit to this regulation. Catholics must have schools where religion is taught. French Canadians must have French schools. They want to preserve their language and their Faith. Bilingual schools must be preserved and protected.' On the other hand, Bishop D.J. Scollard of Sault Ste Marie could write that the 'regulations in whole and in part are preeminently fair, just and equitable, and should satisfy all fair minded men.' Of course the bishop, in company with many English-speaking Catholics, was likely fearful that the bilingual schools question might escalate into the separate schools question, with a revival of the venomous anti-Catholicism last witnessed at the end of the previous century. Harbouring such worries, he would want to remain in favour with the government, and he must have fervently wished that the issue would soon pass into history.[8]

The Ontario Tory leader, struck by an avalanche of mail from every direction, held to his opinion that the 'whole question' was 'simply one of administration.' The government was simply moving to correct a situation which should never have been allowed to develop. As Whitney told Bishop W.A. Macdonell of Alexandria:

the main point is that through negligence, and carelessness, and want of proper inspection many of these schools were allowed to drift, so to speak, until they became in reality French Schools instead of Public or Separate Schools under the provisions of our school laws. Consequently, a great many of the parents to-day think that the condition of things mentioned in Dr. Merchant's Report is the normal condition of affairs, and that they are entitled to have such schools as I have mentioned, instead of such schools being a direct infringement of the law. This increases our difficulty, and the fact that, as we all know, the French people are a very sensitive people, makes the matter still more difficult to deal with.

It is too bad that certain individuals are endeavouring, and will endeavour no doubt, to raise the religious question, or rather will endeavour to make this question a question of religion, when, as you say, it is something entirely different.[9]

Without a doubt, the premier thought that Franco-Ontarians should want to have their children fully competent in English in order to avoid having them fall into the category of second-class citizens. How could they fully participate in the life of Ontario and in the opportunities it afforded if they were not fluent in English? Whitney was offering them help, not threatening harm; 'the Regulation,' he wrote Borden, who was naturally concerned about the strains placed upon national and party unity by this development, 'was intended to cure the defective condition of the [bilingual] schools' as found by Dr Merchant.[10]

The Tory chief was also alarmed by the signs of what he judged to be narrow nationalism that he saw rising out of the dispute. 'I am afraid,' he told concerned historian Thomas Chapais,

that in this Province, and perhaps in your Province, men will interest themselves in this question from other than patriotic motives, and it is quite possible that perhaps for years the people and present Government of Ontario will have to remain under suspicion entirely unjust and unwarranted. ... you may rely upon it that the present Government of Ontario will go a long way and will strain a point even in order to make sure that our French-Canadian fellow subjects shall receive fair play.

Genuinely convinced that his career 'proved conclusively' that he would not intentionally be 'a party to interfering in the slightest degree with any right or privilege of those whose mother tongue' was 'the French language,' the premier was honestly perplexed by the growing intensity of French-Canadian anger. The government was simply taking a firm administrative hold on schools which had existed on sufferance and which were in a deplorable state. Whitney could not understand the position assumed by French-Canadians because, despite his conviction that he was being fair, he did not understand the aspirations of French-Canadians. He shared this shortcoming with many Ontarians, who, in turn, made it politically impossible for him to act other than he did.[11]

After a year of bitter complaints, refusals to comply with the regulation and walk-outs staged by Franco-Ontarian pupils, the Whitney government did retreat a little on the enforcement of the order. Early in 1913, L. Genest of the Ottawa separate school board pointed out a very real administrative difficulty created by the circular: if a student was not competent enough in English at the conclusion of the first form to be promoted, he would then have to stay at that level and would contribute to congestion in the classroom. Probably in response to this sound point – as well as in reaction to the storm of protest – the government decided that, on the approval of the chief inspector, French could be the language of instruction for pupils above the first form who could not understand or speak English. Whitney termed the alteration an 'outcome of the experience of the year that is past.' F.A. Walker in his book *Catholic Education and Politics in Ontario* judges it a loophole 'for a great deal of French teaching,' and he adds: 'it is testimony to the zeal of French Canadian national sentiment that the dispute continued with such passion.' And Whitney was proven unhappily accurate in predicting that he and his government would be viewed with 'suspicion' – if not worse – 'for years' by many French-Canadians.[12]

IV

The feelings of French-Canadians were also stirred in the same period over the question of naval aid to Great Britain, a problem which Whitney readily addressed. In 1909, the premier had already indicated that he favoured the gift of 'one or two Dreadnoughts' to the mother country. Thus, when Borden sought his advice in 1912 on the federal Conservatives' 'course upon the Naval question,' the Ontario Tory was quite prepared to reply:

I am in favour of placing at the disposal of the Imperial Authorities a sum of money sufficient to build two battleships or armoured cruisers of the Dreadnaught [sic] type to be known as Canadian battleships, but to be absolutely under the control and management of the Admiralty subject to any conditions that may be deemed reasonable.

...

it seems to me that *our self-respect as a people can only be kept in good condition by the immediate offer which I have indicated above.*

Because the premier regarded such a move as but a first step in tightening the bonds of empire, he did not view the matter lightly. 'I would submit to defeat without hesitation,' he told Borden, 'rather than give way on the subject.'[13]

Whitney's proposal was made prior to Borden's visit to England in the summer of 1912, when the new prime minister discussed the naval question with Winston Churchill, then first lord of the admiralty. Thus, the Ontarian's advice – which was followed almost to the letter by Borden in his naval aid bill – was offered before the prime minister was subjected to the pressure of personality and memorandum in Great Britain and, possibly, made the federal leader more agreeable to British wishes. Nevertheless, Whitney was not at all anxious to have Churchill visit Canada at this particular juncture. 'People who are apparently timid,' he wrote to Borden, 'fear that an impulsive man like Churchill might create an undesirable effect by urging or asking our people to do something towards the up-keep of the Navy. I think the basis of this feeling is a fear that he might talk as from a pedestal and be inclined to instruct us as to our duty &c.' The premier was worried lest Canadian aid should appear to have been conscripted rather than volunteered.[14]

When the prime minister returned to Canada, the Ontario chieftain was eager to have him quickly announce a policy of naval aid. He assumed that the federal leader now had enough information to prove that a state of emergency did, in fact, exist, and placed himself easily in Borden's shoes:

I would count the days until I was in a position to make a public announcement with regard to an immediate contribution, and my individual opinion is that that contribution should be at least twenty-five, and perhaps thirty, millions of dollars; that the Home Government should be told 'Take this money, build battleships with it, call them ours if you like, put them in your fleet and use them as your own.' And this condition should be added, namely, that the Home Government should continue to build the same number of battle-ships in the future as if our contribution had not been made.

… Delay or hesitation now will in my opinion not only be fatal to the splendid record you have made for yourself but it will be full of danger to the Empire, and also full of grave danger for your Government.

I believe that any attempt at compromise, any attempt in the direction of making a small contribution instead of a large one, will be disastrous. I believe the bolder action will meet with the approbation of our people, and I shiver to contemplate what the people of Ontario will say if any other line of action is adopted.

Whitney then reiterated advice he had offered three months earlier:

Let there be no misunderstanding. I would face defeat squarely on this proposition, and if defeat should come let it come. I cannot bring myself to contemplate the possibilities which

I think I can see in the future both from a Party and an Imperial point of view if there is anything approaching hesitation or weakness now.
... you must rule your Colleagues with an iron hand in this matter.

Strong words, born of equally strong convictions – which were Ontarian to the core. Consequently, the premier must have been immensely pleased by Borden's decision to offer thirty-five million dollars in naval aid to Britain, and profoundly dismayed by the action of the predominantly Liberal Senate, led by George Ross, in blocking the move. 'There is one consolation arising out of the action of the Senate,' he wrote to Frank Cochrane, 'and that is that old man Ross will never have another opportunity of hiding himself from the people. He has shewn conclusively now that he has no regard for political principles and that he has no self respect.' The old political enemies had crossed swords again, this time on territory which once had been common ground.[15]

v

Ross was not the only 'old man' in politics: at the outset of 1913, Whitney was in his seventy-first year and beginning to show signs of age. When the legislative session opened in February of that year, it was R.A. Pyne who braved the cold to meet the lieutenant-governor at the doors of the parliament buildings; the premier had to 'avoid walking owing to an attack of rheumatism.' Undoubtedly compounding Whitney's sense of illness and fatigue was the cold knowledge of A.J. Matheson's death during the previous week. He could take some comfort, however, from the fact that, in the preceding autumn, his party had reversed the results of the general election in Middlesex East and had captured that riding in a by-election in which Rowell's pledge to 'Abolish the bar' had been a key point of debate. That outcome had put him 'in seventh heaven' and, 'disdainful of Rowell,' 'he offered to wager money that the Provincial Opposition would go into the next general election with a new leader.' In the session that followed, however, the Tory leader did not personally present the number of measures which he customarily did, though his cabinet managed to pick up much of the slack as the premier's pace slowed. Nevertheless, he was quick to rise to champion government policies or assault Liberal proposals. Under attack, he stood to defend his three-fifths clause in local option votes and to ridicule Rowell's promise to abolish the bar as a direct encouragement to intemperance, on the grounds that such an abolition would increase the sale of liquor in shops.[16]

At the same time, Whitney continued to display no sympathy to those who wanted alterations in the assessment act so that municipalities might be free to work out their own systems of taxation. He scouted the idea of placing the burden of assessment on land, rather than buildings, by arguing that such a scheme would hurt the poor in both town and country and benefit the wealthy. The Conservative leader had no patience at all with those who urged 'the Henry George scheme of single tax on land': this concept had 'for its avowed object the destruction of all individual ownership of land.' Such ideas had currency because, he argued,

we are living at present in an atmosphere of hysteria with reference to many questions and beliefs; and a certain number of our fellow-mortals, who have apparently strong objections to ordinary exertion for the purpose of gaining a livelihood, spend a great portion of their time puzzling over the discovery of new and startling propositions, and especially of remedies for diseases which perhaps do not exist. As one who has been in touch with public affairs for a number of years, and who has faith in the sober common-sense of the people, I sometimes feel surprised when I observe the readiness of men who desire to get into public notice to advocate measures, the impropriety of which a little serious thought would convince them. However, we are all human and mortal, and due allowance must be made. It is not unreasonable to expect that in the end public opinion will cure these and similar evils.[17]

Whitney not only refused to act on the demands of the single-taxers, he appeared to back away from the implementation of a new workmen's compensation measure in this session, despite the fact that such legislation had been anticipated, for W.R. Meredith had completed his report on the subject. In 1910, the premier had appointed his former leader as a one-man commission to

(1) inquire and report as to the laws relating to the liability of employers to make compensation to their employees for injuries received in the course of their employment; (2) to make such recommendations as he may deem expedient for enactment in this Province; (3) to cause to be prepared and to report a bill, embodying such changes in the law, as, in his opinion, should be adopted.

The Conservative leader had taken this action in response to demands from Ontario's trade unionists for a complete overhaul of Mowat-inspired compensation legislation contained in an 1886 act – under which an employer had to be proven guilty of negligence – and his own recognition of the unceasing growth of Ontario's industrial segment.[18]

Accordingly, Meredith had gradually set to work. He had heard briefs from labour leaders who were eager for dramatic changes, and from representatives of the Canadian Manufacturers Association who acknowledged the need for fresh legislation which would end the need for employers to carry expensive liability insurance. And he listened to arguments from insurance company spokesmen who denounced the prospect of any state intervention in the liability field and from some entrepreneurs who seemed prepared to treat most industrial accidents as unfortunate acts of God for which there could be no compensation. The chief justice also travelled to England and Europe to examine schemes already in operation before he turned to the task of drafting a final report and a bill.[19]

But Meredith's draft bill never proceeded to the floor of the legislature in the session of 1913, and angry labour leaders denounced the Whitney government for yielding to pressure from business interests in failing to act on the matter. In light of later developments, this charge seems to have some foundation. Delay appears to have been caused by Meredith's desire to have a second look at the draft, which had aroused the opposition of manufacturers – not because he proposed compensation without proof of employer negligence but because he proposed a mix of state and private insurance and did not allow for employees' contributions to the compensation fund. As well, unrelated but disturbing revelations late in the session diverted the attention of the legislators and may also account for this measure's being placed, temporarily, on a back burner.

As prorogation approached (and after the celebratory presentation of an automobile to Whitney by his grateful followers), William Proudfoot, Liberal member for Huron Centre, made the most serious charges ever levelled against the Whitney administration. This able Grit debater stated that provincial secretary Hanna had paved the way for a wooden-ware company to take legal action against the Crown and that this had netted the business a very handsome out-of-court settlement. Proudfoot charged that Hanna had acted in this fashion out of gratitude for a five-hundred-dollar gift to his own campaign chest by a member of the company in question prior to the 1908 election. Proudfoot further insisted that Whitney knew all the details of the matter. The premier immediately and vigorously denied the charge of corruption; intimated that the source of Proudfoot's information was the same man who had stolen the Hanna-to-Pyne letter on Bishop Fallon's remarks on bilingual schools; and successfully moved an amendment referring the charges to the house committee on privileges and elections.[20]

In the ensuing investigation it was clearly established that Hanna had not exerted pressure on the attorney-general's department to open the way for the company's suit, but that he had earlier received a campaign contribution from a member of the business. Whitney admitted that he had later been made aware of the gift of money, but he thought that the provincial secretary had only been guilty of an error in judgment in accepting the funds. A stormy debate followed the presentation of the Conservative-dominated committee's report to the legislature. The Liberals argued as if they had discovered another Gamey affair; the Tories insisted upon Hanna's honesty. The public of Grey North responded in a by-election by returning a Conservative for this longtime Liberal riding. The premier took this result as a direct vote of confidence in his administration. By the end of the year the Grits found it difficult to get any response to these charges, even from partisan audiences. The people of Ontario apparently had little reason to doubt the

Conservative explanation. Although it was a very clear blemish on the Whitney record, the Tory chief could rightly insist that he had 'been guilty of no impropriety of any kind.'[21]

The episode had taken its toll in other than political ways, and, when the legislature finally was prorogued in early May, Whitney was near exhaustion. Nor did his condition improve once the legislators had gone home. He decided very regretfully, on doctor's advice, not to make the trip from Toronto to Morrisburg in order to participate in the midsummer centennial celebration of the battle of Crysler's Farm. Initially, only his family, cabinet, and doctors knew about his condition, and they insisted upon a complete rest in Toronto. When this did not achieve any particular result, he was persuaded to take his ease in Algonquin Park, but there he fretted about the interprovincial conference – of which he was a co-host – to be held in Ottawa in late October of 1913. None of his advisers wanted him to attend this meeting, but he went and 'showed nearly all his accustomed vigor.' On his return to the provincial capital, however, he soon suffered a relapse, partly because he continued to worry about the affairs of Ontario.[22]

As a result, it was decided that only a vacation outside the country would provide him with a complete rest. Late in November, he and Pyne, who served as his personal physician, slipped quietly south to Washington. At that point they hoped to select a secluded southern retreat where the premier could rest; while deliberating on this matter, the Tory leader took in the sights of the United States capital. The vacation in the deep south never occurred, however, because Whitney's condition worsened alarmingly in Washington. Hastily retracing their steps, he and Pyne had travelled only as far as New York when it became apparent that further journeying might well prove fatal. The Tory chieftain suffered a severe heart attack in that city – quite conceivably he might already have had a minor one – and Lady Whitney was summoned from Toronto as the year drew to a close.[23]

Meanwhile, the public of Toronto remained remarkably uninformed, and only in January 1914 was there a general realization of the seriousness of the premier's illness. Then, suddenly, it was common knowledge that the blunt Tory leader was not expected to live. But the tough lawyer held on, and by mid-January, his doctors had decided that he could make the trip to Toronto. There he rested in the new general hospital – which existed thanks to his government – for the next eight weeks. In the same building George Ross, beset by chronic rheumatism and old age, lay dying.[24]

IV

The premier's illness kept him from attending the 1914 session of the legislature, the cabinet having decided to meet the house without their leader. Consequently, he was not present when I.B. Lucas piloted Meredith's workmen's compensation bill through the legislature. Lucas, after explaining that the delay in introducing the measure had been occasioned by the government's 'being anxious to secure the best law possible,' described the measure as 'one of collective insurance under state management.' Characterized by a few manufacturers as 'Socialism of the worst kind,' the legislation provided for the creation of a three-man Workmen's Compensation Board.

The Act provided both individual and collective liability. It divided employers into two groups with Schedule I paying a contribution to a state insurance fund while employers in Schedule II would be individually liable. ... There was to be no employee contribution and Section 18 (1) made it illegal for the employer to deduct from wages 'any part of any sum which the employer is or may become liable to pay to the workman as compensation.'

...

One of the more progressive features of the Act was the creation of a state insurance scheme for industries in Schedule I. All industries contributed to an accident fund, the contribution to be determined by the Board. The Board could divide the industries in Schedule I into sub-groups where risks were unequal and determine the contribution of each sub-group. The Board could also levy a special contribution on any industry or individual company which, in the opinion of the Board, had an abnormally high accident rate and where the Board felt these accidents were preventable. The Board could also exclude such a company from Schedule I thereby making it individually liable for compensation.

Equally important, Section 100 (1) entitled workmen to compensation in cases of industrial diseases 'due to the nature of any employment in which he was engaged.'

Under the act, the employer was made responsible in all cases of injury to employees, except those whose disability lasted less than a week; there would be no need to prove employer negligence before filing a claim. Any compensation paid to a worker could not be claimed by his creditors. The government would make a contribution of ten thousand dollars to the board in order to help defray administration expenses. Lastly, there would be a provisional assessment, three months before the act became law, which would provide a special reserve fund.[25]

Many manufacturers, although favourably disposed to a state-operated insurance programme, were less than pleased with the legislation: they had hoped to see the measure modified in line with their ideas when the bill was not presented to the 1913 session, but this was not to be. Aside from a small minority who disliked the entire proposition, most quarrelled with the demand that only they – and not their employees – make payments into the fund, and with the two-tier arrangement of industries. They also disapproved of the special assessment to provide a reserve fund, and many wanted compensation paid out to the victim in a lump sum, not in regular portions as Meredith dictated. But, on balance, this was arguing with the details of the legislation, not the principles. An angry R. McLaughlin, the Oshawa automobile manufacturer, was only speaking for the more extreme opponents when he commented on the act: 'It is simply class legislation, and an attempt to place a heavy burden on Manufacturers which should be borne chiefly by the State'; 'Between Trade Unions, socialism, a part of the press, and politicians of a certain stripe, it will soon be looked upon as a crime to be a millionaire ... Success in life by a Manufacturer is being penalized.' But the *Industrial Banner*, speaking for labour, hailed the act as 'the most far reaching legislation that has ever been enacted by any Government in Canada in the interests of labour.'[26]

It was fitting that Meredith should have had such a close connection with the last major piece of legislation from the Whitney administration, although obviously no one knew at the time that this was the last. From the time that the Morrisburg lawyer had come to office in 1905, the former leader had been a constant source of inspiration and encouragement. This relationship was crowned by the Workmen's Compensation Act; Whitney would have been at one with Meredith's reasoning on the need for the legislation: 'In these days of social and industrial unrest, it is, in my judgment, of the gravest importance to the community, that every proved injustice, to any section or class, resulting from bad or unfair laws, should be promptly removed by the action of remedial legislation, and I don't doubt, that the country whose legislature is quick to discern and prompt to remove injustice, will enjoy ... the blessings of social peace and freedom from social unrest.'[27]

While the cause of workmen's compensation was being advanced, the premier was showing an amazing capacity for recovery. Late in February 1914, his personal secretary was able 'to talk business' with him and 'was delighted at the keenness of his interest.' At the end of the month the Tory chieftain was 'entirely out of danger,' 'able to go out walking daily,' and 'as clear and bright as ever.' By late April, he not only said he felt nearly normal, he acted it: he verbally roasted one of his doctors because of the bill the latter sent and refused to pay the full sum.[28]

As the premier slowly recovered – he did not expect 'to do any real work before next Christmas' – he had to give some attention to politics and his party. Recognizing that he had had a very close brush with death and that the Conservatives were scarcely prepared for such an eventuality, he wrote out a political will indicating his possible heir. Whitney named Foy first and then Cochrane, but he also realized that the former was in ill health and the latter was busy with federal matters. Hence, his mention of these two can be simply construed as a deserved salute to a pair of devoted followers. He followed this with the suggestion of either W.H. Hearst, his minister of lands, forests, and mines, or I.B. Lucas, who had become provincial treasurer on the death of A.J. Matheson; but his choice seemed to lie with Hearst. Why he failed to acknowledge the bright and reliable Hanna remains a mystery, unless vexation caused by the storm over the Proudfoot charges caused him to cross the provincial secretary off the list.[29]

Another problem also presented itself for the convalescing premier's consideration: the desirability of calling a general election. Because the number of seats in the legislature had been increased from one hundred and six to one hundred and eleven, and because many Tories were alarmed by the prospect of a campaign without Whitney at the head, some observers were confident that the old man would be persuaded by party workers to announce an election in which he could still rally the troops. Convinced that it would not be wise to allow the current legislature to run its full life – and likely realizing that, no matter what happened in the future, this would be his last hurrah – the Tory chieftain did just that.[30]

Whitney took virtually no part in the politicking which preceded the polling day of 29 June. In his address to Ontario's electors, he simply placed on record his achievements of the past nine years and left it to his cabinet to make the speeches. The bilingual schools question naturally entered the campaign, but it was scarcely a meaningful point of division between the two parties. What did prove divisive was Rowell's pledge to abolish the bar if a Liberal majority was returned. Much of the campaign revolved around this promise. The remaining portions of Rowell's programme – which included suggestions for strict regulation of hours of work and an attack on slums – were partly obscured by the temperance issue that he himself had raised. The hidden part of his platform showed a distinct awareness of Ontario's urban growth and its attendant problems but, unhappily for him, tended to sound like a pledge simply to extend Conservative policies.

On 23 June – late in the battle – Whitney held one emotion-filled meeting in Massey Hall, which was jammed to the rafters. Temporarily showing signs of the old political brawler, he fervently declared that he was 'an unreconstructed Conservative and an unrepentant one to boot.' He flayed Rowell for his liquor policy and denounced the clergy who had entered the campaign on the Liberal side. But the greatest impact was made when he referred to his recent illness. He told a hushed crowd:

Coming back, my friends, as I have, by God's mercy, from the shadow of the dark valley, I am constrained, nay, compelled, to express the thanks I owe to the people of Ontario. They have given me an opportunity, I think I may say, of being of some service, and they have given me their confidence in full measure, – in full measure, heaped up, pressed down, shaken together, and running over – and as long as my renewed health and strength are vouchsafed to me I shall be at their disposal, and endeavour to give them the same faithful service I have in the past.

There was scarcely a dry eye in the house as Whitney finished his genuine testament of appreciation and dedication.[31]

The noteworthy feature of the election results was that, despite Rowell's vigorous leadership, the Liberal party barely improved its position, adding but three seats to its 1911 total – when it had failed to contest numerous ridings – and

1914 Election Results			
Popular vote			Seats
Conservative	269,203	(54.15%)[32]	84
Liberal	189,022	(38.02%)	25
Other	27,882	(5.61%)	1
Labour-Socialist	11,031	(2.22%)	1
Total	497,138	(100.00%)	111

dropping slightly in its percentage of the popular vote, as did the Conservatives. Possibly, the emotionalism surrounding Whitney's illness and recovery was a factor in the final totals; but, more likely, the outcome can be explained in terms of the old man's powerful grip on the province – and an awesome political machine. He had now been in power long enough for his bluntness and honesty to be a source of fact and fancy, and, in the eyes of the majority of Ontarians who admired and respected him, he apparently could do no wrong. Thus, his party easily overwhelmed the Liberals. Gustave Evanturel, who had broken with Rowell on his liquor policy, won as an Independent-Liberal in Prescott riding, while Allan Studholme was still the Labour member for Hamilton East. With tongue in cheek, Whitney accepted the results as an 'unmistakable shewing by the people of Ontario of the common-sense which they possess in such a marked degree' in judging against the 'intemperate' language of Rowell and his supporters. The very few Conservative losses in particular ridings were more than offset overall by Tory victories in four of the six new ridings. What defeats had been suffered were attributed to lack of preparation and inadequate organization. The premier had his mandate and apparently could proceed. But he did not.[33]

During the summer of 1914, Whitney showed signs of being more like his old self. He grappled with a limited number of administrative problems and fretted over the expenditures of the Ontario Hydro-Electric Power Commission. When the rivalries and tensions of Europe swept Great Britain and the empire into the First World War on 4 August, the premier of Ontario issued a statement wholly consistent with his views of the imperial relationship:

The momentous crisis we now face makes plain what Canada's course must be. That course is to exert her whole strength and power at once in behalf of our Empire. We are part of the Empire in the fullest sense and we share in its obligations as well as its privileges. We have enjoyed under British rule the blessings of peace, liberty and protection, and now that we have an opportunity of repaying in some measure the heavy debt we owe the Mother Country, we will do so with cheerfulness and courage.

Three weeks later deeds followed words when the government of Ontario gave a quarter-million bags of flour to Great Britain.[34]

Whitney, however, witnessed little more than a month of the war. At noon on 25 September, suddenly and unexpectedly, he died. A provincial day of mourning was declared, followed by a large public funeral in Toronto. An eastbound train then transported his body to Morrisburg. There, on a grey fall day, he was buried close to the site of his birth, near the Crysler's Farm battlefield.

10

Conclusion: 'The Propriety of It'

At the height of the public debate over the merits of the 1906 liquor legislation, Whitney had declared to a constituent: 'My chief aim is that when the time comes for me to go out of power, my bitterest enemy will not be able to say that I ever did a public act or took a stand on any public question for any reason other than a strong belief in my own mind of the propriety of it.' Such a statement revealed not only the premier's imperious self-confidence – surely an essential trait in any successful politician – but also a concern for the judgment of history on his actions. It seems fair to suggest that he did not have too much cause for worry on the latter point.

It is a relatively simple task to compile a list of the major achievements of his administration that gave new direction to the province. The University of Toronto was thoroughly reorganized and placed on a sound financial footing, which served as the foundation for that institution's growth in the twentieth century. The premier's initial generosity and foresight, founded on the intelligent advice of others, were being cited almost two decades later in an attempt to prod a later Conservative premier, Howard Ferguson, into an equal effort. A series of statutes gave form to the Ontario Hydro-Electric Power Commission and placed the province in the forefront of 'state socialism' in North America. Despite periodic differences of opinion with Adam Beck, Whitney stood with that dynamic personality – the builder of 'Hydro' – through all the important battles. The Ontario Railway and Municipal Board owed its existence to his administration, and represented a further step in the delegation of governmental authority to a body that could devote its entire energies to matters under its purview, while accumulating useful expertise in the process. The Temiskaming and Northern Ontario Railway, inherited from the Ross government, was continued and extended during the Whitney era, and provided with much-improved leadership in the person of Jacob Englehart. And then there was the workmen's compensation legislation, which set the pace for other Canadian provinces and lifted a burden from the backs of many in Ontario's working class. These were some of the landmark developments that delineated nine years of Tory rule, and beneath were a host of lesser reforms, modifications, and improvements, which have already been noted.[1]

Such a brief statement about the important steps taken by a 'progressive' Conservative administration under Whitney's leadership establishes that, coming to office after thirty-three years of Grit rule, it broke new ground; but it does nothing to answer questions about sources of inspiration. As has already been indicated elsewhere, the premier's years in public life, from 1888 to 1914, roughly spanned an important transitional period in Ontario's history. Jacob Spelt has also described the alteration that occurred in the province during these years:

The dominant aspect of urban development during the three decades between 1881 and 1911 was the rise of modern manufacturing. The central service function not only declined as a factor in town development, but through improved transportation facilities, many places lost their position as a service centre, and their population decreased.

...

... This change was accompanied by a big increase in urban population; in 1911, 52.5 per cent of the population in the province lived in incorporated places, as compared with 31.5 per cent in 1881. The amount of urbanization was even greater in South-Central Ontario on account of the expansion of Toronto.

... In general the occupational structure of the provincial population had become much more urbanized, because the non-rural occupations of 1911 had comprised about two-thirds of the gainfully employed population compared with about one-half in 1881.

Whitney entered politics when agriculture was losing its primacy in Ontario's economy; he died when a modern industrial province with its urban society had been clearly established. Given the census figures for 1901 and 1911, it is reasonably safe to assume that he took up the premiership in 1905 at a time when, statistically, the rural population of Ontario yielded first place to the urban.[2]

Consequently, much of the major and minor legislation of the Whitney era was designed to meet the needs of this new society. In this changing milieu both manufacturer and worker could become honestly excited about the possibilities of hydroelectric power because its cheap development and distribution could mean so much to each of them. George Ross had been conscious of the potential of this technological advance, but from the standpoint of the producers – an exceptionally small group of individuals – and had fathered legislation which favoured them. Whitney was equally aware of the implications of this relatively new source of power, but from the standpoint of the users – the obvious majority – and advanced legislation which favoured them. Ross, an insurance company president, saw this new society largely in terms of his immediate associates. Whitney saw it in terms of the people – and votes; hence he could talk in hostile tones about 'barons' and 'corporations' and draw a ready response. This difference not only distinguished one premier from the other; it also distinguished provincial Liberalism from 'progressive' Conservatism at the century's turn.

Other legislative accomplishments of the Whitney period can be seen in exactly the same light. Liberal legislation dealing with workmen's compensation had left it up to the injured victim to seek redress through the courts, where he had to prove negligence on the part of the employer. The act of 1914 ended this difficult requirement. Again, on a most critical point in this law, there was a significant difference between the Liberal and Conservative positions. The Ross administration had dealt with street railway matters on an *ad hoc* basis by means of a cabinet committee; Whitney's response to this problem had been a railway board which, ideally, after due deliberation, would render decisions that demonstrated understanding and consistency. Nor should the assistance given to the University of Toronto be ignored in this examination. Piecemeal Liberal aid to a faulty structure was enough to keep it from falling down as long as it remained on the periphery of an agricultural society. But with the growth of an urban society that could make substantial demands of the institution, there had to be a change of policy or else the university might well collapse, a point undoubtedly pressed by Meredith. Similarly, the measures presented with respect to the automobile, a minimum age for factory workers, smallpox vaccination, and the inspection of dairy facilities all represented an acknowledgment by the Tories of the existence and growth of the urban manufacturing centre.

It is worth noting that, in the area of liquor regulation, Whitney's government provided enabling legislation for municipalities which permitted them to introduce local option; he did not produce a sweeping enactment of prohibition for the entire province. Regardless of their well-organized and well-rehearsed arguments, the demands of the temperance organizations were not the majority demands of an urban society. S.D. Clark has pointed out in his book *Church and Sect in Canada* that when, in this transitional period of Ontario's history, Methodism took on the trappings of an urban church, it divested itself of many traces of its earlier, rural days: gone were the lay preacher, camp meeting, and revivalist techniques, and in their places were the articulate, educated minister and biblical criticism. Yet Methodism did not rid itself of one of its earlier features: strong support for temperance – or, more correctly, prohibition; and Methodists wanted it to be an important aspect of Ontario Liberalism. The subject troubled Newton W. Rowell, a staunch temperance man, when he came to the Liberal leadership in 1911. In Rowell, Whitney faced the only Liberal leader who was evidently prepared to do even more than the premier in meeting the needs of the developing urban society. But Rowell handicapped himself from the outset of this uneven battle with the Conservative chief by carrying a cross – temperance – instead of a sword. His cry of 'Abolish the bar' was an appeal to another Ontario – witness the stagnant Methodist membership figures and the startling urban growth – and it drowned out his pleas for further legislation in the interests of an industrial province. Embarrassingly for Rowell, with his urban interests, he had to seek the safety of a semi-rural riding, Oxford North, when he assumed the leadership. And in 1911 he was soundly rejected in the chief urban centre of the constituency, Woodstock, and saved only by the rural vote. In 1914, after he had developed an extensive programme for an urban society, he was even more soundly defeated in Woodstock and rescued once more by the farmers of Oxford North. Wisely, Whitney left the question of prohibition to the municipalities, although his provincial secretary constantly tightened the screws on liquor regulations.[3]

The Whitney administration, in broadening the services offered by the department of agriculture, demonstrated that it had not forgotten the farmer and rural society – after all, the premier sat for an agricultural constituency – but its landmark legislation was primarily for the urban centres, which responded with massive support for the Conservative party. Of course, there was a danger in this: the farmer might sense that he was losing his place in society as rural depopulation continued at an uneven rate from the nineteenth into the twentieth century. As a consequence, rebellion in the form of political action could follow. This unease may provide a partial explanation for the upsurge of the Patrons of Industry who, unwittingly, had helped to cut loose some rural Liberals who were later rounded up by Whitney for his party; and it certainly was a factor in the rise of the United Farmers of Ontario. Nevertheless, Whitney was not running a grave risk in catering to the needs of a continually growing majority in the urban centres, although this approach did provoke W.D. Gregory to comment, in 1908, that 'radicals' made up 'the Government majority,' demonstrating 'how meaningless party names' had become.[4]

If much of Whitney's 'progressive' legislation can be explained in terms of the society that was taking shape in Ontario, there remains the problem of explaining how it was that Whitney read the desires of this society so accurately (that he did so can scarcely be doubted in the face of the election results detailed elsewhere in this work). The premier did possess a fine capacity for taking the public pulse; he had sharpened this instinct long before he ever contested the provincial riding of Dundas in 1886. And throughout his career as premier he continually used phrases such as 'the people are with us,' and 'public opinion demands it,' in support of his decisions. And, it would seem, he was quite correct in his assessment.[5]

The evidence of a changing Ontario was all around him and he would indeed have been an ineffective politician had he not seen it. Early in his career, when he fought to retain the municipal right to offer bonuses in order to attract manufacturing enterprises, he was displaying an awareness of the danger of economic stagnation should Morrisburg not gain new industries. As it turned out, Morrisburg was one of many towns which, in this period, failed to broaden its economic base, and it did stagnate. Whitney could not have been blind to these developments and their implications. He witnessed the slow rise of the labour movement in Ontario in the latter part of the nineteenth century and he heard the language of socialism in the early twentieth. For nearly all the years that he was premier, he looked across the floor of the legislature at the man who was the embodiment of some of these changing circumstances: Allan Studholme, the Labour member from Hamilton East. And, like others of his day, the Conservative chieftain argued that concession – not rigidity – would rob socialism of its potency. Thus, when the Power Commission Amendment Act of 1909 roused such a storm of protest, Whitney could reply: 'It is indeed a ghastly joke to charge the Ontario Government with being socialistic, etc., when it is the bulwark in Canada by means of which such influences will be shattered.' He was ready to bend with the wind, not rigidly risk being broken; he was quite prepared to make careful changes to accommodate the new age.[6]

Taking a leaf from the interpretation of American history, H.V. Nelles has argued that one reason for the 'progressive' nature of some Conservative legislation was that the left in Ontario did not present a threat and, therefore, 'reformers could take dead aim on their objective without the disquieting suspicion that their rhetoric might be turned against them' – a circumstance that did not obtain in the United States, where progressives feared they might further arouse 'the stirring masses.' In effect, he is saying that Ontarian 'progressives' possessed a freedom to act because they did not need to fear being unable to stop. Such an interpretation seriously discounts the socialist presence in Ontario as a reason for government action. Yet, in light of Whitney's remarks, the socialist factor has to be given due weight, despite the poor showing of the left at the polls. The premier certainly thought that 'socialistic ideas of various kinds' were 'being presented to our people in glowing terms.' And he was convinced that it was necessary to defy 'all this socialistic craze'; the failure of the left to grow may well reflect Whitney's success in defanging socialism through the legislation of his administration.[7]

Others witnessed the changing situation in the province but did not always comprehend what was occurring or sense what to do. John Cameron of the *London Advertiser* had told J.S. Willison as early as 1898: 'Things have changed. A new electorate has grown up. The middle-class ruler has gone out to a great extent. The crowd are in it as never before.' Arthur S. Hardy wrote of the Conservative upswing in the provincial election of the same year: 'I incline to think that the dregs of the cities and country towns in the new vote went largely in their [the Conservatives'] direction.' The 'dregs' evidently continued to go that route and Hardy was apparently helpless in the face of the tide. If these men could note the altered situation, then why not Whitney? What marked him apart from Hardy, Ross, Graham, and MacKay was that, as C.F. Hamilton of the *News* grudgingly admitted in 1906, the Tory leader possessed 'a certain instinct for what the people want.'[8]

Nor was the province unprepared for intervention by the state under the Whitney administration. The limited efforts of the Mowat regime 'coincided in general with the period which has been described as witnessing the beginning of the social welfare state in Canada.' Dozens of municipalities owned their own utilities before the end of the nineteenth century; in Morrisburg, the town council installed a municipally owned waterworks and electric light plant in 1887, the year before Whitney was first elected to the legislature.[9]

The premier not only witnessed, assessed, and acted, he also took advice and accepted support. Long after the Tory chief was dead, one observer noted: 'much of Whitney's greatness was attributable to those he had the sagacity to gather round him.' And, undoubtedly, members of his cabinet, particularly Beck, Hanna, Foy, and Cochrane, were important figures in the successes of his administration; but, it must be remembered, he chose them and he ruled the cabinet. The most influential person in Whitney's political life, however, was not a member of his cabinet at all but, rather, his former leader, W.R. Meredith, who did much more than simply offer encouragement. Meredith became chancellor at the University of Toronto in 1900, in succession to Edward Blake, and it is worth noting that Whitney's university policy became clearly articulated after that date. In addition, once his former follower became premier, the chief justice carefully scrutinized important bills before they were presented to the legislature and harshly criticized badly worded sections, and he prodded Whitney whenever he thought the reform surge of his government was weakening. In 1906, when the forces of private enterprise first began to muster to battle Whitney on the subject of hydroelectric power development, Meredith urged him to stand firm. The sometime Tory leader had a large hand in the creation of the Ontario Railway and Municipal Board, although the original idea appears to have been Whitney's; and he was the architect of the Workmen's Compensation Act of 1914. Meredith's full influence is impossible to assess, but it has to be conceded that it was large indeed. Nevertheless, it is essential to emphasize that Whitney, undoubtedly anxious to have the chief justice's ideas and criticisms, was not a blind follower of his former leader. He judged his mentor to be the holder of 'strong radical views with regard to many public questions,' and although 'very far removed indeed from being a crank,' some of his positions had to be examined carefully.[10]

Whitney not only rendered large service to his province as a 'progressive' Conservative; his contributions to the Tory party at both the provincial and federal levels were also of significant dimensions. Taking charge of an emaciated group in 1896, he built it into a powerful co-ordinated unit by 1905, pulling many urban labourers in behind him as well as rural Liberals who had become disaffected at the time of the Patrons of Industry. From the date of his electoral triumph the Conservative party in Ontario has only been out of office on two occasions, from 1919 to 1923, and from 1934 to 1943; and those were periods of intense social dislocation. In terms of his party, the Tory leader probably built better than he knew. And, once Whitney had the power of the premier's office behind him, his steady support of Borden undoubtedly did much to keep the latter at the head of the federal party. The provincial leader judged his efforts in the federal campaign of 1911 to have been of critical importance, and that assessment, if not modest, was also not inaccurate.[11]

And it should be remembered that Whitney's accomplishments were achieved without benefit of a host of advisers, political strategists, and public-opinion analysts. He kept his own counsel, seeking guidance only from a few close political friends, and this was done when his administration was, in meeting the needs of Ontario's urban society, taking more than one leap in the dark. But he was insistent that sound policy was much better if produced by a concerned few rather than 'the outcome of that fearful and wonderful thing a convention' – a view entirely in keeping with his autocratic temperament. Possibly this feature of his rule can best be seen in a picture of him leaving a political platform, briefcase in hand, having delivered his speech, and with not a solitary aide in sight.[12]

There was, of course, 'Circular of Instructions, 17,' which did little for national unity. Yet, even on the subject of bilingual schools, Whitney was attempting to improve the lot of French-Canadians, to equip these Ontarians to meet the demands of industrialization in what he viewed, along with the vast majority, as an English-speaking province. That he was blind to the dangerous consequences of his policy indicates that he was typically Ontarian in his outlook and sensitivities. And latter-day labour historians can judge him as having under-performed in the matter of legislation for the working class. But he did see to the tighter regulation of hours and conditions of work in a number of industries; and, of course, there was the workmen's compensation act which, admittedly, did not cover all workers. It should also be noted that contemporary society seems to have thought that his actions in this area were sufficient. Similarly, his inaction on female suffrage, while at times quite graceless, had the approbation of the majority. The premier was shrewd enough to provide the lead when he was reasonably confident that most in the province would follow, but he had no intention of marching ahead only to discover his supporting army had evaporated. That attitude secured many, but not all, of the reforms needed in a less than perfect world.

Whitney's personal honesty, which he forced upon all his followers, resulted in a new standard of political morality for the province of Ontario. Unlike Ross, who cheerfully remained president of an insurance company while occupying the premier's office, Whitney scrupulously divested himself of all external interests when he came to the post. On one occasion he called for new tenders for a contract when it was discovered that one of his ministers was a director of the firm which had entered a successful bid. And he even delivered a lecture to W.R. Meredith when he discovered that the University of Toronto was contracting for building materials without calling for tenders, and insisted that the practice be stopped. He most certainly used patronage to reinforce the position of his government, but he seldom – if ever – was vindictive in its application and he generally strove to give the Grits some representation. At times he seemed to delight in weakening the

Liberals by handing them positions they could not refuse. J.A. Macdonald, editor of the *Globe*, was named to the board of governors of the University of Toronto when the new legislation for that place of learning came into effect. Of course, there was no better way to silence the criticism – or even encourage the praise – of that troublesome Grit newspaper, at least on the subject of this one institution. In the heat of legislative debate or campaign battle, the Conservative leader occasionally made bitter comments about the qualities of his opponents, but, behind the scenes, he never stooped to obtain a political advantage out of the personal misfortunes of those facing him. In most respects he was a gentleman – austere, but a gentle man nonetheless.[13]

Whitney largely lived up to his promise of 'bold enough to be honest ... honest enough to be bold.' Once in 1899, in the gloom of opposition, he had pessimistically commented on his own efforts: 'It will be all the same a hundred years hence.' Just fifteen years later nothing was much the same in Ontario, thanks in part to his efforts and his policies. He had helped to place legislation on the province's statute books which recognized the existence of a new industrial society, now partially shaped by government intervention.[14]

Notes

BP Borden Papers   KP King Papers   MP Macdonald Papers
CAR *Canadian Annual Review*   LP Laurier Papers   WP Whitney Papers

CHAPTER ONE

1 Willison Papers, Whitney to Willison, 12 December 1912
2 Brockville *Daily Times*, 2 February 1888
3 WP, scrapbook, clipping from the Morrisburg *Courier*, 3 February 1888
4 Whitney family Bible (in private hands); parish registers, Williamsburg, Matilda,
   Osnabruck, Edwardsburg, 1790–1886, Liber 'D' 15 and 83. I am indebted to Murray
   Barkley for the latter reference.
      There is confusion surrounding Whitney's birth-year. In biographical sketches, for
   which he must have originally provided the information, the date is given as 2 October
   1843; see J. Smyth Carter, *The Story of Dundas* (Iroquois 1905) 220. Further, the
   Ontario Historical and Archaeological Sites Board plaque honouring him states 1843,
   as does the statue in front of Ontario's legislative buildings. But Whitney's tombstone
   and the above noted records make it clear that 1842 is the proper date.
5 Canada West Census 1861, Agricultural Census, Enumeration District no. 6 of the
   Township of Osnabruck, County of Stormont, 1. In the census of 1861, the Whitney
   family religion is given as Wesleyan Methodist, despite the facts surrounding
   Whitney's baptism. WP, Whitney to J.J. McGannon, 19 November 1907. Carter 363
6 WP, scrapbook, clipping from the *Cornwall Economist*, 20 December 1860
7 Pringle Papers, agreement 'to organise a Volunteer Militia Infantry Company at
   Cornwall,' 20 May 1860; requisition for clothing for the Volunteer Militia Infantry
   Company at Cornwall, March 1863; quarterly report of the Cornwall Volunteer
   Infantry Company, 30 September 1863; pay list of the Cornwall Infantry Company of
   Volunteer Militia for their drill for the year ending 30 June 1865
      Quarterly returns, Volunteer Militia, Canada West, quarterly return of the
   Volunteer Militia Rifle Company of Cornwall under the command of Captain Edward

Oliver, 1 April 1862; quarterly return of the Light Infantry Militia under the command of Captain J.F. Pringle, headquarters at Cornwall, 1 July 1865

G.M. Rose, ed., *A Cyclopaedia of Canadian Biography: Being Chiefly Men of the Time* (Toronto 1886) 726

8 Pringle Papers, pay list of J.F. Pringle's Company of the Cornwall Volunteer Battalion, 8 March 1866 to 31 May 1866; list of the officers, non-commissioned officers, and men of the Cornwall Volunteer Infantry Company who were on active service in 1866

Canada, General Service Medal Registrar, 1866–70: Fenian Raid, Red River, Book A, Military Districts nos. 1 to 4, 43

J.A. Macdonald, *Troublous Times in Canada; A History of the Fenian Raids of 1866 and 1870* (Toronto 1910) 23

9 Ibid, 106–8

10 Rose, ed., *A Cyclopaedia* 725. Morgan Papers, 8381, clipping on Whitney's genealogy

11 Bruce W. Hodgins, *John Sandfield Macdonald* (Toronto 1971) 56–74.

WP, Whitney to W. Gibbens, 25 April 1907; Whitney to J. Pope, 19 March 1909. For Whitney's speech at the unveiling of this statue see *Proceedings at the Unveiling of the Statue to John Sandfield Macdonald, First Prime Minister of Ontario, in Queen's Park, Toronto, November 16th, 1909* (Toronto 1909) 5–12. Rose 726

12 See note 1

13 He was not living with his father when the census of 1871 was taken; see Census of 1871, Province of Ontario, District no. 72, Stormont, Sub-District A. Township of Osnabruck, Division no. 1. 95. For that matter, if the census of 1871 can be trusted, Whitney was residing in neither Dundas nor Stormont counties at that time. That fact puts to rest one Morrisburg story related to the author: that Whitney taught school in north Dundas County in this period. His brother Albert (1840–1927) was counted in this census, although he was living-in with the J.P. Wiser family in Prescott town. That would seem to speak well for the accuracy of the census. A good deal of indirect evidence would suggest that Whitney left Cornwall and the study of law sometime in 1867 and did not return until 1872, at the earliest.

Colquhoun Papers, Whitney to Colquhoun, 15 September 1871. This letter establishes that Whitney was living in Aultsville at this time.

14 Rose, ed., *A Cyclopaedia* 725–6. *The City of Ottawa and Central Canada Directory* (Ottawa 1876) 201. *Brockville Recorder*, 1 June, 14 December 1876, 1 March 1877

15 *The City of Ottawa* 201. Carter, *The Story of Dundas* 162–204. *Brockville Recorder 2 March 1876 and 13 December 1877. Dundas County Herald and St. Lawrence Reporter* (Morrisburg), 18 January 1877

16 *Cornwall Reporter, and Eastern Counties Gazette*, 18 November 1876. *Brockville Recorder*, 1 March 1877

17 Register of marriages, births, and funerals in connection with St John's Presbyterian Church, Cornwall, from January 1833 to January 1863, January, February, March

1846, baptism no. 6; register of marriages, births, and funerals of St John's Presbyterian Church, Cornwall, from January 1863 to January 1892, April, May, June 1877, marriage no. 2

Census of 1871, Province of Ontario, District no. 73, Cornwall, Sub-District C, East Ward 14

Cornwall Reporter, and Eastern Counties Gazette, 13 January and 5 May 1877. *Brockville Recorder*, 10 May 1877

18 Rose, ed., *A Cyclopaedia* 726. *Brockville Recorder*, 20 September and 11 October 1877. Toronto *Mail*, 25 September 1877

Macdonell Papers, J.A. Macdonald to Macdonell, 21 August 1877

19 Ontario, *Sessional Papers*, XII, part III (1880), no. 19, return from the records of the elections to the Legislative Assembly in 1879, 10; Ontario, *Sessional Papers*, XVI, part I (1884), no. 1, return from the records of the general election to the Legislative Assembly in 1883, 12–13.

20 Interview with Fred S. Broder, son of Andrew, 28 June 1960. The statements in this paragraph also rest on comments from various sources and a thorough reading of the Whitney Papers.

21 *Brockville Recorder*, 20 September 1877, 30 January 1879. Toronto *Mail*, 31 January 1882

MP, Whitney to Macdonald, 30 September 1881; J.A. Macdonell to Macdonald, 29 November 1881; J.H. Munroe to Macdonald, 8 June 1882; A. Farlinger to Macdonald, 14 January 1887

22 Toronto *Mail*, 9 and 20 February 1883

23 Carter, *The Story of Dundas* 75–80

24 Rose, ed., *A Cyclopaedia* 726

25 Brockville *Daily Times*, 9 December 1886

26 WP, R. Birmingham to Whitney, 17 December 1886

27 F.A. Walker, *Catholic Education and Politics in Ontario* ([Toronto] 1964) 113–14

MP, Macdonald to T.H. McGuire, 18 June and 4 October 1886; G.B. Boyle to Lady Macdonald, 23 November 1886

28 Walker, *Catholic Education and Politics in Ontario* 117 and footnote 17 on 121

29 WP, literature and notes for addresses at meetings, campaign of 1886.

30 MP, A. Farlinger to Macdonald, 14 January 1887

31 Ibid. *Dundas County Herald and St. Lawrence Reporter* (Morrisburg), 20 January 1887. The Liberal owner of this newspaper, George P. Graham, was to cross swords with Whitney time and time again through the lives of the two men. He later became an MPP, member of the provincial cabinet, leader of the provincial opposition, and, finally, federal cabinet minister. Bowell Papers, Bowell to Whitney, 4 March 1887

32 *Dundas County Herald and St. Lawrence Reporter* (Morrisburg), 20 January 1887; *Brockville Recorder*, 27 January 1887

33 WP, scrapbook, clipping from the Morrisburg *Courier*, 16 December 1887; Toronto *Empire*, 13 January 1888

34 Brockville *Daily Times*, 23 December 1887. WP, scrapbook, clipping from the Morrisburg *Courier*, 30 December 1887; 'Loyal Dundas' letter no. 5
35 WP, scrapbook, 'Loyal Dundas' Letter no. 4
36 WP, D. McCarthy to Whitney, 21 January 1888
37 Toronto *Empire*, 11 February 1888. *Toronto Saturday Night*, 24 March 1888
38 *Toronto Saturday Night*, 24 March 1888. F.D. Reville, *History of the County of Brant* (Brantford 1920) II, 354 and 361. 'Big Thunder' was E.B. Wood, who had sat provincially and federally for Brant South.
39 Toronto *Empire*, 7 March 1888
40 Brockville *Daily Times*, 22 March 1888. WP, Whitney to J.F. Gibbons and W.L. Redmund, 16 March 1888
41 Toronto *Empire*, 13 March 1888
42 WP, G.F. Marter to Whitney, 12 and 18 August 1889; W.R. Meredith to Whitney, 22 July 1889. In the Douglas Library Archives, Queen's University, there is a notebook, catalogued as Whitney Papers, containing voting records and Roman Catholic strength in Ontario constituencies in the late 1870s and 1880s. This handbook, compiled by Meredith, was handed on to Whitney and was left in his Morrisburg law office when he became premier. Thus it did not become part of the Whitney Papers housed in the Public Archives of Ontario.
43 WP, G. Kerr to Whitney, 10 August 1889; J. Leitch to Whitney, 21 August 1889; A.E. Powter to Whitney, 22 August 1889
44 MP, A. Farlinger to Macdonald, 17 March 1890; Whitney to Macdonald, 26 February 1890
45 MP, R. Birmingham to Macdonald, 25 November 1889. Walker, *Catholic Education and Politics in Ontario* 126–67. C.R.W. Biggar, *Sir Oliver Mowat* (Toronto 1905) II, 484–98. J.F. O'Sullivan, 'Dalton McCarthy and the Conservative Party, 1876–1896,' MA thesis (University of Toronto 1949) 70–86, 122–36, 148–50
46 *Toronto Saturday Night*, 8 February 1890. WP, O. Fulton to Whitney, 12 March 1890; D. Fraser to Whitney, 14 March 1890. MP, R. Stephenson to Macdonald, 20 May 1890; J.H. Metcalfe to Macdonald, 24 May and 3 June 1890; J.W. Slaven to Macdonald, 3 June 1890; N.C. Wallace to Macdonald, 27 May 1890.
47 Toronto *Empire*, 6 May 1890, quoting the Morrisburg *Courier*. WP, Whitney to 'Dear Sir,' 16 May 1890. Walker, *Catholic Education and Politics in Ontario* 138.
48 Ontario, Sessional Papers, XXIII, part I (1891), no. 1, 16–17.
49 The Equal Rights figure was arrived at by counting their votes in the ridings of Durham East and Toronto where the movement ran candidates against Tory nominees; Equal Rights captured Durham East. Elsewhere there were Conservatives who ran with the blessing of the Equal Rights movement, but their votes are located in the Conservative column.
50 WP, W.R. Meredith to Whitney, 6 June 1890; A.H.U. Colquhoun to Whitney, 9 June 1890; scrapbook, clipping of Whitney's maiden speech in the legislature. MP, Macdonald to W.E. Sanford, 10 July 1890; M. Bowell to Macdonald, 1 August 1890. Thompson Papers, Father P.J. Noonan to Thompson, 7 June 1890

CHAPTER TWO

1 WP, W.R. Meredith to Whitney, 5 September 1890 and 6 June 1892. Bowell Papers, Bowell to Whitney, 29 December 1891
2 Toronto *Globe*, 2, 28, and 29 April 1891; 4 and 11 March 1892; 14 April and 13 May 1893
3 Toronto *Globe*, 5 March 1892; 1 and 20 May 1893
4 Toronto *Globe*, 21 April 1891
5 WP, W.R. Meredith to Whitney, 31 December 1890; 5 January, 6 March and 16 June 1891; H.H. Ross to Whitney, 23 January 1892. Toronto *Globe*, 23 February 1893. *Toronto Saturday Night*, 13 June 1891
6 *Wiarton Echo*, 2 March 1893
7 S.E.D. Shortt, 'Social Change and Political Crisis in Rural Ontario: The Patrons of Industry, 1889–1896,' in Donald Swainson, ed., *Oliver Mowat's Ontario* (Toronto 1972) 211. Toronto *Globe*, 10 March 1891
8 V.M. Nelson, 'The Orange Order in Canadian Politics,' MA thesis (Queen's University 1950) 138–9. *Wiarton Echo*, 13 July 1893. *A History of the Year 1894 with Especial Reference to Canadian Affairs* (Toronto 1894) 47
9 Toronto *Globe*, 4 December 1893. *Canada Farmers' Sun* (London), 5 December 1893
10 WP, W.A. Willoughby to Whitney, 6 December 1892. Toronto *Globe*, 3 May 1893, quoting James Moody, president of the Winchester Township and Dundas County Patrons of Industry associations. *Brockville Recorder*, 16 November 1893. *Canada Farmers' Sun* (London), 28 November 1893
11 Wallace Papers, Whitney to Wallace, 28 January 1893
12 Laurier urged Mowat to accept the measure, arguing that the ballot 'is such a liberal principle that to refuse to apply it to one class of electors ... can hardly be reconciled with the tenets of the Liberal party.' He also pointed out that such a move would draw the 'most wicked teeth' of the PPA. Liberal journalist John S. Willison, and Richard W. Scott, author of the 1863 Separate School Act, shared Laurier's view. LP, Laurier to Mowat, 29 January 1894; Willison to Laurier, 19 January 1894. Scott to Archbishop John Walsh, 8 February 1894, quoted in Walker 171

Christopher Finlay Fraser, commissioner of public works and longtime Roman Catholic cabinet member, was opposed to Conmee's bill and chose this moment to depart the cabinet for reasons of health. Fraser's health was failing, but he also wanted to be free to speak against the measure, which he did. In the end, however, he supported the legislation. Fraser's place as the Catholic in the cabinet was taken by William Harty, the member for Kingston, who became commissioner of public works on 30 May 1894. *A History of the Year 1894* 44. See also: Scott Papers, Ross to Scott, 27 April 1894
13 *A History of the Year 1894* 45
14 Ibid. 49–50
15 There were ninety-four seats at stake, but Ottawa had dual representation and thus is

counted as a single constituency. Wallace Papers, W.J. Hanna to Wallace, 18 April 1895

16 *Brockville Recorder*, 1, 8, and 15 June 1894

17 There is little agreement among sources on the figures under this heading. For example, S.E.D. Shortt in 'Social Change,' 222, provides figures of fifty Liberals, twenty-three Conservatives, seventeen Patrons, and four Independents. Judging from a footnote in this work, his figures rest in part on the *Canadian Parliamentary Companion, 1897*, and the distribution of seats had changed by that year. The *Canadian Parliamentary Companion* was not published in 1894, and this accounts for part of the confusion. The figures in the present work rest on *A History for the Year 1894*, a compilation from newspapers, and the *Centennial Edition of a History of the Electoral Districts, Legislatures and Ministries of the Province of Ontario, 1867–1968*, compiled by Roderick Lewis (Toronto nd). The totals given here are immediate post-election results and do not take into account Liberal by-election triumphs in London (October 1894), Kingston (January 1895), Algoma West (January 1895), and Haldimand (March 1895). These victories changed the standings to fifty-one Liberals, twenty-four Conservatives, sixteen Patrons, two PPA, and one Independent.

Of the twenty-seven successful Tory candidates, James T. Watt in 'The Protestant Protective Association in Ontario: A Study in Anti-Catholic Nativism,' MA thesis (McMaster University), appendices V and VI, states that six were members of the PPA and one was believed to be; further, another three signed the PPA obligation.

Watt names five successful Patrons as members of the PPA. There is a problem here, however, because he categorizes one of their number as a Conservative when other sources do not, and he calls another one simply a PPA candidate, while Shortt in 'Social Change,' 234, insists that he is a Patron, pure and simple, although he places him in the wrong constituency. Shortt (226) states that only two successful Patrons were members of the PPA. All of this confusion suggests that, despite the work done on the election of 1894, a constituency-by-constituency analysis is needed in which extensive use could be made of local newspapers.

18 Thompson Papers, Thompson to T. Galt, 11 August 1894; W.R. Meredith to Thompson, 1 October 1894

19 Marter sat for Muskoka, 1886–94, and then successfully contested Toronto North. Toronto *Empire*, 6 October 1894. Toronto *Globe*, 5 October 1894

20 WP, W.R. Meredith to Whitney, 4, 10, and 17 October 1894

21 *Canada Farmers' Sun*, 10 October 1894

22 Toronto *Empire*, 24 October 1894

23 Toronto *Empire*, 26 October 1894. Toronto *Mail*, 24 October 1894

24 Toronto *Mail*, 25 October 1894. WP, Whitney to O.A. Howland, 4 January 1895

25 London *Free Press*, 9 and 19 November 1894. Toronto *Empire*, 15 November 1894
Marter's stance on separate schools may have, in part, been inspired by the fact that the Tory candidate, Mayor E.T. Essery of London, was a PPA member. Marter's prohibitionist views were no secret, particularly in light of his unsuccessful legislative efforts on the question, but as leader he converted them into party policy.

E.E. Sheppard was on the platform with Whitney and he did deal with separate schools. He conceded that they could not be abolished, but he did want a stop put to the tinkering with school law: 'we have not got the Separate schools of Sir. O. Mowat and his clique.' Sheppard also called for similarly qualified teachers, identical texts, and the same inspectors for separate and public systems. Essery, speaking last, called for 'one national school' system which, in effect, was a demand for abolition.

26 Toronto *Empire*, 21 November, 6 and 8 December 1894. WP, G.F. Marter to Whitney, 7 December 1894. Wallace Papers, E.T. Essery to Wallace, 28 November 1894

27 WP, Whitney to O.A. Howland, 4 January 1895. Toronto *Empire*, 7 December 1894

28 Toronto *Mail and Empire*, 14 March 1895
Some of the Patrons in Kent West voted to censure their member, Thomas Pardo, for his failure to stay to the Patron platform and his frequent support of Mowat; Toronto *Mail and Empire*, 29 April 1895. Pardo certainly did fit the description that Conservatives gave to the Patrons: he was a Liberal, became a Patron in the 1894 election and defeated the sitting Conservative, and then was the successful Liberal candidate in the 1898 election.

29 Toronto *Mail and Empire*, 4 April 1895
For accounts of the student strike see: R.M. Dawson, *William Lyon Mackenzie King, 1: 1874–1923* (Toronto 1958) 33–6, and W.S. Wallace, *A History of the University of Toronto, 1827–1927* (Toronto 1927) 152–5.

30 WP, W.R. Meredith to Whitney, 27 April 1895; A. Broder to Whitney, 15 February 1896

31 Toronto *Mail and Empire*, 19 February 1896; Toronto *World*, 18 February 1896

32 Toronto *World*, 19 February 1896

33 Ibid. Toronto *Mail and Empire*, 28 February 1896
Thomas Crawford (1847–1932), a Methodist of Irish birth and education, was a member of the legislature from 1894 to 1924, serving as speaker, 1907–11, and as minister without portfolio, 1923–24. He was a lifelong Orangeman who marched in July 12th parades from his Irish boyhood on. He also supported the right of women to vote and sit in elected bodies.

34 Oliver Aiken Howland (1847–1905), a son of Sir William P. Howland – sometime Macdonald cabinet minister and lieutenant-governor of Ontario – was elected to the legislature in 1894 and resigned in 1897. He was mayor of Toronto, 1901–2, and a founder and first president of the Union of Canadian Municipalities. His older brother, William, was mayor of Toronto, 1886–7; see Desmond Morton, *Mayor Howland: The Citizens' Candidate* (Toronto 1973).

35 Mills Papers, G.W. Ross to Mills, 21 February 1896

36 Toronto *Mail and Empire*, 5 March 1896

37 Toronto *Mail and Empire*, 8 April 1896

38 WP, T.S. Edwards to Whitney, 7 May 1896; J. Haggart to Whitney, 12 May 1896; W.H. Montague to Whitney, 13 May 1896. Toronto *Mail and Empire*, 19 and 25 May 1896

39 LP, A. Johnston to Laurier, 17 July 1896. In this letter, Johnston threw some light on

the provincial election of 1894 in Dundas: 'My defeat was principally to be attributed to the break made in the Liberal Party by the Patrons of Industry. They ran a candidate, Mr J.P. Fox, the same man who ran as the third candidate this time, in the last Provincial Election in 1894 and the Liberal party did not run any. About half the Liberals in the Village vote for Whitney the Conservative candidate. Fox had formerly been a Conservative. It was the same in general all over the Province, the people in the Towns and Villages could not be got to vote for a Patron Candidate. Nevertheless this made a great many of the Liberal Patrons very angry and a considerable number of them united with the McCarthy or rather Clark[e] Wallace Conservatives and brought out Fox and voted for him – Broder got 1932, I got 1870 and Fox 494.'

40 Denison Papers, Denison to Lord Salisbury, 2 May 1896. Willison Papers, A.S. Hardy to Willison, 16 July 1896. Mills Papers, W.A. Charlton to O. Mowat, 20 July 1896. wp, G.S. Ryerson to Whitney, 21 July 1896

41 LP, G.W. Ross to Laurier, 25 June 1896

42 LP, A.S. Hardy to Laurier, 4 September 1896; Laurier to A.S. Hardy, 8 December 1896; A.S. Hardy to Laurier, 10 December 1896; Laurier to A.S. Hardy, nd [late 1896]; Laurier to J.S. Willison, 16 December 1896; A.S. Hardy to Laurier, 1 January 1897

43 wp, W.R. Meredith to Whitney, 11 February 1897; A.E. Evanturel to Whitney, 16 September 1897. Interview with W.R. Plewman, 17 May 1961

44 wp, Letterbook A, Whitney to W.H. Montague, 4 April 1897; Whitney to C. Tupper, 5 April 1897; Whitney to A.E. Belcher, 10 April 1897. The three letterbooks in the Whitney Papers have been given neither letters nor numbers to distinguish them. I have designated them A, B, and C, in chronological order, to tell them apart.

45 Toronto *Mail and Empire*, 2 and 5 October 1896. Toronto *World*, 27 and 28 October 1896

46 wp, Letterbook A, Whitney to T. Birkett, 18 June 1897; Whitney to C.V.S. Boudreault, 2 July 1897; Whitney to Shannon, 27 April 1897

47 wp, Letterbook A, Whitney to W.G. Elliott, 19 May 1897; Whitney to R. Birmingham, 15 June 1897; Whitney to L.H. Clarke, 17 June 1897; Whitney to Rev. J.P. Doherty, 28 June 1897

48 wp, Letterbook A, Whitney to R.H. Bowers, 24 July 1897; Whitney to W.J. Crosthwaite, 21 May 1897; Whitney to T. Williamson, 19 June 1897; Whitney to J.W. St John, 1 July 1897; Whitney to P. White, 8 March 1897; Whitney to Dr Steacy, 24 May 1897; Whitney to W.M. McGuire, 22 March 1897; Whitney to W.B. Sanders, 19 March 1897; Whitney to J. Reid, 12 August 1897; Whitney to A.P. Campbell, 18 February 1897; Whitney to Dr Vardon, 19 February 1897; Whitney to H. Eilber, 10 March 1897; Whitney to Dr Reaume, 17 June and 17 July 1897. wp, C.A. Muma to Whitney, 15 March 1897; G.H. Macdowell to Whitney, 20 March 1897

49 wp, Letterbook A, Whitney to R. Birmingham, 11 July, 16 and 20 August 1897; Whitney to J.W. St John, 23 August 1897

50 Gregory Papers, G. Smith to W.L. Smith, 7 March 1897. wp, J. Barr to Whitney, 10 March 1897

51 wp, J.H. Laughton to Whitney, 25 March 1897; Letterbook A, Whitney to S. Griffin, 19 August 1897. LP, G.W. Ross to Laurier, 30 March 1897

52 LP, J.S. Willison to Laurier, 13 December 1896

53 LP, R. Harcourt to O. Mowat, 15 April 1897; G.W. Ross to Laurier, 11 May 1897

54 LP, A.S. Hardy to Laurier, 11 October 1897

55 wp, D. Bechard to Whitney, 8 March 1897; A. Wallis to Whitney, 24 August 1897; Letterbook A, Whitney to S. White, 4 April 1897; Whitney to A. Wallis, 19 August 1897; Whitney to R.H. Bowes, 24 July 1897

56 Willison Papers, J.M. Gibson to Willison, 12 October 1897; A.S. Hardy to Willison, 4 November 1897

57 wp, A.H.U. Colquhoun to Whitney, 6 October 1897. LP, J.M. Gibson to Laurier, 27 March 1897

58 wp, Letterbook A, Whitney to A. Broder, 19 May 1897

59 wp, Letterbook A, Whitney to R. Grass, 24 July 1897; Whitney to J.W. St John, 16 August 1897

60 Toronto *Globe*, 30 November 1897

61 wp, Letterbook A, Whitney to G.S. Ryerson, 24 July 1897. Toronto *Globe*, 3 and 21 December 1897, and 13 January 1898

62 Toronto *Globe*, 18 December 1897. wp, Letterbook A, Whitney to Rev. Dr Coffey, 18 March 1897

63 Toronto *Globe*, 26 and 27 January, 8, 9, and 23 February 1898. Toronto *Mail and Empire*, 26 January 1898

64 Toronto *Globe*, 22 November 1897. See 34–6 in this chapter. Howland voted with the Whitney amendment which was lost, and against the Mowat amendment which carried. The *Globe* was not quite accurate in its charge; nevertheless, Howland's performance was not that of one who had signed the PPA obligation.

65 wp, W.D. McPherson to Whitney, 24 January 1898

66 Toronto *Globe*, 7 February 1898

67 wp, T. O'Hagan to Whitney, 8 February 1898

68 Mills Papers, Letterbook 1, Mills to R. Ferguson, 23 February 1898; Mills to J.R. Gemmell, 19 January 1898; Mills to Daniel Mills, 18 February 1898; Mills to A.S. Hardy, 25 January 1898

69 Willison Papers, S. Lyon to Willison, 17 February 1898; memorandum from A.S. Hardy to Willison, attached to letter of 8 February 1898. LP, A.S. Hardy to Laurier, 18 January 1898; J.A. Halsted to Laurier, 21 January 1898; A.S. Hardy to Laurier, 14 February 1898. Toronto *Globe*, 1 February 1898

70 This figure and the Conservative one were derived from a combination of sources: Ontario, *Sessional Papers*, XXXI, part 1 (1898–99), no. 1; A.J. Magurn, ed., *The Parliamentary Guide and Work of General Reference, 1898–9* (Winnipeg and Ottawa

1898) 142–6; Roderick Lewis, comp., *Centennial Edition of a History* ... Each of these works contains some minor errors.

In the constituency of Russell, which went Liberal and which is included in this total, the election was not held until 18 March.

Included in the Liberal total is W.R. Beatty (Parry Sound), who contested the constituency successfully for the Conservatives in 1894. In 1898, however, a Tory candidate was put up against him and he evidently ran as an Independent; on the first division in the new legislature, he voted with the Liberals. Also in the Liberal figure is T.L. Pardo (Kent West), who had successfully contested the riding in 1894 as a Patron; but, by 1898, he was judged to be a Grit.

71 Included in the Conservative figure is G.N. Kidd (Carleton), elected as a Patron in 1894, but returned as a Tory in 1898, against a Liberal opponent. Also included is J. Tucker (Wellington West), who had been elected as a Patron in a by-election in January 1896. Tucker, 'formerly a Liberal,' was regarded by Whitney as a Conservative supporter by mid-1897. In 1898 he faced only a Liberal opponent.

72 LP, J. Dickson to Laurier, 9 March 1898. Gregory Papers, G. Smith to Gregory, 2 March 1898. Moncton *Daily Transcript*, 5 March 1898

73 Both J. Young (LP, Young to Laurier, 10 March 1898) and J. Charlton (Charlton Papers, Diaries, vol. 10, 1 March 1898) used the expression 'close call.' Willison Papers, J. Cameron to Willison, 5 April 1898. Mills Papers, Letterbook 1, Mills to R. Harcourt, 5 March 1898. Charlton Papers, Diaries, vol. 10, 5 March 1898

74 Moncton *Daily Transcript*, 2 March 1898. LP, D. Hughes to Laurier, 22 March 1898; F.A. Anglin to Laurier, 25 March 1898. Willison Papers, A.S. Hardy to Willison, 29 March 1898. Charlton Papers, Diaries, vol. 10, 1 March 1898. G.M. Grant, 'The Ontario General Election,' *Queen's Quarterly* v (April 1898) 331

75 LP, J.T. Garrow to Laurier, 5 April 1898. Mills Papers, Letterbook 1, Mills to R. Harcourt, 5 March 1898

76 Willison Papers, A.S. Hardy to Willison, 1 April 1898

77 Toronto *Globe*, 4 March 1898. Belcher Papers, Whitney to Belcher, 5 and 10 March 1898.

In 1894, Howland obtained 6073 votes and his opponent 3996; in 1898, Foy received 4464 votes and his opponent 4059.

CHAPTER THREE

1 Toronto *Globe*, 4 March 1898

2 Toronto *Globe*, 14 June and 13 July 1898. In a public letter Hardy gave 'as the substantive reason' for the session the desire to have all constituencies properly represented, something that would not be possible once election trials had taken their toll. Willison Papers, A.S. Hardy to Willison, 12 July 1898

3 Toronto *Globe*, 16 July, 4 and 5 August 1898. WP, W.D. McPherson to Whitney, 25 July 1898; Letterbook B, Whitney to C.A. Muma, 3 August 1898. Gregory Papers,

Willison to G. Smith, 18 and 21 July 1898; Letterbook 1, Gregory to G. Freeman, 15 July 1898

4 Toronto *Globe*, 13 and 15 August 1898. WP, Letterbook B, Whitney to W.G. Elliott, 15 August 1898; Whitney to T.S. Sproule, 11 August 1898

John Dryden (1840–1909), a farmer by occupation and a Baptist by religion, was first elected for Ontario South in the provincial election of 1879, and sat for that riding, with the exceptions noted in this chapter, until his defeat in 1905. He was appointed minister of agriculture on 30 September 1890, and held that position until his resignation on 7 February 1905.

John Morison Gibson (1842–1929), a lawyer of Presbyterian persuasion, sat for Hamilton West from 1879 until 1898, and for Wellington East from 1898 until his defeat in the election of 1905. He was successively provincial secretary, 1889–96; commissioner of crown lands, 1896–99; attorney-general, 1899–1904; and minister without portfolio, 1904–5. Subsequently, he was appointed lieutenant-governor of Ontario in 1908.

5 WP, Letterbook B, Whitney to J.W. Allison, 20 August 1898

6 WP, Letterbook B, Whitney to Dr Montague, 4 October 1898

7 WP, W.D. McPherson to Whitney, 11 May 1898; Letterbook B, Whitney to E. Bristol, 15 December 1898; Whitney to J.J. Foy, 16 November 1898 (internal evidence indicates that this letter should be dated 16 December 1898); Letterbook C, Whitney to Dr H.G. Lackner, 27 May 1899; Whitney to T.W. Crothers, 15 June 1899

8 WP, Letterbook B, Whitney to L.H. Clarke, 11 September 1898; Whitney to W.D. McPherson, 11 and 15 September 1898; Whitney to L.H. Clarke, 22 September 1898

9 WP, Letterbook B, Whitney to C. Calder, 18 September 1898; Whitney to J.B. Dow, 4 November 1898; Letterbook C, Whitney to C. Calder, 2 June 1899; Letterbook B, Whitney to W.D. McPherson, 21 December 1899; Whitney to J. Burns, 3 February 1900; WP, Dr T.E. Kaiser to Whitney, 27 May 1899; S. Griffin to Whitney, 17 August 1900. Gregory Papers, Letterbook 1, Gregory to Laurier, 8 June 1899

10 WP, Letterbook C, Whitney to T.W. Crothers, 9 June 1899. Gregory Papers, Letterbook 1, Gregory to D.E. Cameron, 29 June 1899

11 Gregory Papers, Gregory to W.H. Hoyle, 14 December 1899

12 WP, clipping from the Toronto *Globe*, 30 March 1899

13 WP, J.J. Foy to Whitney, 30 August 1899; Letterbook C, Whitney to A.G. Brown, 19 August 1899. Toronto *Mail and Empire*, 26 April 1898. Willison Papers, A.S. Hardy to Willison, 10 May 1898 and 20 October 1899. Mills Papers, Letterbook 5, Mills to R. Ferguson, 31 October 1899

Hardy did not live long after stepping down from the premiership; he died on 13 June 1901, in Toronto.

14 Gregory Papers, G. Smith to Gregory, 2 March 1898. Mills Papers, Letterbook 5, Mills to R. Ferguson, 31 October 1899. LP, G.W. Ross to Laurier, 18 February 1899

15 WP, Letterbook B, Whitney to Rev. Dr Coffey, 27 October 1899; Whitney to J.M. Gibson, 24 October 1899; Whitney to A.S. Hardy, 18 November 1899.

234 Notes to pages 58–9

Short notes on cabinet ministers Dryden and Gibson appear in note 4 of this chapter.

Elihu J. Davis, the owner of a tanning business who gained his political spurs at the township level, was elected by acclamation for the riding of York North in May 1888. Subsequently, he briefly served as minister without portfolio from 21 July to 28 August 1896, after which he became provincial secretary and registrar until this cabinet shuffle of October 1899. He was commissioner of crown lands until November 1904, when he left the cabinet.

James Thompson Garrow, a lawyer, first captured Huron West in the election of 1890. Appointed in this cabinet rebuilding, he remained a minister without portfolio until January 1902, when he departed for the bench.

Richard Harcourt, another lawyer, came to the legislature for the riding of Monck as a result of a by-election in December 1878. He was named provincial treasurer by Mowat in September 1890, and held that post until exchanging it for education. He retained that position until the resignation of the Ross ministry in February 1905.

William Harty of Kingston was elected to the legislature in a by-election in February 1892. Mowat made him commissioner of public works in May 1894. Subsequent to Ross's shuffle, he served as minister without portfolio until he retired from office in January 1902.

Francis Robert Latchford, a prominent Ottawa lawyer, was elected to the legislature for Renfrew South in a by-election on 14 November 1899, after his appointment as minister of public works. He was personally defeated in the election of 1905, and resigned his office with the rest of the Ross ministry.

James R. Stratton, publisher of the Peterborough *Examiner* and member for Peterborough West, was first elected at the general election of 1886. Appointed provincial secretary and registrar at this time, he resigned the post on 22 November 1904, in part because of the notoriety he gained during the Gamey affair.

16 WP, Letterbook B, Whitney to F.G. Macdiarmid, 28 October 1899; Whitney to G. Taylor, 14 December 1899. Ontario Department of Education Papers, G.W. Ross to W. Atkin, 15 November 1899. Gregory Papers, Letterbook 1, Gregory to G. Smith, 14 and 19 December 1899. Willison Papers, G.W. Ross to Willison, 22 December 1899; J. Young to Willison, 27 January 1900. Mills Papers, Letterbook 5, Mills to G.W. Ross, 23 December 1899

17 Toronto *Mail and Empire*, 1 May 1900. LP, G.W. Ross to Laurier, 22 May 1900. WP, clipping from the Toronto *Mail and Empire*, 10 February 1900. Gregory Papers, Letterbook 1, Gregory to G. Smith, 21 February 1900. Willison Papers, G.W. Ross to Willison, 3 May 1900. Clarke Papers, Clarke to R. Clarke, 20 February 1900

18 Toronto *Mail and Empire*, 13, 14, 20, and 24 September, and 9 November 1900. Toronto *World*, 9 November 1900

H.G. Thorburn, ed., *Party Politics in Canada* (Toronto 1963) 161. It should be noted, however, that each party obtained 50 per cent of the popular vote. See also: A.W. MacIntosh, 'The Career of Sir Charles Tupper in Canada, 1864–1900,' PH D thesis (University of Toronto 1960) II, 559–60 and 578

19 WP, C. Tupper to Whitney, 27 February 1899. Tupper Papers, Letterbook (vol. 21), Tupper to R.R. McLennan, 30 May 1898; Tupper to T.G. Blackstock, 4 March 1899; Tupper to S. Barker, 8 March 1899; Tupper to R. Birmingham, 8 March 1899; Tupper to Whitney, 14 March 1899; Tupper to W.E. Sanford, 8 April 1899; Tupper to S. Barker, 11 April 1899; Tupper to J.E. Seagram, 22 April 1899; Letterbook (vol. 22), Tupper to C.G. Blackstock, 5 July 1899; Tupper to S. Barker, 20 July 1899; Tupper to A.W. Wright, 25 July 1899; Tupper to T.W.H. Leavitt, 26 July 1899
   Barker volunteered for his chore before either funds had been raised or organizers appointed.
20 Tupper Papers, R. Birmingham to Tupper, 22 May 1900; Tupper to R. Birmingham, 25 May 1900. Toronto *Mail and Empire*, 26 May 1900.
   Birmingham shortly regretted his action, but the party, including Whitney, would have nothing to do with him. See: WP, R. Birmingham to Whitney, 2 August 1900; Letterbook B, Whitney to J.W. Walsh, 2 February 1901
21 For a sampling of the difficulties with these Roman Catholics, see: LP, Willison to Laurier, 25 April 1899; P. Ryan to Laurier, 1 May 1899; T. Mulvey to Laurier, 20 November 1899; Laurier to T. Mulvey, 3 January 1899 (internal evidence indicates this letter should be dated 3 January 1900) and 15 April 1900; T. Mulvey to Laurier, 17 April, 4 and 14 July 1900; A. Campbell to Laurier, 21 September 1900. Toronto *Mail and Empire*, 8 May 1900
   Willison Papers, Laurier to Willison, 9 July 1900; J. Crerar to Willison, 11 November 1900. LP, G.W. Ross to Laurier, 4 May 1900; Laurier to G.W. Ross, 7 May 1900; W.J. Boland to Laurier, 14 May 1900. Mills Papers, Letterbook 6, Mills to P. Ryan, 7 July 1900. WP, Letterbook B, Whitney to E. Bristol, 12 July 1900; Whitney to S. Griffin, 26 November 1900; Whitney to T.A. Wardell, 27 November 1900
22 Toronto *Mail and Empire*, 28 May 1901. WP, Letterbook B, Whitney to F.A.E. Evanturel, 19 November 1900; Letterbook C, Whitney to Sister Augustin, 23 March 1899. The information suggested in this last letter was confirmed by a letter from Sister Superior Ste Marie, 12 August 1965. Norah attended the school in 1898–9 and 1899–1900.
23 WP, Letterbook B, Whitney to D.B. McDonald, 27 June 1901; Whitney to T.G. Carscallen, 24 May 1901.
24 Toronto *Mail and Empire*, 14 June, 12 and 13 December 1900; 11 January, 2 and 4 March, 1 May and 1 June 1901
25 WP, copy of a speech made during the budget debate, 26 February 1901; Letterbook B, Whitney to A.J. Matheson, 12 January 1901; G.W. Ross to Whitney, 29 January 1901. Toronto *Mail and Empire*, 7 and 27 February 1901
26 Toronto *Mail and Empire*, 13, 14, and 27 March 1901. See this paper, 3 April 1901, for details of Ross's provision for the University of Toronto.
27 Toronto *Mail and Empire*, 27 March 1901
28 G.M. Grant Papers, G.W. Ross to W. Harty, 19 March 1901. Willison Papers, G.W. Ross to Willison, 30 March 1901

29 Toronto *Mail and Empire*, 13 March, 10, 12, 13, and 17 April 1901. WP, Letterbook B, Whitney to J.E. Wetherell, 24 April 1901

30 WP, Letterbook B, Whitney to Rev. G. Bonsfield, 4 and 5 July 1900; Whitney to J.W. Allison, 9 September 1900; Whitney to J. —— [faded], 30 October 1900. Judging from limited internal evidence, it would appear that they had been living with Whitney not from the time of their marriage, but from the time that Whitney found out they were married.

31 See chapter 2, 45. In 1897, Whitney had suggested the sum of two thousand dollars but, apparently, twenty-five hundred dollars had been the agreed-upon amount. Much of the information concerning Whitney's ongoing financial difficulties is contained in an undated memorandum, written in the third person but in Whitney's hand. Internal evidence would date it about 26 September 1899.
   WP, Letterbook C, Whitney to R. Grass, 26 September 1899; Letterbook B, Whitney to A.B. Ingram, 29 October 1899

32 WP, Letterbook B, Whitney to R. Grass, 20 January 1900; Whitney to M.B. Morrison, 21 August 1900; Whitney to T.A. Wardell, 24 August 1900; Whitney to M.B. Morrison, 24 August 1900; Whitney to T.A. Wardell, 29 August and 7 September 1900; Whitney to M.B. Morrison, 25 December 1900 (the problem could not be forgotten even on Christmas day!); Whitney to T.A. Wardell, 29 January 1901; Whitney to G.E. Foster, 3 August 1901

33 Interview with F.S. Broder, 28 June 1960

34 WP, Letterbook B, Whitney to C. Tupper, 14 October 1899; Tupper Papers, Letterbook (vol. 22), Tupper to Whitney, 23 October 1899; Tupper to S. Barker, 24 October 1899. WP, E. Bristol to Whitney, 18 October 1899

35 Hugh Graham of the Montreal *Star* was one who wanted Foy's federal candidature; see WP, Graham to Whitney, 27 September 1900. Representative replies to Whitney's circular letter can be seen in WP, A.J. Matheson to Whitney, 25 September 1900; H. Carscallen to Whitney, 25 September 1900
   Included in the group which continued to lean on Foy were Joseph Flavelle, W.R. Brock, and E. Bristol; see WP, J.J. Foy to Whitney, 9 October 1900; Letterbook B, Whitney to Bristol, 10 October 1900
   WP, J.J. Foy to Whitney, 1 October 1900; Letterbook B, Whitney to J.J. Foy, 30 September 1900; Whitney to C. Tupper, 1 October 1900; Whitney to H.J. Macdonald, 12 January 1901. Toronto *Mail and Empire*, 2 October 1900

36 WP, Letterbook C, Whitney to W.C. Gibbens, 5 April 1899; Whitney to Rev. Dr Courtice, 23 September 1899; Whitney to A. Wallis, 2 November 1899 (Whitney was disturbed by anti-French editorials in the *News* which, if unanswered, might wrongly be taken as representative of the Conservative view); S. Griffin to Whitney, 2 February and 4 May 1900

37 WP, Letterbook B, Whitney to A.W. Wright, 24 September 1901. Toronto *Mail and Empire*, 1 November 1901. [C.R. Mabee], *Progress or Whitneyism: Which?* (Toronto 1901). Willison Papers, A. Smith to —— [circular], 3 September 1901; A. Smith to Willison, 19 October 1901

38 Tupper Papers, Letterbook (vol. 21), Tupper to G.F. Marter, 17 March 1899. WP, S. Griffin to Whitney, 4 May 1900; R.L. Joynt to Whitney, 6 December 1900; T.A. Wardell to Whitney, 23 December 1900; W.A. Willoughby to Whitney, 27 March 1901; clipping from the Toronto *Telegram*, 28 February 1901; clipping from the Toronto *World*, 23 April 1901; Letterbook C, Whitney to C. Tupper, 15 March 1899; Letterbook B, Whitney to T.A. Wardell, 18 December 1900. Toronto *Globe*, 1 March 1901. Toronto *Mail and Empire*, 1 March 1901

39 WP, R.A. Pyne to Whitney, 19 January and 24 June 1901; Letterbook B, Whitney to W.A. Willoughby, 13 January 1901; Whitney to R.A. Pyne, 17 January 1901

40 WP, J.J. Foy to Whitney, 4 January 1900; A.H.U. Colquhoun to Whitney, 4 January 1900; T.A. Wardell to Whitney, 5 January 1900; Letterbook B, Whitney to J.J. Foy, 5 January 1900. Toronto *World*, 9 and 20 November 1900

41 WP, S. Griffin to Whitney, 30 November 1900; Letterbook B, Whitney to S. Griffin, 25 November 1900; Whitney to J.J. Foy, 25 and 27 November 1900. Toronto *Mail and Empire*, 24 November 1900

42 WP, Letterbook B, Whitney to R. Shaw Wood, 26 November 1900

43 Toronto *Mail and Empire*, 3 and 6 December 1900; Toronto *World*, 6 December 1900

44 WP, R.A. Pyne to Whitney, 19 January 1901; S. Griffin to Whitney, 19 January 1901; Letterbook B, Whitney to Major Beattie, 12 January 1901; Whitney to Captain Robson, 15 January 1901. Wallace Papers, T.W.H. Leavitt to Wallace, 15 January 1901. Toronto *Mail and Empire*, 15 January 1901

45 Toronto *Mail and Empire*, 23 January 1901

46 WP, S. Griffin to Whitney, 25 and 26 January 1901

47 WP, S. Griffin to Whitney, 29 January 1901; T.W.H. Leavitt to Whitney, 4 and 9 February 1901; Letterbook B, Whitney to T.W.H. Leavitt, 28 January 1901

48 Toronto *Mail and Empire*, 25 February and 20 March 1901

49 Toronto *Mail and Empire*, 21 March 1901. Toronto *Globe*, 21 March 1901. WP, Letterbook B, Whitney to J.J. Foy, 8 June 1901; Whitney to E.B. Osler, 11 June 1901

50 WP, Letterbook B, Whitney to G.H. Kidd, 15 July 1901; Whitney to J.J. Foy, 27 May 1901 (internal evidence indicates that the date should be 27 August 1901); Whitney to A.H.U. Colquhoun, 27 August 1901

51 WP, Letterbook C, Whitney to J. Reid, 14 April 1899; Letterbook B, Whitney to R. Grass, 26 December 1899; Whitney to Dr Ryan, 28 May 1900; Whitney to W.H. Montague, 9 June 1900; Whitney to L.H. Clarke, 16 August 1900; Whitney to W.W. Meacham, 15 December 1900; Whitney to R.A. Pyne, 24 July 1901. Gregory Papers, Letterbook II, Gregory to W.H. Hoyle, 7 January 1901

52 John Willison, *Reminiscences: Political and Personal* (Toronto 1919) 327–8

53 WP, memoranda on Lambton East, Lambton West, and Northumberland West. Internal evidence indicates that these documents were written by A.W. Wright in the month of July 1901. The Conservatives took Lambton West in the general election of 1902, while the Liberals retained the other two ridings.

54 Wallace Papers, E.B. Osler to —— [circular], 19 June 1901. E.B. Osler, MP for Toronto West, made the appeal for funds in his capacity as chairman of the executive

committee of the provincial organization. He sought money from Ontario MPS, MPPS, and constituency organizations. Within a month his call produced about five hundred dollars, much of it from Toronto men; consequently, a second letter was sent out. See: WP, R.A. Pyne to Whitney, 25 July 1901

55 WP, R.A. Pyne to Whitney, 19 September 1901; Letterbook B, Whitney to A.W. Wright, 30 July 1901; Whitney to A.J. Matheson, 5 August 1901; Whitney to A.F. Wood, 7 September 1901. Toronto *Mail and Empire*, 16 August and 4 September 1901. Although called the annual meeting, it was the third one held in less than eight months.

56 Toronto *Mail and Empire*, 12 November 1901

57 Toronto *Mail and Empire*, 20 September 1901. Toronto *World*, 20 September 1901. Toronto *Globe*, 20 September 1901. J.S. Hopkins, ed., *Morang's Annual Register of Canadian Affairs, 1901* (Toronto 1902) 445–6

58 WP, R.A. Pyne to Whitney, 20 October 1901; Letterbook B, Whitney to A.J. Matheson, 6 October 1901; Whitney to Dr Ryan, 24 September 1901

59 Ruth E. Spence, *Prohibition in Canada* (Toronto 1919) 193–216. *CAR* (1902) 369–75

60 *CAR* (1902) 378–9

61 Willison Papers, G.W. Ross to Willison, 14 February 1902

62 J. Spelt, *The Urban Development in South-Central Ontario* (Assen 1955) 138–71

63 Merrill Denison, *The People's Power* (Toronto 1960) 28–31. See also: W.R. Plewman, *Adam Beck and the Ontario Hydro* (Toronto 1947) 30–1

64 WP, Letterbook B, Whitney to A.F.H. Cross, 4 May 1901. Toronto *Mail and Empire*, 14 January 1902

65 *CAR* (1902) 46

A small set of papers – largely dealing with the political labours of Dr T.E. Kaiser – was in the possession of G. Challies, once a chairman of the Ontario-St Lawrence Development Commission. Copies of these papers have been filed with the Whitney Papers in the Public Archives of Ontario. In this set is a piece of legislative assembly notepaper on which the Miscampbell amendment was typed. There is also a note in pen indicating the authors of the amendment. See also T.W.H. Leavitt to T.E. Kaiser, 29 January 1902, in the same collection.

Andrew Miscampbell (1848–1905) was first elected for Simcoe East in 1890, and repeated his success in 1894 and 1898. Shortly after this last election he left the lumber business to become manager of the Northern Navigation Company; in mid-1900 he was appointed manager of steamships in the large Clergue enterprise at Sault Ste Marie. Consequently, he sought and won election for the riding of Sault Ste Marie in the 1902 election, only to be unseated and defeated at the ensuing by-election. After that, he was appointed organizer for the provincial Tory party by Whitney, and was a diligent worker in the successful 1905 campaign.

Henry Carscallen (1845–1906) had just left the Liberal party when he was elected as Tory member for Hamilton East in the contest of 1898. He was returned in 1902 and

1905. Prior to his plunge into provincial politics, he had served as a Hamilton alderman for twelve years and, on three occasions, had unsuccessfully contested the mayoralty. A lawyer by profession, he was actively involved in the establishment of the Hamilton blast furnace and was a solicitor for the Toronto, Hamilton and Buffalo Railway. An active outdoor sportsman, he was a vigorous champion of adequate fish and game protection laws.

66 Willison, *Reminiscences* 330
67 Toronto *Mail and Empire*, 21 February 1902
68 Toronto *Mail and Empire*, 5 April 1902
69 Toronto *Mail and Empire*, 6, 7, 9, and 26 May 1902
70 Toronto *Mail and Empire*, 15 and 29 April 1902. Willison Papers, J.M. Gibson to Willison, 26 May 1902
71 Toronto *Evening Telegram*, 15 May 1902. Toronto *Mail and Empire*, 29 April and 6, 7, and 27 May 1902
72 Toronto *Mail and Empire*, 19 and 20 May 1902
73 Toronto *Mail and Empire*, 8, 27, and 29 May 1902. Denison Papers, G.W. Ross to Denison, 24 May 1902
74 These figures and the others were derived from a combination of sources, none of which is completely accurate and all of which, therefore, have to be consulted together: Ontario, *Sessional Papers*, xxxv, part ix (1903), no. 46; Lewis, *Centennial Edition*; several appropriate editions of *The Canadian Parliamentary Guide*; and a variety of newspapers.

The Liberal seats do not include Lennox, which the Grits claimed after the election and which the newspapers conceded to them, but, which, finally, a judicial recount gave to the Conservatives. Consequently, a number of sources show the Liberals as winning fifty-one seats, but this was not so. On the other hand, Renfrew North is counted for the Liberals although the successful candidate died two days after the election, and a by-election gave the riding to the Tories.

Some might choose to arrive at the Liberal total votes in different fashion. No votes were counted for the Liberals in Dufferin and Simcoe West, where only Prohibitionists unsuccessfully contested the ridings with the Tories; nor were there Liberal votes to be tallied in Toronto North, where G.F. Marter failed to win the riding running as an Independent and where the Liberals did not name a candidate.

75 The Conservatives secured one seat, Grey Centre, by acclamation. The Haldimand votes cast for the losing Independent Conservative candidate are counted in the Conservative column. Nevertheless, no matter how one might choose to tally votes from certain grey areas, the fact remains that the Conservatives got a larger share of the popular vote than did the Liberals.
76 The size of the Independent figure is largely caused by the 3,556 votes cast for George Marter in Toronto North.
77 There were four more seats in this election than that of 1898. This occurred because seven new seats were created out of three old ones in northern Ontario.

A curiosity of the election was the candidacy of Miss Margaret Haile for the Socialists in Toronto North, where she obtained eight-one votes. The Socialists also contested the other three Toronto ridings, in addition to Elgin West, Hamilton East and West, London, and Middlesex East. The four Socialist-Labour candidates were in the Toronto ridings.
78 The Conservatives lost Norfolk North when the member was unseated and the Liberals won the by-election.
79 Sifton Papers, Willison to Sifton, 11 May 1902; G.W. Ross to Sifton, 2 June 1902
80 Toronto *Mail and Empire*, 3 and 11 June 1902
81 LP, R. Cartwright to Laurier, 31 July 1902; Laurier to R. Cartwright, 11 August 1902. WP, undated memorandum on coalition offers in Whitney's hand; S. Griffin to Whitney, 8 July 1902; R.A. Pyne to Whitney, 24 July 1902; J.J. Foy to Whitney, 22 August 1902; W.C. Mikel to Whitney, 13 September 1902. *CAR* (1902) 53
82 WP, E. Bristol to Whitney, 18 November 1902; E. Bristol to G.W. Ross, 18 November 1902. Belcher Papers, B. Nesbitt to Belcher, 20 December 1902; Whitney to Belcher, 22 December 1902. LP, G.W. Ross to Laurier, 9 January 1903; Laurier to G.W. Ross, 10 January 1903
83 *CAR* (1903) 126. WP, W.R. Smyth to Whitney, 5 February 1903
84 Hector Charlesworth, *More Candid Chronicles* (Toronto 1928) 138. For a fuller account of this episode see: Charles W. Humphries, 'The Gamey Affair,' *Ontario History* (June 1967) 101–9. See also: *Report of the Royal Commission 're' Gamey Charges* (Toronto 1903); and *CAR* (1903).
85 Sifton Papers, G.W. Ross to Sifton, 19 March 1903
86 LP, Willison to Laurier, 11 July 1903. Charlesworth, *More Candid Chronicles* 140–1. Interview with W.R. Plewman, 17 May 1961
87 Denison, *The People's Power* 32–7. *CAR* (1906) 224
88 Denison, *The People's Power* 37. Plewman, *Adam Beck* 37–9
89 Denison, *The People's Power* 41–2
90 Plewman, *Adam Beck* 40
91 199,749 votes favoured prohibition, while 104,539 were opposed. Under the terms of the referendum, 213,000 favourable votes were required; see *CAR* (1902) 386, and *CAR* (1903) 550 and 552. Charlesworth, *More Candid Chronicles* 192
92 LP, G.W. Ross to Laurier, 6 April 1903; Laurier to G.W. Ross, 7 April 1903. WP, undated memorandum in Whitney's hand.
93 Denison Papers, A.H.U. Colquhoun to Denison, 20 May 1902; G.W. Ross to Denison, 22 September 1903. LP, G.W. Ross to Laurier, 5 October 1903; Laurier to G.W. Ross, 6 October 1903; G.W. Ross to Laurier, 9 October 1903. WP, resolution of the Ontario Liberal-Conservative Association, 3 September 1903; Whitney to J. Chamberlain, 4 September 1903
94 LP, G.W. Ross to Laurier, 9 October and 13 November 1903. Challies collection in WP, Whitney to T.E. Kaiser, 12 and 16 November 1903. Willison Papers, W.D. LeSueur to Willison, 19 December 1903. Gregory Papers, Letterbook III, Gregory to T.C. Smith, 30 December 1903. *CAR* (1903) 152–3

95 *CAR* (1903) 125–6. LP, G.W. Ross to Laurier, 5 January 1904
96 LP, G.W. Ross to Laurier, 12 February 1904
97 *CAR* (1903), 512–15
98 *CAR* (1904) 268–74
99 *CAR* (1904) 263, 278–9, 296–302, and 569–72. WP, J.W. Hughes to Whitney, 21 March 1904. Attached to the letter is a clipping from *United Canada*, 12 March 1904. This paper was owned and edited by a Liberal and had a wide circulation among Catholics of Irish background, particularly in Renfrew. In the clipping, the editor saluted Whitney for avoiding the clutches of the 'freaks and fanatics who ruined leader Meredith' and 'destroyed his party.'
100 Brian D. Tennyson, ed., 'The Cruise of the *Minnie M.*,' *Ontario History* (June 1967) 125–8. *CAR* (1904) 279–85
101 LP, G.W. Ross to Laurier, 9 September and 15 November 1904. *CAR* (1904) 286–7
102 Charles W. Humphries, 'The Sources of Ontario "Progressive" Conservatism, 1900–1914,' *Canadian Historical Association Historical Papers* (1967) 125–6
103 LP, J.K. Kerr to Laurier, 15 November 1904; Laurier to J.K. Kerr, 17 November 1904; J.K. Kerr to Laurier, 20 November 1904; G.W. Ross to Laurier, 20 November 1904; Laurier to G.W. Ross, 22 November 1904; G.W. Ross to Laurier, 2 December 1904; C. Sifton to Laurier, 1 February 1905. *CAR* (1904) 287–92
104 *CAR* (1904) 293–6. WP, G. Smith to Whitney, 24 November 1904
105 Willison Papers, R.E. Sinclair to Willison, 24 November 1904; Willison to W.S. Frost, 14 December 1904; J.B. Pettit to Willison, 21 December 1904; H.I. Strong to Willison, 14 January 1905; W. Mills to Willison, 17 January 1905; A. Shortt to Willison, 19 January 1905 (Shortt did not define the 'evil element.' Lacking power, the Tories were scarcely in a position to be guilty of serious corruption. Presumably Shortt was pre-judging the party's performance in power and probably had men like Gamey and Nesbitt in mind.); S.F. Dixon to Willison, 20 January 1905. Gregory Papers, G. Smith to H. Bourassa, 16 and 19 January [1905]
    W.L. Grant Papers (always cited as W.L. Grant Papers to distinguish them from the G.M. Grant Papers which are cited as the Grant Papers), G.F. Macdonnell to Grant, 20 December 1904. James Cappon, 'The Responsibility of Political Parties,' *Queen's Quarterly* (1904–5) 307–13
106 *CAR* (1905) 202
107 *CAR* (1904) 306–9. *CAR* (1905) 202–4
108 This figure and the others were derived from a combination of sources, none of which is completely accurate and all of which, therefore, have to be consulted together: Ontario, *Sessional Papers*, XXXVII, part X (1905), no. 46; Lewis, *Centennial Edition*; several appropriate editions of *The Canadian Parliamentary Guide*; and a variety of newspapers.
    The Liberal seats include that of E.W. Rathbun of Hastings East, who was classified as either an Independent or an Independent-Liberal. But the Toronto *Globe* of 9 January 1905 judged him to be a Liberal supporter, regardless of the above descriptions.

Included in the total Liberal vote are the ballots cast for two defeated Independent-Liberals who ran in Grenville and Toronto West. Peter Oliver, in *G. Howard Ferguson: Ontario Tory* (Toronto and Buffalo 1977) 29, terms the Grenville candidate a Liberal. In Toronto West, John Hunter ran as an Independent-Liberal on a platform which included items that the Liberals had neglected, but the West Toronto Liberal Association decided not to enter a candidate; see the Toronto *Globe*, 9 and 10 January 1905.

109 The 'Other' vote total would be even smaller were it not for the inclusion of 1735 votes cast for a Prohibitionist candidate in Dufferin where the Liberals did not run, and 2092 votes cast for F.A.E. Evanturel who lost the riding of Prescott. Evanturel, who had held the seat, was a Liberal, but so was winner L.J. Labrosse, who garnered 2093 votes and who was also president of the Prescott County Liberal Association. The Conservatives did not field a candidate in this constituency.

The Socialist vote is not classified separately this time because the results for that group in 1905 were not as noteworthy as they had been in 1902.

110 Toronto *Mail and Empire*, 26 January 1905

111 BP, Whitney to Borden, 27 January 1905. W.L. Grant Papers, G.F. Macdonnell to Grant, 30 January 1905. Minto Papers, T.C. Patteson to Minto, 26 January 1905. The temperature is in Fahrenheit.

112 Wrong Papers, G.W. Ross to Wrong, 9 February 1905. LP, G.W. Ross to Laurier, 6 February 1905

113 Spelt, *The Urban Development* 138–71

CHAPTER FOUR

1 Toronto *Mail and Empire*, 27 January 1905

2 WP, scrapbook on his 1910 trip to England, clipping from the Toronto *News*, 4 February 1905

3 Interview with Fred S. Broder, 28 June 1960

4 Toronto *Globe*, 26 January 1905

5 Toronto *Globe*, 9 February 1905. WP, F.D. Monk to Whitney, 27 January 1905

6 W.L. Grant Papers, C.F. Hamilton to Grant, 10 February 1905. Toronto *Globe*, 9 February 1905, and 19 June 1931 (editorial on Pyne at the time of his death). Toronto *Daily Star*, 8 February 1905

7 Toronto *Mail and Empire*, 8 May 1902, speech delivered at Sault Ste Marie

8 Willison Papers, S.F. Dixon to Willison, 20 January 1905. WP, G.S. Ryerson to Whitney, 15 February 1905, and attached clipping from the *Hamilton Herald*, 13 February 1905. Toronto *Daily Star*, 10 February 1905

9 Scott Young and Astrid Young, *Silent Frank Cochrane* (Toronto 1973) 12–22. Indirect evidence suggesting an arrangement can also be found in the fact that, in addition to Lamarche and the Liberal candidate, an Independent Conservative also contested the 1905 election in Nipissing East. This may represent some Tory discon-

tent with the deal that had been worked out; see: WP, J.M. McIlvenna to Whitney, 13 January 1905.

Cochrane, unlike the rest of the cabinet, was born outside of Ontario, in Clarenceville, Quebec, on 18 November 1852.

10 WP, W.R. Smyth to Whitney, 29 May 1905; T.A. Craig to Whitney, 7 June 1905; Whitney to W.R. Smyth, 3 June 1905

11 Michael J. Piva, *The Condition of the Working Class in Toronto – 1900–1921* (Ottawa 1979) chapter 1

12 Ibid. chapters 2 and 3

13 Ibid. chapter 4

14 Ibid. chapter 5, and 119 in particular

15 *The Canada Year Book 1912* (Ottawa 1913) 14. Calculations are my own.

16 Piva, *The Condition of the Working Class in Toronto* chapter 6

17 *The Canada Year Book 1912* 9 and 10. Calculations are my own.

18 *Fifth Census of Canada, 1911*, I, 74

19 D.A. Lawr, 'The Development of Ontario Farming, 1870–1914: Patterns of Growth and Change,' *Ontario History* (December 1972) 240–2

20 Ibid. 251, quoting the *Farmers' Advocate*, 5 December 1907

21 *The Canada Year Book 1912* 24. Calculations are my own.

22 *Fourth Census of Canada, 1901*, I, 416–17; *Fifth Census of Canada, 1911*, II, 442. Calculations are my own.

23 Donald Avery, *'Dangerous Foreigners': European Immigrant Workers and Labour Radicalism in Canada, 1896–1932* (Toronto 1979) chapter 1

24 *Fourth Census of Canada, 1901*, I, 144; *Fifth Census of Canada, 1911*, II, 42–3

25 Wallace, *A History of the University of Toronto* 148–66

26 University of Western Ontario Archives (UWOA), WP, W.R. Meredith to Whitney, 5 June 1905. In addition to the principal collection of Whitney Papers in the Public Archives of Ontario, there are two minor sets of material. One is now in the University of Western Ontario Archives, and the other is in the possession of the author. The location of any Whitney Papers, other than those in the PAO, will be indicated each time they are cited.

Wallace, *A History of the University of Toronto* 164

27 *CAR* (1905) 293–4

28 In the author's possession (CWH), WP, S.H. Blake to Whitney, 18 May 1905.

W.T. White, then general manager of the National Trust Company – of which J.W. Flavelle was president – was another who lauded Whitney's policy; see: CWH, WP, W.T. White to Whitney, 24 August 1905.

WP, J.W. Flavelle to Whitney, 18 May 1905. Flavelle was in London, England, and Willison cabled the good news about the university to him.

29 *CAR* (1905) 289

30 *CAR* (1905) 265. See also: WP, Whitney to H.P. Dwight, 29 May 1905.

The premier also stepped on the toes of W.F. Cockshutt, Conservative MP for

Brantford, when he blocked a late revision of the charter of the Huntsville and Lake of Bays Railway in which the implement manufacturer had an interest. Whitney's action was based on information to the effect that the charter deliberately misstated the length of the railway and that the portion of the line already constructed was recklessly built. See: WP, W.F. Cockshutt to Whitney, 5 June 1905; Whitney to W.F. Cockshutt, 7 June 1905; Whitney to A.A. Mahaffy, 9 June 1905.

31 CAR (1905) 275. WP, Whitney to E.C. Whitney, 10 May 1905
32 WP, J.A. Macdonell to Whitney, 15 April 1905; Whitney to J.A. Macdonell, 17 April 1905
33 At least one Roman Catholic Conservative nodded in approval of Whitney's biting opinion; see: WP, J.A. Macdonell to Whitney, 20 April 1905
34 WP, Whitney to H.H. Ross, 27 March 1905; Whitney to J.N. Eastman, 30 March 1905; Whitney to W.R. Armstrong, 6 June 1905; W.R. Armstrong to Whitney, 7 June 1905; Whitney to A. Broder, 25 May 1905
35 WP, A.E. Donovan to Whitney, 15 February 1905; J. Leitch to Whitney, 23 June 1905; S.D. Chown to Whitney, 8 February 1905; Whitney to S.D. Chown, 10 February 1905; J.A. Austin to Whitney, 13 February 1905; Whitney to J.A. Austin, 16 February 1905
36 WP, Whitney to G. Pattinson, 16 June 1905; Whitney to P.W. Ellis, 16 June 1905
37 CAR (1905) 289
38 J.A. Macdonald, the managing editor of the Toronto Globe, told Whitney: 'You may have observed that we have had a series of editorials dealing with the University situation. I would like you to be quite convinced that my interest in the University is altogether free from any interest I may have in party politics, and that what I now say in The Globe I said during the term of office of the late Government, and even before I joined The Globe staff at all. I have known the University for a good many years, and for at least a dozen years have been on fairly intimate relations with members of all circles and cliques within the University. In the discussion now going on in The Globe, as well as in the articles of a year ago, for all of which I am myself responsible, the one object is the betterment of the University. Professors and others belonging to conflicting departments come to me with their views. I hear them all, but keep myself absolutely from alliance with any one of them. I think your Government going in at the present time, with no hampering claims, and practically a free hand, have a fine opportunity, and I trust a way may be open for an effective handling of the situation. … The University is a most important charge and I should be glad to render any assistance possible to me through The Globe to any well-conceived plan looking to making the University the great and progressive institution it ought to be.' See: WP, J.A. Macdonald to Whitney, 15 March 1905. An amused Whitney replied: 'I thank you for your kind words, which if rather surprising were none the less agreeable to read.' See: WP, Whitney to J.A. Macdonald, 3 March 1905; the letter was incorrectly dated and should read 3 April 1905.
39 CWH, WP, Whitney to G. Smith, 7 September 1905; Whitney to W.R. Meredith, 25 September 1905

40 *Report of the Royal Commission on the University of Toronto* (Toronto 1906) iv
CWH, WP, J. Loudon to Whitney, 29 September 1905. Whitney replied: 'You will
have seen by the newspapers this morning the conclusion which has been arrived at by
the Government. I have great hope that good results will follow.' See: CWH, WP,
Whitney to Louden [sic], 30 September 1905. The news of the commission got into
the papers in advance of the official government announcement.

41 WP, I.H. Cameron to Whitney, 3 October 1905; Whitney to I.H. Cameron, 3 October
1905

42 WP, N. Burwash to Whitney, nd (internal evidence indicates 4 October 1905);
Whitney to N. Burwash, 6 October 1905

43 WP, N. Burwash to Whitney, 7 October 1905; Whitney to N. Burwash, 9 October
1905. Cody Papers, J.P. Sheraton to Cody, 30 November 1905. Michael Bliss, *A
Canadian Millionaire: The Life and Business Times of Sir Joseph Flavelle, Bart.,
1858–1939* (Toronto 1978) 164

44 CWH, WP, Whitney to W.R. Meredith, 25 September 1905

45 WP, Whitney to Mrs A.D. Brander, 10 July 1905; Whitney to Rev. T.E. Burke, 8
November 1905; Whitney to J.B. Mullan, 23 May 1905

46 *CAR* (1905), 278–9

47 WP, Whitney to W.J. Crothers, 7 March 1905

48 WP, Whitney to M. Bailey, 25 February 1905; Whitney to I. Hilliard, 4 March 1905;
Whitney to J.S. Gallagher, 6 March 1905; Whitney to T. Colquhoun, 14 March 1905

49 WP, Whitney to S.D. Chown, 27 March 1905; Whitney to W.J. Crothers, 7 March
1905

50 *CAR* (1905) 280–3. Bliss, *A Canadian Millionaire* 164–5

51 WP, J.W. Flavelle to Whitney, 28 November 1905 (In this letter, Flavelle offered to
resign from the university commission if Whitney thought that the 'freest' exchange
between them was now impossible.); Whitney to E.C. Whitney, 29 November 1905;
Whitney to E.W. Hagarty, 1 December 1905; Whitney to C. Magee, 4 December
1905. Bliss, *A Canadian Millionaire* 165

52 WP, Whitney to A. Whitney, 16 December 1905; Whitney to E.C. Whitney, 28
December 1905. W.L. Grant Papers, C.F. Hamilton to Grant, 30 November 1905

53 WP, Whitney to G.F. Ruttan, 17 April 1905

54 WP, Whitney to J. Alford, 8 May 1905; Whitney to J. York, 3 June 1905; Whitney to
G.N. Hickey, 2 June 1905; Whitney to C.E. Hickey, 15 June 1905

55 Hector Charlesworth, *I'm Telling You* (Toronto 1937) 32. Charlesworth does not
identify Nesbitt by name, but his description of the Toronto representative leaves no
doubt in my mind. Early in 1906 Nesbitt was out of Whitney's hair, for he resigned his
seat in the legislature; the Conservative who succeeded him in Toronto North was
W.K. McNaught.

56 WP, Whitney to S. Hughes, 20 March 1905; S. Hughes to Whitney, 14 July 1905; S.
Hughes to Whitney, 14 September 1905; Whitney to S. Hughes, 15 September 1905;
Canon J.C. Farthing to Whitney, 29 August 1905.
Hughes continued to be critical of Whitney and, in November, insisted that '15

counties' in Ontario might 'elect opposition members' because of party workers' disgust at the premier's handling of patronage; see: Willison Papers, C.F. Hamilton to Willison, 15 November 1905.

Certainly some people were rewarded for party services rendered. T.W.H. Leavitt, a recognized author as well as a former party organizer, was appointed Inspector of Public Libraries; he replaced a man who was over eighty years of age. Charles Lamarche, who resigned his Nipissing East seat to open a place for Frank Cochrane, was appointed Police Magistrate at Mattawa and Registrar of Deeds for the county; Lamarche replaced a former Liberal member of the legislature, John Loughrin, who had sat for the old riding of Nipissing from 1890 to 1902. Loughrin was dismissed for active partisanship. Scott and Astrid Young state in *Silent Frank Cochrane*, 32, that Loughrin was a defeated candidate in 1902; he was not – rather, he chose not to run. They also insist that he was dismissed because he ran in the 1905 provincial election; he did not.

57 H.V. Nelles, *The Politics of Development: Forests, Mines and Hydro-Electric Power in Ontario, 1849–1941* (Toronto 1974) 157–8. *CAR* (1905) 266

58 wp, F.H. Clergue to Whitney, 11 August 1905; L. Gouin to Whitney, 8 September 1905; Whitney to L. Gouin, 18 September 1905; Whitney to Laurier, 7 October 1905 (or see LP for same letter).

59 wp, W. Mulock to Whitney, 17 February 1905; Whitney to W. Mulock, 24 February 1905; Whitney to C.H. Campbell, 1 March 1905; Whitney to Laurier, 2 March 1905 (or see LP for same letter); R.L. Borden to Whitney, 27 April 1905

60 wp, R.L. Borden to Whitney, 6 December 1904; R.L. Borden to Whitney, 20 January 1905. Robert Craig Brown, *Robert Laird Borden: A Biography, I: 1854–1914* (Toronto 1975) 86–9

61 Willison Papers, C.F. Hamilton to Willison, 4 April and 7 November 1905. wp, J. Leitch to Whitney, 15 August 1905 (Leitch reported that Hugh Graham was 'immensely pleased' with Whitney's leadership). *CAR* (1905) 266–8

62 wp, Whitney to J.A. Macdonell, 28 October 1905. UWOA, wp, W.R. Meredith to Whitney, 13 November 1905

CHAPTER FIVE

1 wp, Whitney to A. Broder, 11 May 1906

2 wp, Whitney to H. Eilber, 27 November 1906. Ontario, *Sessional Papers*, XXXIX, part IV (1907), no. 12, 'Report of the Minister of Education, Province of Ontario for the Year 1906' ii and 175–6.

In 1905, of 5694 teachers in Ontario's rural schools, 954 held temporary certificates or certificates lower than third class; 2904 held third-class certificates; 1693 held second-class certificates; and only 143 teachers held first-class certificates.

Pyne was also concerned about the growing numbers of female teachers, particularly in rural schools, caused by the low salaries which drove away men and made women transitory occupants of teaching posts. 'For the fourth and fifth forms,' he said, 'male teachers are generally necessary. This proposition needs no defence.'

3 *Sessional Papers*, no. 12, 176–8. Toronto *World*, 11 April 1906. *CAR* (1906) 347

4 *Sessional Papers*, no. 12, iii and 177. WP, Whitney to I. Hilliard, 9 February 1906

5 Toronto *World*, 11 April 1906. *CAR* (1906) 347–8.

The two *ex officio* members of the advisory council were the president of the University of Toronto, who was automatically chairman, and the new superintendent of education. Three senate members were elected by the University of Toronto, and one each by Queen's, McMaster, and Ottawa. Four members would represent the public school teachers, two the high school teachers, and one the separate school teachers. Two public school inspectors were also elected by their peers.

6 Toronto *World*, 11 April 1906. *CAR* (1906) 355

7 Toronto *World*, 11 April 1906

8 *Sessional Papers*, no. 12, 178. WP, Whitney to H. Eilber, 27 November 1906; Whitney to Dr F.W. Lewis, 4 December 1906; Whitney to T.W. Crothers, 14 December 1906

9 *Report of the Royal Commission on the University of Toronto* x–xi. The report was virtually complete at the end of March 1906. On 4 April, all the commissioners dined at Goldwin Smith's handsome home and signed the report. See: Willison Papers, J.W. Flavelle to Willison, 31 March 1906.

10 *Report of the Royal Commission on the University of Toronto* xx

11 Ibid. liii–lvii

12 Toronto *World*, 3 May 1906

13 Toronto *World*, 3 May 1906. None of the cabinet attended the banquet.

On 12 April, once the report was public, O.D. Skelton testily asked Adam Shortt: 'How is the Tor. Univ^y Commission going to stretch Loudon to fit his new position?' See: Shortt Papers.

14 WP, G.M. Wrong to Whitney, 4 May 1906; Whitney to G.M. Wrong, 4 May 1906 (or see Wrong Papers for same letter); S.H. Blake to Whitney, 21 May 1906. CWH, WP, W.R. Meredith to Whitney, 2 May 1906; W.R. Meredith to Whitney, 8 May 1906

15 Willison Papers, Whitney to Willison, 12 June 1906.

Meredith, as chancellor of the institution, was an *ex officio* member of the board, as was the president. Other members of the royal commission named to the board were Goldwin Smith, who wanted to beg off because of age and deafness, and D. Bruce Macdonald. Among other appointees were Sam Blake, Sir Charles Moss, and E.C. Whitney (whose nomination attracted some criticism); see: WP, A. Whitney to Whitney, 21 June 1906; G. Smith to Whitney, 10 July 1906; Whitney to G. Smith, 10 July 1906.

WP, J. Loudon to Whitney, 14 July 1906; J. Loudon to J.J. Foy, 16 July 1906

16 WP, Whitney to G.H. Ferguson, 27 June 1906. CWH, WP, G.H. Ferguson to Whitney, 29 June 1906; Whitney to G.H. Ferguson, 3 July 1906. One of the reasons for Ferguson's support of Cody was undoubtedly his long acquaintance with the clergy-

man, which dated from their university days when they shared a room. Initially Ferguson had Stephen Leacock as his roommate, but when his parents saw the future humorist, they insisted tht he find a new companion; Ferguson then moved in with Cody. See: Peter Oliver, *G. Howard Ferguson* 12.

17 G.M. Wrong would have liked to see B.E. Walker offered the presidency. 'Now with ample funds,' Wrong told J.W. Flavelle, 'you can pay the right man his price and, if he can be secured, he is preeminently the right man.' See: Flavelle Papers, 4 May 1906.

The premier would have been delighted had Osler accepted: 'He would make short work of all the little squabbles and intrigues that have been going on and all the people would be prepared to believe that everything and anything he did was right.' See: WP, Whitney to E.C. Whitney, 20 December 1906.

WP, G. Smith to Whitney, 5 November 1906; Whitney to G. Smith, 6 November 1906. Smith also feared that delay would mean that Hutton would leave his mark upon both office and policy at this critical juncture, and thus create 'awkwardness' when the new man was found. He expressed this opinion to Edmund Walker, who was convenor of the board's presidential search committee. See: G.P. de T. Glazebrook, *Sir Edmund Walker* (Oxford 1933) 76.

When Falconer was being considered, his background as a Presbyterian clergyman was viewed by Whitney as 'a distinct handicap.' 'I talked with Borden over the telephone about it,' he told his brother Ned, 'and he speaks in very high terms of him indeed. Of course whoever is chosen will belong to some Church, and no doubt that may cause some little feeling, but I think he is a pretty good man.' See: WP, nd.

18 WP, Whitney to T.E. Burke, 28 March 1906

19 WP, Whitney to T.S. Edwards, 7 April 1906; Whitney to T.E. Burke, 12 February 1906; Whitney to R. Corrigan, 10 April 1906

20 WP, Whitney to S.B. Wilson, 27 March 1906

21 Toronto *World*, 21 March, 5 and 21 April 1906.

The licence fees were scaled as in the table.

Municipality	Tavern	Shop
Cities over 100,000	$1200.00	$1000.00
Cities over 30,000	$700.00	$700.00
Cities over 10,000	$500.00	$500.00
Towns less than 10,000 and over 5000	$450.00	$450.00
Towns less than 5000 and over 2000	$350.00	$350.00
Towns of 2000 and less	$250.00	$250.00
Villages	$250.00	$250.00
Townships	$120.00	$200.00

22 Toronto *World*, 21 March 1906

23 Toronto *World*, 29 March and 4 April 1906. Toronto *Globe*, 29 and 30 March 1906. *CAR* (1906) 331. WP, A.A. Doupe to Whitney, 3 April 1906.

24 Toronto *World*, 5 April 1906
25 Ibid. wp, Whitney to W.F. Thompson, 21 April 1906
26 wp, Whitney to C.B. Powell, 2 April 1906; Whitney to W.J. Hanna, 13 April 1906.
   Toronto *World*, 29 March, 5 and 21 April 1906
27 Toronto *World*, 30 April and 4 May 1906
28 Toronto *World*, 20 and 21 April 1906

CHAPTER SIX

1 For a delightful account of earlier, bribery-laden brawls between Torontonians and the
  railway company, see: Christopher Armstrong and H.V. Nelles, *The Revenge of the
  Methodist Bicycle Company: Sunday Streetcars and Municipal Reform in Toronto,
  1888–1897* (Toronto 1977). Toronto *Globe*, 3 May 1905
2 Toronto *Globe*, 4 and 5 May 1905
3 Toronto *Globe*, 10 and 11 May 1905
4 Toronto *Globe*, 9, 10, and 20 May 1905. *CAR* (1905) 265. The Conservatives held the
  three York ridings, both Ontario North and South, and Halton. Only Peel was Liberal;
  its member was John Smith, the supporter of a limited franchise for females in
  Ontario.
5 Toronto *Globe*, 11, 26, 27, and 29 April and 9 May 1905
6 Toronto *Globe*, 13 March 1906. wp, Whitney to W.R. Meredith, 31 October 1905
7 Toronto *World*, 13 and 24 March 1906. Toronto *Globe*, 13 March 1906
8 Toronto *World*, 18 March 1905; 13 and 24 March 1906. On the first date it was noted
  that Whitney had promised the Lord's Day Alliance delegation that he would view
  their request for no extension of Sunday running rights 'with a sympathetic eye.'
      The premier fully backed Hendrie in the matter of limited franchises. 'When it is
  considered,' he told the legislature, 'that municipal councils may be elected one year
  and turned out of office the next, we should go slow in giving them power to make
  agreements for all time to come. The government will not take the responsibility under
  any circumstances of giving the power to grant any perpetual franchises.' See: Toronto
  World, 7 April 1906
9 Toronto *World*, 13 and 24 March 1906
10 Toronto *World*, 13 March, 11 April, and 2 May 1906
11 Toronto *World*, 11 April 1906. *CAR* (1906) 345
12 *CAR* (1906) 345
13 Toronto *World*, 29 March and 11 April 1906. wp, Whitney to J.S. Hendrie, 2 May
   1906
14 Toronto *Globe*, 8 February 1917 (This issue contains James Leitch's obituary.)
      Brian C. Elkin, 'The Ontario Railway and Municipal Board 1906–1914: A Study of
   a Regulatory Agency Under The Whitney Administration,' major graduate research
   paper (York University 1977) 16–17. Elkin incorrectly states that Leitch had been an
   MPP. Leitch was chairman until 1912, when he was replaced by Donald McIntyre.
   wp, J. Leitch to Whitney, 26 March 1906; Whitney to J. Leitch, 1 June 1906

15 Elkin, 'The Ontario Railway and Municipal Board' 19–20. J.K. Johnson, ed., *The Canadian Directory of Parliament, 1867–1967* (Ottawa 1968), 286. Although elected to the House of Commons in 1891, Ingram had been unseated, and was returned in a by-election in 1892; he was re-elected in 1896, 1900, and 1904. He did not resign his Commons seat until December of 1906, some six months after his appointment to the board. He served as vice-chairman until 1932.

Ingram's appointment was not a certainty – though likely – as late as 2 June, the date of Leitch's appointment. The cabinet was allowed full voice in naming board members, other than Leitch. See: WP, Whitney to A. Broder, 2 June 1906

16 Elkin, 'The Ontario Railway and Municipal Board' 20–2. *CAR* (1906) 107

17 Bryan D. Palmer, *A Culture in Conflict: Skilled Workers and Industrial Capitalism in Hamilton, Ontario, 1860–1914* (Montreal 1979) 210–13. *CAR* (1906) 288–9. WP, Whitney to J. Leitch, 20 November 1906.

Oddly enough, Elkin says nothing about the Hamilton strike, choosing to focus on the much smaller London street railway labour dispute; equally oddly, Palmer makes no use of the Whitney Papers.

18 Palmer, *A Culture in Conflict* 214–15. *CAR* (1906) 289.

The suggestion that a police riot occurred is contained in a letter from a Tory supporter, E.A. Dalley, to Whitney (WP, 7 December 1906). Dalley had a small axe to grind in this letter, but there is no reason to doubt his description of police actions. Considering the case that he is attempting to make, it is strange that Palmer makes no use of this letter.

19 Palmer, *A Culture in Conflict* 216. *CAR* (1906) 289. Palmer fails to identify Gibson or note his long-time Liberal connection. See note 4 to chapter 3, above, for further information on J.M. Gibson.

20 WP, E.A. Dalley to Whitney, 7 December 1906; S.D. Biggar to Whitney, 8 December 1906

21 Carscallen, a one-time Liberal, had been responsible for John Gibson's defeat in 1898 in Hamilton East, and held the seat until his death. He was, however, not from the working class, being a lawyer involved in both the establishment of a blast furnace in the city and the building of the Toronto, Hamilton and Buffalo Railway.

In the by-election, Studholme received 2356 votes, and Tory John J. Scott 1503. In the general election of 1905, Carscallen had 2576; the Liberal 2433; and a Socialist (not Studholme) 375. The Liberals and the Tories ran candidates against Studholme in 1908, but he only faced Conservatives in 1911 and 1914. Studholme held the seat until his death on 28 July 1919.

WP, Whitney to J.J. Scott, 5 December 1906; E.A. Dalley to Whitney, 7 December 1906

22 Albert Tucker, *Steam into Wilderness: Ontario Northland Railway, 1902–1962* (Toronto 1978) 2–9

23 Other commissioners were F.E. Leonard, B.W. Folger, M.J. O'Brien, and Edward Gurney. For further information on these four, see Tucker, *Steam into Wilderness* 9–10.

24 Ibid. 12–17
25 Ibid. 29–32
26 Ibid. 33–8
27 Ibid. 39
28 Toronto *World*, 26 April 1906. *CAR* (1906) 343–4
29 *CAR* (1906) 334
30 Nelles, *The Politics of Development* 161. WP, A. Broder to Whitney, 4 April 1906; Whitney to E.C. Whitney, 6 April 1906; R.L. Borden to Whitney, 19 April 1906; Whitney to R.L. Borden, 20 April 1906
31 WP, S.D. Chown to Whitney, 4 April 1906; J. James to Whitney, 9 May 1906; G. Ritchie to Whitney, 4 April 1906; Whitney to D. Creighton, 5 April 1906; Whitney to H.H. Strathy, 9 June 1906. Nelles, *The Politics of Development* 160–1
    When the government operation of the mine ended, the northern portion of the limit was divided and auctioned off. Nelles bemoans this development because, he argues, the manner of the government's approach to and retreat from its ownership of a mining property was such as to discredit the concept of public ownership of mines in Ontario. He then presses on to speculate about what would have been the impact had the government developed the T&NO railway right-of-way mines. This did not happen for two good reasons: the time was the first decade of the twentieth century and the place was Ontario. To suggest that it might have happened – and to condemn Whitney for not making it happen – is to indulge in radical wistfulness.
32 *CAR* (1906) 335
33 Ibid. Toronto *World*, 24 April 1906
34 Toronto *World*, 15 March and 25 April 1906
35 WP, Whitney to F. Nicholls, 11 January and 14 March 1906; F. Nicholls to Whitney, 29 March 1906; affidavit of R.C. Board, 29 March 1906
36 WP, H.M. Pellatt to Whitney, 9 January and 9 February 1906; F. Nicholls to Whitney, 3 and 6 April 1906; Whitney to F. Nicholls, 7 April 1906; H.M. Pellatt to Whitney, 5 May 1906
37 WP, Whitney to H.M. Pellat, 5 May 1906; H. Wallis to H.M. Pellatt, 5 May 1906; H.M. Pellatt to Whitney, 7 May 1906; Whitney to H.M. Pellatt, 7 May 1906
38 A number of Ontario's premiers have been men from farms and small towns – not just born in such locations, but raised, educated, and employed at home – who, after a period of political apprenticeship, came to the premier's office and contact with the large men of industry and commerce. The reactions of these premiers to this kind of exposure varied widely. Whitney frequently found 'big men' to be foolishly abrasive and his response has been noted. Mitch Hepburn, on the other hand, softened and became very pliable in their hands.
    In his work, *The Politics of Development*, H.V. Nelles suggests that government was reduced in the twentieth century to the role of client of the business community. Aside from the obvious fact that, in virtually every piece of legislation, the government is someone's client – and never everyone's, because there is always opposition which is not just limited to the official opposition – it is hard to argue that the Whitney-

led government moved into this subservient role. Whitney was very much his own man and his government displayed a good deal of responsible independence.

39 WP, Whitney to E.C. Whitney, 7 February 1906; resolution of the Guelph city council, 21 March 1906; resolution of the Toronto board of trade, 22 March 1906; resolution of the representatives of southwestern Ontario municipalities at a meeting held in Galt, 23 March 1906; resolution of West Flamboro township council, 2 April 1906; resolution of Etobicoke township council, 6 April 1906; resolution of Guelph trades and labour council, 9 April 1906; resolution of Toronto district labour council, 9 April 1906. These are just a sampling of the petitions.

40 Plewman in *Adam Beck* (49) states that Meredith worded much of the legislation, and Denison repeats this point in *The People's Power* (52). But doubts about Meredith's authorship of the legislation are created by a remark of his to Whitney in a letter of 8 May 1906: 'I congratulate you on your power bill' (CWH, WP). Meredith could be humorous with Whitney, but not facetious, and this statement makes it appear less likely that he drafted the legislation presented on 7 May. It is likely, however, that he examined the measure prior to its introduction to ensure that it was framed in proper legal language and devoid of error. He had performed this service before for the Conservative administration.

Denison, *The People's Power* 53

41 Denison, *The People's Power* 56–7. On the same occasion, Lieutenant-Governor M. Clark expressed the hope that the investors would be 'permitted to enjoy the legitimate fruits of their enterprise.' His remarks produced angry criticism from public power exponents. But Whitney, who had declined to attend the ceremony, defended the lieutenant-governor and noted that 'every word he uttered there would have been spoken by me, had I been there' (WP, Whitney to E.W.B. Morrison, 11 May 1906). Whitney was convinced that if the Electrical Development Company would just co-operate with the government its prospects would be bright. The company made its own trouble through the intransigence of management and, presumably, would continue to do so until Nicholls and Pellatt had learned the merits of co-operation.

42 CWH, WP, W.R. Meredith to Whitney, 9 May 1906. *CAR* (1906) 180–1. LP, Whitney to H.E. Gordon, 23 May 1906; Whitney to Laurier, 26 May 1906: 'you will see,' Whitney wrote to Laurier, 'that there has been no justification for the alarm manifested in some quarters with reference to the consequences of this legislation. We have no doubt that we will be able to meet the views of the public on this question without any recourse to the necessary powers contained in the Act.' WP, Whitney to Earl Grey, 26 May 1906: 'More or less criticism has been heard of this legislation,' the premier wrote to the governor-general, 'but I am bound to say that it comes from persons either ignorant of the facts or actuated by selfish motives. We are satisfied from data now in our possession that there will be neither expropriation nor development by the Government, but that the Government will be able to arrange so that the demands and wants of the consumers will be satisfied by the Companies at reasonable prices.'

43 WP, J.S. Hendrie to Whitney, 14 May 1906; Whitney to J.S. Hendrie, 15 May 1906

44 WP, Whitney to F. Nicholls, [June 1906]; H. Wallis to Whitney, 23 July 1906. A careful reading between the lines of correspondence between Whitney and brother Ned would indicate that the latter paid for the trip, including the cost to Pyne.

45 WP, Whitney to G.W. Grote, 16 May 1906; Whitney to R.L. Borden, 17 May 1906; S.H. Blake to Whitney, 21 May 1906. *CAR* (1906), 329. W.L. Grant Papers, C.F. Hamilton to Grant, 23 June 1906.

The government, during the 1906 session, also moved to more properly regulate joint-stock companies selling shares in the province, and increased the salaries of civil servants.

46 WP, Whitney to R.L. Borden, 20 April 1906

47 *CAR* (1906) 517. Willison Papers, C.F. Hamilton to Willison, 14 October 1906

48 Willison Papers, C.F. Hamilton to Willison, 11 and 19 November 1906

49 LP, G.W. Ross to Laurier, 23 and 29 October 1906

50 WP, Whitney to H. Clark, 11 September 1906

CHAPTER SEVEN

1 LP, G.W. Ross to Laurier, 3 December 1906. Denison Papers, G.W. Ross to G.T. Denison, 15 January 1907. For a sample of those who had doubts about the wisdom of elevating Ross to the Senate, see: LP, A. Irving to A.B. Aylesworth, 23 January 1907; J. Cumming to Laurier, 30 January 1907. Irving wrote: 'I am oppressed at being told that it is seriously intended to recognize Ross – by taking him into your Government or into the Senate or both ... He is in direct antagonism to true Reform principles – and he should not be touched if your Government wishes to keep the old line of Reformer, as adherents.' Cumming commented: 'A little bird whispers that you are going to appoint the Hon. Mr. Ross to the vacant Senatorship. This is all right. ... but ... don't dream of having him your leader for Ontario and do not under any condition give him a Department. He is the man on the stump and can spin theories but as an Executive Minister to my personal knowledge he is a total failure. He is not entitled to more than the senatorship.'

2 *CAR* (1907) 512. LP, G.P. Graham to Laurier, [mid-December 1906]; Laurier to G.P. Graham, 19 December 1906; W.S. Buell to Laurier, 10 January 1907; G.P. Graham to Laurier, 11 January 1907; G.P. Graham to Laurier [mid-February 1907]; C.M. Bowman to Laurier, 11 February 1907.

Newton W. Rowell was also mentioned as a possible Liberal leader, but this suggestion did not secure a great deal of support.

3 WP, Whitney to E.C. Whitney, 17 January 1907

4 *CAR* (1907) 530 and 532. The grant to rural schools in 1907 was $380,000. In 1904, the grant from the Ross administration had amounted to $118,000.

5 WP, Whitney to J. MacKay, 28 September 1907

6 WP, Whitney to T.W. Crothers, 27 June 1906; Whitney to J.S. Duff, 17 January 1907. *CAR* (1907) 534–5. Crothers astonished everyone by returning a cheque for two

thousand dollars in payment for services rendered; he said he simply wanted $192.00 to cover expenses incurred during the investigation.

7 Nelles, *The Politics of Development* 176. *CAR* (1907) 507–9. WP, Whitney to T.S. Sproule, 1 March 1907. The tax on natural gas was two cents per one thousand cubic feet, with a 90 per cent rebate to businesses using the product of their own wells.

8 *CAR* (1907) 509–10

9 *CAR* (1907) 494–5

10 *CAR* (1907) 495. LP, G.P. Graham to Laurier, 18 November 1907. By the time of this letter, Graham was Laurier's minister of railways and canals. Because there had been no division on the provincial bill, which was passed while Graham was opposition leader, the minister now feared awkward trouble with Whitney over the measure.

11 *CAR* (1907) 496

12 WP, Whitney to E.C. Whitney, 26 March 1907; W.R. Meredith to Whitney, 16 April 1907; Whitney to R.L. Borden, 16 and 19 April 1907; Whitney to F. Cook, 26 April 1907. *CAR* (1907) 497

The land was taken by the federal government under Section 117 of the BNA Act, and Whitney thought there was 'room for strong argument on the other side.' The provincial government was perfectly willing to lease the land, but it wanted compensation for monetary loss in terms of timber licences and dues. F.W. Borden had denied that Ontario was entitled to such compensation.

13 Sifton Papers, Sifton to G.P. Graham, 1 February 1907. Senator Jaffray, president of the *Globe*, denied that he had any money in the Electrical Development Company, but he had invested in the Toronto Electric Light Company, which would, in the private power interests' scheme of things, distribute Electrical Development Company power, and which was inextricably linked with the Nicholls-Pellatt group. J.W. Flavelle, owner of the *News*, was associated with the National Trust Company, which served as trustee for the bondholders of the Electrical Development Company.

WP, extract of a letter from A.M. Grenfell to Earl Grey, 29 March 1907, contained in M. Clark to Whitney, 2 April 1907

14 WP, H.H. Macrae to Whitney, 26 April 1907; Whitney to A. Beck, 26 April 1907; Whitney to S.H. Blake, 29 April 1907; S.H. Blake to Whitney, 30 April 1907. Willison Papers, F. Cochrane to Willison, 3 December 1907. Nelles, *The Politics of Development* 274

15 WP, Whitney to F.W. Taylor, 5 July 1907; F.W. Taylor to Whitney, 1 August 1907; Chaplin, Milne, Grenfell and Co. Ltd. to Whitney, 10 August 1907; Whitney to Chaplin, Milne, Grenfell and Co. Ltd., 13 August 1907

16 WP, Whitney to H.H. Ross, 13 September 1907; Whitney to E.C. Whitney, 9 October 1907. *CAR* (1907) 518. The Electrical Development Company argued that it was being cut out of the lucrative western Ontario market; but, surely, the requirement that its charge be the same as that of Ontario Power was a factor in its decision.

17 Plewman, *Adam Beck* 51. Nelles, *The Politics of Development* 275–81

18 WP, Whitney to C.B. Smith, 2 December 1907; Whitney to E.C. Whitney, 4 Decem-

ber 1907; Whitney to E.C. Whitney, 3 January 1908. Willison Papers, F. Cochrane to
Willison, 3 December 1907. On 5 December 1907, Whitney wrote to Ned: 'I find my
suspicion was right, viz., that what Willison has been saying in the 'News' against the
Power Policy has been really the views of Flavelle and against Willison's inclination.'
Whitney's suspicion may have been correct because, earlier in the year, Willison had
taken a different approach privately. 'Yes,' he wrote to C.F. Hamilton, 'the relations
between B.E. Walker [now president of the Bank of Commerce] and myself are very
greatly strained. He has been the chief apologist for the Electrical Development
Company, the Toronto Electric Light Company and the Canadian Northern Railway
and has been exceedingly troublesome. He has absolutely no public spirit except in the
field of banking and in his own particular pursuits while his arrogance on questions
which he does not understand is intolerable. ... so many corporations centre in the
Bank of Commerce and he is so utterly their slave that he is dangerous. I insisted with
Mr. Flavelle that the account [of the *News*] must be removed and therefore we have
gone to the Dominion Bank. ... I have fought a good many battles in my life and do
not propose to be beaten by Walker and his interests.' See: Willison Papers, Willison
to C.F. Hamilton, 3 May 1907. *CAR* (1907) 523–4
19 Nelles, *The Politics of Development* 281–7. Nelles places considerable emphasis on
these last two efforts by Whitney, as evidence that the premier was still seriously
striving for some sort of accommodation with the Electrical Development Company. I
do not read the situation in quite that way. Whitney was prepared to explore only those
possibilities which fell within his own guidelines. He surely knew that Blake would
not be very helpful, and the premier was determined not to expropriate. These two
efforts represented going another mile, but that mile led nowhere.
   WP, G.S. St Aubyn to Whitney, 30 January 1908; Whitney to G.S. St Aubyn, 6
February 1908. St Aubyn represented some of the English investors in the Electrical
Development Company. Whitney first met him during his 1907 trip to England. St
Aubyn was associated with A.M. Grenfell of the English investment firm of Chaplin,
Milne, Grenfell and Company. Grenfell was the son-in-law of Earl Grey, the
governor-general, and St Aubyn was Grenfell's brother-in-law. This meant that, when
in Ottawa, St Aubyn stayed at Rideau Hall, and this fact helps to explain some of
Grey's hostility to Ontario's electric power policy; see: WP, Whitney to E.C. Whitney,
29 January 1908.
   In the end, entrepreneur William Mackenzie rescued the Electrical Development
Company by means of a corporate shuffle which Nelles explains on 285–6.
20 *CAR* (1907) 525–8. WP, Whitney to T.E. Burke, 17 January 1907; Whitney to J.G.
Bowles, 21 February 1907; Whitney to Mrs S.G.E. McKee, 6 March 1907; Whitney
to W.H. Raney, 11 March 1907; Whitney to W.A. Hanna, 14 March 1907
21 *CAR* (1907) 526. WP, Whitney to W. Wainwright, 22 February 1907
22 LP, G.P. Graham to Laurier, 26 July 1907. Graham insisted that he had accepted the
provincial leadership for only one session; that there would be little confusion caused
by his departure; and that he was the best choice from Ontario for a federal cabinet

post. Some Liberals may well have hoped that he would remain longer as leader of the provincial forces because W.L.M. King has noted an arrangement made for Graham which seems to indicate some expectation that he would stay: 'I am told he rec'd an income from party friends of $3 to 4,000, while leader of [the] opposition in addition to his indemnity.' See KP, diary, 4 September 1907. King goes on: '*The World* of today suggests me as his successor, as leader of the Ont. Opposition ... I have no doubt if I wanted it, I would have little difficulty in securing financial aid toward going into Ont. politics with the hope of ultimate leadership from the start, tho' to be the chosen leader at the outset is absurd & out of the question. Even if offered it would have no attractions or temptations as against my present work for the Dominion & present prospects there.'

WP, Whitney to H.H. Ross, 13 September 1907. The riding not only went to the Tories, but it remained in their possession as long as Whitney was premier.

23 WP, Whitney to A.T. Wilgress, 8 October 1907. Graham Papers, D.C. Ross to Graham, 8 October 1907; M.J. Haney to Graham, 6 December 1907. LP, A. Smith to A.B. Aylesworth, 8 October 1907

24 *CAR* (1908) 297

25 *CAR* (1908) 293. WP, Whitney to E.C. Drury, 1 April 1908

26 *CAR* (1908) 278 and 283. The provincial Liberals did not know quite what to do in this matter and frantically MacKay sent a telegram to Laurier about the federal government's position. See: LP, A.G. MacKay to Laurier, 30 March 1908 (two telegrams); Laurier to A.G. MacKay, 30 and 31 March 1908; C.M. Bowman to Laurier, 31 March 1908. Graham Papers, C.M. Bowman to Graham, 30 March 1908

27 WP, A.E. Little to Whitney, 17 March 1908; J. Mitchell to Whitney, 26 March 1908; F.J. Ramsey to Whitney, 27 March 1908. These letters represent complaints from Tories that the new boundary lines did not aid their cause. On the other hand, the Conservatives of Essex South wanted to be rid of Tilbury and their wishes were met when this village was pushed into Kent West. The Conservative then captured Essex South in the 1908 election for the first time since 1879. Whether or not the shift of Tilbury was responsible for this outcome cannot be settled here, but it probably was a factor in the result. See: WP, W.A. Smith to Whitney, 30 March 1908; Whitney to W.A. Smith, 31 March 1908

28 WP, Whitney to E.A. Dunlop, 13 April 1908

29 *CAR* (1908) 336. W.L. Grant Papers, C.F. Hamilton to Grant, 31 May 1908

30 WP, R.L. Borden to Whitney, 23 January and 19 April 1906; Whitney to R.L. Borden, 20 April 1906; R.L. Borden to Whitney, 2 June 1906; Whitney to R.L. Borden, 4 June 1906; R.L. Borden to Whitney, 11 July 1906; Whitney to R.L. Borden 13 July and 21 September 1906; R.L. Borden to Whitney, 22 and 26 September 1906; Whitney to R.L. Borden, 28 September 1906; R.L. Borden to Whitney, 11 January 1907; Whitney to R.L. Borden, 12 January 1907; R.L. Borden to Whitney, 4 May 1907; Whitney to R.L. Borden, 5 May 1907; Whitney to C.G. O'Brian, 8 May 1908

Whitney left organizational matters to a cabinet committee composed of Foy, Pyne,

Cochrane, and Hanna. Thus, not much that related to party organization crossed his desk once he became premier. The federal Ontario Conservatives later appointed an organizer for their own purposes; he was J.S. Carstairs.

In Prescott riding, the 'result was not brought about without a certain amount of friction between the French and English sections of the Convention, but the English candidate ... finally retired in favor of [George H.] Pharand.' See: WP, C.G. O'Brian to Whitney, 12 May 1908. Pharand then took the constituency in the general election by a mere four votes; it was the first time Prescott had gone Conservative since 1879.

31 Graham Papers, F.G. Inwood to Graham, 7 April 1908. Inwood was appealing to Graham for money for the Ontario Liberal leadership fund, which, at the time the letter was written, was 'a little overdrawn'; the trouble was keeping it 'up to scratch.' Graham promptly gave one hundred dollars. See also: Graham Papers, Private Letterbook B, Graham to W.S. Buell, 13 April 1908; Graham to J. Loughrin, 22 April 1908; Graham to T. McDonald, 19 May 1908; Private Letterbook C, Graham to W.A. Gilmour, 27 May 1908. LP, Laurier to L.M. Jones, 3 April 1908.

The Liberals had trouble in Dundas County trying to find someone to run against Whitney. One Grit was prepared to let the riding go by default to the premier, but George Graham thought they should 'skirmish up some one.' One longtime Whitney opponent in Morrisburg, Tom McDonald, was angered by talk of an acclamation for the Conservative leader. 'No doubt,' he wrote to Graham, 'it was Whitneys [sic] liberality in taking a French and an Irish Catholic into his Cabinet that has set the tide flowing in his direction but they forget that he has also taken in three orangemen in his Cabinet, all of whom attend the orange demonstrations and meetings and join hands in the denunciation of pope and popery. I am sorry to see things drifting in this way as if permitted to continue the Liberal cause will be dead for years to come, but what is equally annoying is to hear some of our best Liberals advocate allowing Whitney to be elected by acclamation in Dundas. I rec'd a letter from the Gen'l Secretary who says that many of our Liberals from Dundas were at Toronto and they all declared nobody could be got to oppose Whitney. Efforts I am told have been made to induce the calling of a Convention but up to the present have been unsuccessful.' McDonald said he would take on the 'angel of righteousness' if only finances permitted and 'would fight him to the death.' In the end, McDonald did run as the Liberal candidate in Dundas. See: Graham Papers, Private Letterbook B, Graham to W.L. Redmond, 4 April 1908; T. McDonald to Graham, 16 April and 5 May 1908.

In the larger arena of the province, MacKay complained that 'the strong men naturally want to go to the Dominion.' See: Graham Papers, A.G. MacKay to Graham, 6 January 1908

32 WP, Whitney to E.C. Whitney, 9 June 1908; S.H. Blake to Whitney, 9 June 1908. Gregory Papers, Letterbook IV, Gregory to W.S. Brewster, 9 June 1908

33 This figure and the others were derived from a combination of sources: Ontario, *Sessional Papers*, XLI, part X (1909), no. 46; Lewis, *Centennial Edition*; and several editions of *The Canadian Parliamentary Guide*.

Conservatives were acclaimed in six constituencies: Addington, Durham East, Lanark South, Muskoka, Simcoe South, and Victoria East; this, naturally, lowered the total votes cast. In Grenville, as in some other ridings, the Conservative candidate (in this case, Howard Ferguson) did not face a Liberal opponent but, rather, an Independent-Conservative; the votes cast for the latter have been counted under the 'Other' heading.

34 The heading 'Labour-Socialist' should not be taken to mean that there was a cohesive party on the left; there was not. This heading simply covers an assortment of left-wing candidates, of whom the only successful one was Allan Studholme, the victor in Hamilton East with 2717 votes.

35 LP, A.G. MacKay to Laurier, 17 June 1908. Graham Papers, D.T. Wright to Graham, 11 June 1908; Private Letterbook C, Graham to J. Cumming, 12 June 1908. Willison Papers, W.T.R. Preston to Willison, 9 August 1908

36 *CAR* (1908) 256. Carl Berger, *The Sense of Power* (Toronto 1970)

37 WP, Whitney to F. Cook, 13 July 1906; Whitney to Captain Kincaid-Smith, 5 June and 23 May 1907; Whitney to Willison, 30 December 1908 (or see Willison Papers for same letter).

38 WP, H.A. Gwynne to Whitney, 9 September 1909. Bodleian Library, Oxford University, Milner Papers, Diary, 10 September 1908. Willison Papers, Whitney to Willison, 14 September 1908. Rudyard Kipling had somewhat different advice for Milner. 'As to Canada ...,' he wrote, 'You will have to face the impact of young, callous, curious and godlessly egotistic crowds who will take everything out of you and put little back. Their redeeming point is a certain crude material faith in the Empire of which they naturally conceive themselves to be the belly-button. ... Canada is a constipating land.' See: Milner Papers, R. Kipling to Milner, [July 1908].

39 *CAR* (1908), 211. WP, Whitney to H.A. Gwynne, 2 December 1908. George Graham was 'particularly pleased with the result in Ontario where the entire force of the Whitney Government was up against' the Liberals. See: Graham Papers, Private Letterbook D, Graham to W.P. Millar, 29 October 1908; Private Letterbook E, Graham to T.A. Burrows, 1 December 1908

40 WP, Whitney to J.J. Foy, 8 October 1908

41 Denison, *The People's Power* 72–4. *CAR* (1909) 372–3. LP, N.W. Harris and Co. to Laurier, 3 June 1909; B.E. Walker to Laurier, 4 June 1909; J.L. Blaikie to Laurier, 11 June 1909; Laurier to J.L. Blaikie, 14 June 1909; E.R. Wood to Laurier, 17 June 1909; Burnett and Co. to Laurier, 8 July 1909; Laurier to A.B. Aylesworth, 3 September 1909; A.B. Aylesworth to Laurier, 15 September 1909; Earl Grey to Laurier, 10 April 1910

42 WP, Whitney to A.J. Dawson, 7 July 1909; Whitney to E. Farrer, 3 August 1909; Whitney to F.W. Taylor, 9 August 1909; Whitney to A.J. Dawson, 14 August 1909; Whitney to P.H. Bowyer, 16 October 1909

43 WP, Whitney to E.C. Whitney, 19 March 1909. *CAR* (1909) 369. Willison Papers, unsigned memorandum in Whitney's handwriting, dated by Willison as 12 April 1909

44 WP, Whitney to P.H. Bowyer, 23 April 1909; Whitney to E.C. Whitney, 27 April 1909; W.F. Nickle to Whitney, 3 May 1909; W.J. McGuire to Whitney, 5 June [1909]; Whitney to W.J. McGuire, 7 June 1909; D. McGregor to Whitney, 15 June 1909; Whitney to D. McGregor, 18 June 1909. *CAR* (1909) 388–9

45 WP, Whitney to Susan C. Millar, 10 March 1905; Whitney to E.C. Whitney, 21 June 1909. Joanne Emily Thompson, 'The Influence of Dr. Emily Howard Stowe on the Woman Suffrage Movement in Canada,' *Ontario History* (December 1962) 265–6

46 *CAR* (1908) 280. WP, Whitney to A.W. Loucks, 30 July 1909; Graham to Whitney, 22 April 1909; Whitney to Graham, 23 April 1909

47 WP, Whitney to Judge R.B. Carman, 6 August 1908; Whitney to A. Mills, 13 March 1908; Whitney to W.J. Hanna, 17 June 1909. Ponton Papers, W. Nesbitt to Ponton, 20 March 1909

CHAPTER EIGHT

1 WP, Whitney to H.A. Gwynne, 6 January 1909; Whitney to N.E. Nichols, 29 April 1909; Whitney to Willison, 10 June 1909 (or see Willison Papers for same letter); Whitney to J. Thomas, 3 August 1909; Whitney to A.J. Dawson, 18 April 1910; Whitney to Captain Kincaid-Smith, 19 April 1910. Willison Papers, Whitney to Willison, 12 January 1910. *CAR* (1909) 50

2 *CAR* (1909) 47, 55, and 60. WP, Whitney to G.E. Foster, 24 April 1909

3 *CAR* (1909) 89–90. *CAR* (1910) 238. WP, Whitney to P.D. Ross, 12 November 1909

4 WP, Whitney to R.L. Borden, 24 and 30 November 1909 (or see Borden papers for same letters). Brown, *Robert Laird Borden* I, 154–63

5 *CAR* (1910) 431–2

6 Plewman, *Adam Beck* 65–7. Denison, *The People's Power* 87–9

7 Walker, *Catholic Education and Politics in Ontario* 192–222. Bishop R.A. O'Connor of Peterborough had explained the Conservative administration's position on this diffcult problem to Archbishop C.H. Gauthier of Kingston on 30 November 1906: 'The government will be willing to go as far as possible quietly, so as not to stir up bigotry and excitement throughout the country.' See Walker 210.

8 The background material was drawn from two sources: Marilyn J. Barber, 'The Ontario Bilingual Schools Issue, 1910–1916,' MA thesis (Queen's University 1964) 1–16; and Walker, *Catholic Education and Politics in Ontario* 126–91. For later developments in this question, see also: Margaret Prang, 'Clerics, Politicians and the Bilingual Schools Issue in Ontario, 1910–1917,' *Canadian Historical Review* (December 1960) 281–307.

   Ontario Department of Education Papers, A. Macdonell, Bishop of Alexandria, to R. Harcourt, 8 October 1903; R. Harcourt to F.R. Latchford, 13 October 1903. Latchford penned his statement at the bottom of this letter and returned it to Harcourt. Bishop Macdonell was successful in having some of the schools moved from the inspectorate of T. Rochon to that of Michael O'Brien. Latchford sat for the riding of

Renfrew South and, from that location, could easily view the developments which Macdonell discussed.

9 Ontario Department of Education Papers, G.W. Ross to G. Grant, 26 November 1897; J.F. White to R. Harcourt, 20 December 1899; W. Prendergast to R. Harcourt, 15 August 1900. Toronto *Mail and Empire*, 17 August 1900.

Ontario Department of Education Papers, J.J. Tilley to J. Millar, 21 May 1900. This bilingual model school operated from 1896 to 1900. In the latter year 'there were but 5 students in attendance, and only three of these intended to teach.' See: Ontario Department of Education Papers, memorandum from J.J. Tilley, 19 December 1905. By 1905, there were appeals from the Ottawa separate school board for a revival of this school. See: Ontario Department of Education Papers, A. McNicoll to R.A. Pyne, 29 November 1905; W.H. Jenkins to R.A. Pyne, 2 December 1905; R.A. Pyne to A. McNicoll, 22 December 1905; P.M. Coté to R.A. Pyne, 13 January 1906; R.A. Pyne to P.M. Coté, 17 January 1906; J.J. Tilley to R.A. Pyne, 19 January 1906. No action was taken immediately by the department of education.

10 Ontario Department of Education Papers, H.F. Sims, A. Fogarty, R. Mackell, T.D. McGee to R.A. Pyne, 5 and 22 June 1906. Walker, *Catholic Education and Politics in Ontario* 232

11 Ontario Department of Education Papers, J.E. Jones to A.H.U. Colquhoun, 7 and 11 September 1908; L.A. Green to A.H.U. Colquhoun, 24 October 1908. Barber, 'The Ontario Bilingual Schools Issue' 18–19. In 1881, the total population of Ontario was 1,926,922, and the French-speaking segment numbered 102,743. In 1911, the total population of Ontario was 2,523,274, while the French-speaking element had grown to about 240,000.

12 Ontario Department of Education Papers, A.H.U. Colquhoun to J.E. Jones, 2 November 1908; J.E. Jones to A.H.U. Colquhoun, 7 November 1908

13 Walker, *Catholic Education and Politics in Ontario* 235–41

14 WP, Judge A. Constantineau to Whitney, 12 January 1910; H. Wallis to Judge A. Constantineau, 13 January 1910; Earl Grey to Whitney, 15 January 1910; J.P. Whitney to Earl Grey, 17 January 1910. In advance of this advice, Grey decided to decline the invitation. Reaume went, but fell ill and returned to Windsor without actually participating in the affair. Beck and other members of the legislature were present at a large public gathering.

15 Lucas Papers, G.A. East to Lucas, 10 February 1910. WP, J.A.C. Evans to Whitney, 29 January 1910

16 WP, Archbishop F.P. McEvay to Whitney, 15 February 1910. Walker, *Catholic Education and Politics in Ontario* 222–7 and 242, quoting F. Dowdall to Archbishop F.P. McEvay, 18 February 1910

17 WP, W.J. Hanna to R.A. Pyne, 23 May 1910. Walker, *Catholic Education and Politics in Ontario* 247–8. Ontario Department of Education Papers, A.H.U. Colquhoun to F.W. Merchant, 4 November 1910. This was scarcely news to Merchant because he replied: 'I began the investigation on Wednesday, Nover 2nd.'

261 Notes to pages 190–3

See: Ontario Department of Education Papers, F.W. Merchant to A.H.U. Colquhoun, 14 November 1910.

18 Oliver, *G. Howard Ferguson* 44–6. Ferguson Papers, clipping from the Kemptville *Advance*, 23 March 1911. WP, Whitney to W.K. McNaught, 13 November 1911

19 WP, R.L. Borden to Whitney, 25 January 1911; Whitney to R.L. Borden, 27 January 1911 (or see Borden papers for same letter). Henry Borden, ed., *Robert Laird Borden: His Memoirs* (Toronto 1938) I, 303

20 WP, Whitney to S.F. Dixon, 15 March 1909; Whitney to J. George, 25 May 1908

21 *CAR* (1911) 96–7. WP, Whitney to A. Broder, 3 February 1911; Whitney to R.L. Borden, 3 February 1911 (or see Borden Papers for same letter); clipping from the *Daily Express*, 22 February 1911

22 WP, Whitney to R.L. Borden, 23 February 1911; R.L. Borden to Whitney, 24 February 1911 (or see Borden Papers for same letters). *CAR* (1911) 97–8

   George W. Ross did not assume the same position as MacKay who led the Liberals in the legislature. The ex-premier stood against the arrangement for much the same reasons as Whitney had given. He also feared that it would 'prove the undoing of the Laurier Government.' See: Denison Papers, G.W. Ross to Denison, 27 February 1911. Other Ontario Liberals did not waver in their support of the federal leader; one of these was Albert Whitney, Sir James's brother. See: LP, A. Whitney to Laurier, 9 March 1911.

23 Whitney Papers, Whitney to R.L. Borden, 3 May 1911; Whitney to R.L. Borden, 9 May 1911 (or see Borden Papers for same telegram). Grey of Howick Papers, Whitney to Grey, 27 April 1911

24 *CAR* (1911) 225. WP, Whitney to R.L. Borden, 1 and 3 August 1911; R.L. Borden to Whitney, 7 August 1911; Whitney to R.L. Borden, 8 August 1911 (or see Borden Papers for same letters). This is just a sampling of a very extensive correspondence that was carried on throughout the election campaign.

   WP, G.C. Wilson to Whitney, 10 August 1911; Whitney to G.C. Wilson, 11 August 1911; Whitney to A.E. Fripp, 14 August 1911. Wilson sat for the provincial riding of Wentworth North and contested the federal constituency of Wentworth; Fripp sat for the provincial riding of Ottawa West and contested the federal constituency of Ottawa.

   J.J. Carrick (Thunder Bay and Rainy River), H. Clark (Bruce North), J.H. Fisher (Brant), A.E. Fripp (Ottawa), W.F. Nickle (Kingston) and G.C. Wilson (Wentworth) all captured Liberal seats. W.J. Paul held Lennox and Addington for the Conservatives. It should be noted that Fripp headed the polls in the dual-member riding of Ottawa and, thus, probably helped to carry his Tory running mate, J.L. Chabot, to victory. Frank Cochrane did not run in the general election but, rather, successfully contested a by-election in Nipissing when this seat was opened for him.

25 Robert Cuff, 'The Conservative Party Machine and the Election of 1911 in Ontario,' *Ontario History* (September 1965) 149–56.

   This information about the grass-roots work in Huron South was supplied by my former student, Kenneth F. Stewart. Merner won the election, defeating the incumbent Liberal, Murdo McLean, and the critical shift in votes occurred in Hay Township, which was occupied, primarily, by German-Canadians. In this riding the 'ethnic' vote was crucial, as was the hard work of Eilber.

LP, A. Smith to Laurier, 26 February 1909; Laurier to A. Smith, 1 October 1909. Graham Papers, A. Darrach to Graham, 3 December 1909
26 WP, Whitney to H.A. Gwynne, 22 September 1911; Whitney to R.L. Borden, 22 September 1911; Whitney to W.T. White, 10 November 1911
27 Scott Papers, Laurier to Scott, 23 September 1911. Aylesworth Papers, Letterbook 19, Aylesworth to H.J. Wright, 25 September 1911. Graham papers, Private Letterbook M, Graham to J.A. Carman, 27 September 1911; Graham to J.S. Graham, 4 October 1911. Gregory Papers, Letterbook VIII, Gregory to E.F. Baldwin, 2 October 1911. KP, R.F. McWilliams to King, 25 September 1911
28 WP, R.L. Borden to Whitney, 25 September 1911; Whitney to R.L. Borden, 27 September 1911 (or see Borden Papers for same letter).

Whitney and his Ontario supporters consistently backed Borden when his leadership was under attack; see: BP, H. Clark to Borden, 4 April 1910. And the premier steadfastly opposed calling a federal convention which might weaken Borden's position or party unity. See: WP, Whitney to P.H. Bowyer, 16 October 1909; Borden Papers, Borden to W.B. Ross, 22 October 1909.

Foster Papers, W.K. McNaught to Foster, 4 October 1911. Foster wanted to be minister of finance in the new Borden government, and pulled all the strings in an effort to obtain the post; he had to settle for the position of minister of trade and commerce. McNaught, a member of the legislature and the Ontario Hydro-Electric Power Commission, was strongly opposed to the idea of White as minister of finance.

BP, undated memorandum signed 'J.P.W.' This note is in Whitney's hand and was apparently written on the morning of 29 September, after the premier had 'slept over' the talk of the night before. Whitney wrote: 'I am taking care that no person will see this but yourself, and I hope that when you have read it you will at once put it in the nice comfort giving little fire that you keep in your room.'
29 Interview with Fred S. Broder, 28 June 1960. 'It was with great reluctance that Mr. Borden dropped Andrew Broder,' Fred Cook reported to Willison. 'It was felt that he would be a great man on the stump, but as a minister in charge of a department it was feared that he would not make a good administrator. Upon reflection this must be obvious to anone [sic] who knows dear old Andy.' See: Willison Papers, F. Cook to Willison, 10 October 1911. WP, Whitney to E.C. Whitney, 20 October 1911. Brown, *Robert Laird Borden* I, 199.
30 KP, A.G. MacKay to King, 30 March 1911.
31 KP, King to V. Markham, 15 December 1911. In one private letter, the premier cited the various reasons he was to offer publicly, and insisted that the Tories would not attempt 'anything like a snap verdict or a trick verdict.' Nevertheless, it is hard to believe that Whitney could not see the likely benefits of staging an election hard on the heels of a federal one. See: WP, Whitney to T.E. Kaiser, 6 October 1911.
32 As the campaign drew to a close, W.D. Gregory wrote: 'The Provincial Elections take

place on Monday, the 11th. I never knew an election any thing like this one. There appears to be no interest taken in it. You will probably have noticed that seventeen Conservatives were elected by acclamation ... I do not think there is a sure Liberal seat in the Province.' See: Gregory Papers, Letterbook VIII, Gregory to A.F. Jury, 8 December 1911.

  CAR (1911) 456–7. For a sound and thorough account of Rowell's leadership of the Ontario Liberals, see: Margaret Prang, *N.W. Rowell: Ontario Nationalist* (Toronto 1975) 91–157.
33 WP, E.S. Wigle to Whitney, 2 October 1911; Whitney to E.S. Wigle, 18 October 1911; Whitney to O.E. Fleming, 18 October 1911; E.S. Wigle to Whitney, 25 October 1911; A. Broder to Whitney, 23 November 1911; A.A. Aubin to Whitney, 28 November 1911. *CAR* (1911) 473–4
34 KP, King to V. Markham, 15 December 1911. Rowell Papers, A.G. MacKay to Rowell, 3 November 1911. MacKay was under considerable pressure to quit. On 23 October, King was able to write to Violet Markham: 'I was offered last week by an influential group in Toronto the Leadership of the Ontario Liberals, if I would take it. I was told that the resignation of the present leader had been obtained and that if I would accept the position the members could be brought into line ... I have thought the matter over very carefully but cannot see my way to an acceptance.' See: KP.
35 This figure and the others were derived from a combination of sources: Ontario, *Sessional Papers*, XLIV, part XIII (1912), no. 49; Lewis, *Centennial Edition*; and several editions of *The Canadian Parliamentary Guide*.
36 This figure does not include the victor in Rainy River, James A. Mathieu. Mathieu ran as a Liberal-Conservative against the sitting Conservative member, William A. Preston. He therefore is listed under the 'Other' heading; but, after his election, he supported the Whitney government and ran successfully as the Conservative candidate in the elections of 1914 and 1919.
  One of the seventeen Conservative acclamations was in Grenville, where Howard Ferguson was the member. On this particular acclamation, Whitney's Liberal brother, Albert, wrote the premier: 'There was an effort to have a man run here, but I told them plainly if there was any such nonsense I would announce my support to Ferguson. Rowell's platform would not go down here.' See: WP, 11 December 1911.
37 The heading 'Labour-Socialist' is simply a device for gathering up left-wing votes; there was not a cohesive party of the left.
38 WP, Whitney to E.C. Whitney, 12 December 1911; Whitney to N. Champagne, 12 December 1911; Whitney to D. McLellan, 26 December 1911; Whitney to A. Whitney, 12 December 1911

CHAPTER NINE

1 *CAR* (1912) 313
2 Toronto *World*, 19 March 1912. *CAR* (1912) 313–14
3 *CAR* (1910) 412. *CAR* (1912) 318

4 WP, R.J. Fleming to Whitney, 3 April 1912. The maximum set for street railway motormen and conductors was not more than six working days in a week or ten hours per day. Toronto *Globe*, 17 February 1912
5 *CAR* (1912) 329 and 343–6
6 F.W. Merchant, *Report on the Condition of English-French Schools in the Province of Ontario* (Toronto 1912)
7 *CAR* (1912) 370
8 WP, J.O. Routhier to Whitney, 20 September 1912; D.J. Scollard to Whitney, 21 October 1912
9 WP, Whitney to W.A. Macdonell, 14 November 1912
10 WP, Borden to Whitney, 16 October 1912; Whitney to Borden, 17 October 1912 (or see Borden Papers for same letters)
11 WP, Whitney to T. Chapais, 16 October and 28 December 1912
12 Ontario Department of Education Papers, L. Genest to Pyne, 1 March 1913. WP, Whitney to J.C. Milligan, 26 September 1913. Walker, *Catholic Education and Politics in Ontario* 281
13 WP, Whitney to G.E. Foster, 14 April 1909; Borden to Whitney, 1 June 1912; memorandum on the Naval Question, 14 June 1912; Whitney to Borden, 22 June 1912 (or see Borden Papers for same letter)
14 Borden, *Robert Laird Borden* I, 335–70. WP, Whitney to Borden, 15 August 1912
15 WP, Whitney to Borden, 18 September 1912; Whitney to Cochrane, 31 May 1913
16 Toronto *Globe*, 5 February 1913. Willison Papers, F.D.L. Smith to Willison, 30 October 1912
17 *CAR* (1913) 339–42. WP, Whitney to J.A. MacCullough, 14 January 1913; Whitney to L.G. Power, 16 January 1913
18 Toronto *Globe*, 30 June 1910, quoted in D. Carter-Edwards, 'Ontario and the Question of Workmen's Compensation, 1909–1917,' graduate research paper (University of British Columbia 1972) 4. Michael J. Piva, 'The Workmen's Compensation Movement in Ontario,' *Ontario History* (March 1975) 42
19 Carter-Edwards, 'Ontario and the Question of Workmen's Compensation, 1909–1917'. WP, Meredith to Whitney, 11 March and 5 July 1912
20 *CAR* (1913) 400–2
21 Johnson Papers, W.M. Johnson to E.F. Boddington, 10 May 1913. WP, Whitney to J.M. Davis, 13 July 1913; Whitney to Flavelle, 26 April 1913.
     Grey North was the riding for which A.G. MacKay had sat. Rowell's 'Abolish the bar' policy, as well as sympathy for a government under attack – a bit of an oddity – probably played a part in the outcome; see Gregory Papers, Letterbook X, Gregory to R. White, 25 July 1913
22 WP, Whitney to A. Broder, 26 August 1913
23 The bulk of the information in the preceding two paragraphs is drawn from a lengthy memorandum written by Pyne and located in the Whitney Papers. See also: WP, Whitney to H. Wallis, 13 December 1913; Pyne to H. Wallis, 15 and 18 December 1913

24 Johnson Papers, Diary, 3 and 4 January 1914. Foster Papers, Diary, 7 January 1914
25 Piva, 'The Workmen's Compensation' 52–3. Toronto *Globe*, 18 March 1914, quoted in Carter-Edwards, 'Ontario and the Question' 27. *CAR* (1914) 391–4
26 Willison Papers, McLaughlin to Willison, 9 February 1914. *Industrial Banner*, 1 May 1914, quoted in Carter-Edwards, 'Ontario and the Question' 29
27 Ontario, *Sessional Papers*, LXV, part XIII (1913), no. 85, 17, quoted in Carter-Edwards, 'Ontario and the Question' 22
28 WP, H. Wallis to Broder, 23 February 1914; Wallis to Miss J.M. Johnson, 28 February 1914; Whitney to R.M. MacGregor, 29 April 1914; Whitney to Dr A. McPhedran, 21 April 1914.
McPhedran billed Whitney for $6,750.00 because that was the sum he charged other knights in Toronto. Whitney sent a cheque for $5,000.00, and said that that was payment in full. It seems likely that E.C. Whitney helped towards the payment of the medical bills; he certainly had contributed money to assist in defraying the cost of the United States trip. See WP, Pyne's memorandum on Whitney's illness.
29 WP, Whitney to J.W. Johnson, 13 May 1914. Hearst Papers, memorandum by Whitney, 17 May 1914
30 KP, F.G. Inwood to King, 2 April 1914. WP, Whitney to J.W. Johnson, 13 May 1914
The riding of Monck was eliminated and the new constituencies were Cochrane, Niagara Falls, St Catharines, Windsor, Toronto-Parkdale, and Toronto-Riverdale; the last two brought the Toronto total to ten. Minor boundary alterations were made elsewhere.
31 *CAR* (1914) 430 and 354
32 This figure and the others were derived from a combination of sources: Ontario, *Sessional Papers*, XLVII, part XII (1915), no. 50; Lewis, *Centennial Edition*; and several editions of *The Canadian Parliamentary Guide*.
Again, the heading 'Labour-Socialist' is simply a device for gathering up left-wing votes.
33 WP, Whitney to S.T. Loucks, 2 July 1914. Foster Papers, Diary, 17 and 18 June 1914. Of the new seats, the Conservatives took Niagara Falls, St Catharines, Toronto-Parkdale, and Toronto-Riverdale, but lost in Cochrane, and in Windsor where J.O. Reaume was defeated because an Independent-Conservative candidate split the Tory vote.
34 WP, Whitney to Beck, 6 August 1911. *CAR* (1914) 459

CHAPTER TEN

1 Ferguson Papers, B.E. Walker to Ferguson, 27 August 1923. Willison Papers, Willison to J.H. Benton, 4 September 1923. Willison declared that 'Whitney hated few men as he hated Adam Beck.' But this seems to be an exaggeration.
2 Spelt, *The Urban Development* 138–9 and 165. See also 103–4 of this work.
3 S.D. Clark, *Church and Sect in Canada* (Toronto 1948) 329–46. Ontario, *Sessional Papers*, XLIV, part XIII (1912), no. 49, 89–91; Ontario, *Sessional Papers*, XLVII, part

XII (1915), no. 50, 109–11. In 1911, Rowell received 876 votes in Woodstock and his opponent 1043, but he carried the riding 2651 to 2091. In 1914, Rowell received 911 votes in Woodstock and his opponent 1478, but he carried the riding 3048 to 2935.

4 For a fuller examination of the degree of urban support for Whitney see: C.W. Humphries, 'The Sources of Ontario "Progressive" Conservatism, 1900–1914,' *Canadian Historical Association Historical Papers* (1967) 120–2.

Spelt, *The Urban Development* 141–3. The author explains: 'For the entire province the number [of farmers] rose from 206,989 in 1881 to 285,608 in 1891. By 1901 the number had declined to 185,415, but it increased again during the next decade; in 1911 it was 226,801.' He then proceeds to note how the farmers of Ontario became increasingly orientated towards, and dependent upon, the urban centre. Of course this development angered some farmers. O.D. Skelton tried to reason (to no avail) with W.C. Good on this point: 'The first chapter [of Good's manuscript] strikes me as being an admirable and balanced treatment of the rural problem. I should be a little more optimistic as to the present status of farming in Canada than you are, but doubtless one's perspective changes when one passes from the study to the plough. One might question, too, whether the cityward drift is due wholly or mainly to the decline in the economic prosperity of the country. Granted that the social causes to which you make reference are of minor importance, and determine which shall go, rather than how many shall go, you do not seem to me to give enough weight to the fact that industrial evolution has meant shearing off from the work of the farm many activities and occupations once carried on by the farm or the village family, and now carried on in city factories. The farmers have simply followed the work, just as the increasing numbers of women in industry reflect the fact that much of the work of the home is now carried on in the factory and shop. You are, of course, familiar with this point of view, and perhaps react from it because it has sometimes been put forward as a sole and sufficient explanation of the decline in rural population. This is natural, but it must, I think be given some consideration. In some degree the increasing proportion of people who live in cities means that a larger proportion of the nation's work (useful or otherwise) is being done in the cities. It may also be true, as you insist, that the money rewards are much greater in the city in relation to the effort expended.' See: Good Papers, O.D. Skelton to Good, 9 January 1918.

Gregory Papers, Letterbook IV, Gregory to W.S. Brewster, 9 June 1908

For a close examination of what happened to Liberal country and town support at the century's turn in two provincial ridings see: Barbara A. McKenna, 'Farmers and Railwaymen, Patronage and Corruption: A Volatile Political Mix in Turn of the Century Elgin County,' *Ontario History* (September, 1982) 206–33

5 WP, Whitney to W.M. Southam, 21 February 1908, in defence of the three-fifths clause; Whitney to T.S. Sproule, 1 March 1907, in reference to the imposition of provincial taxes on mines, mining lands and natural gas wells

6 WP, Whitney to A.J. Dawson, 7 July 1909

7 Nelles, *The Politics of Development* 253. WP, Whitney to J.A. MacCullough, 14 January 1913; Whitney to G.H. Ferguson, 7 November 1912

8 Willison Papers, J. Cameron to Willison, 5 April 1898; Hardy to Willison, 1 April 1898; C.F. Hamilton to Willison, 19 November 1906

9 Splane, *Social Welfare* 11. Splane accepts the judgment of Elisabeth Wallace in her article, 'The Origin of the Social Welfare State in Canada, 1867–1900,' *Canadian Journal of Economics and Political Science* (1950) 383–93.

John Graham Harkness, *Stormont, Dundas and Glengarry. A History, 1784–1945* (Oshawa 1946) 370

10 Willison Papers, M.H. Irish to Willison, 26 June 1923. WP, Meredith to Whitney, 13 November 1905; Whitney to E.C. Whitney, 26 March 1907. CWH, WP, Meredith to Whitney, 9 May 1906.

Whitney and Meredith must have exchanged correspondence while the former led the Conservative party in opposition to the Liberal government, but there is virtually no evidence of this in the Whitney Papers. There was a limited exchange of correspondence once Whitney assumed the premiership. Presumably personal discussions and telephone conversations replaced correspondence once Whitney took up permanent residence in Toronto.

11 McKenna, 'Farmers and Railwaymen.' WP, Whitney to R.H. Pope, 17 June 1907. The premier wrote: 'Since Mr. Borden's decision to remain in public life as Leader, things have been said to me from time to time, suggesting his retirement. ... I want to make it clear ... that at any function or demonstration where I speak, I shall feel impelled to refer to him and his leadership, *past and future*, in terms of highest approbation.' WP, Whitney to D. McLellan, 26 December 1911

12 BP, Whitney to Borden, 11 September 1907

13 WP, Whitney to Meredith, 8 May 1909. In 1913, Whitney would not even personally reply to a letter from an Edmonton Conservative who asked him why MacKay 'resigned the Liberal leadership.' MacKay by that time was living in Alberta and was a candidate in a provincial election. See: WP, H. Wallis to G.C. Benjamin, 20 March 1913

14 WP, Letterbook B, Whitney to R. Grass, 26 December 1899.

Bibliography

This work rests primarily on manuscript materials and contemporary newspapers. Press items, government documents, theses, and secondary sources are cited in the notes. The following is a list of manuscript collections used in the preparation of this biography; the most important, in terms of this study, have been marked with an asterisk.

PUBLIC ARCHIVES OF ONTARIO
Belcher, A.E.; Bristol, E.; Cheeseworth, J.W.; Clarke, C.; Cody, H.J.; Colquhoun, W.; Ferguson, G.H.; Hearst, W.H.; Lucas, I.B.; Mowat, O.; Patteson, T.C.; Pringle, J.F.; Wallace, N.C.; Whitney, J.P.*

Departmental records: education

Church records: Registers of marriages, births and funerals, St John's Presbyterian Church, Cornwall

PUBLIC ARCHIVES OF CANADA
Borden, R.L.*; Bowell, M.; Denison, G.T.; Foster, G.E.; Good, W.C.; Graham, G.P.; Grant, G.M.; Grant, W.L.; Earl Grey of Howick; King, W.L.M.*; Laurier, W.*; McCarthy, D.; Macdonald, J.A.*; Macdonell, J.A.; McLennan, J.; Lord Minto; Morgan, H.J.; Murphy, C.; Pope, J.; Ponton, W.N.; Rowell, N.W.; Scott, R.W.; Sifton, C.; Thompson, J.S.D.; Tupper, C.; Willison, J.S.*

Departmental records: census 1861; census 1871; militia

Church records: Parish registers, Williamsburg, Matilda, Osnabruck, Edwardsburg

UNIVERSITY ARCHIVES
Oxford
Lord Milner

Queen's
Aylesworth, A.B.; Flavelle, J.W.; Gregory, W.D.*; Shortt, A.

Toronto
Charlton, J.; Wrong, G.M.

Western
Coyne, J.H.; Mills, D.; Whitney, J.P.

TORONTO PUBLIC LIBRARY
Denison, F.C.; Johnson, W.M.

Index

Hendrie, John S. 98, 100, 136–42, 155
Hepburn, Mitchell 251n
Howland, Oliver A. 28, 29, 35, 47–8, 229n
Hughes, Sam 119–20, 194
Hutton, Maurice 129
hydroelectric power development 76, 77–8, 85–7, 110, 151–6, 163–8
Hydro-Electric Power Commission (1905 royal commission) 113, 151–2
Hydro-Electric Power Commission of Ontario 154–5, 163, 165, 167, 168, 176, 183, 200, 213, 215

Industrial Banner 211
Ingram, Andrew B. 143, 250n

Jaffray, Robert 147, 254n
Jessop, Dr Elisha 65
Jesuit Estates Act 23

Kaiser, Dr T.E. 78
Keewatin, District of 157–8
Kemp, A.E. 194
King, Mackenzie 183, 196, 256n, 263n
Kipling, Rudyard 258n
Kittson, Henry N. 143
Knox College 115–16

Lamarche, Charles 100–1, 246n
Latchford, Francis 57, 91, 94, 186, 234n
Laurier, Sir Wilfrid 37, 38, 49, 59, 111–12, 121, 155, 158, 159, 174
Leavitt, T.W.H. 59, 67–71, 78, 246n
Leitch, James 142–3
Lennox, T.H. 138
Liberal party (Ontario) 38, 92, 95
Liberal-Conservative party (Ontario) 28–9, 41, 47, 73, 220
Liberal-Conservative Association (Ontario) 69, 72, 92, 95
Liberal-Conservative Union of Ontario 41, 59, 72

liquor regulation 44, 51, 116–19, 129–34, 168–9, 217. *See also* prohibition
London Street Railway strike 143
Lord's Day Alliance 140
Loudon, James 108, 114, 127, 128, 129
Loughrin, John 246n
Lucas, Isaac B. 98, 209, 211
Lynch, Archbishop John Joseph 12

Mabee, C.R. 66
McBride, Richard 157
McCallum, Peter 25
McCarthy, D'Alton 11, 14, 25, 28
Macdiarmid, Finlay 98
Macdonald, Rev. D.B. 114, 115–16
Macdonald, Henry Sandfield 7
Macdonald, J.A. (Toronto *Globe* editor) 128, 174, 222, 244n
Macdonald, Sir John A. (politician) 9, 12, 18, 23
Macdonald, John Greenfield 7
Macdonald, John Sandfield 6, 7, 24
Macdonell, Archbishop Alexander 185–6
MacKay, A.G. 91, 159, 169, 173, 182, 194, 195, 196
Mackenzie, William 77, 86, 110, 136, 178
McLaughlin, R. 210–11
Maclean, William F. 67, 69
Maclennan, John Ban 6
McNaughton, Daniel 24
Macnish, Donald 56
Mail (Toronto) 12, 29
Mail and Empire (Toronto) 65–6, 68, 69, 77
manhood suffrage 17
Manitoba school question 23, 24, 34–7, 47
Manufacturers' Life Insurance Company 85
Marter, George F. 18, 28–9, 30–1, 32, 36, 66–7, 76, 79
Massey, Chester 128

THE ONTARIO HISTORICAL STUDIES SERIES

The Ontario Historical Studies Series is a comprehensive history of Ontario from 1791 to the present, which will include several biographies of former premiers, numerous volumes on the economic, social, political, and cultural development of the province, and a general history incorporating the insights and conclusions of the other works in the series. The purpose of the series is to enable general readers and scholars to understand better the distinctive features of Ontario as one of the principal regions within Canada.

The Biographies of the Premiers

*J.M.S. Careless (ed.), THE PRE-CONFEDERATION PREMIERS
A. Margaret Evans, SIR OLIVER MOWAT (Premier, 1872–1896)
Robert J.D. Page, SIR GEORGE W. ROSS (Premier, 1899–1905)
*Charles W. Humphries, SIR JAMES P. WHITNEY (Premier, 1905–1914)
Charles M. Johnston, HON. E.C. DRURY (Premier, 1919–1923)
*Peter N. Oliver, HON. G. HOWARD FERGUSON (Premier, 1923–1930)
John T. Saywell, HON. MITCHELL F. HEPBURN (Premier, 1934–1942)
Roger Graham, HON. LESLIE M. FROST (Premier, 1949–1961)
A.K. McDougall, HON. JOHN P. ROBARTS (Premier, 1961–1971)
*Published